BISHOP ÆTHELWOLD

His Career and Influence

BISHOP ÆTHELWOLD

His Career and Influence

edited by
BARBARA YORKE

THE BOYDELL PRESS

© Contributors 1988

First published 1988 by The Boydell Press
an imprint of Boydell & Brewer Ltd
PO Box 9, Woodbridge, Suffolk IP12 3DF
and of Boydell & Brewer Inc.
Wolfeboro, New Hampshire 03894-2069, USA

ISBN 0 85115 484 0

British Library Cataloguing in Publication Data

Bishop Aethelwold: his career and influence.
  1. Aethelwold, *Saint, Bishop of Winchester*
  2. Christian saints — Biography
  I. Yorke, Barbara, 1951-
  282'.092'4   BR1720.A3/
  ISBN 0-85115-484-0

Library of Congress Cataloging-in-Publication Data

Bishop Aethelwold: his career and influence.
  Includes index.
  1. Aethelwold, Saint, Bishop of Winchester, ca.
908-984. I. Yorke, Barbara, 1951-   .
BR754.A33B57 1988   270.3'092'4   87-26882
ISBN 0-85115-484-0

⊗ Printed in Great Britain
on long life paper made to the full American Standard
by St Edmundsbury Press, Bury St Edmunds

CONTENTS

LIST OF ILLUSTRATIONS

FOREWORD

This volume had its origin in a series of lectures in Winchester in the summer of 1984 which Canon Paul Britton organised as part of a Saxon Festival to celebrate the millenary of the death of Bishop Æthelwold of Winchester. Kevin Crossley-Holland, who contributed to the lecture series and was at that time writer-in-residence at Winchester School of Art, suggested the idea of producing a volume of essays and made the initial approach to the publishers. It was suggested that I might edit the volume and I set about approaching those who had contributed to the Winchester Saxon Festival and to a programme of lectures given as part of the millenary celebrations in Abingdon which were organised by a local committee under the secretaryship of Miss E. F. Aldworth, Chairman of the Friends of Abingdon. Thus the volume began to take shape, although in the event not all of those who lectured at Winchester and Abingdon wished to write a paper for the volume and other scholars, who were working on different aspects of the period, were invited to contribute as well. The aim has been to approach Æthelwold's life and influence through a number of different areas of study, though inevitably there are some important aspects which it has not been possible to tackle in the space available. It is particularly regretted that at a late stage it proved impossible to include a paper on the architecture of Æthelwold's foundations.

The millenary of Æthelwold's death was also marked by 'The Golden Age of Anglo-Saxon Art' Exhibition at the British Museum. One of the main organisers of the exhibition was Derek Turner, who played an important role as well in the celebrations at Winchester and Abingdon, and organised the temporary return of the Benedictional of St Æthelwold to Winchester Cathedral library. Derek Turner was to have contributed a paper to this volume, but before his initial research was completed he died tragically on 1 August – St Æthelwold's feast day – 1985. However, Dr Andrew Prescott, who as research assistant in the British Library had been working with Derek Turner on aspects of the Benedictional, agreed to continue work on the topic which Derek Turner had begun. He dedicates his paper in this volume to Derek Turner's memory.

I would like to record my personal thanks to Canon Britton and Kevin Crossley-Holland for their role in bringing this volume into existence, and to Amanda Hummel of Boydell & Brewer for her assistance during its gestation. I am also most grateful to all the contributors for their willing co-operation and help with many matters. Finally, I must record my immense debt of gratitude to my husband Robert Yorke, Archivist at the College of Arms, London, for his advice on editorial matters and, above all, for the moral support he has provided.

ABBREVIATIONS

Ælfric	*Vita S. Æthelwoldi, Three Lives of English Saints*, ed. M. Winterbottom (Toronto, 1972)
ASE	*Anglo-Saxon England*, ed. P. Clemoes (Cambridge)
B	W. de G. Birch, *Cartularium Saxonicum*, 3 vols and index (London, 1885-9)
BM Facs.	British Museum Facsimiles
CCM	*Cahiers de Civilisation Médiévale*
Chron. Abingdon	*Chronicon Monasterii de Abingdon*, ed. J. Stevenson, RS, 2 vols (London, 1858)
Councils and Synods	*Councils and Synods, with other documents relating to the English Church, I, 871-1204*, ed. D. Whitelock, M. Brett and C. N. L. Brooke, Part I, 871-1066 (Oxford, 1981)
EETS	Early English Text Society
EHD	*English Historical Documents, c.500-1042*, ed. D. Whitelock, 2nd edn (London, 1979)
Gesta Pontificum	*Willelmi Malmesbiriensis Monachi De Gestis Pontificum Anglorum*, ed. N. Hamilton, RS (London, 1870)
Gesta Regum	*Willelmi Malmesbiriensis Monachi De Gestis Regum Anglorum* ed. W. Stubbs, RS, 2 vols (London, 1887-9)
Hist. York	*The Historians of the Church of York and its Archbishops*, ed. J. Raine, RS, 3 vols (London, 1879-94)
K	J. M. Kemble, *Codex Diplomaticus Aevi Saxonici*, 6 vols (London, 1839-48)
Liber Eliensis	*Liber Eliensis*, ed. E. O. Blake, Camden Society, 3rd series, 92 (London, 1962)
Memorials	*Memorials of St Dunstan, Archbishop of Canterbury*, ed. W. Stubbs, RS (London, 1874)
MGH	*Monumenta Germaniae Historica*
OS Facs.	Ordnance Survey Facsimiles
PL	*Patrologia Latina*
Regularis Concordia	*Regularis Concordia Anglicae nationis monachorum sanctimonialiumque*, ed. T. Symons (London, 1953)
Robertson	A. J. Robertson, *Anglo-Saxon Charters*, 2nd edn (Cambridge, 1956)
RS	Rolls Series
S	P. Sawyer, *Anglo-Saxon Charters: An Annotated List and Bibliography*, Royal Historical Society Guides and Handbooks 8 (London, 1968)

Tenth-Century Studies	*Tenth-Century Studies: Essays in Commemoration of the Millenium of the Council of Winchester and Regularis Concordia*, ed. D. Parsons (Chichester, 1975)
Two Chronicles	*Two of the Saxon Chronicles Parallel*, ed. C. Plummer, 2 vols (Oxford, 1892-9)
Wulfstan, *Vita*	*Vita S. Æthelwoldi, Three Lives of English Saints*, ed. M. Winterbottom (Toronto, 1972)
Wulfstan, *Narratio*	*Frithegodi Monachi Breviloquium Vitae Beati Wilfredi et Wulfstani Cantoris Narratio Metrica de Sancto Swithuno*, ed. A. Campbell (Zurich, 1950)

INTRODUCTION

Barbara Yorke

The main events of Æthelwold's life are relatively well-recorded in contemporary and near-contemporary documents. Æthelwold himself provided some details of his career in his vernacular account of the monastic reforms of the tenth century,[1] but the major biographical sources are two pre-Conquest accounts of his life. There has been much debate about the priority and authorship of the two works. The preface to the shorter Life reveals that its author was Ælfric, a pupil of Æthelwold's at Winchester and later abbot of Eynsham.[2] Ælfric states in his preface that he is writing twenty years after the death of Æthelwold (d.984), and the work is dedicated to Bishop Cenwulf of Winchester (1005-6). The author of the longer Life was identified by William of Malmesbury as Wulfstan Cantor, who was also a pupil of Æthelwold's and a monk of Old Minster,[3] and this identification is now generally accepted as correct.[4] Wulfstan is known to have been the author of a Latin poem on the miracles which occurred after Æthelwold's translation of St Swithun's remains in 971, and there is a close correspondence between a chapter in the Life and part of the preface to the poem.[5] The two Lives contain very similar material, and it is clear that one must be derived from the other, but opinion has varied about which of the two works is earlier. Most recent commentators have been inclined to give priority to Ælfric, and to see Wulfstan's Life as a slightly later expansion of Ælfric's work.[6] However, Michael Lapidge's detailed evaluation of the work of the two authors leads him to the opposite conclusion and he reinforces the view of D. J. V. Fisher that it is Wulfstan's work which was the original composition and that Ælfric's *vita* must be seen as an abridgement

---

[1] The only surviving text of this work, generally known as 'King Edgar's Establishment of Monasteries', is in BL Cotton MS Faustina A. x, and is unfortunately incomplete. The case for Æthelwold's authorship has been forcibly argued in D. Whitelock, 'The Authorship of the Account of King Edgar's Establishment of Monasteries', *Philological Essays: Studies in Old and Middle English Language and Literature in Honour of Herbert Dean Meritt*, ed. J. L. Rosier (Mouton, The Hague, 1970), pp 125-36. For an edition of the text see *Councils and Synods*, pp 142-54, and, for a translation, *EHD*, pp 920-3.
[2] Ælfric ch 1. For a translation of Ælfric's Life, see *EHD*, pp 903-11.
[3] *Gesta Pontificum* p 406; *Gesta Regum* I, 167.
[4] For other views see J. Armitage Robinson, *The Times of St Dunstan* (Oxford, 1923), pp 106-8; R. N. Quirk, 'Winchester Cathedral in the Tenth Century', *Archaeological Journal* 114 (1957), 26-68.
[5] Wulfstan, *Vita*, ch 44, and Winterbottom, p 3 of the same edition. On Wulfstan, see also Quirk, 'Winchester Cathedral', *passim*, and Lapidge, below, ch 4, pp 110-12.
[6] See for instance, the discussion in *EHD*, p 903.

of it.[7] It seems likely, once Dr Lapidge's full arguments are available in print, that this will be the view that prevails.

The accounts of Ælfric and Wulfstan cover many aspects of Æthelwold's life and achievements, but inevitably they are selective, as one of their main functions was to promote the cult of Æthelwold following the translation of his remains in 996.[8] Fortunately, we can also study Æthelwold through the numerous charters and other administrative documents which were produced by his monasteries, and elsewhere, during the tenth-century reforms, as well as through the art and architecture of his foundations.

Æthelwold was born in Winchester during the reign of Edward the Elder (899-924),[9] and subsequent events suggest that his family was both wealthy and eminent. He joined the court of King Athelstan (924-39) as an *adolescens* and was eventually sent by the king to the household of Bishop Ælfheah of Winchester (933-51).[10] Ælfheah ordained Æthelwold as a priest on the same day as his nephew, Dunstan. As a member of Athelstan's court and as a priest in Winchester, Æthelwold would have experienced the beginnings of a monastic revival in England and have met monks from the reformed Benedictine monasteries of Europe, which provided the inspiration for the English movement.[11] When Dunstan was created abbot of Glastonbury, in the early years of King Edmund's reign (939-46), Æthelwold joined him and was received into the monastic order.[2] Glastonbury was the first monastic house in England to be reformed under the influence of the Continental movements, and, probably because of this, was a major centre of royal and aristocratic patronage.[13] Æthelwold eventually wished to leave Glastonbury in order to study the European reforms at first hand, but his request was refused by King Eadred (946-55). Instead, on the advice of his mother, Eadgifu, Eadred made Æthelwold abbot of the derelict monastery of Abingdon which had come into the royal fisc.[14] Æthelwold was able to instigate his own reforms at Abingdon with the help of monks from Glastonbury and former clerks from Winchester and elsewhere.[15] His decision to send one of his monks to study at the monastery of Fleury, so that first-hand information

---

[7] Lapidge, below, ch 4, p 89 n 1, and D. J. V. Fisher, 'The Early Biographers of St Æthelwold', *English Historical Review* 67 (1952), 381-91. It should be noted that much of Ælfric's work consists of abridgements of longer and more complex works (see n 69).

[8] Æthelwold died in 984 and his body was translated in 996, shortly after the dedication of the new east end of Old Minster: Wulfstan, *Vita* ch 41.

[9] Ælfric ch 2, Wulfstan, *Vita* ch 1.

[10] Ælfric ch 5, Wulfstan, *Vita* ch 7, and see Yorke below, ch 3, p 68.

[11] For the intellectual background and Continental connections of Athelstan's court see Robinson, *Times of St Dunstan*, pp 51-8; M. Wood, 'The Making of King Æthelstan's Empire: an English Charlemagne?', *Ideal and Reality in Frankish and Anglo-Saxon Society*, ed. P. Wormald (Oxford, 1983), pp 250-72; and S. Keynes, 'King Athelstan's books', *Learning and Literature in Anglo-Saxon England*, ed. M. Lapidge and H. Gneuss (Cambridge, 1985), pp 143-201.

[12] Ælfric ch 6, Wulfstan, *Vita* ch 9.

[13] Glastonbury was closely associated with the families of Dunstan and King Athelstan (*Memorials* pp 6-20). Edmund and Edgar were both buried there, and members of prominent noble families like those of Athelstan Half-King and Ælfhere of Mercia were patrons and members of the community.

[14] Ælfric ch 7, Wulfstan, *Vita* ch 11, and see Thacker below, ch 2, pp 45-51.

[15] Ælfric and Wulfstan *ibid*.

could be obtained on the religious life there, gives some indication of the standards to which Æthelwold was aspiring.[16]

Æthelwold's wider monastic reforms were carried out after his appointment as bishop of Winchester by King Edgar (*rex Merciorum* 957-9, *rex Anglorum* 959-75) in 963.[17] In the following year, with the support of King Edgar and of the pope, Æthelwold had the clerks of the Old and New Minsters forcibly expelled and replaced by monks from Abingdon.[18] Even Æthelwold's episcopal staff were to be in monastic orders, a policy which ran counter to contemporary English and Continental practice.[19] Ælfric and Wulfstan also record Æthelwold's revival of three great monasteries in eastern England,[20] Peterborough (*Medehamstede*) (966),[21] Ely (970),[22] and Thorney (972),[23] and for all of them separate documentation of Æthelwold's role in their revival survives. There is less certainty about which other English monasteries were refounded by Æthelwold. The reform of St Neots (Cambs) by Æthelwold is recorded in the *Liber Eliensis*,[24] but in other cases the evidence is less clear and it would appear that, while Æthelwold or monks from Abingdon assisted in the reform of several other religious houses, Æthelwold did not exercise the same control over these foundations as he enjoyed in Abingdon, Winchester and in his fenland monasteries. These other foundations lack the extensive range of documents which characterise Æthelwold's most important foundations and so the evidence for Æthelwold's role is more circumstantial. Chertsey (Surrey), for instance, is likely to have been reformed by Æthelwold because it lay within Æthelwold's diocese, its clerks were expelled at the same time as the Winchester clerks, and its first abbot was Ordbriht from Abingdon.[25] Milton Abbas (Dorset) was also reformed in

---

[16] Ælfric ch 10, Wulfstan, *Vita* ch 14. *Chron. Abingdon* I, 129 records that monks were brought to Abingdon from Corbie by Æthelwold to give instruction in chanting.

[17] Ælfric ch 11; Wulfstan, *Vita* ch 16, gives the date of consecration as 29 November.

[18] Ælfric ch 12-14; Wulfstan, *Vita* ch 17, dates the expulsion of the clerks to *sabbato in capito Quadragesime*, i.e. 19 February 964. Permission to expel the clerks had been obtained from Pope John XII by Edgar and Dunstan in 963 (*Councils and Synods* no. 29, pp 109-13), and may have been discussed at a major assembly in England in 964, though the date of the council is controversial; see E. John, 'The Beginning of the Benedictine Reform in England', *Orbis Britanniae and Other Studies* (Leicester, 1966), pp 249-64 and *Councils and Synods* no. 30, pp 113-18.

[19] See Wormald below, ch 1, pp 37-8.

[20] Ælfric ch 17, Wulfstan, *Vita* ch 3-4.

[21] The Peterborough reforms are described in *The Chronicle of Hugh Candidus, a Monk of Peterborough*, ed. W. T. Mellows (Oxford, 1949), espec. pp 27-30, and in Robertson no. 39, a list of the gifts of Æthelwold to Peterborough.

[22] The main source for Æthelwold's work at Ely is the *Libellus quorundum insignium operum beati Æthelwoldi* which seems to have been drawn up between 1109 and 1131 from an Old English record. The *Libellus* survives independently in two twelfth-century manuscripts and a substantial portion of it was incorporated into Book II, ch 1-49, of the *Liber Eliensis*: *Liber Eliensis* pp xxxiv, xlix-liii.

[23] The reform of Thorney is also discussed by Hugh Candidus (*op. cit.* pp 42-3), the property assigned to it is recorded in Robertson, appendix 2, no. 9. See also C. Hart, *The Early Charters of Eastern England* (Leicester, 1966), pp 146-209, and S. Raban, *The Estates of Thorney and Crowland* (Cambridge, 1977), pp 8-12.

[24] *Liber Eliensis* II, 29. The monastery was probably refounded c.980 with monks from Ely and Thorney at which time it was known as Eynesbury. See Hart, *Charters of Eastern England* p 28, and *The Annals of St Neots with Vita Prima Sancti Neoti*, ed. D. Dumville and M. Lapidge (Cambridge, 1985), pp lxxxvii-lxxxix.

[25] The expulsion of clerks from Chertsey is recorded in the 'A' version of the *Anglo-Saxon*

964,[26] and so it too can presumably be included within Æthelwold's sphere of activity. Monks from Abingdon seem to have helped Bishop Oswald of Worcester in his reforms of Pershore, Evesham and, possibly, St Albans, but direct intervention by Æthelwold himself in the affairs of these houses seems unlikely.[27] Nor does Æthelwold seem to have had any hand in the reform of Crowland, as has sometimes been suggested.[28] Æthelwold's main spheres of activity were his own diocese and parts of eastern England where the church had never fully recovered from a loss of land at the time of the Danish settlements. Æthelwold may have hoped at one time to revive other eastern monasteries, such as Oundle, Barrow and Breedon, whose sites he acquired, but in the event these lands were used to endow other foundations.[29]

Æthelwold appointed abbots to his main foundations, but it is clear that he exercised a major supervisory role. The earlier foundations presumably followed a version of the Benedictine Rule which had been followed at Abingdon,[30] but, at a council held in Winchester before Edgar's death, it was agreed that all the English monasteries would adhere to the *Regularis Concordia Anglicae nationis monachorum sanctimonialiumque*.[31] The *Regularis Concordia* is particularly concerned with the liturgy to be observed in the English religious houses, but also lays down a number of other practices which all are to share. There is good reason to believe that Æthelwold was the main compiler of the *Regularis Concordia* and that it reflects his preferences to a considerable extent.[32] The concept of imposing a version of

---

Chronicle (*Two Chronicles* I, 116-18), and see D. Knowles, *The Monastic Order in England* (Cambridge, 1950), p 51.

[26] *Two Chronicles op. cit.*

[27] Knowles, *Monastic Order*, pp 51-2. Knowles is inclined to attribute the reform of St Albans to Æthelwold as its first abbot, Ælfric, was a monk from Abingdon, but Oswald's biographer provides grounds for assigning the reform of St Albans to Oswald (*Hist. York* II, 71, 495 and 505).

[28] For instance in Knowles, *op. cit.*, p 51. However, Crowland seems to have been an independent foundation by Abbot Thurkytel of Bedford, a kinsman of Bishop Oswald: see D. Whitelock, 'The Conversion of the Eastern Danelaw', *Saga Book of the Viking Society* (1941), 174-5, and Raban, *Thorney and Crowland*, pp 8-12.

[29] Hugh Candidus describes how Æthelwold first intended to refound Oundle (Leics.), but transferred his interest to Peterborough which was endowed with the site of the former monastery at Oundle (*Chronicle*, pp 27-8). Æthelwold also acquired the former monasteries of Barrow-on-Humber (Lincs.) (S 782) and Breedon-on-the-Hill (Leics.) (S 749). Barrow was certainly given to Peterborough, and it is likely that that monastery also received Breedon which had formerly been one of its daughter houses.

[30] M. Gretsch, *Die Regula Sancti Benedicti in England und ihre altenglische Übersetzung*, Texte und Untersuchungen zur englischen Philologie 2 (Munich, 1973); *The Rule of St Benedict: the Abingdon Copy* ed. J. Chamberlin (Toronto, 1982); Thacker below, ch 2, pp 54-6.

[31] The council cannot be dated exactly, but a date between 970 and 973 seems likely (*Councils and Synods*, p 135). A new edition of the *Regularis Concordia* has been produced by T. Symons and S. Spath in *Consuetudinum saeculi X/XI/XII monumenta non-Cluniacensia*, ed. K. Hallinger, Corpus Consuetudinum Monasticarum 7.3 (Siegburg, 1984). However, most contributors to the volume have not had access to this edition and so references are to the earlier edition of Symons (see under Abbreviations) unless otherwise indicated.

[32] See Lapidge below, ch 4, pp 98-100. *Regularis Concordia* (pp 4-5) records certain provisions which Dunstan added to the decisions agreed at the Winchester council, and it is possible that Dunstan did not attend the council in person, particularly as only bishops, abbots and abbesses are described as being present (p 3): see F. M. Stenton, *Anglo-Saxon England*, 3rd ed. (Oxford, 1971), pp 449-50.

the Benedictine Rule on all the English monasteries may have been inspired by the legislation of the great Aachen reform councils of 816-19 in which Benedict of Aniane was so influential.[33] Details of many of the practices to be followed seem to have been taken from those of Continental reformed monasteries, and Æthelwold acknowledges in his introduction the help he has received from monks from Fleury and Ghent.[34] However, the relative roles of Ghent and Fleury and the exact nature of their contributions are obscured by the fact that the *Regularis Concordia* is earlier in date than the surviving customals of either of these houses, though the recent discovery and analysis of a Fleury customary which is more nearly contemporary with the *Regularis Concordia* makes it likely that the customs of Fleury were more influential than had been thought previously.[35]

With the exception of New Minster (Winchester) and Milton Abbas, which had been founded as communities of secular clerks within the tenth century, the houses which Æthelwold reformed had been monasteries in the seventh century, but had subsequently come to be served by secular clerks or had fallen into lay hands. Æthelwold could therefore claim that he was simply restoring earlier conditions, and the past history of his foundations was a matter of acute interest to him. His prose tract on 'King Edgar's Establishment of Monasteries' begins with an account based on Bede's *Historia Ecclesiastica* of the Gregorian mission and the first establishment of monasteries in England, and makes it clear that Æthelwold saw the tenth-century reforms as an attempt to recover the high standards of monasticism which could be found in Bedan England.[36] At Æthelwold's foundations the relics of earlier English saints were recovered and their cults revived. The cults of Swithun at Winchester and Æthelthryth at Ely were particularly important, and the miracles they performed were seen as sanctioning Æthelwold's actions.[37] As guardian of the saints' interests, Æthelwold sought to recover the lands which had been granted to the Old Minster and Ely in the pre-Alfredian period, irrespective of the fact that many of the lands had been in other hands for several generations. The archives of Winchester, Ely and Peterborough demonstrate the way in which Æthelwold relentlessly pursued his aims through law-suits, land transfers and purchase, and if his houses did not possess suitable charters from their foundation period for the lands to which they claimed title, new charters were constructed in which the history of the house was carefully rehearsed.[38]

---

[33] See Wormald below, ch 1, pp 15-19, and Thacker ch 2, p 55.

[34] *Regularis Concordia*, ch 5. Dunstan had stayed at St Peter's in Ghent during his period in exile, but Æthelwold had his own connections with Ghent whose abbot Womar was at one time part of his *familia* at Old Minster – see Lapidge below, ch 4, p99 n 67.

[35] See Lapidge below, ch 4, pp 98-100, and Wormald ch 1, pp 30-2.

[36] See n 1, and Wormald below, ch 1, pp 40-2; Thacker ch 2, pp 62-4.

[37] For Swithun, see D. J. Sheerin, 'The Dedication of the Old Minster in Winchester in 980', *Revue Bénédictine* 88 (1978), 261-73. Æthelthryth seems to have been of similar importance to Ely (*Liber Eliensis* II, 1). Æthelthryth's relics and those of her saintly kinswomen, Seaxburg, Eormenhilda and Wihtburg, were translated as part of the monastery's revival (*Liber Eliensis* II, 52-3). See also Thacker below, ch 2, pp 60-3, for Æthelwold's interest in saints' cults at other of his foundations.

[38] The *Codex Wintoniensis* (BL Add. MS 46487) reveals the tortuous history of many of the Winchester estates, and Æthelwold's claims seem to have necessitated a rewriting of many

The financial outlay was enormous; for instance, the restoration of rights which Old Minster claimed over its large estate at Taunton (Som.) was purchased with the gift of 200 mancuses and a silver cup to King Edgar and 50 mancuses to his wife.[39] But even with great wealth apparently at his disposal, Æthelwold could not have succeeded without the support of King Edgar, whose active intervention on Æthelwold's behalf is frequently recorded. After Edgar's death, some aggrieved landowners, particularly in eastern England, were able to have Edgar's decisions overturned or to force Æthelwold to offer them more favourable terms.[40] Edgar may have hoped that Æthelwold's reconstitution of the great fenland abbeys would provide an extension of direct West Saxon influence into an area where the royal house held little land, and a counterbalance to the powerful family of Æthelstan Half-King.[41] Edgar presumably did not foresee the great resentment which Æthelwold's tenurial reconstructions caused amongst the nobility.[42]

Æthelwold was responsible for the reform of nunneries as well as monasteries. Nunneries were also covered by the provisions of the *Regularis Concordia*, and Æthelwold provided an Old English translation of the *Rule of St Benedict* for their benefit.[43] The Nunnaminster in Winchester was probably reformed with the other Winchester communities in 964,[44] and it is likely that Æthelwold was responsible for imposing stricter standards on other nunneries in his diocese.[45] In part, Æthelwold's interest in nunneries can be associated with his support for Edgar's second wife, Queen Ælfthryth, who was given a special supervisory role over the nunneries in the *Regularis Concordia*.[46] Her new foundation of Wherwell (Hants.) was supported by

---

Winchester documents: see E. John, 'The Church of Winchester and the Tenth-Century Reformation', *Bulletin of the John Rylands Library* 74 (1964-5), 404-29, and H. P. R. Finberg, 'The Winchester Cathedral Clergy: their Endowments and their Diplomatic Crimes', *The Early Charters of Wessex* (Leicester, 1964), pp 214-48. At Ely it seems to have been believed that the 'Isle of Ely', which Æthelwold acquired piecemeal from several landowners, represented a dowry which Æthelthryth had received from her husband, Tondbert: E. Miller, *The Abbey and Bishopric of Ely* (Cambridge, 1951), pp 9-17. See also below, Wormald ch 1, pp 39-40, and Thacker ch 2, pp 53-4.

[39] Robertson no. 45.

[40] See, for example, the actions of Leofsige who seized estates of Peterborough and Ely after Edgar's death (*Liber Eliensis* II, 11), and for Thorney estates, see Raban, *Thorney and Crowland*, pp 16-17.

[41] E. John, 'Kings and Monks in the Tenth-Century Reformation', *Orbis Britanniae*, pp 154-80.

[42] D. J. V. Fisher, 'The Anti-Monastic Reaction in the Reign of Edward the Martyr', *Cambridge Historical Journal* 10 (1950-2), 254-70, and E. John, 'War and Society in the Tenth Century: the Maldon Campaign', *Transactions of the Royal Historical Society*, 5th series, 27 (1977), 173-95.

[43] Gretsch, *Die Regula Sancti Benedicti in England*, *passim* and 'Æthelwold's translation of the *Regula Sancti Benedicti* and its Latin exemplar', *ASE* 3 (1974), 125-51. *Liber Eliensis* II, 37 records that Edgar and Ælfthryth gave an estate at Sudbourne (Suffolk) to Æthelwold on condition that he should translate the *Rule of St Benedict* into English.

[44] Wulfstan, *Vita*, ch 22, records the reform of Nunnaminster, but does not date it, though he does place it before the acquisition and reform of Ely (970); see also Ælfric ch 17.

[45] For Romsey, see S 812 and E. John, 'Some Latin Charters of the Tenth-Century Reformation', *Orbis Britanniae*, pp 181-209.

[46] *Regularis Concordia*, p 2. Some uncertainty exists about the number of Edgar's marriages, but it seems most likely that he married twice and that the union with Wulfthryth which produced St Edith was illicit (*Gesta Pontificum*, pp 190-1); see further Yorke below, ch 3, pp 82-4.

estates which had formerly been part of the endowment of the Old and New Minsters of Winchester.[47]

Æthelwold not only took care of the landed endowments of his monasteries, but also of their immediate physical surroundings. In Winchester the south-eastern quarter of the town was reorganised so that each of the religious houses could have its own precinct and be separated from the ordinary citizens.[48] The monasteries were provided with elaborate stone buildings, which showed the influence of contemporary European styles of architecture. Of all Æthelwold's churches, most is known about the Old Minster in Winchester. Its ground-plan has been revealed through excavation and can be supplemented by the written descriptions of Wulfstan and his contemporary Lantfred.[49] When Æthelwold extended the Old Minster, he incorporated both the original seventh-century church and the burial place of St Swithun into it, and so was able to stress through architectural form the continuity with past religious practice which he was so anxious to demonstrate in other ways as well.[50] The new church was dominated by a massive westwork which was probably adjacent to the royal palace and intended, in part, for royal use.[51]

Æthelwold's churches with their large number of altars and side-chapels were intended as settings for elaborate liturgy and processions.[52] The form of church services was a major preoccupation of the *Regularis Concordia*, and Æthelwold appears to have tried to synthesise the best of Continental and English practices in the liturgies of his foundations.[53] Æthelwold's stress on the importance of the monastic office led naturally to a concern with music. Monks from Fleury and Corbie were brought over to instruct the monks of Abingdon in the correct forms of chanting, and their pupils went on to develop new musical forms. At Winchester the art of troping was considerably advanced, the concepts of harmony were introduced and new forms of notation developed to record their advances. The human voice was supplemented with instruments: the organ is mentioned as having been used at Winchester and Ramsey.[54]

The churches were richly decorated with furnishings of gold and silver provided by Æthelwold himself, though sadly none of the major pieces still exist and we have to rely on written descriptions from his foundations.[55]

---

[47] M. A. Meyer, 'Women and the Tenth-Century English Monastic Reform', *Revue Bénédictine* 87 (1977), 51-61.

[48] Robertson no. 49; M. Biddle, '*Felix Urbs Winthonia*: Winchester in the Age of Monastic Reform', *Tenth-Century Studies*, pp 132-9.

[49] Quirk, 'Winchester Cathedral'.

[50] Sheerin, 'Dedication of Old Minster', 261-73, and see n 38 above.

[51] Biddle, '*Felix Urbs Winthonia*', p 138.

[52] H. M. Taylor, 'Tenth-Century Church Building in England and on the Continent', *Tenth-Century Studies*, pp 141-68.

[53] See Prescott below, ch 5, pp 119-47.

[54] See Berry below, ch 6, pp 149-60.

[55] *Chron. Abingdon* I, 343-7, lists the gifts which it was believed Æthelwold had given to the foundation, including a silver *tabula* costing £300, a gold chalice of immense weight, three crosses of silver and gold and many lesser items, though it is unlikely that Æthelwold actually made any of these items as the chronicler claimed. The chronicler notes that many of Æthelwold's gifts were taken to Normandy after the Conquest. (See also Thacker below, ch 2, pp 57-8.) For his gifts to Peterborough, see Robertson no. 39, and to Ely, *Liber Eliensis* II, 3.

Fortunately a few pieces of sculpture and some internal fittings have survived, and, although these would be considered minor works by the Anglo-Saxons, they do give us some idea of the high standards of craftsmanship and iconographical representation to be found in Æthelwold's religious houses.[56] But the major existing tributes to the craftsmen of Æthelwold's foundations are the manuscripts. Pride of place must go to the *Benedictional of St Æthelwold*, produced for Æthelwold's own use and written by his chaplain Godeman, whom Æthelwold later appointed as the first abbot of Thorney.[57] Many aspects of the lavishly decorated *Benedictional* are without parallel. Its text is a skilful synthesis of the two main Continental traditions with English practice,[58] and many of its illustrations are original compositions.[59] Gold is much in evidence, both in the illustrations and in the opening dedicatory verse.[60] The artistic workshops established at Æthelwold's foundations during his lifetime were to continue as influential schools of craftsmen after his death, and had a widespread influence both in England and on the Continent.[61]

Æthelwold's scriptoria also produced less elaborate works to aid the spread of Christian learning in his foundations. Among Æthelwold's gifts to Peterborough at the time of its foundation were twenty-one Latin works, including commentaries on the Bible and on Christian doctrine, grammatical works, saints' lives and Latin verse.[62] Æthelwold established high standards of learning in his foundations and personally provided instruction in the liberal arts at Abingdon and Winchester. Wulfstan, Lantfred, Godeman and other anonymous writers testify to the skills in the composition of Latin poetry and prose which could be acquired at Winchester.[63] These writers favoured the hermeneutic style of Latin writing: a rather ostentatious style which delighted in obscure construction and rarefied vocabulary and whose use in England had been developed by the West Saxon scholar, Aldhelm (bishop of Sherborne 705-9). Æthelwold himself wrote in this style and although only a few examples of his Latin composition survive, it is clear that he was himself a highly proficient writer and translator of Latin.[64]

Æthelwold as well as being a good Latin scholar, wrote in the vernacular and encouraged its use in his foundations. Memoranda on land transactions

[56] See, for instance, *The Golden Age of Anglo-Saxon Art, 966-1066*, ed. J. Backhouse, D. H. Turner and L. Webster (London, 1984), especially pp 94 (metalwork), 115 (ivory), 130 (stonework), 135 (window glass), and 136-7 (tiles), and Coatsworth, below, ch 7, pp 161-93.
[57] BL, Add. MS 49598. There is a facsimile edition: G. F. Warner and H. A. Wilson, *The Benedictional of St Æthelwold* (Roxburghe, 1910).
[58] Prescott below, ch 5.
[59] R. Deshman, '*Christus rex et magi reges*: Kingship and Christology in Ottonian and Anglo-Saxon Art', *Frühmittelalterliche Studien* 10 (1976), 367-405, and E. Temple, *Anglo-Saxon Manuscripts 900-1066* (London, 1976), no. 23.
[60] The dedicatory poem is edited in M. Lapidge, 'The hermeneutic style in tenth-century Anglo-Latin literature', *ASE* 4 (1975), appendix II, 105-7.
[61] Deshman *op. cit.* and Coatsworth below, ch 7.
[62] Robertson no. 39; M. Lapidge, 'Surviving booklists from Anglo-Saxon England', *Learning and Literature in Anglo-Saxon England*, pp 52-5.
[63] M. Lapidge, 'Three Latin poems from Æthelwold's school at Winchester', *ASE* 1 (1972), 85-137, 'The hermeneutic style', 85-90, and below, ch 4, pp 104-12.
[64] See Lapidge below, ch 4, pp 93-101.

might be written in Old English,[65] but Æthelwold was also aware of the value of the vernacular for educating a wider body of people. His compositions in Old English include the tract on the establishment of the monasteries, and a translation of the *Rule of St Benedict*.[66] Æthelwold's Old English is distinctive and, unlike his Latin writings, its primary characteristic is its clarity.[67] It is likely that Winchester possessed a considerable school of Old English studies which played a major part in the development of Standard Old English.[68] Its most illustrious pupil was Ælfric who produced a wide range of homiletic and educational works in the vernacular which played an important part in widening the scope of the tenth-century reformation.[69]

Æthelwold's work as a leading churchman of the tenth century must be viewed in relation to that of the other Anglo-Saxon reformers, principally Dunstan, archbishop of Canterbury (959-88), and Oswald, archbishop of York and bishop of Worcester (Worcester 961-92; York 972-92). All shared aims for the revival of monasticism, Latin learning and the arts, though they did not necessarily favour identical policies or styles. Æthelwold's belief that a bishop's household should be served by monks not canons, his interest in the vernacular and in the earlier monastic history of England places him somewhat apart.[70] The question of whether Dunstan or Æthelwold should be seen as the major influence on King Edgar and the ecclesiastical policy of his reign is the subject of some debate.[71] Dunstan's role in the religious policy of Edgar's reign is enigmatic, for neither of his pre-Conquest biographers discuss his career as archbishop.[72] The importance of his monastery at Glastonbury has already been mentioned, and Canterbury was certainly a major artistic and intellectual centre, though it does not seem to have experienced any major reform in Dunstan's time.[73] Later tradition attributed the reform of various south-western foundations to Dunstan,[74] but none of them have produced anything like the wealth of documentary evidence which survives from Æthelwold's foundations. Although Glastonbury was

[65] See Robertson nos. 31, 37, 38, 39, 40, 45, 49 and 53. It is likely that a vernacular account lies behind Ely's *libellus* (*Liber Eliensis* p xix).

[66] See nn 1 and 43.

[67] See Lapidge below, ch 4, pp 101-3.

[68] H. Gneuss, 'The origin of Standard Old English and Æthelwold's school at Winchester', *ASE* 1 (1972), 63-84, and Lapidge below, ch 4, pp 108-10.

[69] The principle editions of Ælfric's work are *The Homilies of the Anglo-Saxon Church*, Part I, ed. B. Thorpe (London, 1844); *Ælfric's Lives of the Saints*, ed. W. Skeat, EETS 76, 82, 94 and 114 (London, 1881-90); *Ælfric's Catholic Homilies: The Second Series*, ed. M. Godden, EETS, 2nd series, no. 5 (London, 1979). For a recent general assessment of Ælfric's work see E. John, 'The World of Abbot Ælfric', *Ideal and Reality*, pp 300-16.

[70] Wormald below, ch 1, pp 30-42.

[71] The case for Dunstan as the main architect of the tenth-century reformation is argued by Robinson, *Times of St Dunstan*, pp 81-103, and N. Brooks, *The Early History of the Church of Canterbury: Christ Church from 597 to 1066* (Leicester, 1984), pp 243-53. A spirited case for Dunstan's eclipse by Æthelwold is made by John, *Orbis Britanniae* pp 154-80.

[72] For a discussion of the possible reasons see Brooks *op. cit.*

[73] Brooks, *Church of Canterbury*, pp 250-66. Canterbury in Dunstan's time seems to have contained a mixed community of clerks and monks like many of the Continental centres which contained both a bishop's *familia* and a monastic community (see Wormald below, ch 1, pp 37-8). The arrangements of Canterbury therefore differed from those of Winchester and from what was proposed in the *Regularis Concordia*.

[74] Knowles, *Monastic Order*, pp 49-50.

the richest of all the English monastic houses in 1086 and the one from which the greatest number of post-reformation bishops is known to have been appointed,[75] it is noticeable, in the relevant lists printed by Knowles, that overall Æthelwold's refounded monasteries feature much more strongly than the houses associated with Dunstan.[76] Æthelwold and his biographers pay tribute to Dunstan's role as archbishop,[77] but the biographer of Oswald believed it was Æthelwold who was Edgar's chief counsellor.[78] It was after Æthelwold's appointment as bishop of Winchester that the major period of monastic reform began, apparently with the active support of Edgar, and it was Æthelwold who wrote the *Regularis Concordia* and played the major role in the Winchester council. Dunstan's role in the reforms of Edgar's reign remains obscure, but there seems little doubt of Æthelwold's importance.

Æthelwold's relationship with Edgar was more than just that of a bishop with his king. There is a body of evidence which suggests that Æthelwold had acted as Edgar's tutor when abbot of Abingdon,[79] and he has been identified as the so-called 'Edgar A' scribe who wrote a large number of the original charters extant from the period 960 to 963.[80] It would appear that Æthelwold had been in the personal service of King Edgar between 960 and 963, if not before, writing and drafting royal charters, and no doubt helping to guide royal policy.[81] Æthelwold's biographers refer to co-operation between Æthelwold and Edgar on ecclesiastical matters, but they preferred not to discuss Æthelwold's influence on secular affairs. Yet many of Æthelwold's ecclesiastical concerns had an overt political dimension as well, and appear to have been designed to elevate the office of king. The stress on the king's role in the *Regularis Concordia*, the political symbolism of westworks and some of the imagery in the *Benedictional*, all point in this direction,[82] and raise questions about Æthelwold's role in key events of Edgar's reign, such as his second coronation at Bath in 973 with its imperial connotations.[83]

Æthelwold also played a part in the succession disputes of Edgar's reign

[75] Glastonbury had been the pre-eminent West Saxon religious house since the time of Edmund (see n 13), and a number of those who had been monks there had left to join Æthelwold. We tend to know more about Glastonbury than other religious houses because of the researches of William of Malmesbury, so its domination in Knowles' lists may be more apparent than real. I am grateful to Patrick Wormald for this point.

[76] Knowles, *Monastic Order*, pp 697-701 and 702-3. Christ Church and St Augustine's, Canterbury, were also remarkably wealthy, but seem to have produced few bishops.

[77] Æthelwold, in his vernacular account, places most emphasis on the role of King Edgar, but says that he acted with Dunstan's advice: *Councils and Synods* no. 33. See also Ælfric ch 18, and Wulfstan ch 27.

[78] *Hist. York* I, 427, and see Stenton, *Anglo-Saxon England*, pp 449-53. Wulfstan, *Vita* ch 25, stresses the links between Edgar and Æthelwold, and says that Æthelwold was *a secretis Edgari*.

[79] John, *Orbis Britanniae*, pp 159-60, though the evidence is not as clear-cut as has sometimes been believed. See also Lapidge below, ch 4, p 98.

[80] R. Drögereit, 'Gab es eine angelsächsische Königskanzlei?', *Archiv für Urkundenforschung* 13 (1935), 335-436.

[81] S. Keynes, *The Diplomas of King Æthelred 'The Unready' 978-1016: A Study in Their Use as Historical Evidence* (Cambridge, 1980), pp 71-9.

[82] Deshman, 'Kingship and Christology', 399-204.

[83] Dunstan has usually been credited with developing the coronation *ordo* used in 973, and the ideas of rulership contained within it. See Brooks, *Church of Canterbury*, pp 247-8; A. Jones, 'The Significance of the Regal Consecration of Edgar in 973', *Journal of Ecclesiastical History* 33 (1982), 375-90.

and seems to have been a major supporter of Edgar's second wife, Ælfthryth.[84] His support for the claims of her sons over those of their elder half-brother Edward is unequivocal, and when Ælfthryth's son, Æthelred, became king in 978, Æthelwold was one of the young king's major advisors. Æthelwold's death in 984 seems to have been followed by a major change in the alignments at the royal court.[85] It is in these political dimensions of Æthelwold's life and work that his contemporary biographers appear to be most deficient.

Such omissions are not surprising for the lives by Wulfstan and Ælfric were written primarily to promote the cult of St Æthelwold. The first public stage in its promotion was the translation of Æthelwold's body on 10 September 996, some twelve years after his death on 1 August 984. Wulfstan played a prominent part in the events leading up to the translation and in the subsequent development of the cult, and his life of Æthelwold should be seen as one part of his activities on behalf of his former mentor.[86] So it is not surprising that Wulfstan and Ælfric stress Æthelwold's personal piety and adherence to Benedictine practice. He did not drink alcohol nor eat animal flesh, except when obliged to through infirmity.[87] Even as abbot and bishop Æthelwold joined in the manual work of his foundations and narrowly escaped death when a timber fell on him during building works at Abingdon.[88] Miracles during his lifetime and at his tomb bore witness to the sanctity of his personal life.[89]

It is hard to get behind such hagiography to an appreciation of what Æthelwold may actually have been like, though there can be little doubt that he was an exceptional personality. He is traditionally seen as the most austere and severe of the reformers. Wulfstan and Ælfric indicate that Æthelwold expected high standards from those under him and an unquestioning obedience, even if it meant, as it did for one monk, plunging an arm into a boiling cauldron.[90] But we can also see from their work that Æthelwold had won the respect and gratitude of his monks. Æthelwold was evidently a good patron to those who served him, and a significant proportion of his monks received advancement in the church as abbots or bishops.[91] But Æthelwold could also be an implacable and ruthless opponent, as many former secular clerks and landowners knew to their cost. However, one must be careful to judge Æthelwold by the standards of his own time, not by the timeless standards of sainthood. He lived at a time when dishonouring one's enemies was as important as honouring one's friends, at a time when bishops were major figures at court who were expected to accept the standards of the secular aristocracy and who needed influence with the royal house to achieve ecclesiastical innovations. It is inevitable that

---

[84] See Yorke below, ch 3, pp 81-7.
[85] Keynes, *Diplomas*, pp 176-86.
[86] See Lapidge below, ch 4, pp 112-17.
[87] Ælfric ch 20, Wulfstan, *Vita* ch 30.
[88] Ælfric ch 11, Wulfstan, *Vita* ch 15.
[89] Ælfric ch 21-8; Wulfstan, *Vita* ch 32-9, 42-6.
[90] Ælfric ch 10, Wulfstan, *Vita* ch 14.
[91] Abbots Aldulf of Peterborough, Brihtnoth of Ely, Godeman of Thorney, Ordbriht of Chertsey, Ælfric of St Albans, Æthelgar of New Minster and Osgar of Abingdon were all pupils of Æthelwold and sometime monks of Abingdon. Many of Æthelwold's monks later became bishops, see Knowles, *Monastic Order*, appendix IV, pp 697-701.

Æthelwold should remain something of an enigma, but his actions can speak as eloquently as Wulfstan's and Ælfric's prose. Æthelwold was a man who believed fervently in the need to restore the monastic Golden Age of Bede's *Historia Ecclesiastica* and while some of his methods may seem questionable, his strength of purpose, his administrative skills and his ability to inspire others can still impress us a thousand years later.

Æthelwold has not attracted a modern, full-length biography. Assessments of his life have been made by Robinson and Knowles, both of whom, it would be fair to say, did not find their subject entirely to their liking.[92] These studies concentrated on Æthelwold's career in the church, but more recently Eric John, in a series of papers, has stressed the political and social dimensions of many of Æthelwold's reforms.[93] Our assessment of Æthelwold has also benefited in recent years from a growing appreciation of the relationship of the English reforms to similar movements in Europe.[94] The problems in studying Æthelwold are in many ways the problems of studying the tenth-century reformation as a whole. Many of the major texts are not available in modern editions and until this has been achieved a full assessment of the work of Æthelwold and the other reformers will not be possible. The range of papers gathered in this volume also reveals another major problem, for so widespread was Æthelwold's influence, that any study would have to draw on expertise in many different branches of academic study. It is hoped, however, that the volume will go some way to aiding the reassessment of the career and influence of this important, but complex, man.[95]

[92] Robinson, *Times of St Dunstan*, pp 104-22; Knowles, *Monastic Order*, pp 36-56 – 'Ethelwold was throughout of a more austere and intransigent temper than Dunstan' (p 39).
[93] Especially *Orbis Britanniae*, pp 154-80, and 'War and Society', 173-95.
[94] For instance, D. Bullough, 'The Continental Background of Reform', *Tenth-Century Studies*, pp 20-36, and Wormald below, ch 1, pp 13-42.
[95] I would like to thank all the contributors whose papers have helped me to write the Introduction, and Patrick Wormald in particular who has provided me with much helpful advice; however, they bear no responsibility for any errors remaining.

Chapter 1

ÆTHELWOLD AND HIS CONTINENTAL COUNTERPARTS:
CONTACT, COMPARISON, CONTRAST

Patrick Wormald

Æthelwold's life more or less spanned the tenth century, the *siècle de fer*. It is not surprising that this sombre assessment of the age is most familiar in French. On the whole, it was a poor century for French kingship, as the Carolingian dynasty came to an end (if rather less messily than most French dynasties). The phrase was originally coined by Cardinal Baronius, who went on to call it 'leaden' too. This doubtless reflected the Holy See's embarrassment at the alleged antics of its popes, which would give Gibbon as much fun as the seedier late Roman emperors. Elsewhere the outlook was considerably brighter. In Germany and England, the rise of new monarchies was boosted by unprecedented triumphs over old and much-feared enemies. Otto the Great and Edgar the Peaceable were consciously heirs to what the Franks appeared to have lost. Three of the century's more positive aspects are highlighted by the life of Æthelwold. One is the spectacular economic growth, marked by both urbanisation and monetarisation, of the lands controlled by successful rulers. Æthelwold is actually the first Englishman known to have been born in a town, and his Winchester was as conspicuous a beneficiary of commercial development and royal patronage as Otto's Magdeburg. A second is the ordeal, to be seen as a confident effort to channel divine intervention into societies perceived literally as theocracies. Appropriately, the *siècle de fer* was the century *par excellence* of the ordeal: at one end of the German empire, a missionary was said to have converted the Danish king by carrying the hot iron unscathed, and at the other, Otto scandalised the bookish Italian lawyers by formally introducing the judicial duel. An extraordinary incident in Æthelwold's *vita* saw the saint insist that one of his monks who was exceptionally competent in the kitchen (and who later became bishop of Ramsbury) prove the obedience that he had previously

A version of this paper was read at the Anglo-American Conference of Historians in July 1985, as well as at the Winchester festival of summer 1984. I am most grateful to those who have commented on the text in its successive stages: Stuart Airlie, Marilyn Dunn, Simon Keynes, Michael Lapidge, Patricia Morison, Jinty Nelson and especially John Nightingale, who was most generous with his wide knowledge of the primary and secondary literature of tenth-century reform. Over the years, I have learnt much about these matters from the teaching of Karl Leyser and Henry Mayr-Harting: the first rescued me with welcome discretion from a grisly error in my original Winchester lecture, and the second kindly checked the final draft for any more. In a field where so much is *sub iudice* as well as *sub specie aeternitatis*, however, none of these scholars should be thought to endorse all that follows. Finally, I owe much to the acumen and patience of Barbara Yorke and Jenny Wormald, which extended far beyond the calls of editorial and conjugal duty respectively.

'stolen' from Æthelwold in that he had exercised it behind his back, by drawing a morsel from out of a boiling cauldron. The third is the subject of this book. For English historians, the Tenth Century is above all one of 'Reformation', the enforcement of Benedictine observance upon the religious life which, to judge from his memorials, was the main inspiration of Æthelwold's life. On the continent, likewise, the century was pre-eminent among those dubbed 'Benedictine' by Cardinal Newman. It began with the foundation of Cluny; it saw movements of Benedictine reform in most of Latin Christendom; and it concluded with the first stirrings of monastic revival among the Normans – a people, as the apostle of their reform was said to have remarked, hitherto renowned for a rather different kind of interest in monasteries.[1]

But Æthelwold's European context is not just an agreeable backcloth to our portrait. For Æthelwold, as for most major Anglo-Saxon churchmen, continental scenery is an important part of the picture. It is as meaningless to deny religious change its external inspiration, at almost any stage in the history of the British Isles, as it is to monitor modern European economies without regard to Wall Street. Æthelwold's *Regularis Concordia* admitted a debt to continental movements. But, as Professor Bullough has said, '"England and the Continent in the Tenth Century" is one of the unwritten works of early medieval historiography.' Much has been written on the Anglo-Saxon and European reforms in English and continental languages respectively; but there is no Levison to link the two worlds, then and now. Further, the very exercise of cross-channel comparison gives a third dimension to English patterns otherwise visible only in two. This is especially useful for the 'Tenth-Century Reformation', where the sources are so one-sided. We may suppose that the range of reforming ambitions and counter-reforming challenges was broadly the same on the continent as in England (just as it was half a millenium later); so the much richer European material raises a wider range of questions than we can ask of insular evidence alone. Moreover, as I have argued before, 'one of the advantages of considering early English history in the widest possible continental context is that one then sees not only what is (often surprisingly) similar, but also what is significantly different'. A continental perspective brings out precisely those English phenomena which cannot be passed off as manifestations of the *Zeitgeist* (always a temptation in this sort of exercise), and which cry the

---

[1] On the *siècle de fer* see M.T.Gibson, 'The continuity of learning, *c*.850-*c*.1050', *Viator*, 6 (1975), 1. For the battle of the Lech, see Widukind, *Res gestae Saxonicae*, ed. H.-E.Lohmann and P.Hirsch, *MGH, Scriptores rerum Germanicarum* iii 5, p 129; and, for the Battle of Brunanburh, *The Anglo-Saxon Chronicle: MS A*, ed. J.M.Bately, The Anglo-Saxon Chronicle, a collaborative edition, ed. D.Dumville and S.Keynes, III (Cambridge, 1986), p 72. For the *translatio imperii* see Widukind i 34, p 48, and below, pp 31-2 and n 78. For Æthelwold and the ordeal see Wulfstan, *Vita* ch 14, pp 42-3; for Poppo and the Danes, Widukind iii 65, pp 140-1, and for Otto and the lawyers, C.Wickham, *Early Medieval Italy* (London, 1981), p 129. For William of Volpiano on the Normans see *Libellus de Revelatione ... Fiscanensis Monasterii*, PL CLI, col 721; R.Herval, 'Un moine de l'an mille: Guillaume de Volpiano. Ier abbé de Fécamp', *L'Abbaye de Fécamp: Ouvrage scientifique du xiii centénaire, 658-1958* (Fécamp, 1959), has his doubts, but the story is at least *ben trovato*. See also N.Bulst, *Untersuchungen zu den Klosterreformen Wilhelms von Dijon*, Pariser Historische Studien 11 (Bonn, 1973), pp 147-9.

louder for explanation. Such considerations determine the structure of this paper. The first part attempts an introduction to six European reformers, whose names are better known than their records. Three issues follow: a probable instance of continental influence on Æthelwold's objectives; an area where his approach is profitably compared with foreign models; and a discrepancy between him and his continental counterparts, which seems to arise from his *English* background.[2]

I begin, as one so often must with the major themes of medieval European history, in the age of Charlemagne. Among the young bloods at the Frankish court in the 760s was a Visigothic aristocrat apparently called Witiza, but known to Ardo his biographer, to his contemporaries and to history by the significant name of Benedict. Like Æthelwold's, Benedict's spiritual life began at court. But unlike Æthelwold's (at least as reported), Benedict's was a personal conversion born of the realisation that honour was laboriously attained and swiftly lost, which he concealed from his father until he was safely tonsured at St Seine near Dijon (774). His monastic life was at first notably austere: he preferred the models of Basil and Pachomius to St Benedict's Rule, which he regarded as fit only for novices and the sick. Even when he warmed to it, graduating, as Ardo says, from single combat to public warfare, 'he declined a little from the rigour of his first conversion because he had taken on an impossible task, but his will remained the same': to the end of his life, like Æthelwold, he refused four-footed flesh and had chicken soup only when ill. Offered the abbacy of St Seine, he preferred to return to his homeland and found a tiny cell on family property at Aniane. Yet celebrity was thrust upon him, as on so many heroes of monastic history. Aniane had to be rebuilt repeatedly to accommodate his following, which reached three hundred (Ardo among them). He inspired the conversion to religious life of William of Gellone, founder of the ducal house of Aquitaine. He secured a royal charter from Charlemagne, intended (said Ardo) to protect his monastery from the claims of his kin, and in fact guaranteeing the election of its abbot according to St Benedict's Rule. He was given other monasteries to reform or establish. In a probable echo of the original Benedict, he was said at the end of his life to have had twelve monasteries under his rule, and he kept them under close supervision, to the extent of appointing their abbots as Æthelwold did (and as St Benedict had done, whatever his Rule said). It was arguably a tribute to his efforts that the Council of Chalon in 813 expressed satisfaction with monastic standards

---

[2] D. A. Bullough, 'The continental background of the reform', *Tenth Century Studies*, p 20; this paper, marked by deftness of touch as well as weight of learning, is much the best discussion now available in English (though see also n 29 below), but there is perhaps room for more concessions to the 'Anglorum gentis inertiae'. The other quotation is from my 'Bede and Benedict Biscop', *Famulus Christi: studies in commemoration of the thirteenth centenary of the birth of the Venerable Bede*, ed. G. Bonner (London, 1976), p 154, to which this article is in some sense a sequel. The continental literature on almost all matters discussed here is vast. E. Sackur, *Die Cluniacenser in ihrer kirchlichen und allgemeingeschichtlichen Wirksamkeit bis zur Mitte des elften Jahrhunderts*, 2 vols (Halle, 1892-4) may be said to have defined the subject's terms and remains fundamental: I have not henceforth cited its many detailed insights. References to modern literature are generally restricted to (a) works in English, (b) works in foreign languages which seem to me (i) 'strategic', or (ii) in need of rebuttal.

throughout the southern region that was its remit, unlike the four councils held elsewhere in Francia that year.[3]

When Louis, who, as sub-king, had backed Benedict's work in the *Midi*, succeeded his father at Aachen, he founded a monastery for him at nearby Cornelimünster, and invited him to do for Frankish monasticism as a whole what he had already done in the south. The result was a remarkable burst of Aachen legislation, now expertly disentangled and dated 816-19.[4] This for the first time drew a firm line between monks professing the Rule of St Benedict, and canons or 'clerici', living a communal life which nevertheless allowed for the retention of personal property, and for pastoral work in the Church at large. Thus the many communities which had other than truly monastic priorities were given their own code of observance based on the Rule for canons produced two generations before by Chrodegang of Metz.[5] For monks proper, the obligatory Rule of St Benedict was accompanied by an equally binding customary which supplemented and partly superseded it. The liturgy was to be that of St Benedict, but a number of prayers and rituals were added; eating fowl was forbidden except for the sick, as in Benedict of Aniane's own lifestyle, then permitted, on reflection, for eight days at Christmas and Easter, which were then cut to four.[6] Ardo calls this customary a 'capitularem institutum', and there is evidence that it was enforced by *missi*, like other royal legislation. The idea was that 'just as there was one profession for all, so there should also be one health-giving custom [*una salubris consuetudo*]'; the effect was that 'all monasteries were so arrayed *ad formam unitatis* as if they were set up by one master and in one place'.[7]

---

[3] Ardo, *Vita Benedicti abbatis Anianensis* [*VB*], ed. G. Waitz, MGH, *Scriptores* XV(1), ch 1-3, 5-6, 17-21, 24, 30-1, 42, pp 201-4, 205-10, 211-14, 218-19. MGH, *Diplomata Karolinorum* [*DK*], ed. E. Mühlbacher, I 173, pp 231-3. MGH, *Concilia*, II(1), ed. A. Werminghoff, 37: 22, p 278, and cf. *ibid.*, pp 259-60, 289-90. For Æthelwold's appointment of abbots, Wulfstan, *Vita* ch 21, 23, pp 46-7; for St Benedict's theory, *La règle de St Benôit* [*RB*], ed. A. de Vogüé, Sources Chrétiennes, 181-6 (Paris, 1971-2), ch 64, II pp 648-9; and for his practice, *Grégoire le Grand, Dialogues*, ed. de Vogüé, Sources Chrétiennes, 251, 260, 265 (Paris, 1978-80), ii 3, 22, pp 148-51, 202-3. J. Semmler, 'Benedictus II: *Una regula, una consuetudo*', *Benedictine Culture, 750-1050*, ed. W. Lourdaux and D. Verhelst (Medievalia Lovanensia 11, 1983), pp 1-49 is an up-to-date summary of the views of the main modern authority on Benedict of Aniane, with full bibliography of his earlier work. See also R. McKitterick, *The Frankish Kingdoms under the Carolingians, 751-987* (London, 1983), pp 108-24.

[4] *VB* ch 29, 35-9, pp 211, 215-18. CCM I, ed. K. Hallinger, 18-25, pp 433-561; note that what Ardo says about the lightening of 'munera' on monasteries, ch 39, pp 217-18 is reflected in 'Notitia de servitio monasteriorum', *ibid.*, pp 483-99. J. Semmler, 'Zur Überlieferung der monastischen Gesetzgebung Ludwigs des frommen', *Deutsches Archiv* 16 (1960), 310-88 was the pioneering work; note that 10 July 817, the date borne by most MSS of the authoritative text of the monastic decree, was possibly not that of its final promulgation.

[5] MGH, *Concilia*, II(1) 39, pp 307-421. J. Semmler, 'Mönche und Kanoniker im Frankenreiche Pippins III und Karls des Großen', *Untersuchungen zu Kloster und Stift*, Veröffentlichungen des Max-Planck-Instituts für Geschichte 68 (1980), pp 78-111. See also Ch. Dereine, 'Chanoines', *Dictionnaire d'histoire et de géographie ecclésiastique* 12, cols 364-75.

[6] *VB* ch 21, p 209; CCM I 18: 7, 20: 6, 21: 43, 23: 77, pp 435, 458, 481, 534-5. J. Semmler, '"Volatilia": zu den benediktinischen Consuetudines des 9 Jahrhunderts', *Studien und Mitteilungen zur Geschichte des Benediktinerordens* 69 (1958), 163-76.

[7] *VB* ch 36, p 215. For the *missi* see (e.g.) CCM I 14-15, pp 331-54; *Vita Hludowici Imperatoris*, ed. G. H. Pertz, MGH, *Scriptores* II ch 28, p 622; and the texts cited by E. Lesne, 'Les Ordonnances monastiques de Louis le Pieux et la *Notitia de servitio monasteriorum*', *Revue d'histoire de l'Eglise de France* 6 (1920), 173-4.

Benedict's career is marked by several paradoxes. Known as 'Benedict II' to some contemporaries, he has been accused by some later Benedictines of betraying the spirit of the first Benedict's Rule.[8] Hailed by the monks of Cornelimünster in the letter communicating to Ardo the exact date of his death (11 February 821) as 'he … through whom the Lord Christ has restored the Rule of St Benedict in the whole kingdom of the Franks', and the leader of a reform generally represented at the time as a recovery of 'pristine' standards, he is perceived rather as an innovator by modern scholars, for whom the eighth century is still an age of the 'Regula Mixta'.[9] Finally, though the Aachen legislation exists in seven versions distributed through fifty-one manuscripts (albeit only ten from ninth-century Francia), his quest for uniform observance undoubtedly failed; and while his influence on later reformers is clear (Cluniac sources alone tell us his Visigothic name), it has proved impossible to trace the channels of its transmission.[10] In considering these problems, it is necessary, first, to remember that St Benedict himself allowed his abbots considerable discretion, not least as regards the liturgy so considerably expanded by his namesake. Moreover, the latter was only echoing the former in regarding the Rule as one 'for beginners', and in looking beyond it to the models of Basil and Pachomius. In his *Concordia Regularum*, designed to demonstrate its harmony with other rules, he placed *first* St Benedict's *final* chapter, in which the father of western monks directed attention to the superior eastern prototypes; and his encyclopedic *codex* of pre-Carolingian rules was a logical follow-up.[11] His reported ambition to bring monastic life within reach of the many rather than the few corresponds with his master's; and while the second Benedict's concessions to Frankish *mores* over a kin's retention of an oblate's family property might not have been endorsed by the first, his inclusion of a prison for delinquent brethren surely met the spirit of the original Rule's anxiety lest any professed soul be jettisoned.[12] Benedict of Aniane was thus entitled to the name he took because he was the most prolific western student of monastic literature since Benedict of Nursia, and perhaps he understood the Rule's strengths better than anyone before Dom de Vogüé: in its comprehensive range it was a faithful guide to previous *exempla*, while its flexibility made it adaptable to changing spiritual and social needs.

---

[8] See P. Schmitz, 'L'influence de Saint Benôit d'Aniane dans l'histoire de l'ordre de Saint-Benôit', *Il Monachesimo nell' Alto Medioevo: Settimane di Studio del Centro Italiano di Studi sull'Alto Medioevo* 4 (1957), 401-15.

[9] *VB* ch 36, 42, pp 215, 219; *Cartulaire générale de l'Yonne*, ed. M. Quantin (Auxerre, 1854) 25, p 49; *Gesta abbatum Fontanellensium*, ed. S. Loewenfeld, *MGH, Scriptores rerum germanicarum* ch 17, pp 50-1. J. Semmler, 'Pippin III und die fränkischen Klöster', *Francia* 3 (1975), 130-46 summarises his oft-repeated views on early Carolingian monasticism.

[10] John of Salerno, *Vita S. Odonis* [*VO*], *PL* CXXXIII i 22-3, cols 53-4. A. H. Bredero, 'Cluny et le monachisme Carolingien: continuité et discontinuité', *Benedictine Culture* (as n 3), pp 50-75. Neither Aniane nor Cornelimünster had the permanent importance of Cluny, Fleury, Gorze, St Maximin's or Abingdon, and Benedict's *vita* was not preserved outside Aniane itself.

[11] *RB* ch 18, 73, II pp 534-5, 672-5; *VB* ch 2, 38, pp 202, 216-17; *Concordia Regularum Patrum* ch 1; *Codex Regularum*, *PL* CIII, cols 717-22, 393-702.

[12] *VB* ch 2, p 202; *CCM* I 20: 33, 36, 23: 28, 31, pp 466-8, 523-4; cf. *RB* ch 23-28, II pp 542-53. J. Semmler, 'Die Beschlüße des Aachener Konzils im Jahre 816', *Zeitschrift für Kirchengeschichte* 74 (1963), 45-6, 50-1, and cf. *ibid.*, pp 53-4 on alcohol.

Nor was the pre-eminence assigned to the Rule in the Aachen legislation entirely new. Other monastic traditions indeed survived in the eighth century, but so they did in the ninth – as the Rule allowed. And *explicit* references to any other rule than St Benedict's had long since disappeared from Frankish evidence (they are never found in England).[13] St Boniface's councils ordered the reception of St Benedict's Rule for the 'restoration of regular life' in Francia before Benedict of Aniane was born.[14] The reference to the Rule in Charlemagne's charter for Aniane is matched in an earlier original for Hersfeld (775), while both are foreshadowed in the documents of Flavigny.[15] Even if Charlemagne did not ask Monte Cassino for an authentic copy of the Rule, he certainly despatched a copy, and to the Mount of Olives of all places.[16] Above all, there is little difference of principle – as opposed to detail – between the monastic legislation of Louis the Pious and his father. Charlemagne's references to the Rule by name are relatively few, but this hardly means much when it is also absent from Louis' 'Ecclesiastical Capitulary' of 818-19. To judge from a remarkable pair of capitularies where Charlemagne is found scratching his Augustan mane and wondering how St Martin *can* have been a monk when he preceded St Benedict, he was unaware that any other Rule existed.[17] Even the role of the *missi* in 816-19 was pre-figured in 802; and it is evident from the letter in which Alcuin sought a 'third rank', inferior to a monk's but superior to a canon's (the king having observed testily that the community at Tours 'sometimes called themselves monks, sometimes canons and sometimes neither'), that the legislative wedge driven in 816 between monastic and canonical models was already being hammered fourteen years earlier.[18]

In this light, the life and work of Benedict of Aniane were symptomatic rather than innovative: he was just the most thorough of those swept up by the monastic currents that had long been flowing towards a codified Benedictine observance. Yet we do seem to hear a new note in the Emperor Louis' reported concern that in his whole kingdom there should be 'nulla varietas' among monks. It was not one rule but one set of customs that was unprecedented, and controversial. Benedict undoubtedly shared – perhaps

[13] For the eighth century see Semmler (as n 9) and for the ninth, Semmler (as n 12). An exception among Charlemagne's authentic diplomas is *DK* I 98, p 141, an immunity for Farfa of 775; cf. *Marculfi Formulae* I 1, ed. K. Zeumer, *MGH, Formulae*, p 39. For England see my 'Bede and Benedict Biscop' (as n 2), pp 141-6, and H. Mayr-Harting, *Bede, the Rule of St Benedict and Social Class* (Jarrow Lecture, 1976), pp 6-10. Cf. W. Ullmann's review of H. Mordek, *Kirchenrecht und Reform im Frankenreich*, *English Historical Review* 92 (1977), 361-3.

[14] *MGH, Capitularia* [*Cap.*], ed. A. Boretius, I 10: 7, 11: 1, pp 26, 28; cf. *Vita S. Sturmi abbatis Fuldensis*, ed. G. H. Pertz, *MGH, Scriptores* II, pp 371-2, and *CCM* I 13, p 324.

[15] *DK* I 89, pp 128-9; *Collectio Flaviniacensis* 44, *MGH, Formulae*, p 481.

[16] *MGH, Epistolae Karolini Aevi* [*Ep. KA*] III, p 65. For the Monte Cassino letter see *CCM* I 9, pp 139-75, and for the problems it raises, J. Semmler, 'Karl der Große und das fränkische Mönchtum', *Karl der Große, Lebenswerk und Nachleben, II Das geistige Leben*, ed. B. Bischoff (Düsseldorf, 1965), pp 264-6; Charlemagne *had*, in any event, got hold of what apparently was very close to St Benedict's autograph copy: D. Knowles, *Great Historical Enterprises* (Cambridge, 1963), pp 140-1, 168-9.

[17] *Cap.* I 71: 12, 72: 12, pp 161-2, 164 (on which see F. L. Ganshof, 'Note sur les capitula de causis cum episcopis et abbatibus tractandis', *Studia Gratiana* 13 (1967), 3-25). Cf. *Cap.* I 23: 1-16, 25: 3, 28: 13-14, 16, 33: 12, 17, 34: 3-5, 37: 23-4, 138, pp 63, 67, 75-6, 93-4, 101-2, 105, 108-9, 275-80.

[18] *Ep. KA* II 247, 258, pp 400, 416; cf. Semmler (as n 16), pp 266-7.

inspired – the king's passion for uniformity, and this may relate not so much to a specifically monastic conception as to the wider vision of 'Imperium Christianum'.[19] 'Unitas regni – unitas ecclesiae' was the movement's motto, and its failure was simply that of 'Christian Empire' itself. But if many soaring Carolingian ambitions came inevitably to earth, they also left deep ideological imprints. Thus, while Professor Semmler was right to describe the Aachen decrees as 'the first time in the long history of western monasticism that an essentially inner-monastic decree, a *consuetudo*, was a matter of state legislation', he was wrong, as we shall see, to call it 'also the last'.[20]

Among those who did revere Benedict's memory was my second star, Odo of Cluny (d. 942). Odo's *vita* was the work of John of Salerno, whom he had converted from canon to monk. Odo himself told John that he was the son of Abbo, an exceptionally conscientious judge close to Duke William of Aquitaine, in whose household Odo grew up. Abbo had surreptitiously dedicated him to St Martin when no one was watching his cradle, but then withdrew him from 'the ecclesiastical order' and from 'the study of letters' in favour of 'martial exercises' and 'the duties of huntsmen'. However, Odo's spiritual destiny, like Æthelwold's, was foretold by visions, and he proved simply unfit for the young aristocrat's life, returning exhausted from each hunt. Eventually, he was allowed to join the canons of St Martin's Tours, where he developed in St Martin's honour the musical gifts which he shared with Æthelwold.[21] He encountered St Benedict's Rule while browsing in the library, and was so impressed that he misunderstood its provision about sleeping clothed and refused for three years to change for bed. When told of the existence of genuine Benedictine observance under Abbot Berno at Baume in Burgundy, he rushed to enrol. His old patron, Duke William (descendant of Benedict of Aniane's illustrious convert), had founded a further abbey for Berno at Cluny in 909/10; when Berno died, Odo became its abbot (927). John's *vita* is thenceforth devoted to Odo's labours for reform elsewhere: so closely on his travels did he observe St Benedict's injunction that monks should walk with their heads bowed that he was nicknamed 'the digger' and nearly mugged for his water-bottle. His reputation secured an invitation to make peace between Italy's warring dynasts; thus it was probably Odo, more than three centuries after Gregory the Great, who introduced the Rule to Roman monasteries.[22] But most significant were his encounters with the refined gentlemen at the abbey of

---

[19] CCM I 15: 1, p 341; cf. *Cap.* I 138: 3, p 276. See the illuminating discussion by T.F.X. Noble, 'The monastic ideal as model for Empire: the case of Louis the Pious', *Revue Bénédictine* 86 (1976), 235-50.

[20] Semmler (as n 4), 386.

[21] VO Pr., i 3-10, cols 43-8. There is an English translation of the *vita* (and of Odo's *Life of Gerald* – below, n 26): G. Sitwell, *St Odo of Cluny* (London, 1958). For Odo's music see P. Thomas, 'Saint Odon de Cluny et son oeuvre musicale', *A Cluny: Congrès scientifique ... en l'honneur des Saints abbés Odon et Odilon*, Société des amis de Cluny (Dijon, 1950), pp 171-80; it seems to follow from the number of musical works wrongly ascribed to Odo that he was reckoned *maestro*. *A Cluny* is one of the two seminal collections for the modern study of Cluniac monasticism. (For the other see n 31 below.)

[22] VO i 15, ii 7-10, 19, 21-3, cols 50, 53, 60, 64-7, 71-6 (note especially the confrontation over foot-washing in cols 73-4). On Odo in Rome, see G. Ferrari, *Early Roman Monasteries* (Vatican, 1950), pp 30-1, 188, 205, 265, 403, and B. Hamilton, 'The monastic revival in tenth century Rome', *Studia Monastica* IV (1962), 47-9.

Fleury, which was to have such close contacts with English reform. They were decidedly reluctant to abandon the eating of meat, and went so far as to create an artificial fish shortage, which St Benedict himself remedied with a draught of Gallilean proportions. Moreover, members of the community are said to have dissipated the monastic endowment by treating it as personal property, subject to the rights of kin. Their behaviour is strongly reminiscent of the 'pride, gluttony and avarice' at pre-reform Winchester.[23]

The *vita*'s general impression of Odo's priorities is sustained by Odo's own considerable *oeuvre*. This includes an abridgement, itself massive, of Gregory the Great's towering *Moralia in Job*. It is easy to understand Job's importance for Odo, as a man of wealth and status who received the most drastic lesson in the transitoriness of earthly glory.[24] Job is again prominent in Odo's *Collationes*, whose title and subject-matter (the principal vices) recall Cassian, and which has a message for the men of power and pride in Odo's world: his own adolescent problems are echoed in the story of the priest celebrating mass after a hunt who found himself crying 'Tally-Ho!' at the moment of consecration.[25] Above all, there is his extraordinary *Life of Count Gerald of Aurillac*, another exploration of the evanescent boundary between the worlds of flesh and spirit, but with reference to a holy layman whose example should shame sinful clerics into living the life more properly expected of them: 'it is the very greatest praise to keep the disposition of a religious in a secular habit, just as it is the height of ignominy to have sought the world in the garb of a religious'. Gerald was given an unusually literary education for a nobleman because he was a sickly child; and, as with his exact contemporary King Alfred, his life in secular office confused lay and clerical images to a remarkable degree. His chastity was such that he would not be seen naked, and, when laid out in death, his hand flew to the relevant part of his anatomy. He had his men fight with the blunt end of their spears and the flat of their swords, yet was always victorious, and no more shed his own blood than that of others.[26] And a link between Odo's *Life of Gerald* and his own *vita* is that gentle Gerald was reduced to apoplexy when his men boasted of his miracles, while Odo gave the credit for his own miracles to St Martin. Such reticence is a hagiographical *topos*, but here, as in Æthelwold's *Lives*, it has a special significance.[27]

Modern scholars tend to deny Cluny's revolutionary impact. The *vita Odonis* ascribes the way of life at Baume when Odo joined to Benedict of

---

[23] VO iii 8-11, cols 80-3. Cf. iii 4, col. 78 for a brother who claimed that fowl were permitted as having been created on the same day as fish, and choked to death. The parallel between Fleury and Winchester was first drawn by Eric John in his epoch-making article, 'The King and the monks in the tenth-century Reformation', *Orbis Britanniae and other Studies* (Leicester, 1966), 167-73.

[24] *Epitome Moralium S. Gregorii in Job, PL* CXXXIII, cols 105-512; see J. Laporte, 'Saint Odon, disciple de Saint Grégoire le Grand', *A Cluny*, pp 138-43; and F. Lotter, 'Odos vita des Grafen Gerald von Aurillac', *Benedictine Culture* (as n 3), pp 76-95.

[25] Odo, *Collationes, PL* CXXXIII ii 34, col 579; cf. i 36, ii 1, 7-9, iii 9, 24-6, cols 544, 549-50, 554-6, 596-7, 607-10. J. Leclercq, 'L'idéal monastique de Saint Odon d'après ses oeuvres', *A Cluny*, pp 231-2.

[26] Odo, *De vita S. Geraldi Auriliacensis Comitis* [VG], *PL* CXXXIII Pr., i 4-5, 8, 42, ii 8, 16, iii 10, cols 639-40, 644-5, 646-7, 667-8, 675, 679-80, 696; translation as n 22. See Lotter 'Odo's vita' (as n 24).

[27] VG ii 10-13, 20, 23-4, 26, 29-30, 32, cols 676-8, 681-8; VO ii 2, 22, cols 61-2, 72-3.

Aniane: only gradually did Cluniac liturgy expand to its ultimately awesome scale.[28] Again, the arrangement in Cluny's foundation charter whereby the abbey was committed to SS. Peter and Paul, and its immunity protected by papal guarantee, had been anticipated by a number of houses since Pope Nicholas I's privilege for Vézelay c.863, including Gerald's Aurillac and another of Berno's abbeys. Cluny's intimate juridical ties with the papacy, and all that flowed from them, developed over half a century after Odo's death.[29] Likewise, the mighty Cluniac connection was an eleventh-century growth; Odo's 'family' of monasteries looks like that of Benedict of Aniane, and when Berno's will claimed St Benedict himself as offering a precedent for appointed rather than elected abbots, he had a point.[30] Finally, Cluny did not break decisively with secular values. If Odo *was* the son of Count Ebbo (Abbo) of Déols, he effectively inherited the abbacy of the latter's foundation of Bourg-Dieu; even if he was not, his closeness to Duke William gave him all too traditional a claim to the succession at Cluny. Throughout its history, Cluny regularly compromised with the rights of lay proprietors.[31]

Yet Cluny did come to seem a turning-point in monastic history; and it had a case for beginning its days of greatness with Odo. It was he that made the Abbot of Cluny a major European figure for the next two hundred years, and thus began the abbey's lavish endowment by Europe's crowned heads.[32] Cluny's extant series of papal charters also began with Odo, and if there was nothing new about papal protection, its privileges soon had special features. One was that John XI's charter of March 931 and Leo VII's charter for Fleury of 938 covered any other monks seeking Odo's rule; this provision was a corner-stone of what would become the Cluniac connection;

---

[28] VO i 22-3, 32, cols 53-4, 57. See also n 35 below.

[29] *Recueil des chartes de L'abbaye de Cluny* [*Rec. Cl.*], ed. A. Bernard and A. Bruel, 6 vols, Collection de Documents inédits sur l'histoire de France (Paris, 1876-1903) 112, I pp 124-8. Vézelay's privilege from Nicholas I is P. Jaffé *et al.*, *Regesta Pontificum Romanorum* [*J*] 2831, confirmed by John VIII *J* 3189; Gigny's is *J* 3499; for Aurillac's see *VG* ii 4, cols 672-3. See H. E. J. Cowdrey, *The Cluniacs and Gregorian Reform* (Oxford, 1970), pp xiii-xix for Cluniac historiography, pp 4-22 for Cluny's place in the history of papal protection; also E. Boshof, '"Traditio Romana" und Papstschutz im 9 Jahrhundert: Untersuchungen zur vorkluniazensischen Libertas', *Rechtsgeschichtliche Diplomatische Studien zu Frühmittelalterlichen Papsturkunden*, ed. E. Boshof and H. Wolter, Studien und Vorarbeiten zur Germanica Pontifica, 6 (Köln, 1976), pp 1-108.

[30] Berno's will is *PL* CXXXIII, cols 853-8. Cf. above, p 15 and n 3, with Cowdrey, *Cluniacs*, pp 67-75.

[31] J. Wollasch, 'Königtum, Adel und Klöster im Berry während des 10 Jahrhunderts', and H. E. Mager, 'Studien über das Verhältnis der Kluniacenser zum Eigenkirchenwesen', *Neue Forschungen über Cluny und die Cluniacenser*, ed. G. Tellenbach (Freiburg, 1959), pp 19-165, 169-217. Professor Wollasch's all but conclusive case for Odo's origin depends crucially on the thesis that John of Salerno's chronology was artificially distilled from the Lausiac History on which he had previously been working (at the expense of his digestion); and it does not seem to take account of Sackur's own suggestion, *Die Cluniacenser* I, p 44, n 4.

[32] King Ralph's grants: *Recueil des Actes de Robert Ier et de Raoul, Rois de France (922-36)*, ed. J. Dufour, Chartes et Diplômes ... publiés par l'Academie des Inscriptions et Belles Lettres XI (Paris, 1978) 12, 18, 19 A-B, pp 47-52, 77-88: the first of these, the earliest extant royal charter for the abbey, coincides with Odo's assumption of the abbacy. Grants by Kings Hugh and Lothar: *Rec. Cl.* 417, I pp 403-4, and *P. Uk.* (see next note) 81, pp 137-8. Charters of the Burgundian king Conrad (soon after Odo's death): *MGH, Regum Burgundiae ... Diplomata et Acta*, ed. T. Schieffer, 27-9 (943), pp 133-8. However, as pointed out by Cowdrey, *Cluniacs*, p 16, there were earlier and now lost royal and papal grants.

and, in an age when papal diplomatic often meant rubber-stamping drafts from would-be beneficiaries, it looks like Odo's own idea.[33] Another – also a foretaste of the construction of Cluny's later liberty – was that its bulls covered its new acquisitions in detail, instead of simply renewing its rights in general terms like Vézelay's. Both Odo and Leo VII, the pope responsible for four such charters, plus another for Bourg-Dieu, were protégés of Rome's real ruler, Alberic; and it is surely this personal link that explains a type of papal warranty otherwise rare outside Italy. So the 'special relationship' of Cluny and the Holy See, already acknowledged by John XIII over fifty years before John XIX's better-known pronouncement, may itself have been a function of Odo's international stature.[34] Above all, to see Cluniac monasticism as merely the apotheosis of the *Adelskirche* is to view it upside-down. It appealed so powerfully to the high-born not because it came to an accommodation with this world but because its approach to the next offered spiritual standards with which an aristocracy could identify: a display-conscious class was naturally attracted to its elaborate liturgy.[35] And Odo, with his acute – and presumably innate – sensitivity to aristocratic vices, did much to set this tone. His *vita Geraldi* was scarcely plausible even as an ideal of aristocratic life: what nobleman, even if prepared to avoid bloodshed, would forgo heirs of his body? Gerald's reported behaviour was not a gentlemanly blend of accepted norms but a heroic stand against them: we are still in the age of 'Epic' rather than 'Romance'. The fact that Odo confronted 'potentes' with a model at once recognisable and rebarbative epitomises the way in which tenth-century reform, English and European, reached out towards the world of the warrior nobility *without* abandoning its principles, and was for *both* reasons successful.[36]

My next *dramatis persona* is Abbo of Fleury, born at about the time when Odo died, and one of the few major early medieval churchmen specifically said *not* to have been an aristocrat. But Aimo, his biographer, insists that his background was respectable; in particular, one maternal relative was a monk at Fleury and another a 'clericus' in the attached 'schola', which ensured his admission to first the latter, then the former. He became a

---

[33] *Papsturkunden, 896-1046* [*P. Uk.*], ed. H. Zimmermann, 2 vols, Veröffentlichungen der österreichischen Akademie der Wissenschaften 174, 177 (Wien, 1984-5) 64-5, 83, pp 107-10, 140-2; this edition at last makes it relatively easy to see Cluny's papal charters in their diplomatic context. See the discussion of Cluny's 'licence to reform' in Wollasch, 'Berry', pp 100-5, and Cowdrey, *Cluniacs*, p 68.

[34] *P. Uk.* 73-5, 81-3, pp 125-8, 137-42; and cf. 58, pp 96-7 (the first extant papal charter, again coinciding with Odo's election), 67, 95, 130, 188-9, 348, 351, 530, 570-4, pp 111-12, 167-8, 229-31, 370-3, 676-9, 682-6, 1007-10, 1083-90. For Vézelay in the period see *P. Uk.* 3, 28, 68, 227, pp 7-9, 50, 112-14, 449-50, etc. It is interesting that another (Italian) house which made a habit of such detailed confirmations was Subiaco, site of St Benedict's first foundation, and also 'protected' by Leo VII: *P. Uk.* 57, 72, 77, 85, 92, 226, pp 94-6, 120-4, 130-2, 146-8, 162-4, 443-8, etc. On the Odo-Leo-Alberic link see Hamilton (as n 22), 50-1. And for the use of the 'protection' formulae of the *Liber Diurnus*, ed. H. Foerster (Bern, 1958) 64, 89, pp 121-2, 169-70, see L. Santifaller, 'Die Verwendung des Liber Diurnus in den Privilegien der Päpste von den Angfängen bis zum Ende des elften Jahrhunderts', *Mitteilungen des österreichischen Instituts für Geschichtsforschung* 49 (1935), 251-74.

[35] B. H. Rosenwein, 'Feudal War and Monastic Peace: Cluniac history as ritual aggression', *Viator* 2 (1971), 129-57.

[36] R. W. Southern, *The Making of the Middle Ages* (London, 1967 repr.), p 212.

master of at least five of the seven liberal arts, and could echo Boethius' *Consolation of Philosophy* in pleading to Kings Hugh and Robert that he 'wished only for the salvation of the monastic senate'.[37] When Archbishop Oswald of York, himself an alumnus, asked Fleury for an expert to teach his new foundation of Ramsey, Abbo was the obvious choice. He was thus the only major continental reformer who actually visited England (985-7), and his fortunes there were mixed: he got on splendidly with Oswald and Dunstan (whose *vita* was in his baggage, for versification, on the day of his death); but whereas he was given gifts by Ealdorman Æthelwine, he received 'only words' from King Æthelred (then in his anti-monastic phase); and he was later to complain that English food, and specifically English beer, made him permanently fat.[38] Elected abbot on his return to Fleury, he became a major public figure: he was in regular touch with Rome, not only on ecclesiastical issues but also on behalf of the new Capetian kings, and even of a relative who, as he put it, was 'both noble and a sinner but rather a sinner because she was noble than noble because she was a sinner'.[39] After sixteen years, he was persuaded to attempt the reform of a Gascon monastery which had resisted the efforts of his three predecessors to make it live up to its name, Réole (the Rule). He joked that he would go when he was tired of life; the joke turned sour when he was killed in a riot caused by his attempt to impose monastic discipline (1004). Aimo planned to write about Abbo's posthumous miracles, but, in keeping with priorities we found in Odo's *vita*, he preferred to bring up to date the Miracles of Fleury's patron, St Benedict.[40]

Abbo was perhaps the most intellectually distinguished figure of this paper, and his influence on the English, for whom he wrote his *Quaestiones Grammaticales* (criticising their archaic pronunciation of Latin) as well as the famous *Passio* of St Edmund, ran deep.[41] But his most important work was probably his Canon Collection, because of its connection with the remarkable charter which Fleury received from the papacy in 996.[42] Papal

---

[37] Aimo, *De vita et martyrio S. Abbonis abbatis Floriaci coenobii* [VA], PL CXXXIX 1-3, cols 388-90; Abbo, *Apologeticus, ibid.*, col. 461, and cf. *Collectio Canonum, ibid.*, Pr., col. 474. P. Cousin, *Abbon de Fleury-sur-Loire* (Paris, 1953) is a useful introduction to PL CXXXIX; for several episodes in Abbo's career F. Lot, *Etudes sur le règne de Hugues Capet et la fin du Xe siècle*, Bibliothèque de l'Ecole des hautes études 147 (Paris, 1903) remains fundamental, especially ch II-IV and Appendices II-IV, pp 31-157, 266-79.

[38] VA 4-6, 11, cols 390-3, 401; Cousin, *Abbon*, p 73, n 39. Cf. S. D. Keynes, *The Diplomas of King Æthelred the Unready, 978-1016* (Cambridge, 1980), pp 176-86.

[39] VA 11-12, cols 401-3; Abbo, *Epistolae*, PL CXXXIX 1-4, cols 419-23.

[40] VA 16-21, cols 406-14; *Miracula S. Abbonis*, PL CXXXIX, cols 413-14, and cf. *ibid.* cols 801-52.

[41] Abbo, *Quaestiones Grammaticales*, PL CXXXIX, 1, 10-11, cols 521-3, 528-9; cf. D. Norberg, *Manuel Practique de Latin médiévale*, pp 47-8; Abbo, 'Life of St Edmund', ed. M. Winterbottom, *Three Lives of English Saints* (Toronto, 1972), pp 67-87; E. John, 'The World of Abbot Ælfric', *Ideal and Reality in Frankish and Anglo-Saxon Society: Studies presented to J. M. Wallace-Hadrill*, ed. P. Wormald, D. Bullough and R. Collins (Oxford, 1983), pp 303-15.

[42] Abbo, *Collectio Canonum*, PL CXXXIX, cols 471-508, especially 5, 15, 17, 21, 23, 44, cols 479-80, 484-6, 502-4; and cf. *Epistola 14*, cols 440-60; Fleury's privilege is *P. Uk.* 335, pp 655-7. For what follows the pioneering work was J.-F. Lemarignier, 'L'Exemption monastique et les origines de la reforme grégorienne', *A Cluny*, pp 288-334; the basis of his case is available in English translation: 'Political and monastic structures in France at the end of the tenth and

charters of *protection*, which simply guaranteed a church's property, privileges and way of life against infringement by any power, secular or ecclesiastical, must be distinguished from those of *exemption*, which removed from a monastery most or all of its diocesan's rights and responsibilities under ancient canon law. Though protection from a bishop's abuse of his position obviously merged into exemption from his exercise of legitimate duties, which is why the issue has been controversial in that day and in this, there was an important difference between the right to elect an abbot without episcopal interference, or to preserve monastic peace from public ceremonial, and the freedom to choose which bishop would bless an elected abbot or remove a bad one: apart from anything else, the first accorded with St Benedict's Rule and the second probably did not.[43] It seems that charters of exemption were granted to monasteries for about a century and a half after the arrival of St Columbanus on the continent (c. 590), usually by bishops themselves, but occasionally (as in Bedan Northumbria) by popes: whatever a bishop's theoretical rights, suspicion of episcopal power was deeply embedded in monastic primers like Cassian. But the Carolingian age was no time for restrictions on bishops, and exemption was almost forgotten. Papal charters for Frankish abbeys from the mid-ninth century, including Cluny's, offered protection only.

However, circumstances at the end of the tenth century conspired to resurrect exemption. Abbo himself was on appalling terms with the local bishop of Orleans, whose men actually beat him up. For this reason and others, his canon collection read the letters of Gregory the Great, which really involved no more than *protection*, as if they conveyed *exemption*, and he then sought exemption from the pope. His first approach was rebuffed, more probably because his case in recent canon law was weak than because he failed to offer a bribe, as Aimo insinuates.[44] But the next pope, Gregory V,

beginning of the eleventh century', *Lordship and Community in Early Medieval Europe*, ed. F. L. Cheyette (New York, 1968), pp 111-20. Cowdrey, *Cluniacs*, pp 22-36 is an admirably lucid account of these matters, and I have reviewed the pre-Carolingian position in 'Bede and Benedict Biscop', pp 146-9, with references, pp 161-4. I differ from Dr Cowdrey chiefly in attaching much more significance to this pre-Carolingian phase. He was persuaded by the arguments of W. Schwartz, 'Iurisdicio und Condicio', *Zeitschrift der Savigny-Stiftung für Rechtsgeschichte, kanonistische Abteilung* 76 (1959), 34-98, which seemed to me to take insufficient account of the narrative evidence and to postulate far too many forgeries. Schwartz's case was already undermined by E. Ewig, 'Klosterprivilegien des siebten und frühen achten Jahrhunderts', *Adel und Kirche: Gerd Tellenbach zum 65ten Geburtstag*, ed. J. Fleckenstein and K. Schmid (Freiburg, 1968), pp 52-65; it has now been dealt two *coups de grace*: E. Ewig, 'Bermerkungen zu zwei merowingischen Bischoffsprivilegien und einem Papstprivileg des 7 Jahrhunderts für merowingische Klöster', *Vorträge und Forschungen 20: Mönchtum, Episkopat und Adel zur Gründungszeit des Klosters Reichenau*, ed. A. Borst (Sigmaringen, 1974), pp 215-49; and H. H. Anton, *Studien zu den Klosterprivilegien der päpste im frühen Mittelalter*, Beiträge zur Geschichte und Quellenkunde des Mittelalters, ed. H. Fuhrmann, 4 (Berlin, 1976). See also H. Edwards, 'Two documents from Aldhelm's Malmesbury', *Bulletin of the Institute of Historical Research* 59 (1986), 1-19.
[43] *RB* ch 64-5, II pp 648-59; cf. A. De Vogüé, *La Communauté et l'Abbé dans la Règle de Saint Benôit* (Paris, 1960), pp 362-6, 430-2.
[44] *VA* 6-9, 11-12, cols 392-7, 401-3. In the light of this passage, it hardly seems possible to agree with Zimmermann that *P. Uk.* 335 was forged by Abbo, though one can see that he might have forged *P. Uk.* 258, pp 507-9, and perhaps other charters too, in order to secure it.

was the first German to hold the office. The one European abbey which maintained its exemption from all ecclesiastical authority except the pope's throughout the Carolingian period was Fulda; and in the later tenth century other German monasteries received similar bulls, sometimes in conscious imitation of Fulda.[45] This may explain why Abbo's application to a German pope was successful. Fleury's 996 charter removed all diocesan rights: no episcopal function could be performed except by invitation, and its abbot could be tried, even for criminal offences, only by a provincial council or by the pope himself. Whatever the Merovingian background to Abbo's claims, this charter was a watershed in relations between French monasteries and bishops. Within two years, Cluny had a bull which for the first time gave it a choice of visiting prelates; over the following decades, Abbot Odilo and the popes between them established the liberty which ultimately became normative for western monasteries.[46] It can thus be seen that Æthelwold's integration of cathedral and monastery at Winchester ran right against what was soon to become the European trend.

My fourth counterpart to Æthelwold takes us back to the early tenth century and across to the old Carolingian 'Middle Kingdom': the life of Gerard of Brogne is a barometer of political change in this long-disputed area, in that his first royal charter was granted by Charles the Simple shortly before he lost the west Frankish throne, and his next was issued by Henry the Fowler of the ascendant Saxon dynasty, while his major patron was the semi-independent Count Arnulf of Flanders. Gerard's career is especially elusive: no writings of his own survive, and virtually all the sources for his achievements were tendentiously rewritten, including the Brogne charters and his *vita*.[47] Described as *nobilissimus* in our earliest source, he was

---

[45] Fulda's original charter is in *Die Briefe der heiligen Bonifatius und Lullus*, ed. M. Tangl, *MGH, Epistolae selectae in usum scholarum* I 89, pp 203-5; the ninth-century bulls are J 2605, 2668, 2676, 3020, 3466; those of the tenth century, *P. Uk.* 16, 42, 71, 99, 113, 150, 199, 236, 321, 339, 380, 546, 589, pp 28, 71-2, 118-20, 174-5, 198, 274-5, 394-5, 470-1, 626-8, 662, 733-6, 1036-8, 1111-12. Fulda's diplomatic history is highly complex, consisting as it does of two series of privileges, one largely fabricated and the other often interpolated; but even on an adverse verdict, the core of the case made by H. Goetting, 'Die klösterliche Exemption in Nord- und Mitteldeutschland vom 8 bis 15 Jahrhundert', *Archiv für Urkundenforschung* 14 (1935-6), 107-57 seems to stand: it was a somewhat special case because of its problematic relationship with Boniface's archiepiscopal see at Mainz. Other such bulls for German houses include *P. Uk.* 115 (Gandersheim), 124 (Essen), 157 (Bibra), 186 (Hersfeld), 187 (Meißen), 251 (Ellwangen), 264 (Korvey), 265 (Memleben), pp 201-2, 218-20, 291-3, 364-6, 367-70, 494-5, 519-20, 521-2 – the first and last of these referring to Fulda's example. The one possible case in the West Frankish orbit is *P. Uk.* 263, pp 517-19, but it is probably forged: C. Brunel, 'Les actes faux de l'abbaye de Saint-Valéry-sur-Somme', *Le Moyen Age* 22 (1909), 94-116, 179-96. In Italy, the one house with a history like Fulda's is (significantly?) Monte Cassino itself: J 2675A, 3381; *P. Uk.* 9, 18, 151, 244, 287, 302, 310, pp 18-20, 31-2, 275-7, 482-4, 557-9, 586-8, 601-3. See also Santifaller, 251-74, on *Liber Diurnus* 32, 77, 86 (as n 34), pp 93-4, 138-40, 164-7.

[46] *P. Uk.* 351, 530, 558, pp 682-6, 1007-10, 1052-4. Cluny remained on excellent terms with bishops as a class: H. Diener, 'Das Verhältnis Clunys zu den Bischöffen', *Neue Forschungen*, pp 251-352; but the Mâcon diocese was another matter.

[47] Indispensable for Gerard of Brogne is the set of millenary essays in *Revue Bénédictine* 70 (1960), 5-240: one can hardly approach the sources without their aid. For the re-editing of the sources see J. de Smet, 'Recherches critiques sur la *Vita Gerardi*', *ibid.*, 5-61; in what follows, I have also used the papers of J. Wollasch, 'Gerard von Brogne und seine Klostergründung'; A. D'Haenens, 'Gérard de Brogne à l'abbaye de Saint-Ghislain'; J. Laporte, 'Gérard de Brogne à Saint-Wandrille …'; and D. Misonne, 'Gérard de Brogne à Saint-Rémy …', *ibid.*, 62-82, 101-18, 142-66, 167-76.

apparently, like Odo, the son of an important associate of the major local magnate: the magnate in question was Count Robert, brother of the late King Odo and future replacement for Charles the Simple. When perhaps no more than fifteen, Gerard, like Benedict of Aniane, founded a monastery on his own family property, at Brogne near Namur, where an early Carolingian church now maintained only a token sacerdotal presence (913/14). There is as yet no sign of wider reforming intentions. Gerard's priority was to endow his house with appropriate relics, and from Saint-Denis, where Robert was lay abbot, he secured those of St Eugenius, alleged disciple of St Denis and apostle of Spain. On returning to Brogne, he commissioned an account of the resulting miracles; the fact that, like Æthelwold's, these included the preservation of builders who had come crashing to the ground is a reminder of the architectural ambitions which accompanied monastic reform on both sides of the Channel.[48]

But the political dramas of the 920s gave Gerard new political masters and, for him as for Benedict of Aniane, this meant new responsibilities. Count Gislebert of Lorraine invited him to reform Saint-Ghislain, which inspired a collection of this saint's *miracula*.[49] Count Arnulf called him in on a number of restorations, including those at Saint-Bertin (944), whose recalcitrant brethren sought the patronage of the English King Edmund, and St Peter's Ghent (941), where Dunstan was shortly to find his own refuge. For Ghent, we have Arnulf's original diploma, stipulating the adoption of the Benedictine Rule with special reference to the election of abbots, but with a clause reserving comital rights which monks of the Gregorian period tried indignantly to erase.[50] On his own initiative, Gerard offered the relics of St Wandrille to the Normans in return for the abbey's endowment, but the bargain fell foul of the many vested interests involved. Tenth-century reform was everywhere entwined with the cult of the Church's local heroes, and it is symbolic that the *miracula* and *translationes* of others are better evidence for Gerard than his own *vita*.[51] Perhaps it also makes the point that his achievements were more transitory than the others reviewed here; his work at Saint-Rémi Rheims had to be redone from Fleury, and Ghent was to be reformed again by the movement to be considered next. But it is hard to forget the tribute penned three years after his death (959) by Folcuin: 'In recent times, he was the first, and almost the only one, to preserve the norm of regular life in these western areas.'

John of Gorze, my fifth personality, was from Lorraine, also in the Middle Kingdom, and, in the next century, a well-spring of 'Gregorian' reform. He poses the opposite problem to Gerard. His biography, which John of

---

[48] *Ex virtutibus S. Eugenii*, ed. L. de Heinemann, *MGH, Scriptores* XV(2) 2-11, pp 647-50.
[49] *Ex Raineri Miraculis S. Gisleni*, ed. O. Holder-Egger, *MGH, Scriptores* XV(2) 10, pp 583-4, and cf. *ibid.*, pp 576-9.
[50] Folcuin, *Gesta Abbatum S. Bertini*, ed. O. Holder-Egger, *MGH, Scriptores* XIII ch 107, p 628 – and *loc. cit.* for the following quotation in the text. For Dunstan at Ghent, *Vita S. Dunstani auctore Adelardo, Memorials*, pp 59-60. For Arnulf's charter see *Diplomata Belgica ante annum millesimum centesimum scripta*, ed. M. Gysseling and A. C. F. Koch (Brussels, 1950) 53, pp 143-6; discussed by E. Sabbe, 'Etude critique sur le diplôme de Arnoul Ier comte de Flandre pour l'abbaye de Saint-Pierre a Gand', *Etudes d'histoire dédiées à la mémoire de Henri Pirenne par ses anciens élèves* (Brussels, 1937), pp 299-330.
[51] Cf. D. Misonne, 'Gérard de Brogne et sa dévotion aux reliques', *Sacris Brudiri* 25 (1982), 1-26.

St Arnulf's agreed to write at the behest of the other abbots around his deathbed (976), is one of the great *vitae* of the early Middle Ages, but it has not been edited since 1841, nor translated from its very challenging Latin; and the movement he belonged to has inspired surprisingly little modern literature.[52] The obvious exception, Dom Hallinger's study of the Gorze connection in antithesis to Cluny's, may have made matters worse: an early critic had 'the vague feeling that the last word on every detail has not yet been spoken', but one can understand the general reluctance to add to Hallinger's verbal mountain.[53] John was not an aristocrat, but his background was comfortable: he was formally, if in his own view fruitlessly, educated; and when transferring his patrimony to his community, he could price it at thirty pounds of silver. In the *vita*'s account of his life as a layman, and in its *vignettes* of his future colleagues, we find a restless search for spiritual perfection. Like many monastic movements since Egypt, including St Benedict's, the Lotharingians began with experiments in the hermit's life; and John's austerities always transcended the demands of the Rule, though, like Benedict of Aniane and Æthelwold, he expected less of others.[54] The need for spiritual companionship drew him and his like-minded friends together, but they found no local centres of suitably regular life. They had already visited Rome and Monte Cassino, and were on the point of permanent departure for Italy, when Bishop Adalbero of Metz was made to see the shame of losing such men from his diocese, and offered them nearby Gorze. He had previously vowed to restore the once great foundation of Chrodegang of Metz, now the home of just a few who were monastic in dress but little else, with its shrines stained by animal droppings and its walls bare, and with its properties held in benefice by a lay abbot, the ferocious Count Adalbert. John, for his part, cheerfully accepted the bishop's offer because he remained determined to leave and confidently expected the plan to be aborted by Adalbert's veto. However, the new community was somehow established, with Einold, an archdeacon of Toul who had opted for a less Trollopean spiritual life, as abbot, and with John in charge of external administration (933). 'The garb of clerics' was exchanged for the 'monastic habit', and those who survived from the old dispensation were obliged to join the new.[55]

---

[52] *Vita Iohannis abbatis Gorziensis* [*VI*], ed. G.H.Pertz, *MGH*, *Scriptores* IV Pr. (ch 1-6), pp 337-8. There was no commemorative collection in 1976 comparable to that for Gerard (above, n 47), though there is a characteristic meditation by Dom Leclercq in the commemorative volume for Chrodegang of Metz, *Saint Chrodegang: colloque tenu à Metz à l'occasion du douzième centennaire de sa mort* (Metz, 1967), pp 133-52, and though Gerard's volume has an incisive study by J.Choux, 'Décadence et Réforme monastique dans la province de Trèves', pp 204-23. But a conference on Lotharingian reform is apparently in preparation.

[53] K.Hallinger, *Gorze-Kluny: Studien zu den monastischen Lebensformen und Gegensätzen im Hochmittelalter*, Studia Anselmiana 22-5 (Rome, 1950-1): one of the charms of this 1059-page book is its author's repeated protestations that he is cutting material in order to keep it short. T.Schieffer, 'Cluniazensische oder Gorzische Reformbewegung?', *Archiv für mittelrheinische Kirchengeschichte* 4 (1952), 32. The critique of Hallinger has focused on the 'Kluny' end of the antithesis: it is the main target of *Neue Forschungen*.

[54] *VI* ch 9-14, 16-24, 31-2, 45, 51-2, 55-71, pp 339-46, 350-7. For an eremitical spell in the life of Odo see *VO* i 22, col. 53; and for some important distinctions between early and later monastic movements in regard to the hermit's life see H.Leyser, *Hermits and the New Monasticism: a Study of Religious communities in western Europe, 1000-1150* (London, 1984), pp 12-17.

[55] *VI* ch 24-5, 29, 34-44, pp 343-50.

The many parallels here with the circumstances of the refoundation of Abingdon and the purge of Winchester include the possibility that Gorze sources also give too desolate and/or dissolute an impression of pre-reform conditions: Adalbert and the 'brothers of the monastery' had issued a charter amidst Gorze's allegedly unadorned brick and dung-bedecked altars as recently as 922.[56] For this Reformation, as for others, reformers are not always the best authorities.

John was eventually to be abbot of Gorze, but his biography did not reach that point, breaking off with a vivid account of his conduct as Otto's ambassador to the Khalifh of Cordova: chosen for the job as one 'eager to be a martyr', it was no fault of his that he failed to become one.[57] In the hagiographical *tour de force* on John's life as a monk, three things are especially notable. The first is his reading: like Odo's, this comprised Gregory's *Moralia*, which he allegedly had at his finger-tips, and a striking set of early monastic *vitae*, including Anthony, Macarius, Pachomius, Martin, Germanus and even John the Almsgiver. The second is his business acumen, comparable with that of Æthelwold and Abbot Brihtnoth as recorded in the Ely *Libellus*. He used as monastic bursar the skills he had acquired in managing his family property and that of others (and went a step further than most bursars in cleaning the latrines).[58] In a series of confrontations with possessors of lands claimed by Gorze, he showed shrewdness and courage, though it fits with the pattern we have encountered above that achievements put down by his biographer to him were ascribed in a work which John may have written himself to the *miracula* of Gorze's patron, St Gorgonius.[59] The third is Gorze's role as an exporter of reform. The *vita* says something of this: the houses mentioned include St Arnulf's Metz, of which its author was abbot, and there were more, like St Peter's Ghent.[60] But it is clear that Hallinger massively exaggerated Gorze's influence; for example, St Maximin's Trier, the real nucleus of his Gorze connection, as he admits, seems to have reformed itself without much Gorze assistance, and was so much the stronger house at first that Einold was tempted to decamp thither.[61] The very idea of

[56] Wulfstan, *Vita* ch 10-13, pp 39-42, and cf. Thacker, below, pp 45-52; *Cartulaire de l'Abbaye de Gorze*, ed. A. d'Herbomez (Mettensia II: Mémoires et Documents publiées par la société nationale des Antiquaires de France, 1898) 91, pp 167-8; Adalbero's re-foundation charter is no. 92, pp 169-73.

[57] VI ch 115-36, pp 369-77 (esp. ch 117, p 370).

[58] VI ch 83-4, 72-3, 85-90, pp 360-1, 357, 361-2.

[59] VI ch 95-114, pp 364-9; *Miracula Sancti Gorgonii*, ed. Pertz, *ibid.* 8-12, 15, pp 241-3. W. Schultze, 'War Johannes von Gorze historischer Schriftsteller? Eine quellenkritische Untersuchung', *Neues Archiv* 9 (1883), 498-504 argued against John's authorship of these *Miracula* on the basis of the sort of over-elaborate *kritik* of hypothetical *Quellen* then much in fashion; Pertz's suggestion (*loc. cit.*, p 235) that the similarities between the two stories arise from the fact that John of St Arnulf's was using the '*Miracula*', and the discrepancies from the fact that he was supplying the role which John himself had modestly disclaimed in his own work, seems to be much neater and more plausible.

[60] VI ch 66-8, pp 355-6, and cf. Gorze's own link with Rome ch 52-3, pp 351-2. For Ghent, see Hallinger, *Gorze-Kluny*, p 79; and for a less ambitious approach to the Gorze filiation, M. Parisse, *La Nécrologe de Gorze: contribution à l'histoire monastique* (Annales de L'Est, publiées par la Université de Nancy, II 40, 1971).

[61] VI ch 70, 95, pp 356-7, 364; Hallinger, *Gorze-Kluny*, pp 47, 59-60, 95-128, etc. But see E. Wisplinghoff, *Untersuchungen zur frühen Geschichte der Abtei S. Maximin bei Trier von den Anfängen bis etwa 1150*, Quellen und Abhandlungen zur mittelrheinischen Kirchengeschichte 12

a 'Gorze connection' may be misconceived, if what distinguished it from Cluny's was the looseness of its links, for Cluny's especially tight *familia* did not appear until the eleventh century. Yet Hallinger's book is at least a suitably imposing monument to the vitality of monastic reform in the Ottonian *Reich*; and the important point may be that it had no one source. The movement attracted the interest of kings and bishops, and was criss-crossed by spiritual and genealogical affinities; but tenth-century reform did not always need central direction in order to flourish.

Among its offshoots was my sixth man of the hour, Archbishop Adalbert of Magdeburg (d.981). Unlike the others, he was not seen as a saint, and if this is itself a good reason for including him, it also means that he inspired no *vita* and must be more summarily discussed.[62] He was certainly of noble birth and perhaps Lotharingian origin: his father was conceivably the very Adalbert who had been lay abbot of Gorze. If so, he was another who turned against the paternal model, and in about 950 he joined St Maximin's Trier.[63] Like Æthelwold, he was both monk and bishop. A self-confessed failure as missionary to the Russians (though he confirmed and gave his name to the young Slav noble who was to become the martyred St Adalbert of Prague), he was still Otto's choice for his cherished new archbishopric of Magdeburg; as such, he remained, like Æthelwold, a sedulous visitor of monasteries, sometimes arriving at dead of night to ensure that monks got up for Matins.[64] He was also a major historian. His continuation of Regino of Prüm's Chronicle blends interest in reform with devoted support for the Saxon dynasty's claims to God-given hegemony.[65] Here too there is an analogy with Æthelwold. Finally, he was a charter specialist; and his periodic rather than continuous spells in the Ottonian chancery may have a bearing on the

---

(Mainz, 1970), pp 29-30. Important research by Mr Nightingale shows that 'reform' at St Maximin's was an essentially continuous process.

[62] On Adalbert, I have followed D. Claude, *Geschichte des Erzbistums Magdeburg bis in das 12 Jahrhundert*, 2 vols, Mitteldeutsche Forschungen 67 (Köln, 1972-5) I, pp 114-28. See also nn 63-6 below.

[63] The evidence for Adalbert's Lotharingian origin is essentially that the Adalbert who was an enemy of St Maximin's (and whose identity with Gorze's lay abbot is possible rather than likely) is described in Sigehard's *Miracula S. Maximini*, ed. G. Waitz, MGH, *Scriptores* IV ch 16, pp 233-4 as 'huius nostri Adalberti genitor'. G. Althoff, *Das Necrolog von Borghorst: Edition und Untersuchung*, Veröffentlichungen des historischen Kommission für Westfalen 40: Westfälische Gedenkbücher und Nekrologen I (Münster, 1978), pp 268-82 shows that Adalbert was probably the brother of Bertha, foundress of Borghorst, and goes on to argue that its necrology's bias towards the kin of the Billung (her husband's family) and of the 'Nachfahren Widukinds' (Queen Mathilda's family) excludes a Lotharingian origin for the family of Adalbert and Bertha. Can *argumenta ex silentio* be thus deployed on *Libri Memoriales* – especially if Adalbert *senior* was as described in the St Maximin's *Miracula*? 'Adalbertus noster' in a St Maximin's source still seems much more likely to be the future archbishop of Magdeburg than anyone else.

[64] *Thietmari Merseburgensis Chronicon*, ed. R. Holtzmann, MGH, *Scriptores rerum germani-carum*, n.s. iii 11, pp 108-11.

[65] *(Adalberti) Continuatio Reginonensis*, ed. F. Kurze, MHG, *Scriptores rerum germanicarum*, pp 154-79; K. Hauck, 'Erzbischoff Adalbert als Geschichtsschreiber', *Festschrift für Walter Schlesinger*, ed. H. Beumann, 2 vols, Mitteldeutsche Forschungen 74 (Köln, 1974), pp 276-353. Althoff, *Borghorst*, pp 275-6 shows that a lost version of Adalbert's history probably included a quite detailed account of the 816 legislation.

much-debated production of royal charters in tenth-century England. The charters which, like Æthelwold, he drafted for his own house, drew on the remarkable chain of forged documents whereby St Maximin's, in dispute with the local archbishop, extended its privileges back through the Carolingians and Merovingians to Constantine and Helena.[66] The abbey had sustained a traumatic Viking visitation in 882, and though its library may not have been totally destroyed (the one extant manuscript of Benedict of Aniane's monastic encyclopedia was possibly preserved there), its muniments evidently were.[67] English minsters had the same problem, and we shall see that it elicited a similar response.

We must now turn to the three aspects of Æthelwold's policy which a European setting may help us to understand. The first illustrates that continental influence on English reform nicely symbolised by the story in Odo's *vita* of how St Benedict appeared in a vision to announce that he was late for his festival at Fleury, because he had been over in Britain wrestling with demons for the soul of a backsliding brother called Leutfred. Such influence, though never in doubt, has yet to be explored as thoroughly as it could be.[68] One matter on which more can be said is the sources of the *Regularis Concordia*. A lifetime's study persuaded the text's editor, Dom Symons, that Lotharingian or 'Gorze' models predominated over those of Cluny and Fleury; and because Dunstan had been at Ghent, a daughter of the Brogne and Gorze families, whereas Æthelwold's links were with Fleury, he thought that Dunstan must have had a part in the *Concordia*'s composition, despite the strong evidence that Æthelwold wrote it.[69] As Stenton saw, a mixture of traditions is only to be expected in what was an *agreement*, and there were Ghent brethren at the Winchester synod that produced it, so Lotharingian symptoms are no argument against Æthelwold's 'pen'.[70] More important, it is even harder to be sure of anything in this field than Symons stressed. There is no question of extant 'sources': the *Concordia* is earlier in

[66] On Adalbert in the royal service see J. Fleckenstein, *Die Hofkapelle der deutschen Könige, II: Die Hofkapelle im Rahmen der ottonisch-salischen Reichskirche*, Schriften der MGH 16 (ii) (Stuttgart, 1966), pp 37-8; and Wisplinghoff, *S. Maximin*, pp 126-41. Adalbert's charters for St Maximin's are *Diplomata Regum et Imperatorum Germaniae [DO]*, ed. Th. Sickel, *MGH* I 169, 179, pp 250-1, 260-2. The forgeries which inspired the first of these, together with *P. Uk.* 121, pp 212-14, (and which seem to have influenced Adalbert's own *diktat*) are *Urkundenbuch zur Geschichte der ... mittelrheinischen Territorien* I, ed. H. Beyer (Coblenz, 1860) 3, 9, 20, 46-7, 54, 109, pp 1-2, 12-13, 25, 52-3, 60-1, 114.
[67] Wisplinghoff, *S. Maximin*, pp 5-6, 17-18.
[68] VO iii 11, col. 82. K. Leyser, 'Die Ottonen und Wessex', *Frühmittelalterliche Studien* 17 (1983), 73-97 shows what can be done. Art historians have also done much: e.g. R. Deshman, 'Christus rex et magi reges': kingship and Christology in Ottonian and Anglo-Saxon Art', *ibid.* 10 (1976), 367-405.
[69] Symons' work came in three stages: 'The sources of the *Regularis Concordia*', *Downside Review* 59 (1941), 14-36, 143-70, 264-89; the introduction to his edition of *Regularis Condordia*, pp xlv-lii; and 'The *Regularis Concordia*: history and derivation', *Tenth-Century Studies*, pp 37-59: on the whole, each is successively less optimistic about the possibility of establishing continental links.
[70] F. M. Stenton, *Anglo-Saxon England*, 3rd edn (Oxford, 1971), pp 449-50; the phrase, 'Dunstan the mind, Ethelwold the pen' was coined by Edmund Bishop, and has been much quoted. Dunstan's 'mind' remains elusive, and I hope to return to it in a different context elsewhere.

date than any of the other monastic customaries at issue, and the argument has to be based on parallels with later documents. The reason why there are more parallels with Lotharingian than with Cluniac usage may be that statements of the former are themselves earlier, so less liturgically developed, than those of the latter; and they are much more like the *Concordia* in their general scope, so there is more opportunity to find parallels. Since Symons wrote, a more nearly contemporary record of Fleury customs has come to light, increasing the evidence for their influence on the Winchester synod; and while it remains clear that 'the Fleury party was oftentimes outvoted', the most suggestive single echo of continental practice in the *Concordia* points in their direction.[71]

But the most interesting potential parallel to the *Regularis Concordia* lies in neither Lotharingian nor Cluniac customaries but in that of Benedict of Aniane. Half a dozen manuscripts of the 816-19 legislation survive from the last century of the Anglo-Saxon Church, five of its final authoritative form, and one a unique record of the earliest stage in the Aachen proceedings. All appear to date from after 970, but this only shows that they were seen as an integral part of the reforming programme; in one, the Aachen *capitula* and the *Regularis Concordia* are bound together.[72] And though the manuscripts all belong to the same general family, the interest in the material was such as to absorb more than one textual tradition: to revert to the issue of 'fowl', one text allows its consumption for *eight* days after major feasts, one for *four*, while others leave the number to the abbot's decision.[73] One of these manuscripts comes from Abingdon, while three may have a Winchester provenance, so there is a real possibility that the author of the *Concordia* had a particular interest in the Aachen decrees.[74] Symons himself thought their detailed influence on the *Concordia* slight. But he also noted that the so-called *Memoriale Qualiter* was 'the only monastic document of which we can affirm with certainty that it has been extensively used in the composition of the *Concordia*'; and the Abingdon manuscript actually ascribes part of

---

[71] The relevant customaries have been re-edited (with the *Regularis Concordia*) in CCM VII (2,3), ed. K. Hallinger, who also edited the volume of introductory essays, VII(1) (1983-4). The new Fleury customs are ed. VII(2), pp 3-60, and discussed VII(1), pp 351-70; the quotation in the text is from a summary of Symons' position VII(1), p 393, which is, happily for its author, anonymous. For the Fleury echo see Symons, *Tenth-Century Studies*, pp 51-2.

[72] The MSS are Rouen, Bibliothèque Municipale MS U 107 (N. R. Ker, *Catalogue of Manuscripts containing Anglo-Saxon* (Oxford, 1957) 376) (the unique 816 text); Cambridge, Corpus Christi College 57 (Ker 34); Cambridge University Library MS Ll I 14; London, British Library Harley MS 5431; London, British Library Cotton MS Titus A iv (Ker 200); London, British Library Cotton MS Tiberius A iii (Ker 186) (with Aachen *capitula* and *Regularis Concordia* combined); they are listed by J. Semmler, CCM I, pp 434, 506-7, and four were described by M. Bateson, 'Rules for monks and secular canons under Edgar', *English Historical Review* 9 (1894), 690-708 (quotation below at 701). A thorough re-examination is long overdue.

[73] Corpus 57, f. 40v; CUL Ll I 14, f. 108r; in Tiberius A iii the relevant chapter has been erased. For the place of the English MSS in the stemmata of the Aachen decrees and the *Memoriale Qualiter* see CCM I, pp 179-83, 202-18.

[74] For Corpus 57 and Abingdon see Thacker below, pp 54-5, 58-9. Winchester is suggested as the provenance of Rouen U 107 and Titus A iv by Semmler, *loc. cit.*; St Augustine's Canterbury is postulated as the home of Harley 5431 (apparently a continental manuscript), but Ker seems to be right in thinking it the source of Titus A iv (which, however, is allocated to Winchester by Semmler on no ascertainable grounds).

the *Memoriale* to the 'Emperor Louis'. Æthelwold could thus have thought, however wrongly, that he was modelling the English customary on the Carolingians.[75]

More important than liturgical detail is the whole idea of a *consuetudo* for all, endorsed and enforced by secular authority. Adherence to the Rule of St Benedict was universal in tenth-century monasticism, and the general influence of Benedict of Aniane, especially on the liturgy, is as evident in the Lives of Odo or John of Gorze as in England.[76] But England was the only place in post-Carolingian Europe where monastic uniformity was a matter of political principle. As the *Concordia* says: '[The king] urged all to be of one mind as regards monastic usage ... and so, with their minds anchored firmly on the ordinances of the Rule, to avoid all dissension, lest differing ways of observing the customs of one Rule and one country [*patriae*] should bring their holy conversation into disrepute'.[77] These sentiments recall Benedict of Aniane's obsession with the 'forma unitatis'. For the Carolingians, religious uniformity was a function of their pastoral imperialism: diversity of practice was intolerable for a regime seeking to enforce God's law. English kings from Æthelstan's time also thought that God had given them an 'empire', as their charters show. Whatever the exact meaning of Edgar's coronation in 973, its liturgy certainly drew on Carolingian models, and it is surely no coincidence that it took place at Bath, whose hot springs must have recalled those which attracted Charlemagne to Aachen (as the English could have read in Einhard).[78] In pointing to the Anglo-Saxon copies of the Aachen decrees, Mary Bateson long ago suggested that 'what Benedict did at the council of (Aachen), Æthelwold did at Winchester', and it seems more than likely that both Æthelwold and his royal master consciously adopted the Carolingian ideology of a Christian Empire, serving one God, one king and one Rule. In the sixteenth century, English monasticism went down before the principle that 'this realm of England is an Empire'; five and a half centuries earlier, that very principle, differently envisaged, demanded uniform monastic observance.

The continental context is a potential source of influence on English developments.[79] It also puts them in proportion. Scholars have tended to

---

[75] Symons, 'Sources', p 164; and for lack of influence from the Aachen *capitula*, *Tenth Century Studies*, pp 46-7. The *Memoriale* bears the title 'Epitoma Lothwici Imperatoris super regulam Beati Benedicti' on Corpus 57, f. 34v; but it is not, *pace* Bateson, *op. cit.*, to be ascribed to him or his reign: CCM I, pp 177-282 at pp 224-5 (and cf. *ibid.*, pp 7, 200).

[76] Above, pp 20-1 and n 28; cf. VI ch 81, pp 359-60.

[77] *Regularis Concordia* ch 4, pp 2-3; compare the legislative tone of ch 69, p 69. Symons suggested, *Tenth-Century Studies*, p 47 that the reported communication between king and council at Winchester was modelled on that of Louis and the Council of Aachen – albeit the first was by letter and second oral.

[78] For Edgar's 'imperial' coronation see J. L. Nelson, 'Inauguration Rituals', *Early Medieval Kingship*, ed. P. H. Sawyer and I. N. Wood (Leeds, 1977), pp 63-70; and her 'The Second English Ordo', *Politics and Ritual in early medieval Europe* (London, 1986), pp 361-74. For Einhard on Aachen see *Vita Karoli*, ed. O. Holder-Egger, *MGH, Scriptores rerum germanicarum*, ch 22, p 27. Symons was prepared to contemplate the date of 973 for *Regularis Concordia* also, *Tenth-Century Studies*, pp 40-2, and we may note that Louis' 'Imperial Ordinance' (*Cap.* 136, pp 270-3) was issued in the same month as one of the monastic capitularies (July 817): imperial and monastic ideology were cross-hatched on both sides of the Channel.

[79] Note that an English library (Christ Church ?) had a MS of Odo's *Occupatio*: H. Gneuss,

stress the uniquely English features of the 'Tenth-Century Reformation', above all its close links with the king. The *Regularis Concordia*'s provisions on regular prayers for the royal family are unparalleled in other customaries, and it is suggested that the patronage which Cluny had from the pope, or Gorze from the bishop of Metz, was exercised in England by Edgar and his successors. A recent refinement of this thesis dwells on the common interest of king and monks in reform: like Fleury's meat-eaters, the 'corrupt' English houses represented the investment of local aristocracies in the church, and their replacement by authentic monks gave the king grateful representatives in such politically sensitive areas as the West Midlands or East Anglia.[80] Yet further comparison between England and the continent raises doubts about aspects of this approach. For instance, the contrast between reform's defence mechanisms on either side of the Channel can be overdrawn. No reform in monastic history was more closely tied to kingship in theory and practice than that of Benedict of Aniane, and intercession for king and 'patria' had been inherent in the privileges of Frankish monasteries since the days of Marculf.[81] Cluny's foundation charter prescribed prayers for the late King Odo, and King Ralph, his niece's husband, was an early patron of the abbey. Its immunity was confirmed by Louis IV and Lothair; and if royal guarantees seemed irrelevant thereafter, this was because Capetian protection was hardly worth the parchment it was written on (though Robert II was asked and did his best).[82] At Fleury, it was initially the unreformed who tried to use a royal charter against Odo, but the intervention of Duke Hugh of the Franks probably did as much as Odo's arrival on a donkey to undermine resistance. Fleury's 938 bull explicitly approved the past and future exercise of royal authority.[83] Abbo himself was usually a loyal servant of the Capetians, seeking their help against his bishop before he turned to Rome; judging by some parts of his canon collection, he was another of those prototypes of Gregory VII who was less aware than posterity of the way his ideas were going.[84] Gerard of Brogne depended heavily on the support

---

'A preliminary list of manuscripts written or owned in England up to 1100', *ASE* 9 (1981) no. 903, p 57; described by J. Leclercq, 'L'idéal monastique' (as n 25), pp 227-31, and designed to 'fix the wandering mind of monks', it is ed. A. Swoboda, *Odonis abbatis Cluniacensis Occupatio*, Collectio Teubner (Leipzig, 1900).

[80] *Regularis Concordia* ch 16-20, 24-5, 27, pp 12-16, 20-2, 24-5. See the shrewd assessment of F. Barlow, *The English Church 1000-1066* (London, 2nd edn, 1979), pp 319-20; and for the political dimension, E. John, 'King and the monks' (as n 23).

[81] *MGH Formulae* (as n 13) i 1-2, pp 40, 43, etc. J. Semmler, 'Traditio und Königsschutz', *Zeitschrift der Savigny-Stiftung für Rechtsgeschichte, kanonistische Abteilung* 76 (1959), 1-33.

[82] For Ralph's charters see above, n 32; for those of Louis IV, *Recueil des Actes de Louis IV, 936-54*, ed. P. Lauer, Chartes et Diplômes (as n 32) III (1914) 10, pp 30-2, and cf. 20, pp 49-51 (for Bourg-Dieu); for Lothair's, *Recueil des Actes de Lothaire et Louis V, 954-87*, ed. L. Halphen and F. Lot, Chartes et Diplômes II (1908) 7, 8, 12, pp 15-18, 25-7. For Robert II's attempted protection see *Rec. Cl.* 2800, IV, pp 2-4; and cf. 2485, 2711, III, pp 566-8, 733-5. A categorical (perhaps too categorical) account of Capetian incapacity is Lemarignier (as n 42), pp 102-11.

[83] *VO* iii 8, cols 80-1; *P. Uk.* 83, pp 140-2.

[84] *Collectio Canonum* 3-4, cols 477-9. Cf. J. M. Wallace-Hadrill, 'The *Via Regia* of the Carolingian Age', *Trends in Medieval Political Thought*, ed. B. Smalley (Oxford, 1965), pp 38-9; P. Wormald, 'Æthelred the Lawmaker', *Ethelred the Unready: papers from the millenary conference*, ed. D. Hill, British Archaeological Reports 59 (Oxford, 1978), pp 75-6.

of Arnulf of Flanders, and of West and East Frankish rulers behind him; Louis IV's interest in Ghent was marked, which presumably means that it was mutual.[85] Gorze's bull may have verbally echoed a royal charter, and the normal pattern in the *Reich* was for popes to follow the king's cue.[86] And no tenth-century monk was more intimately involved with kings than Adalbert.

Contrariwise, it deserves more emphasis than it often gets that Æthelwold had papal as well as royal approval for drumming the 'clerks' out of Winchester; and though Glastonbury's bull is dubious, the letter in which a Pope John reproved the depredations of an Ealdorman Ælfric at its expense is comparable with those issued in similar circumstances for Cluny.[87] It has been argued that papal protection became more common on the continent because kings were increasingly unable to offer protection themselves. Thus stated, the proposition is somewhat paradoxical: to quote Stalin, 'how many divisions has the Pope?' The growing appeal of papal sanctions in ninth-century Francia is more plausibly linked with the ideological climate of the False Decretals: the Church had a right and duty to safeguard its property, which certainly did not mean that kings did not. In tenth-century Germany, royal and papal protection were seen as complementary, and kings encouraged the reinforcement of their guarantees by popes.[88] At Cluny, the point is not that bulls replaced royal charters, but that, after 987, royal charters were useless; moreover, once exemption became an issue, only bulls would do. On the continent, then, papal privileges were intended as supplements, not substitutes, for secular support; they assumed real prominence, *when*, rather than necessarily *because*, there was little else. Against this background, the relative rarity of bulls like Æthelwold's in pre-Conquest England is unsurprising.[89] Not only was royal power as formidable as

---

Fleury historiography was emphatically 'royalist': *Helgaud de Fleury, Vie de Robert le Pieux*, ed. R. H. Bautier and G. Labory (Paris, 1965).
[85] *Recueil ... Louis IV* 15, 36, 52, pp 38-40, 82-6, 106.
[86] *P. Uk.* 86, pp 147-9; but Otto's extant diploma for Gorze postdates its papal charter: *DO* 70, pp 149-51.
[87] *P. Uk.* 211-12, 282, pp 414-18, 550-1; cf. *Councils and Synods* 29, 36, pp 109-13, 173-4; and for the Cluny parallels *P. Uk.* 58, 189, 530, pp 96-7, 372-3, 1007-10. Zimmermann's suspicion of the Glastonbury privilege (*P. Uk.* 211) may be well-founded (though see next n); but the same can hardly be said of the letter to Ælfric (if there are scant *Liber Diurnus* echoes in it, the same goes for Cluny's no. 530); let alone of *P. Uk.* 307, the famous treaty between King Æthelred and Duke Richard of Normandy. H. Vollrath, *Die Synoden Englands bis 1066* (Paderborn, 1985), pp 449-53, has doubts about the Winchester bull, chiefly because the monks failed to cite it when under attack in 1071; however, Levison showed that the text was at this point furthering the production of Canterbury's notorious forgeries (*England and the Continent in the Eighth Century* (Oxford, 1946), pp 195-9), which is not only proof that it was extant by that time but also a very good reason why it was unavailable at Winchester! Since the only sound text of the privilege, which was addressed to Edgar rather than Æthelwold, was preserved by Archbishop Parker, it seems possible that it never got beyond Canterbury until it was 'copied' into Winchester cartularies much later on. However, Dr Vollrath does give reasons for ascribing the bull to John XIII and to the year 967: *loc. cit.*, and pp 260-8.
[88] Compare the terms of reference to royal initiative in *P. Uk.* 83 (Fleury), 121 (St Maximin's), 124 (Essen), 178 (Quedlinburg), 199 (Fulda), 229 (Ghent) and 211-12 (Glastonbury and Winchester), pp 140-2, 212-14, 218-20, 349-51, 394-5, 450-1, 414-18: there is nothing unusual about Edgar's role. See also Semmler (as n 81), 16-18.
[89] But there may have been more than are now extant: we know of Ramsey's privileges only

Charlemagne's; the movement's ideology was also early, not late, Carolingian; and the proposed relationship of monk and bishop made exemption unthinkable. All pre-Gregorian reformers were royalist by inclination, papalist only by circumstance. In England, none of the relevant circumstances arose.

A second problem is the role of aristocrats as opponents of reform. On the continent as in England, this was real enough, though the continental pattern does not quite justify the modern tendency to replace the Vikings with the aristocracy as the villains of ecclesiastical decline: Odo's *vita* is among other evidence that demoralisation caused by external assault was an important first stage in the process.[90] But the emphasis on freedom of election in privileges of reformed abbeys from Charlemagne's time was usually directed against the claims of founder's kin, as Ardo's gloss on Aniane's charter shows; and in any reasonably endowed house this kin was almost certain to be aristocratic. 'The lordship of lay persons [*saecularium prioratus*]' was the *Regularis Concordia*'s version of the lay abbacy so much criticised on the continent from Carolingian times; again it was noblemen (and also kings) who were the guilty parties, and noblemen (and kings) who swallowed monastic endowments.[91] We catch clear echoes of the putative English alliance of sound churchmanship and good government against the aristocratic threat to both when holy Gerald spurns the Duke of Aquitaine's invitation to desert the king's service for his own, or when Abbo observes that unreformed Réole has so strong a site as to make its owner 'more powerful than the king of the Franks in these parts'. Yet Gerald's Duke of Aquitaine was William, the very founder of Cluny, and reform at Réole was first solicited by Duke William Sanchez of Gascony.[92] We can go too far with Abbo's witty diptych about sin and nobility, and our assessment of reform may be too much affected by our instinctive sympathy for royal and central, rather than aristocratic and local, power.

Consider three chapters in the early history of Lotharingian reform. Bishop Adalbero is a curiously ambivalent figure in the Gorze evidence. He was very nobly born indeed, and his responsibilities as lord to holders of Gorze benefices cut right across his commitment to the abbey, so that he had to be sharply nudged to keep his promises; but this did not permanently tarnish

---

because they are mentioned in the abbey *Chronicon*, ed. W. Macray, Rolls Series (London, 1886), pp 99, 171, 176; and Ramsey is one of only two Anglo-Saxon abbeys with such a detailed history of its own. A full study of pre-Conquest *Papsturkunden* in England is an urgent desideratum.

[90] VO iii 2, 8, cols 76, 80; cf. *Virtutes S. Eugenii* (as n 48) 2, p 647, and above, n 67; also the Council of Trosly, J. Mansi, *Sacrorum Conciliorum nova et amplissima collectio* XVIII ch 3, cols 270-2.

[91] F. J. Felten, *Äbte und Laienäbte im Frankenreich: Studien zum Verhältnis von Staat und Kirche im früheren Mittelalter*, Monographien zur Geschichte des Mittelalters, ed. F. Prinz and K. Bosl, 20 (Stuttgart, 1980) puts the important case that lay abbots only became unacceptable (and so noticed) in the changed ideological climate of Carolingian times. He hardly does justice to the English evidence which I marshalled in 'Bede, *Beowulf* and the conversion of the Anglo-Saxon aristocracy', *Bede and Anglo-Saxon England: papers in honour of the 1300th anniversary of the birth of Bede*, ed. R. T. Farrell, British Archaeological Reports 46 (Oxford, 1978), pp 50-5; and in *Bede and the conversion of England: the charter evidence* (Jarrow lecture, 1984), pp 19-23.

[92] VG i 32, 35, cols 660-1, 663-4; VA 16, 20, cols 406, 410.

his fame as its second founder.[93] Another to fall foul of John (and St Gorgonius) in pursuit of Gorze claims was Boso II, descendant of the abbey's ninth-century lay abbots. Boso was actually the brother of the King Ralph whose support was so useful to Cluny; but we now know that Ralph's support was no less self-centred than Boso's opposition, just because one was a king, the other not.[94] Finally, there is the curious story of Count Gislebert of Lorraine and St Maximin's Trier. For John's *vita* he was a supporter of reform, but Adalbert gives the credit to King Henry the Fowler, while the St Maximin's account itself has the monks appealing vainly to Henry against the oppressions of the count, whose attitude is altered by a nocturnal visit from St Maximin in person. The latest discussion favours Adalbert's version. But Gislebert's subsequent rebellion (on which Adalbert is a detailed and hostile authority) gave him better reasons for selecting his facts than the other sources; and the St Maximin's story has the ring of truth – not least in that the same sort of tale was told in the presumably independent account of the count's part in the reform at St Ghislain (which has itself been discounted because of his 'bad character').[95] The fact is that there was room in the behaviour of all powerful men, whether bishop, king or nobleman, for inconsistency, tunnel vision and bad conscience; equally, self-interest advised no one to annoy saints, living or dead. So it is in England: Æthelwine, *amicus Dei* for Byrhtferth of Ramsey, was no friend to Ely; and Ælfhere, Ramsey's villain, was at least a patron of Glastonbury. There was no 'pro-monastic' nor 'anti-monastic' party as such; and *if* Ælfhere supported the queen's faction after Edgar's death, Bishop Æthelwold was probably his ally.[96]

One important trend in the study of the early medieval Church since the discovery of the *Eigenkirche* has been to relate what reformers criticised to the structure and values of élite society. But neither in England nor on the continent can reform be seen as an attack on the aristocracy as a class. On the contrary, the participation of the aristocracy was ultimately a much more important reason for the success of tenth-century reform than any amount of royal or papal support: one could almost say that the reason why there *was* a tenth-century Reformation was that a very large number of aristocrats betrayed their class-interest in the Church. Cluny had roughly

---

[93] *VI* ch 35-42, 95-103, 110-14, pp 346-9, 364-7, 368-9; *Miracula S. Gorgonii* 8-11, 15, pp 241-3. These matters are discussed by M. Parisse, 'Varangéville, prieuré de Gorze', *Saint Chrodegang* (as n 52), pp 153-67; I have also learnt much about Gorze's ninth-century history from S. R. Airlie, 'The political behaviour of the secular magnates in Francia, 829-79', Oxford D.Phil. thesis (1985), pp 194-205.
[94] *VI* ch 104-9, pp 367-8; *Miracula S. Gorgonii* 12, p 242; for King Ralph and Cluny see Wollasch, *Neue Forschungen*, pp 142-7.
[95] *VI* ch 95, p 364; *Adalberti Chronicon* (as n 65), pp 159, 160-1; Sigehard, *Miracula S. Maximini* (as n 63) 12, p 232; *Miracula S. Gisleni* (as n 49) 10, pp 583-4. See Wisplinghoff, *S. Maximin*, p 31; D'Haenens (as n 47), 116-17.
[96] *Liber Eliensis* ii 7, 11, 27, 30, 35, 49, 55, pp 80, 90, 101, 104, 110, 116, 126-7; as against *Chronicon Ramsey* (as n 89) 22, 25, 28, 40, 41, 49, 58-60, pp 29-39, 49-50, 52-5, 68, 72, 78-80, 90-107; and *Vita Oswaldi, Hist. York.* I, pp 443-6. D. J. V. Fisher, 'The anti-monastic reaction in the reign of Edward the Martyr', *Cambridge Historical Journal* 10 (1952), pp 266-70 saw this very clearly; see also A. Williams, '*Princeps Merciorum gentis*: the family, career and connections of Ælfhere, ealdorman of Mercia', *ASE* 10 (1982), 166-72; and Keynes, *Diplomas of Æthelred*, pp 163-76.

equal numbers of royal and papal charters by the late eleventh century, but its colossal cartulary is mainly a monument to the Burgundian nobility. There were over 80 outright lay gifts to the abbey in the seventeen years before Odo's abbacy, over 140 during it; and it was Cluny documents that gave Georges Duby his mirror of '*La Société Mâconnaise*'.[97] If England looks different, that is bacause Anglo-Saxon diplomatic is so king-centred. As it is, almost all secular wills include bequests to reformed houses, and the records of Ely and Ramsey show much more than the aristocratic backsliding they are famous for.[98] Above all, Benedict of Aniane, Odo, Gerard of Brogne and Adalbert were themselves of high birth, and reacted consciously (or sub-consciously) against their background; the ambience of Fleury and Gorze was equally aristocratic; and we should surely say the same for Æthelwold and his colleagues. Christianity has always inspired spectacular renunci-ations of wealth. It was meant to. Pressures building up inside the walls of privilege can be as explosive as the resentments of those shut out of them. 'The alternation of headlong violence with abrupt acts of remorse and atonement' was a feature of the age, because a heroic society, with a cult of the grand gesture and of the struggle against odds, faced an as yet quite unresolved tension between a brutal reality and the intolerably immediate ideals of the New Testament. The essence of 'Cluny' and what it stands for was that such reactions were now given a communal focus which was both spiritually and socially élitist.[99] The religious history of the Barbarian West remains unintelligible unless we reckon with tormented aristocratic minds as well as vested aristocratic interests. One tormented mind was probably Æthelwold's.

If the continental perspective adds depth to our perception of English developments, it also isolates what is odd. The distinctively English feature of English reform is not so much the part played by kings at the expense of aristocrats in a community like unreformed Winchester, as the character of the reformed community that took its place. It has long been acknowledged that there was no real European parallel to the cathedral-monastery which Æthelwold created by installing monks in the Old Minster and which he specifically allowed for in the *Regularis Concordia*; but much more atten-tion has been given to the question of when and how Worcester and Canterbury followed suit than to noting how very odd an arrangement it

---

[97] *Rec. Cl.*, p xxix, n 1, pp 113-278, 278-529. Something of the same impression is made by the cartularies of Aniane, *Cartulaire des abbayes d'Aniane et Gellone*, ed. A. Cassan and E. Meynial (Montpelier, 1900) II, pp 133-450; of Fleury, *Recueil des chartes de l'Abbaye de Saint-Benôit-sur-Loire*, ed. M. Prou and A. Vidier, Documents publiés par la société historique et archéologique du Gâtinnais (Paris, 1900) I, pp 119-92; and of Gorze, ed. d'Herbomez (as n 56), pp 173-222.

[98] *Liber Eliensis* ii 11, 13, 15, 29, 31, 34, 59, 60, 61, 62, 63-4, 66, 67, 68, 69-70, 74, 81, 83, 88, 89, pp 86-7, 91, 92, 103, 105, 108, 130-1, 131-2, 132-3, 133-6, 136-7, 138, 139, 139-40, 140, 143-4, 150, 151, 157-8; *Chronicon Ramsey* (as n 89) 25, 28, 31, 32, 34-8, 50-1, 53-4, 63, 80-1, 90, 106-7, pp 51, 52-5, 57, 58, 62-7, 81-2, 83-5, 111-12, 145-7, 153-4, 173-4.

[99] The quotation is from Southern, *Making of the Middle Ages* (as n 36), p 83; the reference is to the Jerusalem pilgrimage particularly, and one of Abbo's Fleury pupils was son (one of a 'copiosa filiorum caterva') to Hugh, an Aquitainian aristocrat who was among the first Frenchmen to make the journey: *VA* 10, cols 397-8. For the atmosphere of Cluny in this later period see J. Wollasch, 'Parenté noble et monachisme réformateur: Observations sur les "conversions" à la vie monastique aux XIe et XIIe siècles', *Revue Historique* 264 (1980), 3-24.

was in European terms.[100] When reform again came to English cathedral closes under Edward the Confessor, Chrodegang's Rule for canons was used: why did Æthelwold not do the same (confining his monastic zeal to the New Minster next door)? The monastic life was certainly thought superior to the canonical, which is why John of Salerno was grateful for his own con-version. By Gregorian times, canons were under acute suspicion, an attitude which coloured most of the rewritten sources for Gerard of Brogne. The reason why the survivors at Gorze had to become monks was that Gorze and the other houses concerned had (or were believed to have) once been monasteries, and while one might graduate from 'cleric' to monk, it was quite wrong to move in the opposite direction. Whatever else they were, however, these houses were *not* cathedrals. On the continent, the canonical life was the only model proper for a bishop's *familia*. One of Benedict of Aniane's motives for drawing so careful a line between the respective spheres of monk and canon was to isolate the former from the cares of the Church in the world, which also explains his well-known ban on monastic education for anyone other than oblates; the last thing he had in mind was the mingling of Martha's life with Mary's (to borrow Abbo's image).[101] Behind the quest for exemption lay the conviction that a bishop's world was different from a monk's, and bad for him; and if the Rule envisaged the diocesan's intervention in a real crisis, it certainly said as little as possible about it. But the clearest indication of Æthelwold's eccentricity is what happened at Magdeburg.[102] Adalbert was a monk and the new archbishopric was to be based on the abbey of St Maurice, but it was never once suggested that the monastic community could simply become the cathedral chapter. The chap-ter *had* to consist of canons, though this meant the transfer of most of St Maurice's monks to a brand new foundation, and a haunted conscience for those who remained, thereby exchanging a superior for an inferior mode of life. For all the extra problems which it would have spared a project that already had its fair share, the Winchester option was not contemplated. Yet Æthelwold turned a cathedral chapter into a monastery. All the signs are that if Dunstan and Oswald hesitated to follow him, this was because they had been abroad, and knew what continental practice was.

Understanding Æthelwold's extraordinary policy requires awareness that monastic reformers were inspired by more than just the Rule of St Benedict. Like St Benedict himself, Benedict of Aniane, Odo and John of Gorze looked beyond 'the Rule for beginners' to the original pioneers of monasticism, Anthony, Pachomius, Basil and the eastern fathers whose teaching was purveyed by Cassian. Moreover, with Odo, Abbo, Gerard and John, there is a marked interest in local saints, native or imported, whose miracles one way or another eclipsed their own.[103] Æthelwold felt exactly the same sense of

---

[100] Most recently, P. H. Sawyer, 'The charters of the Reform movement: the Worcester archive', *Tenth-Century Studies*, pp 87-93; and N. P. Brooks, *The Early History of the Church at Canterbury* (Leicester, 1984), pp 245-53. Note the parallel to the case made out for St Maximin's by Wisplinghoff (above, n 61).

[101] *CCM* I 23: 36, p 526 (cf. 21: 5, p 474); Abbo, *Liber Apologeticus*, PL CXXXIX, col. 464 (but *cave* the misprint!).

[102] On this see Claude (as n 62) II, pp 200-7; *Gesta Archiepiscoporum Magdeburgensium*, ed. W. Schum, *MGH, Scriptores* XIV ch 8, pp 380-1; and Thietmar, *Chronicon* iv 65-8, pp 205-9.

[103] Above, pp 15, 19-20, 23, 26, 28, and nn 3, 21, 25, 40, 51, 58-9; Odo's loyalty to the

debt to the saints of the past: he hushed up his own miracles but trumpeted those of Swithun; and 'Æthelwold's preaching was greatly assisted by the heavenly signs of the holy bishop Swithun'. Swithun perhaps served the same purpose as a common focus of loyalty for reformed and unreformed alike as Martin or Gorgonius.[104] What was special in England was that the reformers had in Bede's *Ecclesiastical History* their own 'gallery of good examples' such as continental reformers found in the Desert Fathers, *combined with* an inspiring account of their 'very special dead'. We should thus expect to find that Bede loomed large in the views of Æthelwold and his circle.[105] And further evidence of their sensitivity to the English past comes in the very singular sets of charters from Abingdon and Winchester during or shortly after Æthelwold's time.[106] At the chronological end of each series stand diplomas or writs of the period whose authenticity is beyond much dispute. But they tend to make historical claims, and, as at St Maximin's, these claims are supported by documentary chains, extending back to the seventh century in Winchester's case, and the ninth in Abingdon's. Not only are these chains highly suspect, but it also looks as if they were fabricated at the time the claims were made, because some of the links are extant in hands of this date.[107] Such a thoroughly historical approach to forgery is met nowhere else in Anglo-Saxon diplomatic, so it is at least suggestive that the houses concerned were those most closely associated with Æthelwold.

---

admittedly special case of St Martin was such that, though mortally ill at Rome itself, he was granted a sufficient recovery to return to unreformed Tours, where he died, *Martino duce*, within the saint's octave: *VO* iii 12, cols 83-6.

[104] Wulfstan, *Vita* ch 14, 26, 33, 35, 37, 38, pp 42-3, 49, 52-3, 54-5, 55-6; Ælfric ch 18, p 25 expresses the position in characteristically lapidary style: 'quod Æthelwoldus verbis edocuit, hoc Suuithunus miraculis decoravit'. (It will have become obvious that I accept Dr Lapidge's case for the priority of Wulfstan's *vita* over Ælfric's.) Mr Nightingale's thesis has a full discussion of the reconciliatory rôle of patron saints in Lotharingian reform.

[105] It is a point of some interest that the earliest calendars to celebrate the feast of Bede as well as St Augustine of Canterbury on 26 May have a Winchester provenance (apart from one simply ascribed to 'Wessex'): F. Wormald, *English Kalendars before AD 1100*, Henry Bradshaw Society lxxii (1934), pp 34, 118, 132, 160. For Æthelwold and the Saints of England see D. W. Rollason, 'The shrines of saints in later Anglo-Saxon England: Distribution and Significance', *The Anglo-Saxon Church: Papers on History, Architecture and Archaeology in Honour of Dr H. M. Taylor*, ed. R. Morris, Council for British Archaeology Research Report 60 (London, 1986), pp 32-43; also Thacker, below, pp 61-3.

[106] These charter series are as follows (beginning with the latest, then following chronological order from earliest to penultimate): Downton, S 891, S 229, S 275, S 540, S 821; Taunton, S 1242 (cf. S 806), S 254, S 373, S 443, S 521, S 825; Chilcomb, S 946, S 325, S 376, S 439, S 817 (and cf. H. P. R. Finberg, *The Early Charters of Wessex* (Leicester, 1964), no. 27); Alresford, S 814, 242, 284, 375; Abingdon, S 878, S 93, 166, 183, 567, 658, 673, and cf. S 786 (Pershore). The Winchester series is discussed by Finberg, *op. cit.*, pp 214-48, and the 'Orthodoxorum' collection by Keynes, *Diplomas of Æthelred*, pp 98-101. See also Thacker, below, pp 51-4. This is not to say that the *historical* claims were fraudulent, nor to deny that the compilers had access to genuine material: merely to assert that the documents we have that purport to date from before Æthelwold's time were never 'issued' (whatever the process involved) by the kings to whom they are ascribed, while those allegedly dating from the mid tenth century onwards sustain the case made here whether genuine or bogus. I hope to return to this matter on another occasion.

[107] Viz. SS 376, 443, 540, and cf. Pershore's S 786 (its first abbot, Foldbriht, was a disciple of Æthelwold's: Wulfstan, *Vita* ch 11, p 41).

Further, more or less authentic texts for Ely and Peterborough refer explicitly to Bede's testimony; the second of these was very probably Æthelwold's own work, and the first has clear connections with him.[108] In other words, the ideology of reform in Æthelwold's favoured abbeys was powered by a bright vision of England's religious history.

There is, however, decisive evidence that Æthelwold had this sort of historical vision: nothing less than a historical work from his own pen. As presented in *English Historical Documents*, this work, now securely attributed to Æthelwold, looks no more than what the editor calls it: 'An Old English account of King Edgar's establishment of monasteries', though it is notable as such for an enthusiasm about Edgar's kingship comparable with Adalbert's commitment to the Ottonians.[109] In fact, it is – or rather was – much more. The extant text begins with a moving account of the conversion of the English and the foundation of many monasteries, taken from Bede. Before the story passes on to Edgar's reign itself, there is a lacuna, perhaps of one leaf in the manuscript, conceivably of three; we thus lack at least 500, or as many as 1500, words – just over a fifth, or just under a half, of the total. The last word before the break is: 'AC – BUT'. It would seem that what is missing is an account, perhaps quite detailed, of what Æthelwold thought had gone wrong with English monasticism since Bede's day; and it is a fair guess that he here gave the Vikings more of a rôle than seemed appropriate in the *Regularis Concordia*. Even as the text stands, he represents what happened in the tenth century as a return to Bede's Golden Age; and this is the final clue to the idiosyncratic course that reform took at Winchester.

It should be remembered that some of the sources represent Benedict of Aniane's reforms, however misleadingly, as a restoration of the monastic *status quo ante*. Wherever, then or later, canons were replaced by monks, this was because of a conviction that such places had formerly been monasteries: indeed, where this could not be established – as in Odo's Tours, thanks partly to the confusion caused by Alcuin's agonisings – monasticisation never happened.[110] Now, as Bede told the story, almost everyone who was anyone in the first century of the English Church was what he rightly or wrongly called a monk; as if this were not enough, Bede quoted Pope Gregory's injunction in his '*Responsa*' that Augustine must continue,

---

[108] SS 779, 782; D. Whitelock, 'The authorship of the account of King Edgar's establishment of monasteries', *Philological Essays: Studies in Old and Middle English Literature in honour of Herbert Dean Meritt*, ed. J. L. Rosier (The Hague, 1970), pp 132-3; J. Pope, 'Ælfric and the Old English version of the Ely privilege', *England before the Conquest: Studies in primary sources presented to Dorothy Whitelock*, ed. P. Clemoes and K. Hughes (Cambridge, 1971), pp 85-113.

[109] *EHD* 238; *Leechdoms, Wortcunning and Starcraft of Early England*, ed. O. Cockayne, Rolls Series (London, 1866) III, pp 432-44, now re-edited *Councils and Synods* 33, pp 142-54, which is the edition used here. As Whitelock suggests, it was probably designed as a prologue to Æthelwold's translation of the Rule, which it follows in the MS (London, British Library Cotton MS Faustina A x). For Edgar's kingship see pp 146-7.

[110] See the very pertinent discussion (from the point of view of this paper) by G. Oexle, *Forschungen zu monastischen und geistlichen Gemeinschaften im westfränkischen Bereich*, Münstersche Mittelalterschriften 31 (München, 1978), pp 112-18 (St Denis), 120-33 (St Martin's) and 134-62 (Lyons). Some places definitely regarded as one-time monasteries nevertheless escaped re-monasticisation, including Agaune: Dereine, 'Chanoines' (as n 4), col. 367 (a reference I owe to my colleague, Marilyn Dunn).

as a bishop, to live the life of a monk with a monastic *familia*, and was so impressed by the arrangement that he twice wrongly compared it with the set-up at Lindisfarne. Further, in his great letter to Bishop Ecgberht, he warmly urged that corrupt and fraudulent monasteries be turned into bishoprics that would do pastoral good.[111] Æthelwold's historical introduction to English monasticism (which is roughly what it was) clearly quotes the relevant Response in its description of Augustine's community at Canterbury; and Symons thought that the *Regularis Concordia* bore traces of the Letter to Ecgberht.[112] On the continent, the monastic chapters established by Boniface and his colleagues were eventually overborne by the Aachen prescription.[113] But in England such arrangements had been endorsed by the national apostle, and a pope at that. The first historian to take the now discredited view that Gregory introduced the Rule of St Benedict into England was Aimo. It is at least a good guess that Abbo had heard this asserted in England.[114] In short, I suggest simply that what Æthelwold did in the Old Minster, unusual even in England and in continental terms bizarre, was because he was himself a historian, soaked in the writings of a historian far greater than he. By the same misinformed logic as prevailed with one-time 'monasteries' in Europe, all English religious communities, including cathedrals, had long ago been 'monastic', and they must all, including cathedrals, become monastic again. The exceptional hold which monasticism now took on the English Church, and which it gradually extended (with Norman help), must be put down to the immortal picture of its origins painted by Bede the monk. This is as striking an illustration as any in English history of how one historian's vision of the past can determine the future. For Æthelwold himself, there is a final possibility. We know that he believed in the English vernacular, at least for the benefit of the 'ignorant', and that he did as much as anyone after Alfred to make Old English into a literary language.[115] He must have been familiar with the famous words in which Alfred, himself drawing on Bede, described how English 'warfare and wisdom' had once flourished together. Perhaps he aimed to recreate this lost age under Edgar's imperial rule, in the hope (vain as things turned out) that his people could avoid the barbarian onslaught of which Bede had warned, and which Alfred had barely repelled.

It is possible to write early English history without much reference to the Anglo-Saxons' neighbours: great scholars have done so. But something is thereby lost. For Æthelwold, it is a nice point that only from the continental angle can we see how much more than Benedictine *pietas* went into the

---

[111] *Bede's Ecclesiastical History of the English People*, ed. B. Colgrave and R. A. B. Mynors (Oxford, 1969) i 27, iv 27, pp 78-81, 434-5; *Two Lives of Saint Cuthbert*, ed. B. Colgrave (Cambridge, repr. 1985) ch 16, pp 208-9; *Epistola Bede ad Ecgbertum episcopum*, ed. C. Plummer, *Baedae Opera Historica* (Oxford, 1896), pp 413-18.

[112] *Councils and Synods*, p 145; Symons, *Tenth-Century Studies*, pp 44-5. In a paper forthcoming in *Journal of Ecclesiastical History*, Antonia Gransden strengthens the case for the influence on Æthelwold of the Letter to Ecgberht.

[113] R. Schieffer, *Die Entstehung der Domkapiteln in Deutschland*, Bonner historische Forschungen 43 (Bonn, 1976), pp 171-92.

[114] *VA* 4, cols 390-1.

[115] *Councils and Synods*, pp 151-2. Note the English language versions of the Winchester charters, SS 806, 817, together with that for S 779, discussed by Pope (above, n 108); and cf.

pursuit of monastic reform, from the dream of Christian Empire to the realisation of a great historian's convictions by what was arguably the second most creative historical intelligence that the Anglo-Saxons produced. It is also a satisfying paradox that the effect of viewing Æthelwold from the standpoint of his cross-channel counterparts is to sharpen rather than blur the contours of his intellectual personality, and to bring out a sensitivity to English tradition perhaps even stronger than Dunstan's or Oswald's. Æthelwold was not only the first Englishman known to have been born in a town; he was also the first, after King Alfred, to act decisively on the principle that National Sin (and especially *trahison des clercs*) would mean National Punishment. In neither respect, as the world of learning in 1980s Britain scarcely needs reminding, was he the last.

Wulfstan, *Vita* ch 31, p 51. See the seminal article by H. Gneuss, 'The Origin of standard Old English and Æthelwold's school at Winchester', *ASE* 1 (1972), 63-83.

Chapter 2

ÆTHELWOLD AND ABINGDON

Alan Thacker

Abingdon was Æthelwold's first major appointment. He was abbot there for some eight years, from c.955 to 963, and even after that he probably continued to supervise the affairs of the house fairly closely from Winchester. Æthelwold made Abingdon for a while the leading English monastic community; indeed apart from Glastonbury, where he himself was trained, there was at first probably no other, and Abingdon seems to have supplied monks for most if not all of his major foundations.[1] The monastery became immensely rich; Ælfric and Wulfstan, Æthelwold's biographers, state that by the time the saint departed to Winchester it had been transformed from a neglected *monasteriolum* to a great establishment with an endowment assessed at over 600 hides.[2]

To put this achievement in perspective it is necessary to consider the earlier history of the community which Æthelwold raised to greatness. It has generally been argued that there was little continuity between the pre-Æthelwoldan establishment, always insignificant, and the rich and powerful monastery which he left in 963.[3] That, however, is to render Æthelwold's achievement too dramatically, and indeed to disregard the version of events current in Æthelwold's own day. King Æthelred II's undoubtedly authentic charter to the community, dated 993, assumes that there had been a seventh-century monastery of St Mary at Abingdon, founded by the West Saxon king Caedwalla (685-8) and possessed of the *rus* known as *Abbendun*. After being attacked by the Vikings it had been unjustly transformed into an *aedificium regale*, but restitution had been made to Æthelwold by Kings Eadred (946-55), Eadwig (956-9), and Eadgar (959-75).[4] Æthelwold, then, is presented as restoring the impoverished and deprived community which he had been given to its original, or at least pre-Viking, condition. Our estimate of his impact on Abingdon must in part depend on the extent to which this picture can be taken at its face value.

The principal problem in evaluating the early history of Abingdon lies in the nature of the sources. Though much may be gleaned from the writings of

I should like to offer my warmest thanks to the organisers of the Millenium of St Æthelwold at Abingdon for inviting me to give an earlier draft of this paper as a lecture, and to the British Academy for the award of a research grant which made possible its completion for this volume.

[1] E.g. Winchester, Chertsey, Ely, Thorney. See below, pp 58-9.
[2] Ælfric ch 7, 17; Wulfstan, *Vita*, ch 11, 21.
[3] E.g. F. M. Stenton, *The Early History of the Abbey of Abingdon* (Reading, 1913), esp. pp 2-3, 31-2, 45, 50-1.
[4] *Chron. Abingdon* I, 358-66; S 876.

Æthelwold himself, from his biographers, and from William of Malmesbury, inevitably it is necessary to take account of the lengthy history of the abbey composed by its own monks in the twelfth and thirteenth centuries making use of archives now lost. The earliest recension was written before 1117, and takes the form of a narrative interspersed with numerous charters generally (though not always) relating to estates granted to the abbey.[5] Later in the thirteenth century this work was revised: a number of new charters were added and existing texts embellished by the addition of witness lists.[6] A third text, much shorter and less important, consists of a history of the abbots written in the late twelfth or thirteenth century.[7] The difficulty is that many of the Abingdon diplomas, especially those relating to the early history of the community, are notorious forgeries, that is to say they either represent reworkings of genuine early documents or simply record current Abingdon tradition in charter form.[8]

Such problems led Sir Frank Stenton, the greatest of Abingdon's modern historians, to claim despairingly that 'utter obscurity overhangs the history of the abbey' before the time of Æthelwold.[9] He was only prepared to accept the most basic outline of the Abingdon record: a community which had been founded by a West Saxon nobleman called Hean in the early eighth century was destroyed by the Danes and later replaced by 'a little monastery established on a royal estate'.[10] More recently, however, it has been suggested that Stenton was unduly pessimistic and that more credence is to be attached to the traditions preserved in the Abingdon chronicle than he allowed.[11] Almost certainly there was an early monastery with endowments in two main areas. The more important was the estate of *Earmundesleah*, according to local tradition assessed at 80 hides and granted by a West Saxon *regulus* called Cissa. The name *Earmundesleah* is now lost but probably originally it designated the abbey's holdings in the vicinity of Abingdon. It was still known in the tenth century but already by then was becoming obsolete.[12] The abbey was also believed to have been granted a group of territories some twenty miles south of Abingdon, around Bradfield, Basildon, and Streatley. They seem to have been lost at an early date and were certainly not claimed by the community in or after the tenth century, an indication that the charter recording this grant may represent an authentic tradition.[13]

In the eighth and early ninth centuries the community thus endowed came increasingly under the influence of Mercia rather than Wessex, but its history remained tied up with kings. Æthelred's charter tells of an Abbot Hrethun who obtained privileges from Pope Leo (795-816) and King Coenwulf

[5] BL Cotton MS Claudius C IX; Stenton, *Abingdon Abbey*, pp 1-3.
[6] BL Cotton MS Claudius B VI; Stenton, *Abingdon Abbey*, pp 1-3.
[7] BL Cotton MS Vitellius A XIII; *Chron. Abingdon* II, 267-95. For other texts relating to the early history of Abingdon see M. Biddle, M. T. Lambrick, J. N. L. Myres, 'The Early History of Abingdon and its Abbey', *Medieval Archaeology* 12 (1968), 30-1.
[8] See esp. S. Keynes, *The Diplomas of King Æthelred the Unready, 978-1016* (Cambridge, 1980), pp 10-13; M. Gelling, *Early Charters of the Thames Valley* (Leicester, 1979).
[9] Stenton, *Abingdon Abbey*, p 7.
[10] *Ibid.*, p 50.
[11] Biddle *et al.*, 'Early Hist. of Abingdon', 26-69.
[12] M. Gelling, *Place-Names of Berkshire, II*, English Place-Name Society 50 (1974), 443-4.
[13] *Chron. Abingdon* I, 11-13; Gelling, *Thames Valley*, nos. 10-11; S 239, 252.

(796-821),[14] and Mercian rulers seem to have been especially associated with estates at Culham and Andersey island. Offa (757-96) is said to have obtained Andersey from the community in the eighth century and to have used it as a residence.[15] Two sisters of King Coenwulf seem to have lived at Culham in the early ninth century and to have bequeathed it to the abbey where they were reputed to have been buried.[16] At that time too the abbot of Abingdon is said to have regained Andersey island from the Mercian king by an exchange.[17] There seems no good reason to reject these traditions out of hand, and they find some confirmation in the fact that Culham long remained very closely linked with the abbey.[18] Moreover, it is significant that Culham continued to have royal associations in the tenth century, when King Athelstan (924-39) lived there.[19]

In the mid ninth century Abingdon passed once again under the control of the West Saxon royal house. Shortly afterwards it suffered from Viking attacks, though the community was later at pains to stress that its charters and holy relics were hidden and preserved, to be rediscovered at the restoration attributed to Æthelred I (865-71).[20] Of Æthelred himself the Abingdon chronicler has naturally nothing but good to report, but his younger brother Alfred (871-99) received an uncharacteristically bad notice:

> Like Judas among the twelve, heaping evil upon evil, he violently seized the vill in which the abbey was sited, ... with all its appurtenances, thus rendering a very poor return to the Conquering Lord, through whom he had obtained victory over the Danes at Ashdown.[21]

It was Alfred, then, who first deprived the community of most of its property. Though some lands, including Culham, seem later to have been regained, the great estate of *Earmundesleah* and much else remained in royal hands and under Athelstan became the site of a favoured royal residence. By then some of this territory was being bestowed upon the king's associates; in 931, for example, Athelstan granted one of the community's early possessions at Watchfield to his thegn Ælfric. Significantly, however, Ælfric returned the estate to the church at Abingdon, and it seems possible that this reversion was a condition of the grant.[22] Certainly Athelstan revived the fortunes of the church in other ways. He and members of his court were said to have made several grants to the community,[23] of which the largest and best attested

---

[14] Stenton, *Abingdon Abbey*, p 8; *Chron. Abingdon* I, 21-3; S 876.

[15] *Chron. Abingdon* I, 18-21; II, 273; *VCH Oxon* VII, 31-2, 35.

[16] *Chron. Abingdon* I, 18-21; Gelling, *Thames Valley*, no. 263; S 184.

[17] *VCH Oxon* VII, 31-2, 35.

[18] It is included in Coenwulf's grant of privileges for all estates belonging to the monastery, which may have an authentic basis: Gelling, *Thames Valley*, no. 18; *Chron. Abingdon* I, 25-7; S 183.

[19] *VCH Oxon* VII, 31-2; below, pp 48-9.

[20] *Chron. Abingdon* I, 31-50.

[21] *Ibid.* I, 50 (author's translation). For a recent discussion of Alfred's annexation of the Abingdon lands see R. Fleming, 'Monastic Lands and England's Defence in the Viking Age', *EHR* 100 (1985), 247-65, esp. 251-1.

[22] *Chron. Abingdon* I, 72-3; S 413.

[23] *Chron. Abingdon* I, 60-72; S 408-10, 1546; Stenton, *Abingdon Abbey*, pp 33-9. Though the charters are dubious (Gelling, *Thames Valley*, nos. 34-6; Keynes, *Diplomas of King Æthelred*, pp 10-13), they nevertheless reflect a tradition that Athelstan was a notable benefactor.

was the grant of 40 hides at Uffington by the great ealdorman Athelstan
Half-King, himself probably of the royal house and the foster-father of
King Edgar.[24] Abingdon was also the scene of the famous embassy sent to
Athelstan by Hugh, duke of the Franks in 926, at which the king received
treasure and relics of astonishing richness. Some of these, such as the
fragments of the Cross and the crown of thorns, were given to Malmesbury
abbey, Athelstan's favourite foundation, but other items, including, it seems,
a nail used at the Crucifixion and a finger of St Denis, were given to
Abingdon, where they were conserved in a silver reliquary and performed
many miracles of healing.[25]

Here then is undoubted evidence that the post-Viking church at Abingdon
was still an important one connected with a royal residence and in receipt of
royal gifts. A further sign of Athelstan's interest is the appointment there of
a German cleric, Godescalc, as *presbyter*.[26] The king seems to have recruited
educated Germans for his more important churches, perhaps because of the
shortage of literate native clergy; there were Germans in the episcopal
familia at Winchester and Canterbury, while at London Bishop Theodred
was probably himself of German descent and was surrounded by German
clerics.[27] Athelstan was interested in ecclesiastical reform and significantly
both Dunstan and Æthelwold were educated at his court. Indeed, it has
recently been suggested that Æthelwold felt particular affection for the king,
that he looked upon him in some special sense as his lord.[28] If so, he may have
regarded Abingdon as an especially appropriate centre for the establishment
of his reformed community.[29] In sum, the seeds of Abingdon's later greatness
were probably sown in Athelstan's reign. Yet despite all this the king does
not bulk large in Abingdon tradition; his church of St Mary, though important, was non-monastic and hence less interesting to the reformers than
the pre-Viking community.

Athelstan's policies towards the church seem to have been continued by
Edmund I (939-46). Like his predecessor, Edmund granted out portions of
the ancient endowment to his followers, perhaps also with the intention that
they revert to the community. One doubtful instance of this is the grant of
10 hides at Appleton, described as part of *Earmundesleah*, to Athelstan

---

[24] *Chron. Abingdon* I, 69-70; Gelling, *Thames Valley*, no. 37; Robertson, *Anglo-Saxon
Charters*, no. xxii; S 1208. On Athelstan Half-King see C. Hart, 'Athelstan Half-King and his
Family', *ASE* 2 (1973), 115-44.
[25] They were still there in the twelfth century, when they were scrutinised and recorded by
Abbot Faritius. The Abingdon chronicle wrongly claims that everything was given to Abingdon; its
relic list in fact contains only one item which accords with William of Malmesbury's account of
the envoys' gifts – the holy nail; the other item expressly said by Faritius to have been given by
Athelstan, the finger of St Denis, was unknown to William: *Chron. Abingdon* I, 88; II, 155-8;
William of Malmesbury, *Gesta Regum Anglorum*, ed. W. Stubbs, RS, 2 vols (London, 1887-9),
II, 150-1; M. Wood, 'The Making of King Æthelstan's Empire: an English Charlemagne?', *Ideal
and Reality in Frankish and Anglo-Saxon Society*, ed. P. Wormald *et al.* (Oxford, 1983),
pp 266-7.
[26] *Chron. Abingdon* I, 64-6; Gelling, *Thames Valley*, no. 36; S 409, 1546.
[27] Wood, 'King Æthelstan's Empire', p 261.
[28] *Ibid.*, pp 257-8, 270-1. See Ælfric ch 5; Wulfstan, *Vita* ch 7.
[29] The fostering of devotion to the Holy Cross at Abingdon in Æthelwold's time may also be
significant here. Devotion to the Holy Cross was a particularly noticeable element in Athelstan's
piety: Wood, 'King Æthelstan's Empire', p 270; below, pp 59-60.

Half-King, who was alleged to have restored it to the church.[30] More circumstantial, however, is the grant to Ælfhild in 940 of Culham, one of the community's few remaining pre-Viking possessions. Under the terms of this transaction the community seems to have agreed to a temporary alienation of part of its endowment in return for being confirmed in possession of Ælfric's land at Watchfield. The recipient, Ælfhild, described as a matron of royal birth, is said to have obtained the estate on the same terms as those on which Coenwulf granted it to his sisters, namely that it was to revert to the church after her death.[31] That may imply that Ælfhild was a descendant of the Mercian royal house, former benefactors of the community; at all events she seems to have been closely associated with Abingdon, since she was a patron of the cult of St Vincent which later flourished there.[32]

After Edmund's death in 946 the church at Abingdon apparently suffered a total eclipse; it was described as deserted, its possessions given over to royal lordship. The reasons for this are unclear, and the Abingdon chronicler himself confessed that he could not explain it, emphasising that he included the tale only because he found it in the *antiqui libri* which were his source.[33] Undoubtedly the story tallies with the statement of Æthelwold's biographers that in 955 King Eadred gave the saint 'a waste and deserted little monastery, consisting of poor buildings and possessing only 40 hides'.[34] Nevertheless, we should beware of giving too much importance to the break; the gap between 946 and 955 was only brief, and Ælfric and Wulfstan's description of the church which Æthelwold was granted seems unduly dismissive. Though viewed from the perspective of the reformed abbey's vast possessions 40 hides may have seemed mean enough, it was still sufficient endowment for a substantial ecclesiastical foundation.

What kind of community was the earlier church? According to Abingdon tradition it was founded as a monastery within the strict definition of the term, but well before Æthelwold's time, indeed probably well before the Viking invasions, it had become a secular minster. At some point, then, the monks of the original foundation had given way to a group of secular priests or canons, who lived in separate houses drawing separate incomes from the communal property, and who, in the tolerant circumstances of the ninth-century Anglo-Saxon church, may even perhaps have married. One indication that this was indeed the case at Abingdon is the reference to Godescalc, Athelstan's German cleric there, as *presbyter* rather than as abbot.[35] More significant, however, is a description in the *De Abbatibus*

---

[30] Though if so it had been lost before the Conquest: *Chron. Abingdon* I, 100-1; Gelling, *Thames Valley*, no. 43; S 480; *VCH Berks* I, 369; IV, 336.

[31] The memorandum stating that Ælfhild held Culham on the same terms as Coenwulf's sisters occurs only in Cotton Claudius B VI: *Chron. Abingdon* I, 91-3; Gelling, *Thames Valley*, no. 269; S 460.

[32] *Chron. Abingdon* I, 92; below. For an unconvincing suggestion that Edmund established Ælfhild as abbess of a revived nunnery of St Helen's see M. Meyer, 'Patronage of the West Saxon Royal Nunneries in Late Anglo-Saxon England', *Revue Bénédictine* 91 (1981), 345.

[33] *Chron. Abingdon* I, 120.

[34] Ælfric ch 7 (trans. *EHD* I, 905); Wulfstan, *Vita* ch 11. This does not tie in with what the Abingdon chronicler tells us of grants made to the community in Athelstan's time, though it does correspond with the undoubtedly authentic grant by Athelstan Half-King.

[35] *Chron. Abingdon* I, 64-6; Gelling, *Thames Valley*, no. 36; S 409.

Abbendoniae of what survived in Æthelwold's time of the old foundation:

> When he received the abbacy of Abingdon at the command of King
> Eadred, Æthelwold ... found the monastery which Abbot Hean had
> built entirely destroyed by the heathen; but twelve dwelling-places for
> monks and twelve chapels which Abbot Hean had built were still
> intact and he ordered that they be preserved intact.[36]

Elsewhere the same author states that it was in those little dwellings that the
'monks' ate and slept, and that there was no cloister, only a high wall
surrounding the 'monastery'.[37] Though attributed to the time of the founder,
all this sounds like the domestic arrangements of twelve canons, each living
separately with his own household, arrangements which would have characterised many, perhaps all, of the grander ecclesiastical communities in the
period before reform.

   Such a community must have had a large dependent territory or *parochia*
over which it exercised certain well-defined rights, including a monopoly
over burials, claims to church scot, etc.[38] The area of this *parochia* would
have corresponded with the administrative unit focused on the estate with
which the church was associated, in this instance, presumably, the great
royal estate of *Earmundesleah*.[39] Though minster churches decayed and often
disappeared after the Conquest, they generally left traces in the form of dues
deriving from their ancient rights, from which their early *parochiae* may be
reconstructed. At Abingdon the situation is complicated by later entitle-
ments accruing to the great monastery founded by Æthelwold, but there are
perhaps a few indications of rights which survived from an earlier period.
Pensions were paid to the abbey from a wide variety of churches throughout
Berkshire (and indeed beyond), and of those the payments from churches in
the Abingdon area, in particular in the later hundreds of Hormer, Sutton,
and Ock,[40] may well have had ancient roots. They included Appleton,
Tubney, Milton, Sutton Courtenay, Wittenham, and Bessels Leigh.[41] It is
especially interesting that pensions were due from the churches at Bessels
Leigh and Appleton, two places undoubtedly within the ancient territory of
Earmundesleah. At Bessels Leigh, whose place-name uniquely preserves
elements from *Earmundesleah*, the chapel, together with neighbouring
Tubney, paid an annual pension of 5s in the twelfth century (it had risen to
22s in 1291).[42] At Appleton, just to the west, the abbey had a portion in the
church, which also paid a small pension. That is particularly significant,
since Appleton was not held by the abbey at the Conquest and indeed does
not seem to have belonged to it since the ninth century.[43] A further indicator

---

[36] *Chron. Abingdon* II, 277 (author's translation).
[37] *Ibid.* II, 272-3.
[38] J. Blair, 'Secular Minster Churches in Domesday Book', *Domesday Book: A Reassessment*,
ed. P. H. Sawyer (London, 1985), 104-42; 'Minster Churches in the Landscape', *Anglo-Saxon
Settlements*, ed. D. Hooke (Oxford, forthcoming).
[39] Blair, 'Minster Churches in Landscape'.
[40] For the medieval hundreds see O. S. Anderson, *English Hundred Names: The S-W Counties*
(Lund, 1939), pp 212-13.
[41] *VCH Berks* II, 59-60; IV, 336, 340, 363, 372, 377, 379-80, 382, 394; PRO, SC Hen VIII/109.
[42] *VCH Berks* IV, 393-4; Gelling, *Place-Names of Berks II*, 442-4.
[43] *VCH Berks* IV, 336, 340; above. Cf. Bessels Leigh where the abbey had a small estate at the

BOUNDARIES

County
Medieval hundred
Medieval parish
Chapelry, etc.

CUMNOR

North Hinksey

South Hinksey

APPLETON

BESSELS LEIGH

Woolton

TUBNEY

LONGWORTH

St Helen Without

Radley

MARCHAM

ABINGDON

Andersey Island

CULHAM

Drayton

SUTTON COURTENAY

Appleford

GOOSEY

MILTON

0 1 2 3 4 5 ml
0 2 4 6 8 km

ABINGDON AND ITS ENVIRONS

of the ancient minster status of Abingdon lies in its relationship with the church at Culham. As has already been stressed Andersey and Culham were the site of a Mercian royal residence, closely linked with Abingdon from the eighth to the tenth centuries. In the light of that connexion Culham's later status is very interesting: it was a peculiar wholly under the abbot's jurisdiction, both for ecclesiastical and criminal pleas. The chapel there was under the abbot's sole control and the diocesan was wholly excluded. Abingdon tradition expressly records that the abbot not only appointed the priest but bestowed upon him the chrism, a function reserved to old minsters in Kent. That traces of such an important early right should only survive at Culham is not altogether surprising, for Culham is one of the very few places that maintained a virtually unbroken link with the abbey from pre-Viking times.[44]

Conquest and only recovered full possession in the time of Abbot Faritius: *VCH Berks* IV, 394-5; *Chron. Abingdon* II, 288.
[44] *VCH Oxon* VII, 35.

One problem in all this is the status of the parish church of St Helen. According to Abingdon tradition this was also on the site of a seventh-century monastic foundation, the nunnery established by Hean's sister Cilla in honour of the Holy Cross and St Helen. These traditions have recently been re-examined and have been thought to have some historical basis. It has even been suggested that the original minster parish was focused not on St Mary's (the abbey) but on St Helen's.[45] Now it is true that St Helen's had an extensive medieval parish including, beside Abingdon itself, the dependent chapelries of Dry Sandon, Shippen, Radley, and Drayton. Moreover, a thirteenth-century *compositio* in the abbey's cartulary refers to *mortuaria* appertaining to the church and its dependencies.[46] It is therefore clear that in the Middle Ages St Helen's served part at least of the original *parochia* focused on Abingdon, by then much eroded through the formation of new parishes on various lesser territories within the original vast royal estate. On the other hand the grants of King Athelstan and Athelstan Half-King are expressly said to be to the church of St Mary, which must by then have been Abingdon's principal church. Probably indeed it was the only one, for Abingdon tradition records that Helenstow had been deserted from the eighth century.[47] One explanation for this would seem to be that at some indeterminate date, probably after the revival of the Benedictine community, the parish responsibilities of St Mary's were assigned to new churches;[48] St Helen's, established on the site of the former nunnery by 995, became the parochial centre for that portion of the original *parochia* in and adjacent to Abingdon, while the more distant northern parts of Hormer hundred were assigned to the church at Cumnor, one of the abbey's oldest possessions.[49] A somewhat analogous process seems to have taken place at Gloucester. There, however, the parish church of St Mary was undoubtedly a possession of the abbey of St Peter,[50] whereas at Abingdon (at least by the twelfth century) the abbot, though he held the advowson, did not have the rectory.[51]

---

[45] Biddle *et al.*, 'Early Hist. of Abingdon', 29.

[46] Bodl. MS Lyell 15, fol. 67; J. Haslam, *Anglo-Saxon Towns in Southern England* (Chichester, 1984), p 57. But see below, n 54.

[47] *Chron. Abingdon* I, 7-8; II, 270; above, pp 45-6. The first reference to the later parish church of St Helen's is in a charter of c995, where it is described as an *ecclesia*: *Chron. Abingdon* I, 394; S 883.

[48] The reformers, though they favoured monastic ownership of churches, generally preferred monks not to act as parish priests: U. Berlière, 'L'Exercice du Ministère Paroissial par les Moines dans le Haut Moyen Age', *Revue Bénédictine* 89 (1927), 236-40. The practice, however, continued to be widely tolerated, and in England Eadgar seems to have tried to protect the rights of parochial churches: G. Constable, 'Monastic Rural Churches and the Cura Animarum in the Early Middle Ages', *Settimane di Studio del Centro Italiano di Studi sull' Alto Medioevo* 28 (1982), 349-89; *The Laws of the Kings of England from Edmund to Henry I*, ed. and trans. A. J. Robertson (Cambridge, 1925), p 21.

[49] Cumnor church, which was immediately adjacent to the abbey's great grange at Cumnor Place, belonged to the community in 1086. It had a large minster-like parish with dependent chapelries at North and South Hinksey and Wootton: *Calendar of Papal Letters* V, 351; *VCH Berks* IV, 398-415. I am grateful to Dr John Blair for this point.

[50] A. T. Thacker, 'Chester and Gloucester: Early Ecclesiastical Organization in Two Mercian Burhs', *Northern History* 18 (1982), 207-9.

[51] *VCH Berks* IV, 446-7. About 1225 the abbot promised to take no further rights in the church of St Helen's, which the community then held at farm from the papal subdeacon, Stephen de Columna: *Salisbury Charters and Documents*, ed. W. Rich Jones and W. Dunn

Nevertheless, there are indicators that St Helen's may have originally belonged to the abbey. First, in the twelfth century it paid dues of 3 marks to the keeper of the infirmary;[52] secondly, it is not mentioned in Domesday Book, possibly because then it was held by the abbey;[53] thirdly (and most significantly), the abbey seems always to have possessed the burial rights in Abingdon.[54] A very interesting case brought before the papal court in the late fourteenth century shows that even at that late date St Helen's had no burial rights of its own and that its parishioners had to be buried in the monks' cemetery.[55]

Almost certainly, then, the church which Æthelwold came to rule and reform in 955 had only ten years before been a substantial minster associated with an important royal residence. The famous reference to a waste and deserted *monasteriolum* was less than just. But Æthelwold's biographers were not interested in unreformed minsters; they wished to call attention to Eadred's new endowments rather than to stress what had descended from Athelstan's day: 'the rest of the land of that place [i.e. Abingdon], amounting to 100 hides, which the king was holding *iure regale*, ... was also given to the abbot and brethren [of the new community]'.[56] The implication is that this was a restoration of the lands confiscated by Alfred, and that those lands were co-extensive with the local hundred.[57] There are, however, problems with this interpretation. Ælfric and Wulfstan do not name the lands included in Eadred's 100 hides; they merely imply that they were appertaining to the royal vill of Abingdon. The Abingdon chronicler is much less reticent. He records a grant of very dubious authenticity, purporting to be that of 955, in which the estates are said to be the *villa* of Abingdon with its appurtenances, and various other *terrae appenditiae*, including Ginge, Goosey, Worth, and Cumnor.[58] According to Abingdon tradition, most of these territories were ancient possessions of the pre-Viking community. Cumnor was probably part of the original territory around Abingdon;[59] Worth and Ginge were supposed to have belonged to the abbey by the ninth century, and were perhaps also part of its original endowment;[60] Goosey was said to have been obtained by exchange from Offa.[61] These lands, however, did not form the compact group needed to make up an administrative unit

---

Macray, RS (London, 1891), pp 168-9. St Helen's was, in fact, appropriated in 1261: J. Townsend, *History of Abingdon* (London, 1910), p 64.
[52] *Chron. Abingdon* II, 328.
[53] *VCH Berks* II, 4.
[54] The *mortuaria* appertaining to the church in the later thirteenth century were even then reserved to the abbey: Bodl. MS Lyell 15, fol. 67. Cf. a further agreement dated 1284: Townsend, *Hist. of Abingdon*, pp 64-5.
[55] *VCH Berks* II, 56-7; *Cal. Papal Letters* IV, p 371; V, pp 5-6, 354. The abbot and monks claimed that 'of ancient custom' they had the right to exact for each body buried in their cemetery a candle and a farthing, together with all oblations and other emoluments arising out of obits and anniversaries.
[56] Ælfric ch 7-8 (trans. *EHD* I, 905); Wulfstan, *Vita*, 11.
[57] Stenton, *Abingdon Abbey*, pp 47-9.
[58] *Chron. Abingdon* I, 124-7; Gelling, *Thames Valley*, no. 64 (where it is classed as a complete forgery); S 567; B 906.
[59] *Chron. Abingdon* I, 8; *VCH Berks* IV, 318.
[60] *Chron. Abingdon* I, 24-7; Gelling, *Thames Valley*, nos. 17-18; S 166, 183.
[61] *VCH Berks* IV, 482; above, n 17.

such as a hundred; nor do they comprise the whole of the original royal estate focused on Abingdon. The nature of Eadred's grant must therefore remain unclear, though one point in the Chronicler's favour is the fact that the abbey did not obtain jurisdiction over the hundred in which it lay and where eventually it had its largest holdings (that is, Hormer hundred) until the reign of Edward the Confessor.[62]

There is some uncertainty about whether Eadred's grant actually took effect. The king died very soon after the refounding of Abingdon, and his successor Eadwig's later reputation as an opponent of reform has encouraged the view that at Abingdon he withdrew his support from the new foundation.[63] Now it is true that Æthelwold himself did not have a high regard for Eadwig: 'through the ignorance of childhood he dispersed his kingdom and divided its unity, and also distributed the lands of holy church to rapacious strangers'.[64] Nevertheless, it seems premature to attribute any failure to implement Eadred's grant to Eadwig's hostility. Eadwig is named as a benefactor of Abingdon in the charter of 993 and in the tradition of the community itself.[65] Neither Ælfric nor Wulfstan mentions any break in monastic life at Abingdon during his reign, and it was, moreover, precisely then that his brother Eadgar was being educated there under Æthelwold's personal supervision.[66] It must too be significant that after the division of the kingdom in 957 Æthelwold continued to attend Eadwig's court and to attest his charters, rather than deserting him (as one might expect) for his pupil Eadgar.[67] The most serious difficulty about Eadred's grant is that almost all the estates expressly named in the surviving version were the subject of later grants by Eadwig and Eadgar. Holdings such as Ginge and Worth were among those whose titles later caused the community most anxiety, and it may be that this is indeed a reflection of something unsatisfactory in the original diploma.[68]

Probably, then, Æthelwold's community remained in being at Abingdon during Eadwig's reign, even if it experienced difficulties in obtaining all that Eadred granted. Though Eadred's plan to build a new church was not pursued,[69] there is no reason to doubt the twelfth-century chronicler's statement that Æthelwold at first retained the buildings already on the site.[70] Nevertheless, it was clearly Eadgar who was remembered as the greatest of Abingdon's benefactors. Æthelwold himself praised the king's generosity to the monastery, which he 'endowed greatly with all things' to rival many of the houses advanced by his ancestors, and which he much enlarged with 'a

---

[62] Stenton, *Abingdon Abbey*, p 48; E. John, *Orbis Britanniae* (Leicester, 1966), pp 195-6.

[63] John, *Orbis Britanniae*, pp 189-91.

[64] *EHD* I, 920. For the ascription of this text to Æthelwold see D. Whitelock, 'The Authorship of the Account of King Eadgar's Establishment of Monasteries', *Philological Essays in Honour of H. D. Meritt*, ed. J. L. Rosier (The Hague, 1970), pp 125-36.

[65] S 876; *Chron. Abingdon* I, 168.

[66] *EHD* I, 921.

[67] John, *Orbis Britanniae*, p 191; Gelling, *Thames Valley*, nos. 67, 86, 93; S 607, 658, 663.

[68] S 567, 583, 654, 673, 757.

[69] Or was it? Eadwig's grant of the forest of Hawkridge 'ad architectandam sanctam Dei Genetricis ecclesiam quae sita est in Abbandune' suggests that work could have been going on in his reign: *Chron. Abingdon* I, 183-5; S 607. I am grateful to Barbara Yorke for this point.

[70] *Chron. Abingdon* I, 277.

great company of monks'.[71] Eadgar's grants during Æthelwold's abbacy and afterwards are too numerous to mention in detail, but they included extensive lands in Wiltshire and Oxfordshire, as well as 50 hides at Marcham in Berkshire, some of which must surely have once been part of the ancient royal estate at Abingdon. By the time that Æthelwold left for Winchester, the abbey had acquired an enormous endowment of some 600 hides.[72]

At the core of the grants of Eadgar and his two predecessors there lay what seems to have been regarded as a restoration of land wrongfully detained from the church of St Mary since the ninth century. Almost certainly therefore these grants involved not only the cession of royal land but also the suppression of the rights of laymen who had received grants of portions of that land from the king. This emerges clearly from the famous (and undoubtedly authentic) diploma of 993, in which King Æthelred (978-1016) referred to the *hereditas* and *libertas* granted to the church at Abingdon by his predecessors Eadred, Eadwig and Eadgar.[73] Æthelred concedes in perpetuity the right of the monks freely to elect their own abbot, in full accordance with privileges allegedly conveyed to Abbot Hrethun by Pope Leo III and King Coenwulf. He also grants that the *agri ad usus monachorum*, restored to the monks by Eadgar, Eadwig, and Eadred, should enjoy the same perpetual liberty from outside interference. There follows a clause, beginning *tempore siquidem*, which refers to lands (*rura*), formerly devoted to God and restored *per hoc modernum privilegium*, but at some time in the past usurped and held by others under *hereditaria karta*. Recently this has been held to apply solely to Abingdon lands granted away in the 980s,[74] but even if that was the prime concern there seems to be no reason why the clause should not also have embraced earlier encroachments on the monastery's ancient endowment. In sum, it looks as if Æthelwold's foundation at Abingdon had been buttressed by earlier grants of privileges and had probably from the beginning been forced to defend itself against secular claims to its restored property. So even if we may not go as far as John[75] in claiming as authentic the supposed prototypes of the 993 charter,[76] it does seem likely that something similar to them must once have existed. That, of course, is very important since it suggests that two of Æthelwold's principal concerns, the maintenance of free abbatial elections in accordance with the Rule of St Benedict and the exclusion of all forms of secular domination, were already making an impression at Abingdon in its early days.

Related to the search for the restoration of privileges was the development of an active historiographical tradition. One aspect of this tradition was undoubtedly the exaltation of an earlier monastic golden age in England, the era of Bede and the saints, and a corresponding undervaluing of the more recent post-Viking past. But there was also another more practical preoccupation: to establish and revive claims to the community's historic rights and endowments. To investigate the past requires learning, and in establishing

[71] *EHD* I, 920-3.
[72] Ælfric ch 17; Wulfstan, *Vita*, 21; *Chron. Abingdon* I, 255-343; S 734.
[73] S 876.
[74] Keynes, *Diplomas of King Æthelred*, pp 98-102.
[75] John, *Orbis Britanniae*, pp 181-207.
[76] S 658, 673.

a school at Abingdon in his early days,[77] when he had Eadgar under his
tutelage, Æthelwold was able to provide the necessary precondition for that
learning. Such moves must have helped to engender the tradition soon to be
represented in the charter of 993 and eventually to reach its full development in the Abingdon Chronicle. The 993 charter was clearly preceded by
earlier ones, which probably already provided the essentials, the allusions to
Caedwalla, Pope Leo, and Coenwulf, and to a large and privileged pre-Viking
landed endowment. It is difficult to believe that that tradition does not owe
something to Æthelwold himself. One possible parallel to the lengthy historical preamble of the 993 diploma is provided by the foundation charter
of Ely, another of Æthelwold's communities.[78] The charter is dated 970, and
if not authentic must at least go back to the tenth-century exemplar predating Ælfric's English version.[79] Its preamble praises the foundress's uncorrupt
and miracle-working remains, and alludes to Bede's account of her life in the
Ecclesiastical History, before going on to describe the later desertion of the
site, its incorporation in the royal fisc, and its purchase by Æthelwold from
Eadgar. Similarly, in the Thorney foundation charter, which appears to be
substantially genuine, there is a version of the story of the holy hermits
Tancred and Torhtred, and their sister Tova, who had earlier occupied the
site of the abbey.[80] Even if such charters were not drawn up in the *scriptoria*
of the beneficiaries, they clearly reflect common historiographical preoccu-
pations, most likely to have originated with their common founder. In this,
as in much else, Abingdon seems to have led the way.

The new community which Æthelwold gathered round him at Abingdon
was drawn from diverse backgrounds. Naturally it included monks from
Glastonbury, where Æthelwold had studied under Dunstan and where there
was already a community following authentic monastic norms. Others,
however, had been canons of Winchester and London, and the Abingdon
chronicler stresses that Æthelwold's reputation for holiness attracted 'men
from various parts of England ... to follow a stricter mode of life'.[81] Contact
was soon established with the great French monasteries reformed under the
influence of Cluny: Corbie, for example, provided monks to teach a new
rule of chanting and reading.[82] The dominant influence, however, was Fleury,
to which, his biographers relate, Æthelwold sent one of his senior monks,
Osgar (later to succeed him at Abingdon), 'there to learn the customs of the
rule and then expound them by teaching to his brethren at home'.[83] Some
indication of the monastic culture thus established is provided by one of the
few surviving books from pre-Conquest Abingdon, an early eleventh-century

[77] As at Winchester: Ælfric ch 20; Wulfstan, *Vita*, ch 31.
[78] S 779; *Liber Eliensis* II, ch 5.
[79] N. Brooks, 'Anglo-Saxon Charters: the Work of the Last Twenty Years', *ASE* 3 (1974), 230;
J. Pope, 'Ælfric and the Old English Version of the Ely Privilege', *England Before the Conquest*,
ed. P. Clemoes and K. Hughes (Cambridge, 1971), pp 85-113; John, *Orbis Britanniae*,
pp 210-33.
[80] C. R. Hart, *The Early Charters of Eastern England* (Leicester, 1966), pp 165-186; S 792.
[81] *Chron. Abingdon* I, 129. Cf. Ælfric ch 7; Wulfstan, *Vita*, 11.
[82] *Chron. Abingdon* I, 129; J. Armitage Robinson, *The Times of St Dunstan* (Oxford, 1923),
p 111, n 2.
[83] Ælfric ch 10 (trans. *EHD* I, 906); Wulfstan, *Vita*, 14.

manuscript now in the library of Corpus Christi College, Cambridge.[84] The manuscript begins with the rule of St Benedict, heavily glossed and apparently one of the most frequently read items in the manuscript.[85] A second section comprised material associated with the Carolingian reformer Benedict of Aniane,[86] including the decrees of the reforming synods of Aachen (816-19) held under his influence, and the *Memoriale qualiter*, a text slightly predating Benedict, though long attributed to him.[87] These items contain few glosses and were presumably less read. The manuscript also includes a copiously annotated kalendar, a version of Usuardus's *Martyrologium*,[88] and the *Diadema Monachorum*, a work by Benedict's pupil Smaragdus.[89] All this could well have been obtained from one of the great continental reformed monasteries, such as Fleury, and indeed at Abingdon it was believed that the community had received the rule of St Benedict from the French house.[90] Æthelwold certainly knew and used a text from Fleury; he based his translation of the rule of St Benedict which he made about 970 on such a version.[91] But interestingly the text in the Abingdon manuscript seems to derive from two different exemplars: one Carolingian, based upon St Benedict's original, the other English, dependent on the eighth-century Worcester manuscript which is the earliest surviving text of the Rule.[92] That is perhaps a further reminder that Æthelwold and his followers looked to the age of Bede as well as to the continent in their search for exemplary monastic custom.

Æthelwold is generally regarded as the most austere of the three great reformers,[93] and indeed he himself seems to have been personally ascetic, following a strict diet and abstaining from the flesh of animals and birds.[94] His biographers report that he established good usages by admonishing the obedient and correcting the foolish with rods: 'he was as terrible as a lion to the disobedient and undisciplined but gentler than a dove to the gentle and humble'.[95] Various rather grim miracles were told of him: at Abingdon, for

---

[84] Cambridge, Corpus Christi College 57; N. Ker, *Medieval Libraries of Great Britain* (2nd edn, London, 1964), pp 2-3.

[85] CCCC 57, fol. 2-32v; R. I. Page, 'More Old English Scratched Glosses', *Anglia* 97 (1979), 29.

[86] *Ibid.*, fol. 33-40v. On Benedict of Aniane see P. Schmitz, 'L'Influence de Saint Benoit d'Aniane dans l'Histoire de l'Ordre de Saint-Benoit', *Settimane di Studio del Centro Italiano di Studi sull' Alto Medioevo* 4 (1957), 401-15, and in this volume Wormald, ch 1, pp 31-2.

[87] For editions of the main texts see *Memoriale Qualiter*, ed. D. C. Morgand and *Synodorum Aquisgranensis Decreta Authentica* and *Regula Sancti Benedicti Abbatis Anianensis*, ed. J. Semmler, *Corpus Consuetudinum Monasticarum* I, ed. K. Hallinger (Siegburg, 1963), pp 177-261, 451-81, 501-36. For the augmented version of the Aachen decrees see *Collectio Capitularis Benedicti Levitae Monastica*, ed. J. Semmler, *ibid.*, pp 537-54.

[88] CCCC 57, fol. 41-92; *Martyrologium Usuardi Monachi*, ed. J.-P. Migne, *PL* 123, col. 599-992; 124, col. 9-860.

[89] CCCC 57, fol. 95 *ad fin*. For other manuscripts containing similar material see M. Bateson, 'Rules for Monks and Canons after the Revival under King Edgar', *English Historical Review* 9 (1894), 690-708.

[90] 'Fecit ... venire regulam Sancti Benedicti a Floriaco monasterio': *Chron. Abingdon* II, 278.

[91] M. Gretsch, 'Æthelwold's Translation of the Regula Sancti Benedicti and its Latin Exemplar', *ASE* 3 (1974), 125-51.

[92] J. Chamberlin, *The Rule of St Benedict: The Abingdon Copy* (Toronto, 1982), pp 9-11; Gretsch, 'Æthelwold's Translation', 134; Bodl. MS Hatton 48.

[93] Stenton, *Abingdon Abbey*, 6-7; Robinson, *Times*, 104.

[94] Ælfric ch 6, 20; Wulfstan, *Vita*, ch 9, 30.

[95] Ælfric ch 19 (trans. *EHD* I, 909); Wulfstan, *Vita*, 28.

example, he tested the obedience of one of the monks of the kitchen by ordering him to plunge his hand into a boiling cauldron in which he was preparing food. He was obeyed and, of course, the monk came to no harm, but the story emphasises rigour and discipline and is very unlike the stories told of, say, Cuthbert.[96] Yet despite this reputation for austerity, at Abingdon Æthelwold was remembered gratefully for mitigating the strict provisions of the Benedictine rule, adherence to which, it was feared, would attract only the poor. In particular, it was claimed, the susceptibilities of the gentry were accommodated by the relaxation of the rule which prescribed that bedding should consist only of mattress, blanket, coverlet, and pillow, to permit the monks of Abingdon to sleep under fur bed covers.[97] Benedict's dietary requirements were also apparently relaxed. Besides the usual vegetables and pulses Æthelwold allowed his monks cheese and, it seems, fried food and some meat,[98] a practice not in accordance with the rule itself or the *Memoriale qualiter*,[99] and probably more lenient than contemporary custom at Fleury.[100] Drink too was quite generously provided; the monks' daily allowance of beer was regulated by a large bowl known as the *bolla* of St Æthelwold, which contained about one and a half gallons and from which the monks filled their mugs. On feast days mead was also allowed – a sester between six at dinner and between twelve at supper. Though such measures may not be absurdly generous, it is perhaps revealing that they attracted men because they were regarded as exceptionally austere.[101]

Æthelwold, then, though he himself adopted the strictest continental practice, permitted some compromises with contemporary aristocratic standards. Further light on the atmosphere prevailing at Abingdon, at least in its early days, is thrown by Ælfric's account of King Eadred's visit to the monastery to lay the foundations of the community's new church. That visit was the occasion of a famous miracle story. Æthelwold invited the king to dine in the refectory with his companions, who included some Northumbrian envoys. The king ordered plenty of mead to be served to his guests and caused the doors to be closed so that none could leave the banquet prematurely. The feast apparently lasted the whole day and was adorned by a suitable wonder: the supplies of mead were constantly renewed. The inevitable result is solemnly recounted in Ælfric's Life; by evening the king's Northumbrian guests had become swinishly drunk and been forced to

[96] Ælfric ch 10; Wulfstan, *Vita*, ch 14.
[97] *Chron. Abingdon* II, 279.
[98] *Ibid.* I, 345-6; II, 279. The provision of meat and fried food is only mentioned in *De Abbatibus*, and is entirely discounted by M. D. Knowles, *The Monastic Order in England* (2nd edn, Cambridge, 1963), pp 716-17.
[99] RSB 55; *Memoriale Qualiter*, p 255. The Aachen decrees of 817, however, permitted the eating of fowl in the octaves of Christmas and Easter: *Synodi Secundae Aquisgranensis Decreta*, ed. Semmler, ch 43 (p 481). Though the final version of 818/19 specified the number of days as four, Abingdon, uniquely, expressly granted eight [CCCC 57, fol. 40v]: *Regula S. Benedicti*, ed. Semmler, ch 77 (p 534). I am grateful to Patrick Wormald for this point.
[100] The customs of Fleury mention fried food but not meat: G. Chenesseau, *L'Abbaye de Fleury* (Paris, 1931), pp 72-3.
[101] *Chron. Abingdon* I, 346-7; II, 279. Drink seems also to have been generously provided at Fleury where even on Good Friday a cup of wine, the *caritas vini*, was allowed to mitigate the strictness of the fast: Chenesseau, *Fleury*, pp 72-3.

withdraw.[102] The story is significant not only as evidence of the quality of the miracles recorded at Abingdon but also because it shows the newly reformed community still fulfilling the functions of Athelstan's *aedificium regale*.

Æthelwold was a mighty builder, and at Abingdon the church whose foundations Eadred had come to lay in 955, though long in construction, eventually developed into a 'glorious minster'.[103] Although it may have languished in the years immediately after Eadred's death, with Eadgar's accession to the whole kingdom in 959 new energy was infused into the enterprise and orders went out that the church be completed within three years.[104] Nothing remains of that building, and contemporary accounts are not very satisfactory. Ælfric refers unhelpfully to a 'noble temple ... which can better be shown than described', and the twelfth-century history of the abbots offers a most curious description: 'The chancel was round, the church itself was also round, having twice the length of the chancel. The tower also was round.'[105] It seems reasonable to suppose from this emphasis on circularity that the building was centrally-planned, or at least that it contained apsidal elements. One possibility is that like Æthelwold's re-constructed Old Minster at Winchester it had a large circular or perhaps double-apsed west work with a complex of chapels and facilities for the display of relics and for royal ceremonial.[106] Certainly at the very least the centralised plan suggests that the palatine chapel at Aachen was one model in the founder's mind.[107]

Though we know little about the actual form of Æthelwold's church at Abingdon, we are much better informed about its ornaments, which were of exceptional richness and splendour. They included certain magnificent items attributed to Æthelwold himself,[108] pre-eminent among which was the golden-plated wheel which supported twelve lamps and from which were suspended numerous little bells. Æthelwold was also believed to have made an object referred to as the *tabula supra altare*, perhaps an altar table or retable, again of gold and silver, which was enriched with sculptured figures of the twelve apostles and cost the enormous sum of £300. Other treasures included three crosses of gold and silver, each four feet in length, texts to adorn the church

---

[102] Ælfric ch 8; Wulfstan, *Vita*, ch 12. Cf. the feast in the presence of King Æthelred and his court, celebrating Dunstan's dedication of the new works at Winchester in 980: Wulfstan, *Narratio*, pp 67-8, ll 57-110.

[103] *EHD* I, 921.

[104] Ælfric ch 9, 11; Wulfstan, *Vita*, ch 13, 15.

[105] *Chron. Abingdon* II, 277-8 (author's translation); Biddle *et al.*, 'Early Hist. of Abingdon', 44-7.

[106] Excavations were carried out at the site of the Norman church in 1922, but no report was ever produced. Evidence was found of a church beneath the medieval building which looks like a conventional late Saxon basilica, perhaps 200ft long: Biddle *et al.*, 'Early Hist. of Abingdon', 60-7. There is, however, no guarantee that this longitudinal structure was Æthelwold's, and indeed it has recently been suggested that it may represent a late eleventh-century building: E. Fernie, *The Architecture of the Anglo-Saxons* (London, 1983), pp 108-10. And, of course, Æthelwold's structure may not have been the only church at Abingdon; he could well have retained the earlier minster alongside his new church: R. Gem, 'Towards an Iconography of Anglo-Saxon Architecture', *Journal of Warburg and Courtauld Institutes* 46 (1983), 8.

[107] Fernie, *op. cit.*, p 109. For a strong argument that Æthelwold's building was an aisled rotunda, consciously evoking the 'royal symbolism' of Aachen, see Gem, *op. cit.*, 7-12.

[108] Though he is most unlikely personally to have made them: C. Dodwell, *Anglo-Saxon Art* (Manchester, 1982), p 49.

made of silver and precious stones, and various sacred vessels – candlesticks, thuribles, vases and the like – for use in the *opus dei*. Most of this had been lost by the twelfth century. The sculptured *tabula* had been broken up by Abbot Vincent (1121-30) to pay Henry I for the liberty of the market at Abingdon and of the abbey's hundred of Hormer; the gold and silver crosses had been destroyed in the reign of Stephen; much else had been seized after the Conquest and sent back to Normandy – including a great quantity of vases and ornaments and the golden wheel, the precious materials of which were valued at £40 after its destruction.[109] Even so, the chronicler's account gives some impression of the immense material splendour of the first of the great reformed monasteries, a fitting environment for the lavish ceremonial introduced by the monks from Corbie and later reflected in the elaborate provisions of the *Regularis Concordia*. The reformers' ideals involved display as well as austerity; their's was an aristocratic world where king and magnates would have felt very much at home.

Abingdon of course has especial importance in that it was the model house which provided a pattern for Æthelwold's other great foundations.[110] Its customs must have influenced the *Regularis Concordia*, in the formulation of which Æthelwold played a leading part.[111] The saint's contacts with Fleury, established at Abingdon, are reflected in the presence at Winchester of monks from that community,[112] and it is significant that in the Abingdon manuscript the rule of St Benedict is coupled with the *Memoriale qualiter*, the only text known to have been used extensively in the *Regularis Concordia*.[113] The combination in that document of a strong Anianian background with an equally strong 'native element', looking back to the age of Gregory and Bede, is characteristic of Abingdon and other Æthelwoldian *milieux*.[114] Though Æthelwold himself ruled the community directly only for some eight years, he almost certainly maintained close contact with it after his departure and in some sense may still have been regarded as its superior. His biographers tell of his regular visitation and close supervision of the monasteries which he founded,[115] and at Thorney indeed he even retained the abbacy, operating through a nominated representative, his chaplain Godeman.[116] At Abingdon itself his successor, Osgar, was a trusted pupil, who seems to have remained a close associate and witnesses several of Æthelwold's more important charters.[117] Monks from Abingdon were probably involved in most of Æthelwold's foundations in the first years of his episcopate.[118] This is particularly likely in

---

[109] *Chron. Abingdon* I, 343-4; II, 278.
[110] The abbey's exemplary role is emphasised in the Old English account of King Eadgar's establishment of monasteries, attributed to Æthelwold himself: *EHD* I, 920-3. Cf. the monastery of Inde (Cornelimünster), which exemplified the reforming ideals of Benedict of Aniane: Ardo, *Vita*, ed. G. Waitz, *MGH Scriptores*, XV (1) (Hannover, 1887), ch 38-9, pp 215-17.
[111] T. Symons, '*Regularis Concordia*: History and Derivation', *Tenth-Century Studies*, pp 42-3.
[112] *Regularis Concordia*, p 3.
[113] *Ibid.*, pp xlviii, 11-12, etc.
[114] *Ibid.*, pp 4, 19; Symons, '*Regularis Concordia*: History and Derivation', pp 46-8.
[115] Ælfric ch 19; Wulfstan, *Vita*, ch 27-8.
[116] *VCH Cambs* II, 210.
[117] Ælfric ch 7, 10, 17; Wulfstan, *Vita*, ch 11, 14, 21; S 782, 787, 835; B 1270, 1280; K 622.
[118] Robinson points out that four of the five monks named in Ælfric ch 7 and Wulfstan, *Vita*, ch 11 became abbots: *Times*, p 110.

the case of the four foundations mentioned in the Chronicle annal for 964, namely Winchester cathedral priory, Winchester New Minster, Chertsey, and Milton Abbas.[119] Monks from Abingdon accompanied Æthelwold to Winchester where they formed the personnel of the new monastic establishment which replaced the ousted canons of Old Minster,[120] and at Chertsey a thirteenth-century cartulary records that Æthelwold ordered the abbot and convent of Abingdon to send thirteen monks to rebuild the church and community there.[121] Almost certainly, therefore, similar arrangements were made at New Minster and Milton Abbas. It seems likely too that Brihtnoth, the first abbot of Ely, had been among the original band of monks who accompanied Æthelwold to his new cathedral (in 970 he was prior of Winchester), and that therefore he had been trained by Æthelwold at Abingdon.[122] Godeman, Æthelwold's representative at Thorney, also a former pupil and a monk of Winchester, was from a similar background, as perhaps were several other leaders of Æthelwold's connexion.[123]

In thus establishing a network of communities under his own close supervision, Æthelwold was following the example of Continental reformers, including not only the Lotharingians, but also Odo of Cluny and Benedict of Aniane himself.[124] Æthelwold's personal influence was considerable, and it is worth pondering the degree of uniformity established in his monasteries. One area where comparison can be attempted is the cult of the saints. By the twelfth century, when under Abbot Faritius its collection was listed, Abingdon was rich in relics, though some at least of these were of recent acquisition.[125] Those which were most revered, however, dated from the later tenth century. They included an iron cross, later known as the *Crux Nigra*, found by Æthelwold's workmen inside a sarcophagus dug up near the spot which in Abingdon tradition was considered the site of the nunnery of St Helen. This object was identified with the miracle-working cross formed from a nail of the True Cross, believed to have been buried with Hean's sister Cilla, the foundress of the nunnery.[126] It is known from a drawing in a thirteenth-century Abingdon manuscript, and has been interpreted as an early Anglo-Saxon disc-headed pin dating from the late seventh or early eighth century.[127] Whatever we make of the traditions relating to the early history of St Helen's (and it is worth remembering that such pins have been

---

[119] *Two Chronicles*, I, pp 116-17.

[120] Ælfric ch 13-14; Wulfstan, *Vita*, ch 16-17.

[121] BL Cotton Vitellius A XIII, fol. 35. Ordberht, the monk appointed abbot of Chertsey in 964, is presumably the Abingdon monk named in Ælfric ch 7; Wulfstan, *Vita*, 11.

[122] Others such as Ealdwulf at Peterborough and Ælfric at St Alban's are more doubtful: *Heads of Religious Houses: England and Wales, 940-1216*, ed. D. Knowles, C. N. L. Brooke, and V. C. M. London (Cambridge, 1972), pp 59, 65.

[123] *Liber Vitae: Register and Martyrology of New Minster and Hyde Abbey*, ed. W. de Gray Birch, Hampshire Record Society, 1892, p 24.

[124] P. Schmitz, *Histoire de l'Ordre de Saint Benoit*, I (Gembloux, 1943), pp 148-62, 192-8; D. A. Bullough, 'The Continental Background of the Reform', *Tenth-Century Studies*, pp 20-36, esp. 31-3; Wormald, ch 1, pp 15-22.

[125] On this list see I. G. Thomas, 'The Cult of Saints' Relics in Medieval England' (unpublished University of London Ph.D. thesis, 1975), pp 150-57. Thomas takes the view that most of the relics listed had only recently been acquired, but see below.

[126] *Chron. Abingdon* I, 7-8; II, 269-70.

[127] Biddle *et al.*, 'Early Hist. of Abingdon', 27-8, plate III; BL Cotton MS Claudius B VI, fol. 5v.

found at other early ecclesiastical sites),[128] it seems reasonable to suppose that the story was current in Æthelwold's time, and that the veneration of the cross in the new community represents an attempt to link it with early monasticism at Abingdon.

Devotion to the Holy Cross may have been a feature of Æthelwold's communities. The Abingdon chronicler records a miracle worked by an Abingdon crucifix at the time of the Danish invasions; according to this singularly horrific story the image on the cross came to life, and 'with marble arms and flexible fingers' extracted stones from the walls of the refectory in which it had been placed and drove away the invading Danes. A second story tells of the image on the same cross responding to a solitary brother when he pronounced grace in the refectory.[129] Interestingly, a similar anecdote is related of Dunstan in Osbern's Life, which describes the Christ-figure on a crucifix speaking in defence of the saint at a council in Winchester.[130] The story was retold in the *Liber Eliensis* and linked with Æthelwold and Brihtnoth, his abbot of Ely.[131] Clearly the motif had a certain currency among twelfth- and thirteenth-century hagiographers; but since it seems also to represent some common element in the piety of Æthelwold's foundations, it may perhaps be older and owe something to the saint's early experiences at the court of Athelstan and at Abingdon.

One other cult at Abingdon can be ascribed to Æthelwold's time: that of the Spanish martyr Vincent.[132] His relics, which were believed to consist of an arm, a thigh-bone, part of a shoulder-blade, and a rib, were in fact the only ones located at Abingdon in the early eleventh-century resting-place list.[133] Local tradition is not altogether consistent as to how they arrived there. The Abingdon Chronicler ascribed their presence to King Eadgar, but the author of the later and probably less reliable *De Abbatibus* offers a more dramatic account: they were, he says, stolen from Glastonbury with the head of St Apollinaris in the time of Abbot Osgar.[134] It is true that Glastonbury claimed to possess relics of St Vincent and the head of St Apollinaris; they had been given by Eadgar with the gold and silver shrine in which the king himself later rested.[135] On the other hand Abingdon tradition tells of a chapel dedicated to the saint built by Ælfhild, the recipient of an apparently genuine

---

[128] Thus Biddle *et al.*, 'Early Hist. of Abingdon', 26-9, 33. For a more sceptical view of the traditions about St Helen's see Stenton, *Abingdon Abbey*, pp 3-4.
[129] *Chron. Abingdon* I, 47-9.
[130] *Memorials*, p 113.
[131] *Liber Eliensis* II, ch 51.
[132] For a general survey of the cult see L. de Lacger, 'Saint Vincent de Saragosse', *Revue d'Histoire de l'Eglise de France* 13 (1927), 307-58. In England the saint appears in the *Old English Martyrology*, ed. G. Herzfeld, EETS, Original Series, 116 (London, 1899), pp 28-9. See J. Cross, 'Saints' Lives in Old English: Latin Manuscripts and Vernacular Accounts: the Old English Martyrology', *Peritia* 1 (1982), 51-8. Ælfric also wrote a life: *Ælfric's Lives of Saints*, ed. W. W. Skeat, EETS, Original Series, 114 (London, 1900), p 443.
[133] D. W. Rollason, 'Lists of Saints' Resting-Places in Anglo-Saxon England', *ASE* 7 (1978), 90.
[134] *Chron. Abingdon* II, 48, 280. The version in the history of the abbots seems more likely to be a fabrication, since there is no reference to the head of St Apollinaris in Faritius's relic-list: Thomas, 'Cults', pp 150-1.
[135] William of Malmesbury, *The Early History of Glastonbury*, ed. J. Scott (Woodbridge, 1981), ch 62.

charter from King Edmund in 940 and possibly still alive in 966.[136] It looks therefore as if Eadgar may have come into possession of relics of St Vincent and divided them between Glastonbury and Abingdon. Whether Æthelwold himself had any role in this is difficult to say. He is not known to have shown interest in the collection of foreign relics at his other communities, except perhaps at Thorney, to which according to local tradition he gave relics of the otherwise unknown martyr Enicius.[137]

Æthelwold used relic cults to enhance the prestige of his foundations. By reviving local pre-Viking cults he could recall the past glories of a stricter and more observant age and enlist local sentiment for his reforms. The process initiated with the cross at Abingdon was continued elsewhere. At Chertsey, for example, an *inventio* helped to link the new community with its early Anglo-Saxon past: according to the thirteenth-century cartulary already mentioned, one of the monks received a revelation of the location of the bodies of the monks of Chertsey slaughtered by the Danes, as well, it seems, as the relics of St Frithewold, the founder, and two other figures associated with its early history, St Becca and St Edor, all of which were removed and placed in a wooden shrine.[138] Similar proceedings seem to have characterised most of Æthelwold's major foundations. At Ely he was responsible for reviving the cults of St Æthelthryth, the foundress, and St Sexburg, her sister and successor in the abbacy.[139] At Thorney, he or his representative Godeman translated *inter alia* SS. Tancred, Torhtred, and Tova, in local tradition three siblings who lived as hermits near the site of the abbey.[140] At Winchester, which associations with the West Saxon royal house perhaps rendered special, Æthelwold seems to have looked primarily to saints of a relatively late period. At the Old Minster, though he encouraged devotion to early bishops such as Birinus (634-c.650) and Haedda (676-?705), he paid more attention to those connected with the royal house, including Beornstan (931-4), Ælfheah (934-51), and above all, Swithun (852-62).[141] His most significant act was the translation of St Swithun in 971 from his tomb outside the west end of the minster to a splendid shrine within, after attention had been called to the saint's efficacy by a succession of miracles beginning in 968. The importance attached to this event can be gauged by the fact that the principal reliquary, made at the king's command, was composed of silver, precious stones, and three hundred pounds of tested gold, and that the actual placing of this splendid receptacle on an altar within the church was preceded by a three-mile barefoot procession.[142] The motives behind this special attention are clear: it showed the old order

[136] *Chron. Abingdon* I, 91-2; Gelling, *Thames Valley*, no. 269; Robertson, *Anglo-Saxon Charters*, no. xlii; Thomas, 'Cults', p 151.
[137] Thomas, 'Cults', p 237; *Liber Vitae Hyde*, p 289. Cf. Ælfsige's obtaining relics of St Florentius for Peterborough: Hugh Candidus, *Chronicle*, ed. W. T. Mellows (London, 1949), pp 49, 51.
[138] Cotton Vitellius A XIII, fol. 35v. The chronicler expressly mentions *cronicae predicti monasterii anglico ideomate* as his source.
[139] *Liber Eliensis* II, ch 52.
[140] Thomas, 'Cults', p 236; *Liber Vitae Hyde*, pp 284-6.
[141] Wulfstan, *Narratio*, pp 61-177, esp. p 73, ll 259-66; Rollason, 'Resting-Places', 91.
[142] R. N. Quirk, 'Winchester Cathedral in the Tenth Century', *Archaeological Journal* 114 (1957), 41-2; Wulfstan, *Narratio*, pp 141, ll 5-18; 143, ll 64-8.

blessing the new and helped to reconcile some at least of the expelled canons and the families from which they (and probably Swithun himself) were drawn.[143] At Nunnaminster, a comparatively recent foundation, a similar policy was applied; there Æthelwold was responsible for the translation of Eadburg, daughter of the founder Edward the Elder, to another new and costly shrine.[144]

Æthelwold further enhanced the relic collections of his new communities by appropriating the remains of early monastic or eremitic saints whose cult sites were not under the supervision of a major ecclesiastical centre.[145] St Wihtburg, for example, was removed from Dereham to Ely, in the teeth of local opposition.[146] Thorney was enriched by the bodies of several early saints, including Botulf and Athulf from Icanho,[147] Cissa, Guthlac's successor at Crowland, Hunna, priest of Æthelthryth of Ely, and most notably of all, Benedict Biscop from Monkwearmouth.[148] Only at Peterborough does Æthelwold seem not to have been personally involved in relic-collecting, but there his reforming colleague, Oswald of Worcester, supplied remains of St Wilfrid, Wilfrid's successor Tatberht, and other early saints from Ripon, perhaps when he visited the community with King Edgar, soon after its refoundation.[149]

William of Malmesbury and the twelfth-century chronicler at Thorney lay stress on Æthelwold's activities as a relic collector. But his activities were not random. If he could not find a suitable local saint from the early period with which to enrich his new foundations he went elsewhere; always, however, he was anxious to draw attention to the pre-Viking past, preferably to the time of Bede and the founding fathers of English monasticism. At Abingdon this attitude is represented primarily by the cult of the Black Cross, but probably from an early period there was also interest there in the saints of the age of Bede. The best evidence of this comes from the copious additions to the kalendar in the early eleventh-century manuscript now in Cambridge.[150] These seem to have been made at various periods throughout the earlier eleventh century, since they include the obits of Anglo-Saxon monks and of most of the pre-Conquest abbots. The numerous augmentations of the feast days generally relate to early saints, though they also include a

---

[143] D. J. Sheerin, 'The Dedication of the Old Minster, Winchester, 980', *Revue Bénédictine* 88 (1978), 261-73; Quirk, 'Winchester Cathedral', 28-68.

[144] L. Braswell, 'St Edburga of Winchester', *Medieval Studies* 33 (1971), 292-324.

[145] Cf. the account in the Thorney *De translatione sanctorum* of Æthelwold's request to Eadgar 'ut sanctorum corpora, quae in destructis et neglectis tunc locis, quondam vero nobilibus et alto opere aedificatis aeclesiis, absque veneratione erant, ad ea quae suo tempore construxerat monasteria transferri permitteret': *Liber Vitae Hyde*, p 286.

[146] *Liber Eliensis* II, ch 53.

[147] There is evidence that Æthelwold originally intended Botulf to go to Ely, but Eadgar intervened and the body was divided between Thorney and the king himself. Only the head went to Ely: Thomas, 'Cults', pp 234-5; *Liber Vitae Hyde*, pp 286-8.

[148] Thomas, 'Cults', pp 231-9; *Liber Vitae Hyde*, pp 288-9; *Gesta Pontificum*, pp 376-9; *English Benedictine Kalendars After* AD1100, ed. F. Wormald, Henry Bradshaw Society 78 (London, 1938), pp 129-30; Rollason, 'Resting-Places', 91.

[149] *Hist. York* I, 462; Hugh Candidus, *Chronicle*, p 31; *Two Chronicles* I, p 117; Thomas, 'Cults', pp 198-203.

[150] CCCC 57; above. The additions are published by M. R. James, *Descriptive Catalogue of the Manuscripts in the Library of Corpus Christi College, Cambridge*, 2 vols (Cambridge, 1912), pp 114-18.

number of contemporary commemorations, such as St Æthelwold himself (an especially elaborate entry), St Dunstan (d.988), St Ælfheah (d.1012), and the second translation of St Bertin (1052).[151] The earlier saints may perhaps be taken to reflect Æthelwold's own interests. Prominence is given, for example, to the relatives of St Æthelthryth of Ely (herself included in Usuardus's text), with the inclusion of SS. Sexburg, Werburg, and Æthelburg of Brie, and there is also an important Winchester group comprising SS. Swithun, Birinus, and Hedda[152] from the Old Minster, St Judoc from the New Minster, and St Eadburg from Nunnaminster. Seventh-century saints and bishops, such as Botulf, Chad, Wilfrid, Honorius and Deusdedit, and the Venerable Bede himself were also commemorated. Some at least of these entries may reflect the early presence of appropriate relics. By the twelfth century the abbey had fragments of SS. Swithun, Birinus, Judoc, and Chad, none of which is said to have been obtained by Abbot Faritius and all of which could have been given by Æthelwold himself.[153] In particular, the second translation of St Swithun, between 971 and the death of Eadgar, was the occasion for the division of the saint's remains, only some of which were placed in Eadgar's precious reliquary. Such a division would have been an especially appropriate moment for the distribution of some portion of the relics to other favoured institutions, including Abingdon.[154]

Æthelwold was a learned man; his role in compiling the *Regularis Concordia* and his translation of the rule of St Benedict into the vernacular suffice to demonstrate that.[155] One part of his learning was historical; he looked back to the golden days of the early Anglo-Saxon church, when true monasticism flourished in England. At Abingdon these interests gave birth to a remodelling of the community's traditions. Essentially Æthelwold's actions there were interpreted as a restoration, a calling back into being of the seventh-century foundation, its relics, its endowments, its privileges. That community was deemed finally to have been extinguished by the attacks of the Danes and the depredations of King Alfred. No matter that it had probably long been a minster; for Æthelwold and his followers the pre-Viking past was all of a piece and all monastic. The stimulus to renew this past came from the continent, where the reformed monasticism pointed the way to primitive purity. Here again Abingdon's role was crucial: it provided the means by which Æthelwold experimented with the legislation of Benedict of Aniane and the customs of Fleury, Corbie, and elsewhere, before he produced the monastic code which was to establish the norm in all his foundations. As the forerunner Abingdon was, in a sense, the mother house and exemplar of Æthelwold's connexion, the largest and most influential of all those established by the trio of saintly reformers. From the saint's

---

[151] His cult was presumably popularised in Winchester by Grimbald (d.901), who had been a monk at Saint-Bertin, and was closely associated with the foundation of New Minster.

[152] Hedda's entry refers to Bede's account of his miracles in the *Ecclesiastical History*.

[153] *Chron. Abingdon* II, 158. It is significant that Aldhelm, whose relics were obtained by Faritius (*Chron. Abingdon* II, 46, 157), is not among the saints added to the Abingdon kalendar.

[154] Quirk, 'Winchester Cathedral', 41-2, 56-9.

[155] *Ibid.*, 30.

experience there sprang much that was to become uniform throughout his communities. Abingdon reflected and perhaps helped to engender Æthelwold's characteristic combination of devotion to the continental reform with an equally strong feeling for the native monastic past and the holy figures associated with it.

Chapter 3

ÆTHELWOLD AND THE
POLITICS OF THE TENTH CENTURY

Barbara Yorke

Æthelwold's biographers, Wulfstan and Ælfric, were not interested in the
secular aspects of Æthelwold's life.[1] Their subject was Æthelwold's career as
monk, bishop and church reformer, and their aim was to prove Æthelwold's
sanctity, both through his life in the church and through the miracles
performed during his lifetime and at his tomb. Kings and queens show
Æthelwold due respect and patronage, but the details of their lives and
court intrigues have no place in these hagiographies. Æthelwold's life is
shown pursued in isolation from the temporal world. Details are provided of
Æthelwold's monastic *familia*, but we know next to nothing of his temporal
family or of his relations with the secular nobility. The biographers have
done a good job, but there are hints that Æthelwold must have been a man
of the world as well as of the cloister. Monasteries like Ely and Thorney
could only be revived with the aid of large sums of money,[2] and secular
clerks, like those of the Old Minster, needed the threat of secular coercion
to make them yield their place to monks.[3] The great feast which Æthelwold
provided at Abingdon for King Eadred and his court is one of the clearest
indications of a dimension to Æthelwold's life on which his biographers
were reluctant to dwell.[4] Alcohol flowed all day at Abingdon on this occasion, and the Northumbrians in the party at least ended up completely
intoxicated. A churchman like Æthelwold was expected to adapt himself to
the way of life of the royal court when the king came calling, not the other
way around.

We would be well-advised to take heed of these hints in the biographies
that there was a secular dimension to Æthelwold's life which they did not
choose to discuss. Even the most cursory examination of medieval church
life makes it apparent that major churchmen frequently had an intimate
involvement in contemporary politics and that their careers were often tied
up with those of secular kinsmen or allies. Recent studies of queens,[5] and
other members of the Anglo-Saxon nobility,[6] have stressed that in the tenth

[1] See Introduction, above, p 11.
[2] *Ibid.*, pp 3-6.
[3] Wulfstan, *Vita* ch 16-18; Ælfric ch 12-14.
[4] Wulfstan, *Vita* ch 12; Ælfric ch 8.
[5] P. Stafford, 'The King's Wife in Wessex, 800-1066', *Past and Present* 91 (1981), 3-27, and
Queens, Concubines and Dowagers: The King's Wife in the Early Middle Ages (London, 1983).
[6] C. Hart, 'Athelstan "Half King" and his Family', *ASE* 2 (1973), 115-44, and A. Williams,
'*Princeps Merciorum gentis*: the family, career and connections of Ælfhere, ealdorman of
Mercia, 956-83', *ASE* 10 (1982), 143-72.

century ties of kinship and mutual obligation were all important, and that many ostensibly ecclesiastical matters could have a political dimension.[7] Above all, we get a feeling that a secular dimension is missing from the contemporary accounts of Æthelwold's life when we compare them with the account of the life of his near-contemporary Dunstan by the mysterious 'B', whose exact identity remains unknown, but who appears to have been a priest and a member of Dunstan's entourage.[8] Whereas Wulfstan and Ælfric display a Bedan reticence in discussing matters of political controversy, 'B' comes closer to Eddius Stephanus in his willingness to show Dunstan's involvement in secular affairs and the effect they had on his ecclesiastical career. An analysis of Dunstan's route to high office in the church helps to highlight matters which we should also take into consideration when assessing the life of Æthelwold.

Dunstan's life reveals how important family connections could be in establishing an ecclesiastical career. Dunstan was born into a well-connected, West-country family, of which at least three other members became bishops. Æthelhelm, who according to Dunstan's second biographer, Adelard, was Dunstan's uncle, was appointed bishop of Wells in c.909, and was subsequently promoted to Canterbury (923x925).[9] Dunstan was also related to Ælfheah the Bald, who was created bishop of Winchester in 935,[10] and to Cynesige, who may have become bishop of Berkshire in c.928, and was certainly bishop of Lichfield from c.946 to 964.[11] Dunstan's career was aided initially by his influential relatives. His uncle Æthelhelm secured his introduction to Athelstan's court,[12] and from there Dunstan moved to the *familia* of his kinsman Ælfheah the Bald in Winchester.[13] It was Ælfheah who dissuaded Dunstan from marriage and persuaded him to follow the monastic life instead.

Dunstan's career in the church was aided and shaped by relatives already well-established in the ecclesiastical hierarchy. One reason for the success of the family as a whole was their kinship with King Athelstan, though the exact form of the relationship is unknown. According to 'B', Dunstan's kinswoman Æthelflæda was of royal stock and related to King Athelstan.[14] As Dunstan is not said to have been related to any other of the West Saxon kings, it is most likely that the family connection was through Athelstan's

---

[7] See above, nn 5 and 6, and D. J. V. Fisher, 'The Anti-Monastic Reaction in the Reign of Edward the Martyr', *Cambridge Historical Journal* 10 (1950-2), 254-70.

[8] *Memorials*, pp 3-52, and on 'B', see N. Brooks, *The Early History of the Church of Canterbury: Christ Church from 597 to 1066* (Leicester, 1984), pp 245-6.

[9] *Memorials*, p 55. Adelard says that Æthelhelm was Dunstan's *patruus*, i.e. his paternal uncle. On Æthelhelm, see J. Armitage Robinson, *The Saxon Bishops of Wells*, British Academy Supplemental Papers 4 (1918), pp 6, 28-31, and M. A. O'Donovan, 'An interim revision of episcopal dates for the province of Canterbury, 850-950: part I', *ASE* 1 (1972), 31-2.

[10] *Memorials*, p 13, and O'Donovan, 'Episcopal dates: part II', *ASE* 2 (1973), 111-12.

[11] *Memorials*, p 32, and O'Donovan, 'Episcopal dates: part II', 95.

[12] *Memorials*, p 55. According to Adelard, Dunstan was in Æthelhelm's household before he went to the royal court.

[13] *Ibid.*, pp 13-14.

[14] *Ibid.*, pp 17-18. Æthelflæda is described as *regali ex progenie orta*, and also as Athelstan4u *neptis*. *Neptis* could mean niece, however, it is unlikely that Athelstan, who was thirty at his accession, had a sibling who could have provided him with a niece old enough to help Dunstan in his youth. *Neptis* was probably used with the more general meaning of kinswoman.

mother, Ecgwynna.[15] Dunstan's family were presumably supporters of Athelstan in the disputed succession on Edward the Elder's death.[16] Ælfheah was one of the priests in Athelstan's household at the time of his coronation,[17] and Athelstan's bid for the throne may have been aided by Archbishop Æthelhelm, who anointed Athelstan as king on 4 September 925.[18] If Æthelhelm was Dunstan's uncle, he was presumably related to Athelstan as well. The relationship between the family of Dunstan and their kinsman Athelstan was likely to have been reciprocal. They supported his claim to the throne from positions within the church, and, after he became king, Athelstan was in a position to advance his kinsmen further.

Dunstan's first major appointment came from King Edmund, who tended to promote men who had previously been favoured by his half-brother, Athelstan. Edmund chose Dunstan, in the first instance, as one of his chief counsellors. Court intrigue succeeded in having Dunstan dismissed, but Edmund reinstated him, after he became convinced, through his narrow escape from death in Cheddar Gorge, that Dunstan had been wronged. It was at this point that Edmund created Dunstan abbot of Glastonbury.[19] The promotion to Glastonbury was not a random choice, but one which took account of family connections. The main land holdings of Dunstan's kin seem to have lain in Somerset, and Dunstan is reputed to have been born at Baltonsborough, some four miles from Glastonbury.[20] Dunstan studied at Glastonbury as a boy,[21] and other members of the family, including Æthelhelm and Ælfheah, may have been members of the community.[22] Æthelflæda, kinswoman of both Dunstan and King Athelstan, possessed a house in Glastonbury where Athelstan visited her, and she may have left this and other estates to Dunstan after her death.[23] The choice of Dunstan as abbot of Glastonbury was a logical extension of existing family interests.

Unfortunately none of Dunstan's biographers have much to say about relatives of Dunstan who pursued secular careers. When Dunstan was at Athelstan's court he was in the company of other young male relatives (*consanguini*) who became jealous of his manifold talents, plotted against him and dumped him in a muddy pool, but we hear nothing of the subsequent careers of these kinsmen.[24] The only relative of Dunstan who pursued a secular career of which anything is known is his brother Wulfric, whom

[15] On Ecgwynna see further below, pp 69-70. Dunstan, his father Heorstan (*Memorials*, p 6) and Athelstan, all share the name-element *stan* which is relatively rare among the West Saxon nobility (although Athelstan was also the name of the eldest son of King Æthelwulf of Wessex).
[16] See below, pp 71-3.
[17] Robinson, 'Saxon Bishops', pp 32-3.
[18] *Memorials*, pp 55-6. Adelard implies that Dunstan was living with his uncle at the time of the coronation.
[19] *Ibid.*, pp 21-5.
[20] J. Armitage Robinson, 'Memorials of Saint Dunstan in Somerset', *Proceedings of the Somersetshire Archaeological and Natural History Society* 1916 (62), 1-3.
[21] *Memorials*, pp 6-10.
[22] Robinson, 'Saxon Bishops', 32-3.
[23] *Memorials*, pp 17-18. However, Dunstan only appears as Æthelflæda's heir in the post-Conquest accounts of his life, where her name has become Ælfgyva (*op. cit.*, pp 85-7, and 178). According to these versions, her legacy made Dunstan's reform of other West Saxon monasteries possible.
[24] *Memorials*, pp 11-13.

Dunstan placed in charge of Glastonbury's estates.[25] Dr Hart has suggested that this Wulfric can be identified with a thegn of the same name who witnessed charters between 943 and 956.[26] Wulfric thegn possessed estates in Wiltshire, Dorset and Gloucestershire, and seems to have been connected through marriage with Ælfwine, brother of Ealdorman Ælfhere of Mercia. Wulfric made Ælfwine heir to some of his estates with reversion to Glastonbury.[27] If, as seems likely, this thegn was Dunstan's brother, his career provides an indication of how Dunstan's family connections could have been extended through the marriages of his relatives.

The biographies of Dunstan contain valuable indications of how an ecclesiastical career might be shaped by kinsmen and pre-existing family interests. It is therefore much to be regretted that Æthelwold's biographers were such good Benedictines that they tell us next to nothing about Æthelwold's temporal family. We do not even know the names of his parents, though we do know that Æthelwold was born in Winchester during the reign of Edward the Elder.[28] Ælfric's homily on St Swithun suggests that Eadsige, one of the clerks of the Old Minster who subsequently became a monk, was related to Æthelwold, but we do not know of any other kinsmen.[29] It is possible though to make some general observations about the status of Æthelwold's family.

Æthelwold is unlikely to have been related to the royal family as he is never addressed in charters by any of the royal house as 'kinsman'.[30] However, there seems little doubt that he was of noble birth. Like Dunstan, Æthelwold followed the normal career pattern of an aristocratic youth, and spent a period in the *comitatus* of King Athelstan.[31] Æthelwold was later to refer to Athelstan as his lord, and he owned an estate of sixty hides at Harting (Sussex) which he had received from the king.[32] Young nobles went to the court in the hopes of getting preferment, and it was Athelstan who arranged for Æthelwold to enter the *familia* of Bishop Ælfheah in Winchester, of which Dunstan was already a member.[33]

The great wealth of Æthelwold, which is apparent in his later career, may also tell us something about his family. It is not possible to provide a total of all the money which Æthelwold paid out to acquire estates, privileges and works of art for his foundations, but the full figure must have run to several thousands of pounds. A silver *tabula* which Æthelwold gave to

---

[25] *Op. cit.*, p 28. Wulfric has the title *procer*.

[26] C. R. Hart, *The Early Charters of Northern England and the North Midlands*, Studies in Early English History 6 (Leicester, 1975), pp 371-2. However, Professor Sawyer prefers to identify Wulfric thegn with a member of the family of Wulfric Spot – *Charters of Burton Abbey*, ed. P. H. Sawyer, Anglo-Saxon Charters II (London, 1979), p xlviii.

[27] Williams, 'Ælfhere', 146, 154-5. Dr Williams is inclined to support Dr Hart's identification.

[28] Wulfstan, *Vita*, ch 2; Ælfric ch 2.

[29] *Ælfric: Lives of Three English Saints*, ed. G. I. Needham (London, 1966), pp 64-5.

[30] Neither is Dunstan ever described as such in charters; however, Dunstan may only have been related to Athelstan and he does not appear in any of Athelstan's charters.

[31] Wulfstan, *Vita*, ch 7; Ælfric ch 5.

[32] *Liber Eliensis*, pp 75-6. The information comes from a summary of Edgar's privileges for Ely (S 779), but as the details are not in the full text of the grant nor in the *Libellus*, from which the compiler of the *Liber Eliensis* took his information about Æthelwold's acquisitions, the exact source of the statement is not known.

[33] Wulfstan, *Vita*, ch 7; Ælfric ch 5.

Abingdon in honour of King Edgar alone cost three hundred pounds,[34] and the rights which Æthelwold secured for the Old Minster estate at Taunton (Somerset) involved an outlay of over two hundred and fifty mancuses.[35] There is no parallel in Anglo-Saxon England for this scale of expenditure by someone not of the royal house. Although some of Æthelwold's wealth may have come from those who supported his church reforms and from the possessions of his monasteries, it is unlikely that all of it can be accounted for in this way. Some of Æthelwold's wealth must have been inherited and be evidence for the high social status of his family.

Although we do not have exact details about Æthelwold's family, it is a fair assumption that it must have included people of great importance in Winchester where Æthelwold was born. The nearest we can hope to come to Æthelwold's family background is by looking at the events and allegiances of Winchester during the time that Æthelwold can be presumed to have been growing up in his parents' home, that is in the latter part of the reign of Edward the Elder and the early years of King Athelstan. There are obviously limits to what can be learnt of this period, but Winchester does seem to have played a significant role in the disputed succession on Edward the Elder's death which requires some elucidation. Edward the Elder had complicated the succession by marrying three times and producing sons by all three marriages, though those of the third marriage (to Eadgifu) were too young to be serious contenders in 924.[36] Edward's eldest son was Athelstan, who had been born some five years before Edward's accession in 899.[37] His mother was Ecgwynna, who, as we have seen, may have been related to Dunstan's family.[38] William of Malmesbury, perhaps drawing on a verse panegyric of Athelstan, described her as *illustri foemina*,[39] but he also knew a claim that she was no more than Edward's concubine, and of low birth.[40] These slurs on Athelstan's parentage were not just a gloss of the twelfth century, as Hrotsvitha of Gandersheim had evidently heard something similar and contrasted the union unfavourably with that of Edward and his second wife, Ælfflæd.[41]

---

[34] *Chron. Abingdon* I, 344-5, with details of other gifts from Æthelwold to Abingdon. See also Thacker, ch 2, pp 57-8.

[35] Robertson 45, pp 92-5; S 806. Edgar received two hundred mancuses and his wife was given fifty; in addition Edgar was given a silver cup worth five pounds.

[36] *Gesta Regum*, pp 136-7.

[37] *Op. cit.*, p 145, reveals that Athelstan was thirty years old when he was acclaimed king; Athelstan was recognised as king in Mercia in 924, but was not crowned until 925 (see below, p 71).

[38] Above, pp 66-7.

[39] *Gesta Regum*, p 136. M. Lapidge, 'Some Latin poems as evidence for the reign of Athelstan', *ASE* 9 (1981), 62-71, has shown that the passages quoted by William are not from a Latin poem of the time of Athelstan, but were composed in the twelfth century. However, this does not rule out the possibility that William's verses are reworkings of an earlier poem, as argued by M. Wood, 'The Making of King Athelstan's Empire: an English Charlemagne?', *Ideal and Reality: Studies presented to J. M. Wallace-Hadrill*, ed. P. Wormald, with D. Bullough and R. Collins (Oxford, 1983), p 256. See also the comments of S. Keynes, 'King Athelstan's books', *Learning and Literature in Anglo-Saxon England: Studies presented to Peter Clemoes*, ed. M. Lapidge and H. Gneuss (Cambridge, 1985), p 144, n 15.

[40] *Gesta Regum*, pp 142 and 155-6.

[41] Hrotsvitha, *Gesta Ottonis* II, 75-97; *Hrotsvithae Opera*, ed. P. de Winterfield, *MGH Scriptores Rerum Germanicarum* (Berlin, 1902), pp 206-7. Edward's and Ælfflæd's daughter,

According to William of Malmesbury, who is the only writer to deal with the matter, Ælfflæd was the daughter of *Ethelmi comitis*.[42] The most likely candidate for identification as Ælfflæd's father is Ealdorman Æthelm/ Æthelhelm of Wiltshire, whose death is recorded in the *Chronicle* for 897.[43] However, it has been suggested that Ælfflæd's father was not Ealdorman Æthelhelm, but Æthelhelm the elder son of King Æthelred I, who was Edward's first cousin.[44] The marriage, it has been proposed, could be seen as a political necessity, following the challenge to the throne by Æthelwold, brother of Æthelhelm, on King Alfred's death. Although Edward soon expelled Æthelwold from the kingdom, his position was not completely secure until the latter's death in 902.[45] The hypothesis that Ælfflæd was a descendant of Æthelred I makes good sense in the context of the early years of Edward's reign, but there is no other support for it. There is no evidence that Ealdorman Æthelhelm and Æthelhelm ætheling were the same person,[46] and it would appear that William of Malmesbury definitely had the former and not the latter in mind. If Ælfflæd had been the daughter of Æthelhelm ætheling, she and Edward would have been within the prohibited degrees of kinship for marriage, and, although there had been a recent irregular union in Edward's family,[47] it is more likely than not that Edward would not have attempted, or have been permitted, to marry such a close relative. Nevertheless, it is possible that Edward's marriage with Ælfflæd was designed to strengthen his position in Wessex by a union with an important noble house, and that, as Hrotsvitha believed, Ælfflæd, whom Edward had married after he became king, had greater status than Ecgwynna, his spouse or concubine of the period when he was an ætheling.[48]

The different views which William of Malmesbury discovered about the status of Ecgwynna may well reflect the views of rival supporters for and against her son, Athelstan: indeed, they seem to prefigure arguments about the succession of Edgar's sons which hinged upon the different status of his two wives.[49] There are some indications that Athelstan had been recognised as Edward's eventual heir before the death of King Alfred.[50] However, when

---

Eadgyth, married Otto I, hence Hrotsvitha's interest.

[42] *Gesta Regum*, p 137.

[43] *Two Chronicles* I, 91, *sa* 898. For other details of Æthelhelm's career, see S. Keynes and M. Lapidge, *Alfred the Great: Asser's Life of King Alfred and other contemporary sources* (Harmondsworth, 1983), p 328.

[44] Stafford, *Queens, Concubines and Dowagers*, pp 43-4.

[45] *Two Saxon Chronicles* I, 92-5.

[46] No acknowledgement of kinship is made in a grant of land from King Alfred to Ealdorman Æthelhelm (S 348). Æthelhelm ætheling is known only from King Alfred's will, see Keynes and Lapidge, *Alfred the Great*, pp 173-8, and 313-16.

[47] Alfred's brother Æthelbald had married his stepmother Judith: see P. Stafford, 'Charles the Bald, Judith and England', *Charles the Bald*, ed. M. Gibson, J. Nelson and D. Ganz (Oxford, 1981), pp 137-51.

[48] Above, n 41. On marriage and concubinage, see Stafford, *Queens, Concubines and Dowagers*, pp 62-71, and M. Ross, 'Concubinage in Anglo-Saxon England', *Past and Present* 108 (1985), 3-34.

[49] See below, pp 82-4.

[50] William's account of a ceremony in which King Alfred appears to have recognised Athelstan as his eventual heir (*Gesta Regum*, p 145), receives support from a tenth-century acrostic poem which also seems to anticipate the succession of Athelstan. Dr Lapidge has suggested that the

Edward died on 17 July 924, it was his son Ælfweard, his eldest son by Ælfflæd, who succeeded him.[51] It may have been the intention that Ælfweard would succeed in Wessex, but that Athelstan would become king of the Mercians on his father's death. Athelstan's sojourn in the household of Ealdorman Æthelred of Mercia and his wife Æthelflæd (aunt of Athelstan) suggests that he was being groomed for this position,[52] and the Mercian Register records his election to the Mercian throne in 924.[53] But the original intentions for the disposal of the throne on Edward's death are obscured by the events which actually occurred, for in the event, Ælfweard died some sixteen days after his father.[54] Athelstan became king of both the Mercians and the West Saxons, but his coronation did not take place until 4 September 925, over a year after Ælfweard's death.[55] This delay in itself suggests that there was opposition to Athelstan in Wessex,[56] and opposition is likely to have centred around Edwin, the surviving son of Edward and Ælfflæd. The one place which William of Malmesbury mentions as a centre of resistance to Athelstan is Winchester, where there was apparently a plot, instigated by a nobleman called Alfred, to have Athelstan captured and blinded.[57]

It is not surprising that Winchester should have been a centre of support for Ælfweard and Edwin. Edward had shown particular favour to Winchester after his accession to the throne of Wessex and marriage to Ælfflæd. He had founded the New Minster on a site adjacent to the Old Minster, and one of

poem may have been written by John the Old Saxon to commemorate the ceremony which William describes – Lapidge, 'Latin poems', 72-83.

[51] Ælfweard appears as Edward's successor, with a reign of four weeks, in a West Saxon Regnal List in the *Textus Roffensis*, Rochester, Cathedral Library, MS A.3.5, fols 7v-8r. There is also a reference to Ælfweard having ruled in the *Liber Vitae* of New Minster (Winchester): *Liber Vitae: Register and Martyrology of New Minster and Hyde Abbey, Winchester*, ed. W. de Gray Birch, Hampshire Record Society (London, 1892), p 6.

[52] *Gesta Regum*, p 145.

[53] *Two Chronicles* I, 105, and II, 121. For a discussion of events in this period which reaches some different conclusions, see A. Williams, 'Some Notes and Considerations on Problems Connected with the English Royal Succession, 860-1066', *Proceedings of the Battle Conference on Anglo-Norman Studies* I, ed. R. Allen Brown (Ipswich, 1978), 149-51.

[54] *Two Chronicles* I, 105, where we are also told he died at Oxford. The regnal list in the *Textus Roffensis* gives him a reign of four weeks (see n 51).

[55] The date of Athelstan's coronation is established by a charter issued on the same day (S 394), and by references to his reign as having lasted fourteen years, seven months and three days in two versions of the West Saxon regnal list: see J. Armitage Robinson, *The Times of Saint Dunstan* (Oxford, 1923), pp 31-6.

[56] S 395 records an assembly of 925 at which no West Saxon bishops or abbots were present, and so may be evidence for a period when Athelstan was recognised as king in Mercia, but had not yet been accepted in Wessex: see Robinson, *Times of Saint Dunstan*, pp 42-5. A comparison could be drawn with the delay in Edward the Elder's coronation because of Æthelwold's rebellion. King Alfred died on 26 October 899, but Edward was not crowned until 8 June 900: Keynes and Lapidge, *Alfred the Great*, pp 291-2.

[57] William refers to the opposition of Alfred in his general assessment of Athelstan's reign (*Gesta Regum*, p 142), and later discusses his actions in greater detail, with an excerpt from a spurious charter (*ibid.*, p 153: S 436). The charter is reproduced in full in William's *Gesta Pontificum*, pp 401-3. The charter was presumably drawn up at Malmesbury and made use of traditions preserved there. In spite of his rebellion Alfred was buried at Malmesbury (*Gesta Regum*, p 152). Malmesbury was particularly favoured by Athelstan for royal burials (n 70), and so it is possible that Alfred was a member of the royal house.

its functions was to serve as a royal mausoleum.[58] At the time of Edward's death, the New Minster already contained the bodies of Edward's father and mother, of his brother Æthelweard and of a son, Ælfwine.[59] With the help of Edward's patronage, Winchester became a major literary and artistic centre, particularly after the appointment of Frithestan as bishop in 909.[60] A direct link between Frithestan and Queen Ælfflæd is provided by the gold-embroidered vestments, later presented to the shrine of St Cuthbert, which carry the inscriptions ÆLFFLÆD FIERI PRECEPIT ... PIO EPISCOPO FRIÐESTANO.[61] The embroidery may have been carried out at the Nunnaminster, another Winchester religious establishment which enjoyed royal patronage.[62] Winchester must have expected and supported the accession of Ælfweard on his father's death. Memory of his brief reign was kept alive in Winchester, and he was buried, like his father, in the New Minster.[63]

A New Minster document suggests that Winchester continued to support the cause of Edwin after Ælfweard's death. The only document of Athelstan's reign in which Edwin appears is a lease from the New Minster community, which survives in a contemporary copy.[64] Edwin's status as a king's son is stressed by use of the term *cliton*, which makes its earliest recorded appearance in this document.[65] Although *cliton* was frequently used in the tenth century as a synonym for ætheling, its use was not consistent. In one tenth-century poem it was used to translate *rex*,[66] and in one of King Eadred's charters a distinction was drawn between Eadwig *cliton* and Edgar ætheling.[67] The New Minster charter may have been using *cliton* in a similar sense to indicate that Edwin should be considered as Athelstan's successor, and the foremost of the æthelings. The New Minster lease provides evidence for the championing of Edwin's cause in Winchester, and the presence of Edwin

---

[58] M. Biddle, '*Felix Urbs Winthonia*: Winchester in the Age of Monastic Reform', *Tenth-Century Studies*, pp 123-40, and B. A. E. Yorke, 'The Bishops of Winchester, the Kings of Wessex and the Development of Winchester in the Ninth and Early Tenth Centuries', *Proceedings of the Hampshire Field Club and Archaeological Society* 40 (1984), 67-9.

[59] *Liber Vitae*, pp 6 and 14, where Æthelweard is wrongly identified as a son of Edward.

[60] F. Wormald, 'The "Winchester School" before St Æthelwold', *England Before the Conquest: Studies in Primary Sources Presented to Dorothy Whitelock*, ed. P. Clemoes and K. Hughes (Cambridge, 1971), pp 305-13, and M. B. Parkes, 'The Palaeography of the Parker Manuscript of the *Chronicle*, Laws and Sedulius, and Historiography at Winchester in the Late Ninth and Tenth Centuries', *ASE* 5 (1976), 149-71.

[61] E. Plenderleith, C. Hohler and R. Freyhan, 'The Stole and Maniples', *The Relics of Saint Cuthbert: studies by various authors*, ed. C. F. Battiscombe (Oxford, 1956), pp 375-432. According to Durham tradition, the embroideries were presented to the shrine of St Cuthbert by King Athelstan, but for reservations about this tradition see Keynes, 'King Athelstan's books', pp 177-8.

[62] There is no definite evidence that the embroideries were made at Nunnaminster, but their designs have close connections with contemporary Winchester art (see n 60) and the embroidery is most likely to have been carried out by women.

[63] *Liber Vitae*, p 6, and see n 51.

[64] S 1417. The land is leased, with the king's permission, to a *minister* called Alfred – particularly interesting in view of William's statement that a nobleman called Alfred was behind the resistance to Athelstan in Winchester (n 57).

[65] D. N. Dumville, 'The ætheling: a study in Anglo-Saxon constitutional history', *ASE* 8 (1979), 7-10.

[66] *Ibid.*, p 9, n 6. The poem is the *Breviloquium Vitae Beati Wilfredi* of Frithegod.

[67] S 569. The charter comes from the thirteenth-century Burton cartulary, but appears to be genuine: Dumville, *op. cit.*, p 10.

among the New Minster witnesses may mean that Edwin actually lived in Winchester in the early years of Athelstan's reign, perhaps under the protection of its religious communities. It may be coincidence, but it was shortly after the death of Bishop Frithestan of Winchester,[68] that Edwin fled the country and was drowned off the coast of Flanders, possibly with Athelstan's connivance.[69]

Athelstan certainly showed less partiality for Winchester than his father had done, and this helps support the view that he had been opposed there. His reservations about Winchester can be seen in his rejection of the New Minster as a place of royal burial. Edward and Ælfweard had been buried in the New Minster, but Athelstan's two cousins, who were killed at the battle of *Brunanburh* in 937, were buried at Malmesbury, where Athelstan himself was buried in 939.[70] When Frithestan retired as bishop of Winchester in 931, Athelstan was careful to secure the loyalty of the see. The new bishop was Beornstan, a priest from Athelstan's own household,[71] and on Beornstan's death in 934, Athelstan again chose one of his own priests, Ælfheah the Bald, kinsman of Dunstan and so possibly of the king as well.[72] The importance of the Winchester see seems to have increased greatly after Ælfheah's appointment, and he regularly attested royal charters in second place, after the archbishop of Canterbury. It was in his household, of course, that Æthelwold began his ecclesiastical career after a period at Athelstan's court.[73] Although there had originally been a preference in Winchester for the succession of Ælfweard or Edwin, which Æthelwold's family might be presumed to have shared, once Athelstan was securely established both sides would wish for reconciliation in their own best interests. The succession of Athelstan would not necessarily have been disastrous for Winchester nobles who had originally favoured a different candidate, but it would not have marked a major advance in their fortunes, as it may have done for the family of Dunstan. In the light of subsequent events, we should take account of the possibility that the families of Æthelwold and Dunstan may have supported different candidates in the succession dispute on Edward the Elder's death.

Athelstan died apparently unmarried in 939. His single status is surprising and may indicate an alliance with his father's third wife, Eadgifu, whereby

[68] Frithestan retired as bishop of Winchester in 931 and died probably in the following year, though it is possible he survived until 933: O'Donovan, 'Episcopal dates: part II', 109-11.
[69] Edwin's death is dated to 933 in the 'E' version of the *Chronicle* (*Two Chronicles* I, 107), and by the Flemish chronicler Folcwine (O. Holder-Egger, *Folcwini diaconi gesta abbatum S. Bertini Sithensium*, MGH Scriptores 13 (1881), ch 107, p 629). William tells how Edwin was put to sea in an untrustworthy boat after a rebellion against Athelstan (*Gesta Regum*, pp 156-7), and that Athelstan founded the community at Milton (Abbas, Dorset) to expiate his half-brother's death (*Gesta Pontificum*, p 186).
[70] *Gesta Regum*, p 151. Athelstan's cousins, Ælfwine and Æthelwine, were the sons of his uncle Æthelweard, who had been buried in New Minster (n 59). It is possible that Malmesbury had always supported Athelstan's claim to the throne: the acrostic poem which looks forward to the young Athelstan becoming king may have been written by John the Old Saxon, who seems to have ended his days at Malmesbury – see Lapidge, 'Some Latin poems', 72-83, and n 50 above.
[71] O'Donovan, 'Episcopal dates: part II', 110-11, and Wood, 'King Athelstan's Empire', 256-7.
[72] *Op. cit.* For Ælfheah, see above, p 66.
[73] See n 33.

on Athelstan's death the succession of one of Eadgifu's sons was assured.[74] Certainly neither of Athelstan's half-brothers seems to have shown any inclination to alter the balance of power at court when they came to the throne, and many of those appointed to office by Athelstan improved their positions under Edmund and Eadred. Oda, for instance, who had been appointed to the bishopric of Ramsbury by Athelstan, was elevated to Canterbury by Edmund, and played a major role in the witans of both Edmund and Eadred.[75] Dunstan became not only abbot of Glastonbury, but a major advisor to both kings, and during Eadred's reign had charge of part of the royal treasury.[76] Among the laity, the family of Athelstan Half-King seems to have been particularly favoured, and during the reigns of Edmund and Eadred extended the areas under its control at the expense of other leading members of the nobility.[77]

Æthelwold's career up to the end of Eadred's reign follows a similar pattern. From Winchester Æthelwold moved to Glastonbury, and after studying under Dunstan for several years, was placed in charge of the lapsed monastery at Abingdon by Eadred, shortly before the king's death.[78] Wulfstan and Ælfric tell us that Æthelwold had wished to leave England to study in one of the continental reformed houses, but that the queen-mother, Eadgifu, had persuaded Eadred to give Abingdon to Æthelwold instead.[79] Æthelwold's desire to leave Glastonbury could be seen as reflecting dissatisfaction with Dunstan's management, but the move to Abingdon was made with Dunstan's permission, and presumably with his co-operation, as other members of the Glastonbury community went with Æthelwold.[80] Up to the time of Eadred's death, Æthelwold appears to have been a protégé of Dunstan and his family, and shared in the continuing success of his patrons.

The pattern of development changed with the accession of Eadwig, the elder son of Edmund, in 955. Dunstan's biographer 'B', who was probably a member of Dunstan's household at the time, provides a dramatic description of a confrontation on the day of Eadwig's coronation, when, he says, the young king withdrew from the celebratory banquet in order to enjoy the 'caresses of loose women', a mother and her daughter. At the instigation of Archbishop Oda, Dunstan and his kinsman Bishop Cynesige remonstrated with the king and forced him back to the banquet.[81] Not surprisingly there were repercussions. Dunstan was forced into exile,[82] and Eadwig's displeasure

---

[74] Williams, 'English Royal Succession', pp 150-1.

[75] For summaries of Oda's career, see Hart, *Charters of Northern England*, pp 347-50, and Brooks, *Church of Canterbury*, pp 222-6.

[76] *Memorials*, pp 29-32.

[77] Hart, 'Athelstan "Half King"', 118-26.

[78] Wulfstan, *Vita*, ch 9-11; Ælfric ch 6-8. See Thacker ch 2, p 47.

[79] Wulfstan, *Vita*, ch 10; Ælfric ch 7. Æthelwold is said to have wished to study more fully the scriptures and monastic life, and there must be a strong likelihood that he wished to go to Fleury where he later sent Osgar (Wulfstan, *Vita*, ch 14; Ælfric ch 10).

[80] *Ibid.* In his account of the monastic reforms, Æthelwold says that Glastonbury was the only monastery to live according 'to the right rule' before Abingdon was founded, and pays tribute to Dunstan's work as a monastic reformer (*Councils and Synods*, pp 142-54).

[81] *Memorials*, pp 32-3. J. Nelson, 'Inauguration Rituals', *Early Medieval Kingship*, ed. P. Sawyer and I. N. Wood (Leeds, 1977), p 66, n 99, argues that the coronation took place on 27 January 956.

[82] *Memorials*, pp 33-4. S. Keynes, *The Diplomas of King Æthelred 'The Unready', 978-1016: A Study in Their Use as Historical Evidence* (Cambridge, 1980), p 49, shows, from the charter

with Cynesige is presumably reflected in the fact that Cynesige witnessed very few of Eadwig's charters.[83] Eadwig proceeded against others as well, including his grandmother Eadgifu, whose property was confiscated.[84] New appointments restricted the powers of Athelstan Half-King,[85] and may have forced his eventual retirement to become a monk at Glastonbury.[86] His son Æthelwold succeeded him in the East Anglian ealdormanry, but did not achieve the full power of his father.[87]

A rift seems to have developed between Eadwig and some of the most important lay and ecclesiastical nobles of the reigns of his father and uncle. The idea that Eadwig was trying to assert his independence from them receives support from the large amount of land granted away by the king at the beginning of his reign. 'B', who obviously wrote from a certain point of view, wrote of Eadwig's folly in losing *sagaces vel sapientes* and favouring the *ignaros quosque sibi consimiles*.[88] 'B' spoke selectively for Eadwig did continue in office a number of men appointed by his father and uncle, including Æthelsige, ealdorman of Central Wessex, and Edmund, ealdorman of the Western Shires, for both of whom little biographical information survives.[89] But as 'B' indicates, Eadwig did bring forward a number of individuals of his own choosing, including several who were *consimiles* in the sense that they were related to Eadwig. The royal kinsmen included the brothers Ælfgar and Byrhtferth, who appear among the top of the witnessing *ministri* from 956,[90] and Byrhthelm who became bishop of either Wells or Selsey in 956, and was promoted to Winchester either late in 958 or in 959.[91]

evidence, that Dunstan went into exile soon after the coronation.

[83] Hart, *Charters of Northern England*, pp 312-13, and Keynes, *op. cit.*

[84] *Memorials*, p 36, where it is recorded that the estates were restored to Eadgifu by Edgar after Eadwig's death. The confiscation of Eadgifu's property is also referred to in a grant of land made by Eadgifu to Christ Church, Canterbury: F.E.Harmer, *Select English Historical Documents of the Ninth and Tenth Centuries* (Cambridge, 1914), 23, pp 37-8.

[85] Athelstan Half-King seems to have administered, in addition to his large East Anglian ealdormanry, the ealdormanries of South-East and Central Mercia following the deaths of Athelstan (949) and Ealhhelm (951), probably with the aid of suffragans (Hart, 'Athelstan "Half King"', 124). The appointment of Athelstan Rota to the ealdormanry of South-East Mercia in 955 (Hart, *Charters of Northern England*, pp 299-300), and of Ælfhere to that of Central Mercia in 956 (Hart, *op. cit.*, p 260) could be seen as a deliberate attempt by Eadwig to reduce the Half-King's power.

[86] Hart, 'Athelstan "Half King"', 128, places his retirement in the summer of 956. However, Simon Keynes, in a forthcoming paper, will argue that the Half-King continued in office until the division of the kingdom in 957, and that his decision to retire had a direct connection with the events of that year.

[87] Hart, 'Athelstan "Half King"', 128-9.

[88] *Memorials*, p 35.

[89] Hart, *Charters of Northern England*, pp 290-1 and 331-2.

[90] Hart, *op. cit.*, pp 254-5. Ælfgar first appears in charters in 951 and witnesses regularly from 956 among the top attesting thegns, followed by his brother Byrhtferth. Ælfgar is described as a kinsman of King Edgar in S 651, and in the account of his death in the 'A' version of the *Chronicle* for 962 (*Two Chronicles* I, 114).

[91] There has been much confusion about the identity of the various Bishop Byrhthelms who were in office during Eadwig's reign, and full discussions can be found in D.Whitelock, 'The Appointment of Dunstan as Archbishop of Canterbury', *Otium et Negotium: Studies in Onomatology and Library Science Presented to Olaf von Feilitzen*, ed. F.Sandgren (Stockholm, 1973), pp 233-36, and Brooks, *Church of Canterbury*, pp 238-40. S 683 and 695 make it clear that Bishop Byrhthelm of Winchester was related to King Edgar, and he is probably the same

Particularly favoured were the brothers Ælfheah and Ælfhere, the sons of Ealdorman Ealhhelm of Mercia.[92] Ælfhere was appointed ealdorman of Mercia early in 956,[93] and Ælfheah, who had the position of royal seneschal in the first part of Eadwig's reign, was given the ealdormanry of Central Wessex in 959.[94]

Eadwig was inclined to favour his own relations rather than some of those who had been the chief counsellors of his father and uncle, and this policy helps us to interpret the disagreement which took place at Eadwig's coronation. Although 'B' wrote of Eadwig leaving the coronation feast in order to entertain 'loose women', the mother and daughter to whom he refers were in fact Eadwig's own kinswomen. Eadwig married the daughter, Ælfgifu, though he was obliged to renounce the marriage in 958 because of their consanguinity.[95] It is possible to learn more about the background of Ælfgifu and her mother, Æthelgifu.[96] The *Codex Wintoniensis* contains the will of a wealthy West Saxon noblewoman called Ælfgifu, who died during King Edgar's reign.[97] The Ælfgifu of the will is described as a kinswoman of King Edgar (and so presumably of his brother Eadwig as well) in charters for two of the estates which she bequeathed in her will.[98] Ælfgifu had evidently been married as she is described in the charters as *matrona*, but there are no references to a husband or children in the will. Certain details we can learn about the testatrix Ælfgifu are therefore compatible with what we know about Queen Ælfgifu, and the likelihood that the two women are one and the same has been accepted by a number of historians.[99] In the will, Ælfgifu refers to a man called Æthelweard who, judging from the context in which he appears, was probably her brother.[100] The only Æthelweard active in this period who is known to have been a royal kinsman is the Æthelweard who was appointed ealdorman of the Western Shires in 973, and who was responsible

---

Byrhthelm who was granted land by his kinsman, King Eadwig, in 956 when *ad episcopalem gradus electus* (S 615).

[92] Williams, 'Ælfhere', 145. Ealhhelm's parents are not known, but there are several references to the family's royal blood (*op. cit.*, n 4). Ælfheah's wife Ælfswith also seems to have been of royal descent (S 662).

[93] Hart, *Charters of Northern England*, p 260. When Ealhhelm died his ealdormanry seems to have been taken over by the Half-King (see n 85); the sons of the Half-King and Ealhhelm therefore all had some claim to the same ealdormanry.

[94] Williams, 'Ælfhere', 148. Hart, 'Athelstan "Half King"', 127, suggests that Athelstan had expected his eldest son, Æthelwold II, to succeed to the ealdormanry of Central Wessex.

[95] The 'D' version of the *Chronicle sa* 958 records that Archbishop Oda separated King Eadwig and Ælfgifu because they were too closely related: *Two Chronicles* I, 113.

[96] Æthelgifu is named by 'B' as the chief instigator of Dunstan's exile (*Memorials*, p 33), and for another reference to her see below, p 80.

[97] D. Whitelock, *Anglo-Saxon Wills* (Cambridge, 1930), 8, pp 21-3; S 1484.

[98] S 738, a grant of ten *cassati* at Newnham Murren (Oxon), and S 737, a grant of ten *cassatae* at Linslade (Bucks). Both grants were made in 966.

[99] For instance, Whitelock, *Wills*, p 118-19; Stafford, *Queens, Concubines and Dowagers*, p 108; and Brooks, *Church of Canterbury*, p 225. One of the estates which was given to Ælfgifu by Edgar (Marsworth, Bucks), was later granted by Edgar and Ælfthryth to Ely (*Liber Eliensis*, p 116). The fact that Ælfthryth was associated with Edgar in the grant suggests that the estate came to her, and it may have been one of the estates reserved for the support of royal women.

[100] Whitelock, *Wills*, p 21: 'I grant the estates at Mongewell and Berkhampstead to Ælfweard and Æthelweard and Ælfwaru in common for their lifetime'. Ælfwaru is identified elsewhere in the will as Ælfgifu's sister.

for a Latin version of the *Anglo-Saxon Chronicle*.[101] In his translation Æthelweard records that he was the great-great-grandson of King Æthelred I, which would mean that Ælfgifu, if she was his sister, would have been Eadwig's third cousin once removed.[102] This degree of kinship would have justified Oda's separation of the couple under some systems of reckoning.[103]

It is likely that Eadwig's marriage to Ælfgifu was connected with the support he gave to other royal relatives during his reign. Ælfheah, Ælfhere and Byrhthelm may all have been related to Ælfgifu and Æthelweard, as well as to Eadwig and Edgar. Ælfheah left an estate in his will to a kinsman called Æthelweard,[104] and Ælfheah's son, Godwine, is described in the foundation charter of Eynsham Abbey as the kinsman of Æthelmær, the son of Ealdorman Æthelweard.[105] Æthelmær also endowed his foundation at Eynsham with an estate which had been left to his father by his kinsman, Bishop Byrhthelm.[106] It is therefore possible that Ælfheah, Ælfhere and Byrhthelm were also descended from King Æthelred I.[107] We seem to have here the promotion of a close-knit kin-group, comparable to the families of Athelstan Half-King and Dunstan. No wonder that those already established in power feared the promotion of this kin-group and, in particular, the marriage of Eadwig to one of its members.

But the person who had most to lose from Eadwig's marriage to Ælfgifu was Eadwig's brother, Edgar. Edgar's chances of succeeding to the throne would have been weakened considerably if Eadwig and Ælfgifu had a son. Their child would have been able to claim royal descent through both parents and so might be considered more 'throneworthy' than Edgar himself. Fraternal succession had occurred among the sons of Æthelwulf and among the sons of Edward the Elder, though the elements of accident and design which brought it about are hard to balance.[108] It may be that Edgar and others at the royal court, such as Dunstan and Oda, believed that Edgar was Eadwig's heir presumptive and that any marriage – and particularly a marriage to a woman of royal birth – was a challenge to a tacit or explicit

---

[101] For a general review of his career, see *The Chronicle of Æthelweard*, ed. A. Campbell, pp xii-xviii. Ælfgifu's will reveals that one of her brothers had a wife called Æthelflæd, and it used to be thought that a manumission by Ealdorman Æthelweard and his wife Æthelflæd provided support for the equation of Ealdorman Æthelweard with Ælfgifu's brother (Whitelock, *Wills*, p 119). However, a recent redating of the manumission makes it too late for Æthelweard the chronicler (Keynes, *Diplomas of King Æthelred*, p 192, n 139).

[102] *Chronicle of Æthelweard*, pp 38-9. 'B' says that Eadwig intended to marry either Æthelgifu or Ælfgifu (*Memorials*, p 32), and this may be an indication that it was Æthelgifu through whom the royal descent could be traced.

[103] Brooks, *Church of Canterbury*, p 225.   [104] Whitelock, *Wills*, 9, pp 22-5.

[105] S 911.   [106] *Op. cit.*, and Whitelock, 'The Appointment of Dunstan', p 235.

[107] Æthelred I had two sons, Æthelhelm and Æthelwold, but no children of either brother are definitely known. There are other members of the royal house recorded in the ninth century who could have had descendants still alive in the tenth century. They include Osferth and Oswald, both of whom are described as *filius regis* in ninth-century charters, and could be sons of one of Alfred's brothers: Keynes and Lapidge, *Alfred the Great*, p 322, n 79. Osferth seems to have been one of the most powerful ealdormen during the reign of Edward the Elder: Hart, *Charters of Northern England* p 355. Alfred's son, Æthelweard, had two sons, Ælfwine and Æthelwine, both of whom died at the battle of Brunanburh, and it is not known whether they had any children (see n 70).

[108] See Williams, 'English Royal Succession', pp 144-67 *passim*.

agreement along these lines.[109] The opposition to Eadwig's marriage may contain the key to the circumstances which culminated in Edgar becoming king of the Mercians and Northumbrians in the summer of 957.

It may always have been intended that Edgar would rule as a subking in Mercia under Eadwig. A Mercian charter of 956 describes Edgar as *regulus*,[110] and the 'D' version of the *Chronicle* states that Edgar became king in Mercia at the same time that Eadwig succeeded to the throne of Wessex.[111] In 957, Edgar became fourteen, and so could have been considered to have come of age and able to rule in his own right.[112] The 'B', 'C' and 'E' versions of the *Chronicle* record the accession of Edgar ætheling to the Mercian throne in this year, as if it was a perfectly peaceful and expected event.[113] None of the contemporary or near-contemporary sources speak of a battle or anything resembling civil war,[114] though some do hint of a crisis in 957 which Eadwig had to neutralise by concessions to those whom he had opposed. 'B', who was probably with Dunstan in Flanders at the time, relates that 'the northern people' rejected Eadwig because of his failure to listen to Dunstan and other wise counsellors, and that, as a result, 'in the witness of the whole people the state was divided between the kings as determined by wise men, so that the famous river Thames separated the realms of both'.[115] The reality of the division is shown by the witness lists of the two courts for the rest of Eadwig's reign. The bishops and ealdormen whose offices lay south of the Thames attested Eadwig's charters and those based north of the river attested Edgar's.[116] But the division of the kingdom was not as equal as 'B''s account implies, for, although Edgar ruled as 'king of the Mercians and Northumbrians', Eadwig remained *rex Anglorum*; Edgar had to recognise his brother's overriding authority.[117]

Exactly what happened in 957 remains unclear, but Edgar seems to have been able to use the bad feeling in some quarters against Eadwig, and probably the incipient nationalism of the Mercians, to draw important concessions from Eadwig which strengthened his position as heir presumptive.[118] Those whom Eadwig had opposed benefited from these developments. Eadwig was obliged to allow Dunstan to return from exile and to take up

---

[109] Although Dumville, 'The ætheling', 1-33, has shown that 'there seems to have been no regular institution of "the designated heir"' (p 33), there were some circumstances in which a successor might be chosen. The choice of Alfred as Æthelred I's *secundarius* is one of the best attested instances: *Asser's Life of King Alfred*, ed. W. H. Stevenson (Oxford, 1904, repr. 1959), ch 29, p 24.

[110] S 633, a grant by King Eadwig to the monastery of Worcester of five *cassati* at Phepson (Worcs).

[111] *Two Chronicles* I, 112-13.

[112] Williams, 'English Royal Succession', p 155. Unfortunately it is not clear whether there was a fixed time at which an Anglo-Saxon noble came 'of age'.

[113] *Two Chronicles* I, 112-13. A lawsuit records in passing that the Mercians chose Edgar as king in this year: Robertson 14, pp 90-9.

[114] All the more dramatic accounts of confrontation between the two brothers come from post-Conquest accounts, e.g. Osbearn, *Memorials*, p 102.

[115] *Memorials*, p 36, trans. *EHD*, p 901.

[116] Hart, *Charters of Northern England*, pp 322-3.

[117] *Ibid.* Bishop Æthelwold evidently regarded the division of the kingdom as Eadwig's decision and responsibility, see p 79, n 123.

[118] Williams, 'Ælfhere', 163-4.

residence in Edgar's kingdom, where he was created a bishop.[119] In 958 Archbishop Oda formally dissolved the marriage of Eadwig and Ælfgifu.[120] Although the dissolution must have been a blow to Ælfgifu's kinsmen, the positions of the most prominent members of the family were not affected adversely by the events of 957 and 958. Ælfhere retained his position as ealdorman of Mercia under Edgar, and it was in the period following the division that Ælfheah was created ealdorman of Central Wessex.[121] Nor was the balance of power changed on Eadwig's death in 959 when Edgar succeeded to the whole kingdom.[122]

The events of Eadwig's reign have necessitated a somewhat lengthy digression, but we can turn now to examine Æthelwold's position on the political crises of the period 955 to 959. At first sight, Æthelwold appears to display the hostility towards Eadwig which we would have expected from someone closely associated with Dunstan. In his own account of King Edgar's establishment of the monasteries, Æthelwold criticised Eadwig for 'the dispersal of the kingdom and division of its unity' and 'the distribution of the lands of holy churches to rapacious strangers', though criticism is tempered by the recognition that Eadwig did this through 'the ignorance of childhood'.[123] The biographers, however, give no clear indication that Æthelwold himself was one of those who suffered from a confiscation of churchlands; they merely observe that the rebuilding of Abingdon which was begun in the reign of Eadred was not completed until the reign of Edgar.[124] Other sources suggest that Eadwig was well-disposed towards Æthelwold and Abingdon. The large number of charters for Abingdon from Eadwig caused the monks of a later period to regard Eadwig as one of their greatest royal benefactors.[125] The grant of privileges which Abingdon claimed to have received from Eadwig is probably a forgery,[126] but the other charters in his

---

[119] Whitelock, 'The Appointment of Dunstan', p 233. At first Dunstan does not seem to have been appointed to any specific see. He became bishop of Worcester after the death of Cenwald (probably in 958), and by 959 was holding London as well.

[120] The 'D' version of the *Chronicle* records that 'her on þissum geare Oda arce biscop to twæmde Eadwi cyning – Ælgyfe forþæm þe hi wæron to gesybbe': *Two Chronicles* I, 113. Oda ceased attesting royal charters during 957 and witnessed only one charter of 958 (S 650). While his absence could be connected with the illness which caused his death on 2 June 958, it could also be the case that Oda was unwelcome at the royal court because of his opposition to Eadwig's marriage: Brooks, *Church of Canterbury*, pp 224-5.

[121] Hart, *Charters of Northern England*, pp 257 and 260. Williams, 'Ælfhere', 158, suggests that Ælfhere and Ælfheah followed different policies in 957, and that Ælfhere played a major part in securing Mercia for Edgar.

[122] Some leading ecclesiastics and laymen who had been prominent in Eadwig's reign did suffer under Edgar. Archbishop Byrhthelm was deposed to make way for Dunstan (Whitelock, 'Appointment of Dunstan', pp 236-47), the thegn Wulfric Cufing had an estate confiscated by Edgar (Hart, *Charters of Northern England*, pp 370-1) and another prominent thegn, Æthelgeard, abruptly ceased witnessing charters on Edgar's accession (*ibid.*, p 285).

[123] *Councils and Synods* 33, pp 142-54; trans. *EHD* p 290.

[124] Wulfstan, *Vita*, ch 11-13; Ælfric ch 7-9. Sir Frank Stenton suggested that Eadwig had vetoed Eadred's grant of a hundred royal hides of royal property based on Abingdon: F. M. Stenton, *The Early History of the Abbey of Abingdon* (Reading, 1913), pp 48-9, and see Thacker ch 2, pp 51-3.

[125] *Chron. Abingdon* I, 168.

[126] S 658. For a discussion of this charter see M. Gelling, *The Early Charters of the Thames Valley*, Studies in Early History 7 (Leicester, 1979), 93, p 51.

name have no obviously dubious features.[127] One of the charters grants a wood for the building of the church of St Mary at Abingdon, and so it would appear that the rebuilding of Abingdon continued during Eadwig's reign.[128] Eric John has assembled a body of information which suggests that it was during Eadwig's reign that Æthelwold tutored Edgar at Abingdon.[129] His discussion throws important light on relations between the two men, for Eadwig is hardly likely to have entrusted his brother's education to Æthelwold if the latter had shown him the sort of hostility which he had received from Dunstan.

Æthelwold's attitude towards Eadwig's wife, Ælfgifu, provides a clearer contrast with the policies of a number of his contemporaries in the church. For unlike Oda and Dunstan, Æthelwold appears to have recognised the marriage of Ælfgifu and Eadwig as legitimate. The only document of Eadwig's reign in which Ælfgifu is acknowledged as Eadwig's wife is an Old English memorandum from Abingdon.[130] The document records an exchange of land between Æthelwold as abbot of Abingdon and the royal kinsman Bishop Byrhthelm. The witnesses include Ælfgifu *ðaes cininges wif* and Æthelgifu *ðaes cyninges moður*. The will of Ælfgifu also suggests an alliance between Ælfgifu and Æthelwold.[131] Æthelwold and his foundations are major beneficiaries. Old Minster, New Minster and Abingdon each received an estate under the will,[132] and the Old Minster, where Ælfgifu intended to be buried, had the reversion of two other estates.[133] The residue of Ælfgifu's possessions was granted jointly to Æthelwold and the abbot of New Minster for the upkeep of their foundations and the relief of the poor. But most striking of all, is a personal legacy to Æthelwold with the injunction 'and pray him that he will always intercede for my mother and for me'.[134] The evidence in the will, in conjunction with the Abingdon memorandum, suggests that Æthelwold may have taken an active role in championing the legitimacy of the union of Eadwig and Ælfgifu, and in securing an appropriate settlement for Ælfgifu after the separation.

Æthelwold also seems to have enjoyed close relations with other members of the royal kindred who were advanced by Eadwig. His links with them can be traced from Eadwig's reign, but become more apparent during the reign of Edgar. Bishop Byrhthelm, the royal kinsman, was a patron of Abingdon; he gave an estate at Stowe (Northants) to the monastery,[135] as well as participating in the exchange of lands referred to above.[136] Ælfhere and his brothers

---

[127] S 583, 584, 605, 607 and 663. See E. John, *Orbis Britanniae, and Other Studies*, Studies in Early History 4 (Leicester, 1966), pp 158-9.
[128] S 607 – the wood was at Hawkridge (Berks).
[129] John, *Orbis Britanniae*, pp 158-60.
[130] Robertson 31, pp 58-9; S 1292.
[131] Whitelock, *Wills* 8, pp 20-3, and see above, pp 76-7.
[132] Old Minster received an estate at Princes Risborough (Bucks), New Minster an estate at Bledlow (Bucks), and Abingdon an estate at Chesham (Bucks).
[133] Mongewell (Oxon) and Berkhampstead (Herts).
[134] Æthelwold was granted an estate at *Tæfersceat* which has not been identified.
[135] *Chron. Abingdon* I, 234. The estate had been granted previously by King Eadwig to his kinsman Byrhthelm (S 615), and see n 91.
[136] See n 130. Byrhthelm exchanged land at Kennington (Berks), which he had been given by Eadwig (S 614) for land at Curbridge (Oxon) belonging to Abingdon.

were also patrons of the house,[137] and Æthelwold's appearance as a witness in royal charters, towards the end of Eadwig's reign, seems to have coincided with the appointment of Ælfheah as ealdorman of Wessex.[138] But Æthelwold's links with the family of Ælfhere are most clearly revealed by their common interest during Edgar's reign in trying to ensure the succession of one of the sons of Edgar's marriage to Ælfthryth.

When Edgar married Ælfthryth in 964 or 965, he already had an heir, Edward, who was probably the son of his first marriage to Æthelflæd Eneda.[139] Not much is known of Æthelflæd or her family, though a link with the family of Athelstan Half-King has been suggested.[140] Ælfthryth also had links with the Half-King's family, for she was the widow of Æthelwold, the Half-King's eldest son.[141] Little is known about the affiliations of Ælfthryth's own family,[142] but throughout her period as queen, and later as queen mother, Ælfthryth enjoyed an association with Æthelwold which was to their mutual advantage. Their alliance may have begun before Ælfthryth married Edgar, for Ælfthryth *matrona*, who persuaded Edgar to sell an estate at Stoke, near Ipswich, to Æthelwold, is usually assumed to have been the future queen.[143] After her marriage, Ælfthryth acted as intercessor for Æthelwold with the king on a number of occasions. As a result of an intervention which enabled Æthelwold to recover various lands and privileges of the Old Minster's estate at Taunton, Æthelwold presented her with fifty mancuses of gold 'in return for her help in his just mission'.[144] Ælfthryth gave Æthelwold an estate at Holland (Essex) for his monastery at Ely,[145] and was joint donor

---

[137] Ælfheah gave estates at Compton Beauchamp (Berks) and Farnborough (Berks) to Abingdon: *Chron. Abingdon* I, 78-9 and 157-8. Ælfhere sold an estate at Kingston (Lisle?, Berks) to Abbot Osgar of Abingdon: Robertson 51, pp 106-7, S 1216. A thegn called Eadric, whose Berkshire estates seem to have come into the possession of Abingdon, may have been their brother: Williams, 'Ælfhere', 154. Ælfhere's brother-in-law and associate, Ælfric *cild* was a major benefactor of Æthelwold's foundation of Thorney: C. Hart, *The Early Charters of Eastern England*, Studies in Early English History 5 (Leicester, 1966), pp 169-70, 178-9.

[138] S 660, a grant to New Minster (959), and S 586, a grant to Ealdorman Ælfheah (956 for 959), are both witnessed by Æthelwold in the company of other abbots. He also witnesses S 658, the dubious grant of privileges to Abingdon.

[139] Some doubt exists about the parentage of Edward. Eadmer in his *Vita Dunstani* states that Edward was the legitimate son of Edgar by Æthelflæd Eneda (*Memorials*, pp 210-14). Eadmer was particularly interested in the problem of Edward's legitimacy and instigated a special enquiry into the matter (see below, n 157), so his testimony commands respect. However, Osbearn, writing a generation before Eadmer, recorded that Edward was the result of an illegitimate liaison between Edgar and a nun of Wilton (presumably Wulfthryth, the mother of St Edith) (*Memorials*, pp 111-12).

[140] Hart, 'Athelstan "Half King"', 124 and 130.

[141] Hart, *op. cit.*, and *Charters of Northern England*, pp 272-4.

[142] Her father was Ordgar who was appointed Ealdorman of Devon soon after her marriage to Edgar (*Two Chronicles* I, 119), but nothing is known of his previous history. The name-element *Ord* is relatively rare among the West Saxon nobility of this date, and it is all the more surprising to find it also occurring in the name of Ordmær, father of Edgar's first wife, Æthelflæd. Possibly Æthelflæd and Ælfthryth were related. For information on the subsequent history of Ordgar's family, see H. P. R. Finberg, 'The House of Ordgar and the Foundation of Tavistock Abbey', *English Historical Review* 58 (1943), 190-201. For a possible link between Ælfthryth's family and Æthelwold, see n 162.

[143] *Liber Eliensis* II, 111-13; Æthelwold subsequently used the estate to endow Ely (S 781).

[144] Robertson 45, pp 92-5; S 806.

[145] *Liber Eliensis*, p 105. The estate had been given to Ælfthryth by Queen Eadgifu.

with Edgar of lands at Marsworth (Bucks)[146] and Sudbourne (Suffolk) to the same foundation.[147] Another of Æthelwold's refounded monasteries, Peterborough, preserved a tradition that Ælfthryth acquired the monastery for Æthelwold from the king. According to Hugh Candidus, Ælfthryth hid in Æthelwold's closet to find out what she could do which would help him most. When she heard Æthelwold praying to God that he should be allowed to refound Peterborough, Ælfthryth leapt out and promised to engage the king's support.[148] Ælfthryth continued to protect Æthelwold's interests after his death. In a surviving writ, she refuted a claim that Æthelwold had acquired a title deed unjustly, even though the complainant was one of her own relatives.[149]

Ælfthryth received not only Æthelwold's gratitude for her support, but more solid benefits as well, like the fifty mancuses she received for her help with the Taunton estate.[150] She was also able to win favourable terms for one of her relatives whose land was repossessed by the Old Minster.[151] The nunnery Ælfthryth founded at Wherwell (Hants) was supported by estates which seem to have been given originally to New Minster, and were no doubt transferred to Wherwell with Æthelwold's co-operation.[152] How far Æthelwold was responsible for the creation of Ælfthryth's special position as protectoress of the nunneries, in parallel to Edgar's role as protector of the monasteries, is not known, but Æthelwold's account of the reform of the monasteries and the *Regularis Concordia*, which may also be regarded as his work, are notable for the stress they place on the importance of the role of the queen.[153] The position of protectoress was not a merely nominal one, and Ælfthryth used her office to intervene in the affairs of nunneries. At Barking, for instance, Ælfthryth expelled the abbess and replaced her with a nominee of her own.[154]

But the strongest sign of Æthelwold's support for Ælfthryth is the extent to which he was prepared to campaign for the succession of one of her sons, which could only be achieved by denigrating the claim of their elder half-brother, Edward. Æthelwold's position is revealed in the grant of privileges which he obtained from King Edgar for the reformed New Minster in Winchester.[155] The privileges seem to have been drawn up, presumably by

---

[146] *Op. cit.*, p 116. The estate had belonged to Queen Ælfgifu and had been returned to Edgar in her will (see n 99).

[147] *Op. cit.*, p 111. The estate was given to Æthelwold on the condition that he made an Old English translation of the Rule of St Benedict: see above, Introduction p 6.

[148] *The Chronicle of Hugh Candidus*, ed. W. T. Mellows (Oxford, 1949), pp 27-9.

[149] F. E. Harmer, *Anglo-Saxon Writs* (Manchester, 1952), 108, pp 396-7.

[150] Robertson 45, pp 92-5.

[151] *Op. cit.* When Æthelwold recovered the large Taunton estate, Ælfthryth's kinswoman, Wulfgyth, and her husband, Leofric, stood to lose an estate. However, at Wulfgyth's request, Ælfthryth persuaded Æthelwold to allow them a life interest in the estate. The writ referred to in n 149 was occasioned by Leofric's attempt to regain permanent possession of the estate after Æthelwold's death.

[152] M. A. Meyer, 'Patronage of the West Saxon Royal Nunneries in Late Anglo-Saxon England', *Revue Bénédictine* 91 (1981), 343-5.

[153] *Councils and Synods* 33, pp 142-54, and *Regularis Concordia passim*. See Introduction, pp 6-7.

[154] M. A. Meyer, 'Women and the Tenth Century English Monastic Reform', *Revue Bénédictine* 87 (1977), 54-6.

[155] S 745; *Councils and Synods* 31, pp 119-33; John, *Orbis Britanniae*, pp 271-5, and Lapidge

Æthelwold, in 966, and to have been presented to New Minster at a major court occasion in that year, which was attended by all the bishops and ealdormen, and even by Edgar's aged great-grandmother, the dowager Queen Eadgifu. The ceremony must have taken place not long after the birth of Edmund, the first son of Ælfthryth and Edgar.[156] Edmund is included among the witnesses as *clito legitimus prefati regi filius*, and is given precedence over his elder half-brother, who is merely described as *eodem rege clito procreatus*. Ælfthryth is also given a prominent place in the document and witnesses before the bishops, after the king and archbishop. It is stressed that she is *legitimus prefati regis coniunx*.[157] At Winchester, a distinction seems to have been made between Edmund and Edward. Both were sons of Edgar, but only Edmund was *legitimus*, and his mother was Edgar's *legitima coniunx*.

Seen from this point of view, many of Æthelwold's actions which enhanced Ælfthryth's position as queen, can be interpreted primarily as attempts to advance the position of the princes who were her sons. To make Ælfthryth protectoress of the nunneries, not only gave Ælfthryth considerable personal power, but helped to distance her further from her predecessor, Edward's mother, who had not enjoyed such a privileged position.[158] The extent to which Æthelwold was prepared to put his resources at the disposal of Ælfthryth and her sons, can be illustrated from Robert Deshman's study of the political iconography of tenth-century Anglo-Saxon art.[159] Deshman has shown that the *Benedictional of St Æthelwold* contains the earliest European representation of the coronation of the Virgin as queen of heaven. In the miniature of the death of the Virgin, the hand of God is shown lowering a crown on to the Virgin's head, while an angel flies down with a sceptre. In conclusion, Deshman comments: 'the pervasive regal character in the manuscript's iconography as well as the specific resemblances to Ottonian propagandistic iconography suggests that Bishop Æthelwold, who was an important figure in King Edgar's court, might have commissioned his

---

ch 4, pp 95-6.

[156] Edgar married Ælfthryth in either 964 or 965 (*Councils and Synods* 31, p 131, n 2), and Edmund died in either 970 or 971 (*Two Chronicles* I, 118-19). This is the only charter in which Edmund appears.

[157] According to Eadmer, who had a special investigation into the subject made by Prior Nicholas of Worcester, Edward was legitimate, but had been born before his father or mother had been consecrated (*Memorials*, pp 214 and 422-4). Ælfthryth is presumably described as *legitima* in the New Minster charter because, unlike Æthelflæd, she was a consecrated queen at the time of the birth of her first son, and this was interpreted at Winchester as giving her sons a better claim to the throne (Nelson, 'Inauguration Rituals', p 65). Ælfric, the biographer and former pupil of Æthelwold, defines ætheling in such a way as to suggest that the status of the mother could affect the ætheling's standing (Stafford, 'The King's Wife', 24). That the Winchester views were not universal is shown by the events after Edgar's death (see below, pp 84-5), and by an entry in London, British Library, Cotton Tiberius B v, vol. 1, 23r, written in 969, in which Edward, Edmund and Æthelred are all described as *æthelingas syndon Eadgares suna cyninges* (Dumville, 'Ætheling', 4-5).

[158] Ælfthryth's special role was stressed at Edgar's coronation in Bath in 973. While Edgar hosted a banquet of the secular nobles and bishops, Ælfthryth presided over a similar entertainment for the abbots and abbesses. The banquet is described in the *Vita Oswaldi*: (*Hist. York* I, 438).

[159] R. Deshman, '*Christus rex et magi reges*: Kingship and Christology in Ottonian and Anglo-Saxon Art', *Frühmittelalterliche Studien* 10 (1976), 367-405, especially 397-9.

Benedictional with some political motive in mind'.[160] Æthelwold may have had more than one political interest to promote through the Benedictional, but his interest in the queen of heaven fits well with his concern to promote the cause of the contemporary queen on earth.[161] The Benedictional is the first western manuscript to depict the consecration of the queen of heaven; one of the claims of Ælfthryth's supporters was that her sons had the best claim to the throne because she was the only legitimate, that is, the only consecrated, queen of Edgar.

The origins of Æthelwold's alliance with Ælfthryth are obscure,[162] but the succession of Ælfthryth's sons was also a cause which was supported by the royal kinsmen, Ælfheah and Ælfhere. Ælfheah died in either 971 or 972, and his will seems to have been drawn up shortly before.[163] In the will, Ælfheah leaves estates to Ælfthryth *ðaes cyninges wifae*, who was one of the witnesses, and to the older and younger æthelings. To avoid any ambiguity, Ælfheah carefully defined the elder ætheling as 'the king's son and her's', i.e. Edmund. Presumably the younger ætheling was Edmund's brother, Æthelred, though this is not specified. But what is clear is that Edward was excluded altogether and Ælfheah shows through his careful definition that he did not regard him as an ætheling, a prince eligible for the throne. Ælfheah also refers to Ælfthryth as his *gefaeðeran*, which Professor Whitelock defined as a word denoting 'the relationship between godparents and parents, or between godparents of the same child'.[164] Presumably either Ælfthryth was godparent to one of Ælfheah's children, or Ælfheah was godparent to one of the æthelings. Either case reinforces the link between Ælfthryth and the family of Ælfheah. Ælfheah's kinswoman, Ælfgifu, was also close to Ælfthryth *paera hlaefdigan*, to whom she left in her will a necklace of a hundred and twenty mancuses, an armlet of thirty mancuses and a drinking-cup.[165] Ælfgifu also left an estate and an armlet of thirty mancuses to the ætheling whom she does not identify further. Ælfgifu's will was drawn up after 966, and therefore dates to after the birth of Edmund.[166] As Ælfthryth is among the beneficiaries, it is most probable that the ætheling is her son, and it would appear that Ælfgifu followed Ælfheah in not recognising the claims of Edward.

In spite of the arguments mustered by the supporters of Ælfthryth's sons, Edward did become king on Edgar's death in 975. Although Ælfthryth's surviving son, Æthelred, could number Bishop Æthelwold and Ælfhere of

[160] *Op. cit.*, p 399.

[161] Æthelwold also gives particular prominence to St Æthelthryth in the *Benedictional*. While St Æthelthryth as founder of Ely would naturally receive particular attention from Æthelwold, a parallel may have been intended between Æthelthryth and Ælfthryth: both were queens and patrons of nunneries.

[162] See n 142. In view of the rarity of the name-element *Ord*, which occurs in the names of Ælfthryth's father (Ordgar) and brother (Ordulf), it is interesting to note Ordbriht, who was a clerk at Winchester who joined Æthelwold at Abingdon and later became abbot of Chertsey and bishop of Selsey (Hart, *Early Charters of Northern England*, pp 350-1). If Ordbriht was a member of Ordgar's family, it would help to explain the alliance between Æthelwold and Ælfthryth.

[163] Whitelock, *Wills* 9, pp 24-5 and 121-5.

[164] *Op. cit.*, p 123.

[165] *Op. cit.*, 8, pp 20-3.

[166] See n 98.

Mercia among his supporters, Edward also had powerful men to back him, including Dunstan and Æthelwine of East Anglia, a son of Athelstan Half-King.[167] Dunstan was evidently unimpressed by the case Æthelwold could muster for the precedence which should be accorded to the son of a consecrated queen, and preferred to give his support to the cause which was backed by the family of Athelstan Half-King with whom he had had a long association.[168] Ælfhere seems to have reacted violently to the accession of Edward and to have attacked monastic houses which were associated with Dunstan and Æthelwine.[169] The culmination of the resistance to the new king was the murder of Edward on 18 March 978.[170] None of the sources explicitly implicate Ælfhere in the murder, though the *Vita Oswaldi* blamed the 'nobles and chief men' who supported Ælfthryth.[171] Certainly the murder brought about the result Ælfhere desired, for Æthelred succeeded to the vacant throne.

Although we know that Æthelwold had worked for the succession of Ælfthryth's sons during the reign of Edgar, we have no information about his reaction to Edward's accession or to his actions during Edward's brief reign. However, after Æthelred's succession his support for Ælfthryth, who probably played an important role during Æthelred's minority, is evident once again.[172] In 980 there was a major ceremonial occasion in Winchester to celebrate the completion of the new west front of the Old Minster, and the dedication ceremony seems to have been taken as an opportunity for a general reconciliation of the leading lay and ecclesiastical nobility.[173] It was in the period after Æthelred's succession that Æthelwold aided Ælfthryth in the foundation of Wherwell,[174] and, on at least one occasion, Ælfthryth and Æthelred stayed with Æthelwold at Ely and royal government was carried on from the monastery.[175] Æthelwold may well have been a very influential figure in the first few years of Æthelred's reign, and it may be significant that it was soon after Æthelwold's death in 984 that Æthelred asserted his independence, dismissed his mother from the court, and tried to recover some

---

[167] P. Stafford, 'The Reign of Æthelred II, A Study in the Limitations on Royal Policy and Action', *Ethelred the Unready: Papers from the Millenary Conference*, ed. D. Hill, British Archaeological Reports 59 (Oxford, 1978), pp 21-6, and Keynes, *Diplomas of King Æthelred*, pp 163-76.

[168] Various sources give Dunstan a major role in procuring the coronation of Edward: see Keynes, *op. cit.*, p 166, n 48. According to Gaimar, Dunstan had refused to recognise Edgar's marriage to Ælfthryth, and had upbraided the couple for adultery: Stafford, *op. cit.*, p 23, n 37.

[169] Fisher, 'Anti-Monastic Reaction', 254-70, and Williams, 'Ælfhere', 159-70. Although some of the sources present the disturbances during Edward's reign as a reaction to the monastic reform of Edgar's reign, secular issues seem to have been at the heart of them. The *Vita Oswaldi* presents Ælfhere and Æthelwold as being in direct confrontation (*Hist. York*, pp 399-475).

[170] For the date of Edward's murder, see Keynes, *Diplomas of King Æthelred*, p 233, n 7.

[171] *Hist. York*, p 449. The author had reasons for disliking Ælfhere, as he had attacked Oswald's foundations in the West Midlands because they impinged on his rights as ealdorman of Mercia (Williams, 'Ælfhere', pp 158-70). The evidence for the murder of Edward is judiciously reviewed by Keynes, *op. cit.*, pp 166-74.

[172] Stafford, 'The Reign of Æthelred II', p 27, and Keynes, *op. cit.*, p 176.

[173] D. J. Sheerin, 'The Dedication of the Old Minster, Winchester in 980', *Revue Bénédictine* 88 (1978), 261-73.

[174] See n 152.

[175] *Liber Eliensis*, p 146.

of his father's gifts to the monasteries.[176] When Æthelred was obliged later to renounce his mistreatment of the monasteries, he acknowledged that the death of Æthelwold had been a decisive breaking point in his reign:

> The death of Æthelwold deprived the country of one whose industry and pastoral care administered not only to my interest but also to that of all the inhabitants of the country, the common people as well as the leading men.[177]

In his support for Ælfgifu and Ælfthryth, Æthelwold departed from the political alliances of his erstwhile mentor, Dunstan, who consistently supported policies which were also favoured by the family of Athelstan Half-King. What is also striking is that, in supporting Ælfgifu and Ælfthryth, Æthelwold was obliged to take up positions which, on the basis of tenth-century canon law, could be described as questionable. Whatever may have been the motives of Oda and Dunstan in opposing the marriage of Eadwig and Ælfgifu, one cannot deny that the couple did come within the prohibited bounds of kinship, at least according to some systems of reckoning. Yet Æthelwold apparently recognised their union and seems to have gone out of the way to stress it in an Abingdon document. Nor can one easily deny that Edward the Martyr had a better claim to inherit the throne on his father's death than his two half-brothers. Although his mother had not been a consecrated queen, her marriage with Edgar seems to have been legitimate, and Æthelwold's claims to the contrary appear as opportunist special pleading. Wulfstan and Ælfric present Æthelwold as a strict disciplinarian;[178] in his expulsion of the clerks from Old Minster he took a much sterner line than the other monastic reformers did in their bishoprics.[179] Yet when involved in secular politics, Æthelwold seems to have been prepared to follow a laxer line. The reasons which took him into secular politics must have been compelling ones.

Of course, Æthelwold was not alone in his support for Ælfgifu and Ælfthryth, and we have already had occasion to remark that Æthelwold's policies were also those of Ælfhere and Ælfheah and other royal kinsmen, who were probably also related to Ælfgifu. Eadwig seems to have deliberately favoured this kin-group, and in so doing challenged the prime positions of those who had been particularly powerful in the reigns of Athelstan, Edmund and Eadred. Before the end of Eadwig's reign, Ælfhere and Ælfheah were in competition with the sons of Athelstan Half-King for the leading ealdormanries, and the rivalry of the two families seems to have resulted in open warfare during the reign of Edward the Martyr. Æthelwold's relationship with the family of Ælfhere and Ælfheah seems to have lain at the heart of his excursions into secular politics and we must seek an explanation for it.

One thing which Æthelwold did share with the kinsmen of Ælfhere was a strong association with Winchester. Æthelwold, as we have seen, was born

---

[176] Keynes, *Diplomas of King Æthelred*, pp 176-7.
[177] S 876. The translation is from Keynes, *op. cit.*, p 176.
[178] Wulfstan, *Vita*, ch 28, and Ælfric ch 19, say that Æthelwold was *terribilis ut leo* to the disobedient and undisciplined. See also Introduction, pp 11-12.
[179] P. Sawyer, 'Charters of the Reform Movement: the Worcester Archive', *Tenth-Century Studies*, pp 84-93, and Brooks, *Church of Canterbury*, pp 251-3.

in Winchester, was in the *familia* of the bishop as a young man, and later returned to Winchester as bishop. Æthelwold's severity towards the clerks of Old Minster may be accounted for by the strength of his local connections, and at least one of the clerks was apparently related to him.[180] His two immediate predecessors also had links with the family of Ælfhere. Bishop Ælfsige (951-58) described Ælfheah as *minnan leofon freond* in his will.[181] Ælfsige bequeathed a large estate at Crondall (Hants) to Ælfheah,[182] and appointed him protector of his will and guardian of his kinsmen, a role that was usually filled by the king.[183] When Ælfsige was elevated to Canterbury in 958, his successor at Winchester was Bishop Byrhthelm, a royal kinsman who also seems to have been related to Ælfhere and Ælfheah.[184] Ælfgifu was probably also a member of this kin-group. In her will she was particularly generous towards the Old Minster, where she was to be buried, but also made bequests to the two other major religious houses in Winchester.[185]

One of the controversial political issues which Æthelwold supported, the marriage of Eadwig and Ælfgifu, also received support in Winchester. The only document besides the Abingdon memorandum in which Ælfgifu was recognised as a legitimate royal wife, is the *Liber Vitae* of New Minster (Winchester).[186] Ælfgifu appears among the list of *feminarum illustrium* who were remembered in the community's prayers. She is described as *coniunx Eadwigi regis*, and the two royal widows who appear above her in the list, Ealhswith and Eadgifu, are described in the same way as the *coniuges* of Alfred and Edward. The New Minster was not new to controversy, and we have already seen how, in the reign of Athelstan, it was only in a New Minster document that Edwin, the son of Edward the Elder and Ælfflæd, was recognised as an ætheling.[187] It was also in a New Minster charter, the grant of privileges from King Edgar, that the opportunity was taken to assert that Edmund, the son of Edgar and Ælfthryth, had a better claim to the throne than his half-brother, Edward.[188]

There were three major political crises during Æthelwold's lifetime: the disputed succession on the death of Edward the Elder; the resistance to Eadwig following his marriage to Ælfgifu; and the rival claims to the throne of the sons of Edgar. Certain features link the three periods of crisis. One is the involvement of Dunstan, or members of his kin-group, in all three issues. To be sure, not much is known of their role at the time of Athelstan's succession, but the kinship of the family to Athelstan, and the favour shown to them by the king, suggest that they played a positive role on Athelstan's behalf. The family of Athelstan Half-King appears to have been in alliance with that of Dunstan. Athelstan's success saw the advancement of this family as well, and both groups suffered a diminution of influence under Eadwig. After Edgar's death, Dunstan and Æthelwine, son of the Half-King, were united in their support for Edward.

[180] See above, p 68.
[181] Whitelock, *Wills* 4, pp 16-17.
[182] This estate had been granted by King Alfred in his will to Æthelhelm, son of Æthelred I, from whom Ælfheah may have been descended: see n 107.
[183] Williams, 'Ælfhere', 149, n 30.   [184] See above, pp 75-7.
[185] See above, p 80.   [186] *Liber Vitae*, p 57.
[187] See above, pp 72-3.   [188] See above, pp 82-3.

The three crises are also linked by opposition in Winchester on all three occasions to the policies espoused by the families of Dunstan and the Half-King. Winchester is the one place where resistance to Athelstan is recorded, and where the cause of Edwin was kept alive. The marriage of Ælfgifu and Eadwig was recognised in Winchester, and the sons of Edgar and Ælfthryth were supported as his heirs in preference to their elder half-brother. On both the last issues, Winchester was acting in support of a group of royal relatives, some of whom were descended from King Æthelred I, who frequently seem to have been in direct confrontation with the families of Dunstan and the Half-King. It was the death of Ælfweard which had helped Athelstan, and the families who rose with him, to power. It seems very likely that the family of royal kinsmen, who were later in opposition to the families of Dunstan and Half-King, were supporters of Ælfweard and Edwin, and that they found their prospects weakened when Athelstan, the rival half-brother, took the throne of Wessex.

When we say that Winchester supported certain issues, we really mean that they were causes which won the support of the leading clergy of Winchester and of the leading lay families. We know regrettably little about the latter, though they may have included members of the royal kin-group discussed above. One member of a major, aristocratic, Winchester family who can be identified with certainty is Æthelwold. Although Æthelwold's support for the issues espoused by Ælfhere and Ælfheah could be interpreted as opportunism on Æthelwold's part, a desire to improve his position in the ecclesiastical hierarchy by joining himself to the rising powers of Eadwig's reign, it may be that there were older and stronger links which bound him to the descendants of Æthelred I and other royal kinsmen. Æthelwold seems to have inherited wealth and ties with the Winchester religious houses through his family: he may also have inherited political allegiances which had their roots in the rivalry between the sons of Edward the Elder in which Winchester seems to have played a significant part.

We began by contrasting the *Lives* of Dunstan and Æthelwold. Their biographers took very different attitudes to portraying their subjects in relation to the secular world, so that from reading them one receives an impression that Dunstan was far more involved in secular politics than Æthelwold. However, it appears that in life the two men were not so different after all. Æthelwold had political causes to espouse as well, and was apparently as single-minded in their pursuance as he was over the need for church reforms. As in Dunstan's life, it appears that inherited ties are likely to have played a major part in directing Æthelwold's involvement in the affairs of the royal family. Their different family backgrounds may help to explain why Æthelwold and Dunstan, who seem to have agreed on many ecclesiastical matters, followed such different, indeed opposing, lines in the political disputes which occurred between the accessions of Eadwig and Æthelred II.[189]

[189] I would like to thank Dr Simon Keynes and Dr Ann Williams for reading an earlier draft of this paper and making many helpful comments, though they bear no responsibility for the final version.

Chapter 4

ÆTHELWOLD AS SCHOLAR AND TEACHER

Michael Lapidge

The main outlines of the life of Æthelwold are well known to us from the near-contemporary hagiographies of two of his most devoted pupils and followers:[1] Wulfstan's *Vita S. Æthelwoldi* (written c.996),[2] and the somewhat later abbreviation of that *uita* by Ælfric (1006).[3] Other contemporary Winchester sources add a wealth of detail and anecdote concerning the influential bishop. Thus the *Translatio et miracula S. Swithuni*, composed at the Old Minster c.975 by Lantfred, a monk of continental (probably Fleury) origin and a colleague of Æthelwold, contains several interesting glimpses of Æthelwold at work.[4] So, too, does Wulfstan's *Narratio metrica de S. Swithuno* (composed 992 x 994, but published c.996), a hexametrical version of Lantfred's *Translatio*; although Wulfstan's poem follows the outline of Lantfred's work, it includes a number of additional eye-witness glimpses of Æthelwold and, in particular, a detailed account of Æthelwold's pro-gramme of building-works at the Old Minster.[5] In all these works Æthelwold is seen as a scholar of considerable learning and a teacher of exacting standards. Unfortunately, however, none of them gives us a satisfactory account of Æthelwold's own education and training. We know from Wulfstan that Æthelwold studied with Dunstan at Glastonbury in the 940s,[6] and that

---

[1] In spite of prevailing confusion on the question of the priority of the Wulfstan and Ælfric *uitae*, there is (in my view) no conceivable doubt that Wulfstan's is the earlier and original composition, Ælfric's a later abbreviation of it. The evidence for this view had earlier been presented by D. J. V. Fisher, 'The Early Biographers of St Æthelwold', *English Historical Review* 67 (1952), 381-91, and is set out at length by Winterbottom and Lapidge, *Wulfstan of Winchester* (as cited below, n 2). The evidence, briefly, is that the date of Wulfstan's *uita* can be fixed fairly precisely to c.996, whereas Ælfric's *uita* dates from a decade later; that in all his known Latin writings Ælfric may be seen abbreviating the work of others; and that sentence-by-sentence analysis of the two *uitae* reveals unmistakeably that Ælfric in his work preserved the sentence-structure of Wulfstan's text but persistently struck out what he regarded as its unnecessary verbiage (on Ælfric's rejection of stylistic ostentation and unnecessary verbiage, see below, p 108).
[2] I quote (by chapter number) from the edition and translation of M. Winterbottom and M. Lapidge, *Wulfstan of Winchester: The Life of St Æthelwold* (Oxford, forthcoming), a critical edition based on the five known manuscripts of Wulfstan's text as well as on the numerous later medieval redactions of the work (including Ælfric's).
[3] *Three Lives of English Saints*, ed. M. Winterbottom (Toronto, 1972), pp 17-29.
[4] I quote (by chapter number) from my forthcoming edition in *The Cult of St Swithun*, Winchester Studies 4.2 (Oxford).
[5] Wulfstan's *Narratio* is quoted from my own edition in *The Cult of St Swithun* (cited above, n 4). The account of Æthelwold's building-works is in the *Epistola specialis* (dedicated to Bishop Ælfheah), lines 35-124.
[6] Wulfstan, *Vita S. Æthelwoldi*, ch 9: 'cuius [*scil.* Dunstani] magisterio multum proficiens.'

he learned there 'skill in the liberal art of grammar and the honey-sweet system of metrics';[7] but no surviving work provides first-hand evidence of this proficiency.[8] Furthermore, we have no direct evidence concerning what books he studied, and how, and what classical and patristic literature he read. If we wish, therefore, to flesh out the skeletal information on Æthelwold's scholarly activity provided by Wulfstan, we are obliged to turn to two sorts of evidence: writings which can (with varying degrees of certainty) be attributed to Æthelwold, and the indirect view of his interests and learning which can be gleaned from the writings of his pupils.

In our search for evidence of Æthelwold's literary activity we may best begin with a curious attestation to a charter of King Edgar, issued in 966 in favour of a thegn named Ælfhelm.[9] Whereas attestations by bishops to Anglo-Saxon charters normally employ such common verbs as *roboraui*, *confirmaui*, and so on, Æthelwold's attestation is recorded by the singular and unusual verb *karessi*: 'ego Æþelwold episcopus karessi.' As far as I can discover, this verb is unique among attestations to Anglo-Saxon charters. The word itself is a coinage from the Greek χαράσσω; but instead of being derived from the latinisations of this word then current (such as *charaxo* or *craxo*),[10] the form *karessi* is seemingly based directly on the Greek word and presupposes a present-tense form **karasso*, whence *karessi* is taken to be the preterite form. The form is spurious (the termination *-essi* is not Greek) but highly revealing: it indicates that the author of this attestation had some pretence to Greek learning. And given that the form is unique, there is no obvious reason to dissociate it from Æthelwold himself.[11] In other words, this unique attestation may provide evidence that Æthelwold was a practitioner of the 'hermeneutic' style which characterises the vocabulary of much tenth-century Anglo-Latin writing.[12]

If the verb *karessi* in an attestation to one of Edgar's charters is an indication of Æthelwold's personal involvement in the production of that charter, there are grounds for looking elsewhere among Anglo-Saxon charters for evidence of Æthelwold's authorship.[13] The question of individual

---

[7] *Ibid.*: 'didicit namque inibi liberalem grammaticae artis peritiam atque mellifluam metricae rationis dulcedinem.'

[8] For an elegiac couplet possibly composed by Æthelwold, see below, p 96.

[9] S 739 (B 1175). P. Sawyer (ed.), *Charters of Burton Abbey*, Anglo-Saxon Charters II (London, 1979), no. 21.

[10] On the occurrence of this word in Insular Latin texts see M. Herren, 'Insular Latin *c(h)araxare* (*craxare*) and its Derivatives', *Peritia* 1 (1982), 273-80; as Herren notes, this form of the word is common in Anglo-Saxon charters from the reign of Athelstan onwards.

[11] One must of course exercise caution in this matter, for it would seem that, in general, verbs of attestation are used irrespective of the bishop to whom they are attached (see S. Keynes, *The Diplomas of King Æthelred 'the Unready' 978-1016: A Study in their Use as Historical Evidence* (Cambridge, 1980), p 27, n 43). Nevertheless, the uniqueness of the verb *karessi* suggests that some personal preference lies behind it; it may, indeed, indicate that Æthelwold was the draftsman of the charter, given the lexical range of the verb χαράσσω.

[12] See M. Lapidge, 'The Hermeneutic Style in Tenth-century Anglo-Latin Literature', *ASE* 4 (1975), 67-111. As I have explained on numerous occasions, the word 'hermeneutic' (first used in this context by Alistair Campbell) refers to Greek-based vocabulary drawn from glossaries of the 'Hermeneumata' type, and has nothing to do with modern *Hermeneutik* nor with hermetic seals, etc.; cf., however, the obtuse remarks of F. Barlow in *The Greatest Englishman: Essays on St Boniface and the Church at Crediton*, ed. T. Reuter (Exeter, 1980), p 28, n 35.

[13] I previously suggested ('The Hermeneutic Style', p 89) that several charters (especially S 658

authorship must be considered within the wider context of tenth-century charter production for, as Simon Keynes has noted,[14] there are some fifty tenth- and eleventh-century charters in which a formula of attestation implies some role in the drafting or copying of the charter. However, in a majority of cases the formula may simply be empty verbiage: thus in the charters of Eadwig for 956 the word *dictaui* (and its compounds) occurs frequently, usually without a direct object, and probably implies no more than *roboraui* and the like;[15] the same is probably true of the formula *dictando titulaui* which is found frequently in charters of the first half of the eleventh century.[16] When these exceptions have been made, we are left with a tiny group of charters in which the phrasing of an attestation may well imply authorship, and which merits examination. First, a charter recording a grant of Reculver by King Eadred to Christ Church, Canterbury, dated 949 and bearing this attestation by Dunstan:[17]

> Ego Dunstan indignus abbas rege Eadredo imperante hanc domino meo hereditariam kartulam dictitando conposui et propriis digitorum articulis perscripsi.

> I Dunstan, an unworthy abbot, at the command of King Eadred composed this charter of inheritance by means of dictation and copied it out with the joints of my own fingers.

The formulation of this attestation is unique among Anglo-Saxon charters and its wording is so explicit that it cannot be argued away as an empty variation of (say) *dictaui*. There is nothing in the body of the charter to arouse suspicion;[18] furthermore, Dunstan's description of himself as *indignus abbas* has a ring of authenticity, for he described himself in exactly those words in a poem undoubtedly composed by him.[19] Nevertheless, there may be grounds for doubting the authenticity of the attestation.[20] The charter survives in two single-sheet copies, neither of which — on palaeographical grounds — can be thought contemporary with 949: Canterbury, DC, Chart. Ant., R. 14,[21] probably copied during the last third of the tenth century, and London,

---

and S 673) which claimed to be 'dictated' or 'written' by Æthelwold might indeed be his productions; these suggestions are, however, invalidated by a more thorough analysis of forms of attestation in Anglo-Saxon charters (see below, pp 93-4).

[14] *Diplomas*, pp 26-8.

[15] *Ibid.*, p 63, n 113.

[16] *Ibid.*, p 27, n 43.

[17] S 546 (B 880).

[18] See P. Chaplais, 'The Anglo-Saxon Chancery: from the Diploma to the Writ', in *Prisca Munimenta: Studies in Archival & Administrative History presented to Dr A. E. J. Hollaender*, ed. F. Ranger (London, 1973), pp 43-62, at 48: 'In so far as the textual authenticity of the charter is concerned, no decisive argument against it can be advanced'.

[19] See Lapidge, 'The Hermeneutic Style', pp 108-9 (the words 'INDIGNVS ABBAS' form part of the telestich of the acrostic poem); cf. also M. Lapidge, 'St Dunstan's Latin Poetry', *Anglia* 98 (1980), 101-6, at 102.

[20] Cf. the remarks of D. Whitelock in *EHD* (first edition, London, 1955), p 341: '... the forger's motive is obvious when a document claims the sanctity of having been drawn up by St Dunstan himself'. The question is treated in detail by N. Brooks, *The Early History of the Church of Canterbury* (Leicester, 1984), pp 232-6.

[21] See *OS Facs.* I. 15.

British Library, Cotton Augustus ii. 57,[22] written in an imitative script which is difficult to date but which is probably of the eleventh century. And if neither of the surviving single-sheet copies can be thought contemporary with 949, there are grounds for regarding the document as a Canterbury forgery of the later tenth century. However, the wording of Dunstan's attestation is so explicit that the simplest explanation may be that the Canterbury forger was basing himself on a text drafted or copied by Dunstan while he was abbot of Glastonbury:[23] in which case the Reculver charter may still provide evidence of Dunstan's role in the production of charters.[24]

Another formula of attestation which merits attention is one in the name of Bishop Oswald of Worcester. It occurs in a charter of King Edgar dated 961 which survives as an original single sheet, now BL Cotton Augustus ii. 39.[25] As it stands the charter is the production of two scribes:[26] the first, who wrote the body of the charter (up to and including the bounds) in Square minuscule script; and the second, who copied the block of eight attestations following the bounds in a form (style I) of Anglo-Caroline script. The first scribe is well known to students of Anglo-Saxon diplomatic as 'Edgar A', since his work as been identified in a group of five charters of King Edgar;[27] but it is the block of eight attestations copied by the second scribe which must interest us here. All these attestations are couched in florid language, but the eighth and last attestation is particularly striking in this respect:

> Ego Oswold legis dei catascopus hoc eulogium propria manu depinxi.

> I Oswald, superintendent of God's law [i.e. bishop], fashioned this codicil (or: testament) with my own hand.

Here once again the language of the attestation is precise and is not to be dismissed as empty verbiage. The word *depinxi* probably owes its occurrence here to Aldhelm;[28] its lexical range at this time may include the process of composition (in this case, of drafting) as well as the actual scribal act of

---

[22] See *BM Facs.* III. 15. The script of Augustus ii. 57 is Anglo-Saxon Square minuscule, but is featureless and does not fit into the definable dating-patterns of Square minuscule. The most reasonable explanation of the featurelessness of the script is that it was written by an eleventh-century scribe in imitation of an earlier model. I am very grateful to David Dumville for advice on this matter.

[23] Brooks, *The Early History*, p 235.

[24] In which case the Aldhelmian language of the Reculver charter merits detailed examination, in view of the hermeneutic style of Dunstan's other writings (see Lapidge, 'The Hermeneutic Style', p 96); see further C.R.Hart, 'Danelaw Charters and the Glastonbury Scriptorium', *Downside Review* 90 (1972), 125-32, and *idem*, *The Early Charters of Northern England and the North Midlands* (Leicester, 1975), pp 18-22.

[25] S 690 (B 1066); for a facsimile see *BM Facs.* III. 23.

[26] See T.A.M.Bishop, *English Caroline Minuscule* (Oxford, 1971), p 9 and pl 11.

[27] The charters in question are S 687, 690, 703, 706 and 707; see Keynes, *Diplomas*, pp 70-9. Because two of these charters are in favour of Abingdon, 'Edgar A' has previously been considered an Abingdon scribe (see P.Chaplais, 'The Origin and Authenticity of the Royal Anglo-Saxon Diploma', in *Prisca Munimenta*, ed. Ranger, pp 28-42, at 42), but, as Keynes has stressed (*ibid.*, p 70), 'by itself this does not constitute sufficient reason for locating the scribe there'. For further discussion of S 687 see below, pp 94-5.

[28] Cf. Aldhelm, prose *De uirginitate*, ch lx: 'uenustum pudicitiae uultum componens diuersis uirtutum coloribus ... depinxi' (*Aldhelmi Opera*, ed. R.Ehwald, MGH, Auctores antiquissimi 15 (Berlin, 1919), p 321); ch xxxii: '... purpureus genarum rubor uelut stibio depinxit' (*ibid.*, p 273). Aldhelm here uses the word in its primary Classical Latin sense of 'to paint'.

copying.[29] More precise in meaning is *eulogium*. The Classical Latin form of the word is *elogium* (which here is spelled with *eu-* to give it a spurious flavour of Greek learning, on the model of words such as εὐλογία, etc.), which is a word used by Roman jurists to describe an additional or supplementary clause in a written deposition.[30] The eight attestations to Edgar's charter are just such a supplement or *e(u)logium* to his written deposition; in other words, the author of the attestation knew precisely the juridical connotations of the word *e(u)logium*. That this author was Oswald himself is suggested by the use of the extremely unusual grecism *catascopus* (κατάσκοπος).[31] That Oswald liked to describe himself in his role as bishop by outlandish grecisms is proved by his attestation as *aecclesiarches* (ἐκκλησιάρχης) in a later charter.[32] It is not surprising that Oswald should have used such grecisms, for he had at one time been a student of Frithegod, the foremost proponent of Greek-based vocabulary in tenth-century England.[33] In other words, the precise use of the term *elogium* coupled with the exceptional grecism *catascopus* suggests that it was indeed Oswald who drafted the eight attestations which are appended to this charter,[34] though it is most unlikely that it was he who copied them into the surviving single-sheet copy (Cotton Augustus ii. 39).[35]

If Dunstan and Oswald were involved in the drafting of royal charters, there is reason to suspect that Æthelwold – who was *a secretis* with King Edgar[36] – was similarly involved. The evidence is less decisive than in the cases of Dunstan and Oswald, but it is worth reviewing. One might recall at the outset Æthelwold's attestation of S 739 discussed above – namely the unique form *karessi* – which could conceivably mean either 'I drafted' or 'I copied'. But unfortunately the charter is preserved only in a thirteenth-century cartulary, so we have no way of knowing whether he 'copied' the

---

[29] See *Dictionary of Medieval Latin from British Sources*, ed. R. E. Latham and D. R. Howlett (Oxford, 1975-), s.v. 'depingere'.

[30] See *Oxford Latin Dictionary*, ed. P. G. W. Glare (Oxford, 1968-80), s.v. 'elogium, 2.'; and note the example there cited from Ulpian: 'idcirco elogium huic edicto subiectum est'. This is precisely the meaning which *e(u)logium* bears in the Oswald attestation; cf. however E. John, *Orbis Britanniae and other Studies* (Leicester, 1966), p 83: '*Eulogium* is a synonym for *singrapha* and is another pompous word meaning diploma.' It is nothing of the sort.

[31] It occurs here in Anglo-Latin for the first time; its occurrences in two charters of later composition (S 673 = B 1047 and S 811 = B 1319) are indebted to the Oswald attestation here in S 690.

[32] S 1341 (K 625); the subsequent occurrence of the word in S 1384 (K 1313) is clearly indebted to its occurrence here; otherwise the word *ecclesiarches* is not recorded in Anglo-Latin sources.

[33] *Chronicon Abbatiae Rameseiensis*, ed. W. D. Macray, RS (London, 1886), p 21: 'cuidam uiro Frithegodo nomine, qui omnium sui temporis, ut putabatur, in Anglia tam seculari quam diuina scientia peritissimus habebatur, traditus est instruendus [*scil.* Oswald]'. On Frithegod's excessive use of grecisms see Lapidge, 'The Hermeneutic Style', pp 78-81.

[34] These same eight attestations recur verbatim in two other charters ostensibly issued in the same year, namely S 688 (B 1067) and S 689 (B 1080), both of which, however, survive only in cartulary copies and are not above suspicion. The block of eight attestations does not otherwise occur outside Edgar's charters of 961; and recall that this was the year in which Oswald was first elevated to the episcopacy.

[35] The scribe who copied the eight attestations into Augustus ii. 39 committed a number of spelling errors (*priamus* for *primas*, *blebi* for *plebi*, *trofheum* for *tropheum*) which are unlikely to stem from Oswald himself.

[36] Wulfstan, *Vita S. Æthelwoldi*, ch 25.

(lost) original; and there is otherwise nothing exceptional in the wording of this charter which could serve as the basis for stylistic analysis. Other charters which claim to be the production of Æthelwold are open to various doubts. Thus a charter dated 955 according to which King Eadred grants Abingdon to Æthelwold is subscribed by Æthelwold in the words 'ego Adeluuold prefati cenobii abbas congaudens dictaui';[37] but the charter is spurious and the formula *congaudens dictaui* is so widespread that it can carry no implication of Æthelwold's authorship.[38] Similarly a charter of Edgar dated 964 is attested by Æthelwold in the words 'ego Athelwold Wintoniensis ecclesie episcopus hanc cartam dictitans rege suisque precipientibus perscribere iussi';[39] but again, as Simon Keynes has shown, this formula occurs frequently in charters between 963 and 1028, and hence no strong arguments concerning authorship can be based on it.[40] Æthelwold is also alleged as the author of two similar charters from the Abingdon cartularies, the first of which (dated 959) is witnessed in the words 'ego Æþelwold abbas hoc eulogium manu propria apicibus depinxi',[41] where the formula of attestation has evidently been lifted from that of Oswald discussed above, and the second of which (dated 958 for 959) bears the attestation 'ego Æþeluuold abbas Abbendunensis cenobii hoc sintagma triumphans dictaui'.[42] These two Abingdon charters belong to a larger group of five charters, all of which begin with the word 'Orthodoxorum' and all of which are forgeries based on an authentic charter of King Æthelred dated 993.[43] No reliance can be placed on their claim to be the productions of Æthelwold, therefore. The final attestation which claims to be the production of Æthelwold takes us back to the previously mentioned 'Edgar A' charters. One of the 'Edgar A' charters – S 687, the earliest of the five – bears the following attestation by Æthelwold: 'ego Aþelwold abbas depinxi'.[44] The charter is dated 960 and is preserved as an original single sheet.[45] We have seen that the word *depinxi* could refer either to the act of drafting or of copying. There is no reason to assume that Æthelwold *copied* the charter, and hence that he is identical with the scribe known at 'Edgar A';[46] but there may be reason to think that he drafted it. Æthelwold is a witness to all the charters copied by 'Edgar A', but only in S 687 does his attestation contain the word *depinxi*; furthermore,

---

[37] S 567 (B 906); the charter is preserved only in the twelfth-century *Chronicon monasterii de Abingdon*.

[38] See Keynes, *Diplomas*, p 26 and n 38.

[39] S 730 (B 1138, K 513).

[40] *Diplomas*, pp 26-7 and n 39. The earliest charter in which the formula occurs is S 712 (B 1112) dated 963; there the formula is attached to Bishop Athulf and Æthelwold is not among the witnesses.

[41] S 658 (B 1046, K 1224).

[42] S 673 (B 1047, K 1221). Note that Bishop Æthelstan here attests in the words lifted from Oswald's attestation ('ego Æþelstan legis Dei catascopus hoc eulogium propria manu depinxi'), where the forger has not understood the precise connotation of Oswald's term *e(u)logium*.

[43] The others are S 786 (B 1282), 788 (B 1284) and 812 (B 1187). The charter of Æthelred on which they are based is S 876 (K 684); see Keynes, *Diplomas*, pp 98-9.

[44] S 687 (B 1055, K 481).

[45] *BM Facs*. III. 22.

[46] R. Drögereit ('Gab es eine angelsächsische Königskanzlei?', *Archiv für Urkundenforschung* 13 (1935), 335-436, at 416) made the suggestion that Æthelwold was identical with 'Edgar A', but there is no hard evidence which could be adduced in support of the suggestion.

S 687 stands apart from the others in the group in respect of its diplomatic formulae, some of which were adapted from charters of the 940s and 950s.[47] Thus, although there is nothing exceptional about the wording of S 687, its claim to be drafted by Æthelwold may be genuine.

Concerning the authorship of one very famous royal charter there is much presumption in favour of Æthelwold, but no decisive evidence. This is the so-called 'New Minster Foundation Charter',[48] an extensive document which is preserved as BL Cotton Vespasian A. viii, a lavish manuscript of thirty-two folios (that is, four quires of eight); the text of the charter (3v-33v), copied in gold lettering, is preceded by an illumination showing King Edgar, flanked by the Virgin and St Peter, offering his charter to Christ seated on high (2v) and by an elegiac couplet describing Edgar's adoration of Christ (3r).[49] The form of the charter, which bears the date 966 and which was intended to record the king's establishment of Benedictine monks at the New Minster, is unique among Anglo-Saxon charters.[50] So too is the text, which in broad outline follows the normal structure of an Anglo-Saxon charter (with pictorial and verbal invocation, proem, dispositive section, blessing and sanction, dating clause and witness-list), but which is much amplified by, for example, the inclusion of a long section (chs xii-xiii) on how the monks are to behave in accordance with the *Regula S. Benedicti*, and by a lengthy rhetorical elaboration in rhyming prose of what in a normal charter would be the invocation:

> Fruebatur letabundus creatoris tripud*io*. et angelorum alacriter
>   utebatur consort*io*.
> Non eum corporalis debilitabat inbecill*itas*. nec animi affligebat
>   anxi*etas*.
> Non typo leuis raptabatur superb*ie*. sed suo se coniungens auctori
>   humilis pollebat mirif*ice*.
> Non eum inanis tumidum uexabat gl*oria*. sed deuotum creatoris
>   magnificabat mem*oria* (ch ii).

This is possibly the earliest surviving example of rhyming Latin prose from Anglo-Saxon England.[51] In keeping with the flamboyance of the prose in this document is its lavish display of grecisms: *basileus* (vi), *carisma* (xv), *cataclisma* (iv), *cosmus* (i), *macrobius* (iii), *melancolia* (xii), *policrates* (ii), *singraphe* (xxii), *thema* (prol.) and *tirannos* (xiv). Some of these words –

[47] Keynes, *Diplomas*, p 71.
[48] S 745 (B 1190, K 527); also ptd *Councils and Synods*, pp 119-33.
[49] There is a description of the manuscript and its illumination in F. Wormald, 'Late Anglo-Saxon Art: Some Questions and Suggestions', in his *Collected Writings I: Studies in Medieval Art from the Sixth to the Twelfth Century*, ed. J. J. G. Alexander, T. J. Brown and J. Gibbs (London, 1984), pp 105-10, at 108-10 and pls 96-8.
[50] Wulfstan (*Vita S. Æthelwoldi*, ch 21) records the fact that Æthelwold produced for Abingdon a 'book of privileges' which was 'sealed with gold leaves' (*laminis aureis sigillata*) – that is, presumably, written like Vespasian A. viii in gold lettering – but this book has not survived.
[51] See, in general, K. Polheim, *Die lateinische Reimprosa* (Berlin, 1925), who does not, however, discuss Anglo-Latin authors. Excepting the New Minster charter, the earliest example of Anglo-Latin rhyming prose is found in Lantfred's *Translatio et miracula S. Swithuni*, composed at the Old Minster c.975. One wonders if there is a connection between the use of rhyming prose in the New Minster charter and Lantfred's presence at Winchester; but we have no means of knowing if he was there as early as 966. There are other links between the prose of Æthelwold and Lantfred; see below, p 97.

such as *macrobius* (μαϰϱόβιος, 'long-lived') and *policrates* (πολυϰϱατής, 'very mighty') – are exceptionally rare. Bearing in mind Æthelwold's delight in grecisms revealed in his *karessi*-attestation, it is worth looking further for evidence of his hand in the production of the New Minster charter. First, there is his lengthy and unusual attestation:

> Ego Aþelwold, ecclesie Wintoniensis episcopus, regis gloriosissimi beniuolentiam abbatem mea altum mediocritate et alumnos quos educaui illi commendans crucis signaculo benedixi.

> I Æthelwold, bishop of the church of Winchester, blessed the generosity of the glorious king [Edgar] with the sign of the cross, commending to him the abbot [Æthelgar] raised by my humble self, as well as the pupils whom I trained.

The unusual nature of this attestation, with its insistence that it was Æthelwold who 'raised' the abbot of the New Minster (that is, Æthelgar) and 'trained' the monks who were to be installed there, has suggested to previous commentators that it was Æthelwold himself who drafted the New Minster charter.[52] And if it was Æthelwold who drafted it, then the elegiac couplet which precedes the body of the charter acquires a special interest, for although we know from Wulfstan that Æthelwold was a skilled metrician, no surviving Latin verse of his has as yet been identified. The elegiac couplet is as follows:

> Sic celso residet solio qui condidit astra;
>   rex uenerans Eadgar pronus adorat eum.

The couplet is too brief to allow any conclusions to be drawn about Æthelwold's metrical technique;[53] its importance lies solely in the suspicion that it may have been composed by him. In any case this suspicion receives some confirmation from the various links between the New Minster charter itself and other documents associated with Æthelwold.

One such document is a curious letter preserved as part of the letter-collection in BL Cotton Tiberius A. xv (? Canterbury, s. xi^in).[54] The letter in question is addressed by a bishop who describes himself as 'ego sancti .N.

---

[52] See Wormald, 'Late Anglo-Saxon Art', pp 109-10; John, *Orbis Britanniae*, pp 271-5, esp. 273, n 1; D. Whitelock, 'The Authorship of the Account of King Edgar's Establishment of Monasteries', in *Philological Essays: Studies in Old and Middle English Language and Literature in Honour of Herbert Dean Meritt*, ed. J. L. Rosier (The Hague, 1970), pp 125-36, at 131-2; and Keynes, *Diplomas*, p 81, n 163.

[53] One distich is not enough on which to base conclusions about the poet's training, but it should be noted that he was apparently familiar with the diction of Vergil and the Late Latin poets; note, for the hexameter, the phrases in Prudentius, *Psychomachia* 875 ('Hoc *residet solio* pollens Sapientia') and Vergil, *Ecl.* II.61 ('*condidit* arces', where *condidit* occurs in the fifth foot, as here); and for the words *pronus adorat* in the pentameter, Caelius Sedulius, *Carmen Paschale* II.193 ('*pronus adoraret*, cuius super aethera sedes') and Alcimus Avitus, *Carm.* I.143 ('factorem *pronus adora*').

[54] The collection is partly printed by Stubbs, *Memorials*, pp 354-404. Stubbs prints only the English letters from the collection, but the collection as a whole deserves attention; cf. the remarks of C. Hohler, *Tenth-Century Studies*, p 74, who describes the collection as the 'one major monument of scholarship from the period'.

confessoris atque pontificis coenobii archimandrita et gratia Dei antistes' to someone who is described as a count or duke (*marc<h>ioni*) and who is said to be 'adorned with the apex of the dukedom' (*ducatus apice adornato*).[55] The letter concerns two clerics 'grown old in wickedness' who stole a certain gospel-book from the church in question (described once again as a *coenobium*) and then sold it to the count for three mancuses; the bishop asks the count to return the book. Who is the bishop and who is the count? The bishop is clearly writing from England (the letter is being delivered through the agency of the bishop of Sherborne). In the late tenth century (the date is controlled by the date of the manuscript) there were four English cathedrals which were also monastic: the Old Minster, Winchester, as established by Æthelwold; Worcester, where Oswald soon followed Æthelwold's example; Christ Church, Canterbury; and Sherborne.[56] But the church in question was dedicated to a confessor who was also a bishop; and of these, Christ Church was dedicated to the Saviour, and Worcester and Sherborne were both dedicated to St Mary. The Old Minster, however, although formally dedicated to SS. Peter and Paul, was, after the translation of St Swithun in 971, widely known as the church of St Swithun; and St Swithun was both a bishop and a confessor. It is likely, therefore, that the author of the letter was the bishop of Winchester. And given that Æthelwold had expelled the secular clerics from the Old Minster in 964, it would hardly be surprising if two of them should have absconded with a gospel-book which Æthelwold, some years later, was doing his best to reclaim.[57] (The identity of the count is less easy to ascertain.)[58] In any case there are several features in the letter which link it to other Winchester writings of the time.[59] The style of the letter is much indebted to Aldhelm for its phrasing[60] and the author also uses occasional alliteration which he may have learned from

---

[55] *Ibid.*, pp 361-2.

[56] See D. Knowles, *The Monastic Order in England*, 2nd edn (Cambridge, 1963), p 621.

[57] If Æthelwold *is* the author of the letter, it must date between 971 and 984 (it can hardly date before 15 July 971, for it was on that day that St Swithun was translated, and the church could not have been described as 'St Swithun's' before then).

[58] The letter provides a few clues: he is addressed by the title *marc<h>io*; he is said to be *utriusque uitae ... ornamentis insignito*, which implies that he had some clerical status, probably that of a lay-abbot; and he is said to have Danes/Vikings living in his territories (*a Danis uestris*). (The original letter contained the name of the villa or estate where the gospel-book was purchased by the count, but this name has dropped out in transmission.) Probably a count of Flanders is in question, for in the tenth century the counts of Flanders used the title *marchio* in their diplomas and were lay-abbots of St Bavo's, Ghent. Stubbs (*Memorials*, p 361, n 1) conjectured Count Arnulf I of Flanders (918-65), but this conjecture is unlikely in view of the fact that St Swithun was not translated until 971. During the period 971 x 984 the count of Flanders was Arnulf II (965-88), and he is the probable addressee; however, the claims of the counts of Normandy and Brittany also deserve attention.

[59] Note that the phrase *utriusque uitae* is used in an anonymous letter sent from Fleury to Dunstan at Winchester (*Memorials*, p 376). I have argued at length in *The Cult of St Swithun* that the author of this letter, who refers to himself as .L., is to be identified with Lantfred, on the grounds that the letter is in rhyming prose and that it shares a number of features of diction and vocabulary with Lantfred's *Translatio et miracula S. Swithuni*.

[60] The phrase *rumor ... percrebrescit* is from Aldhelm's Letter to King Geraint of *Dumnonia* (*rumor ... percrebruit*: *Aldhelmi Opera*, ed. Ehwald, p 482); the antithesis *quod plurimorum est ... quod paucorum est* is from the salutation of the prose *De uirginitate* (*ibid.*, p 228). The word *archimandrita* is also Aldhelmian (*ibid.*, pp 242 and 287).

Aldhelm (e.g. *plagas passim peruolitans percrebrescit* or *cadentibus culmini-busque carie confractis*). More interesting are the grecisms in the letter, in particular the phrase *pro policrati amore pantorumque agiorum* ('for the love of the Mighty One and of all saints'). The use of the word *policrates* here is a strong link with the New Minster charter, for the word is otherwise unattested in Anglo-Latin sources. Also suggestive is a verbal link with the *Regularis concordia*.[61]

We are on somewhat firmer ground with respect to Æthelwold's author-ship of the *Regularis concordia*.[62] In the first place, Ælfric produced for his monks at Eynsham (shortly after 1005) an abbreviated and modified redaction of the *Regularis concordia* that is known as Ælfric's 'Letter to the Monks of Eynsham';[63] and in the preface to that 'Letter' Ælfric explained that the *Regularis concordia* had been compiled in the first instance by Æthelwold: 'ideoque haec pauca de libro consuetudinum, quem sanctus Athelwoldus Wintoniensis episcopus cum coepiscopis et abbatibus tempore Eadgari felicissimi regis Anglorum undique collegit'.[64] Secondly, the *prohemium* of the *Regularis concordia* explains that King Edgar had been taught by 'a certain abbot': *abbate quodam assiduo monente* (c. 1 [1]). One might ask who the abbot was and why he was not named. From Byrhtferth's *Vita S. Oswaldi* we learn unambiguously that Edgar had received his instruction from Æthelwold: 'instructus idem rex ad cognitionem ueri regis ab Æthelwoldo sanctissimo episcopo Wintoniensis ciuitatis';[65] given this information, it becomes clear that Æthelwold had refrained from naming himself as Edgar's instructor out of simple modesty. The *Regularis concordia*, then, was writ-ten by Æthelwold. Of course in the work of compilation Æthelwold drew on the advice of others; he states in the *prohemium* (c. 5 [5]) that he had laid under contribution the advice of monks from Fleury and Ghent ('accitis Flor<iac>ensis beati Benedicti necnon praecipui coenobii quod celebri Gent nuncupatur uocabulo monachis'). Although he does not name his advisers we can easily guess their identity: of monks from Fleury Æthelwold was in immediate contact with his disciple Osgar, who had studied at Fleury, and with Lantfred, a foreign monk who had probably come to Winchester from Fleury and who subsequently returned there;[66] of monks from Ghent, recall that Womar, an abbot of St Peter's in Ghent, spent some time among Æthelwold's *familia* at the Old Minster where he was remembered with

[61] The description of the dilapidated monasteries rebuilt by the count (*Memorials*, p 362: 'insuper etiam *coenobia* et delubra, maceriis penitus cadentibus culminibusque carie confractis solotenus iam *diruta*') recalls the opening of the *Regularis concordia* (ch 2 [2]: 'sacra *coenobia* diuersis sui regiminis locis *diruta*').

[62] Ed. T. Symons and S. Spath in *Consuetudinum saeculi X/XI/XII monumenta non-Cluniacensia*, ed. K. Hallinger, Corpus Consuetudinum Monasticarum 7.3 (Siegburg, 1984), pp 61-147; this edition now supersedes that of T. Symons, *Regularis Concordia* (London, 1953). I quote (by chapter number) from the new edition of Symons and Spath, but give references to chapter numbers of Symons's earlier edition in square brackets.

[63] 'Ælfrici abbatis epistula ad monachos Egneshamnenses directa', ed. H. Nocent, in *Con-suetudinum saeculi X/XI/XII monumenta non-Cluniacensia*, pp 149-85; this edition (from which I quote) supersedes that of M. Bateson in *Compotus Rolls of the Obedientiaries of St Swithun's Priory, Winchester*, ed. G. W. Kitchin (London and Winchester, 1892), pp 171-98.

[64] 'Ælfrici abbatis epistula', ed. Nocent, p 155.

[65] *Hist. York* I, pp 426-7.

[66] See above, n 59.

special affection.[67] But although Æthelwold mentions Ghent – no doubt out of deference to Womar - it was the monastic customs of Fleury which left the deepest impress on the *Regularis concordia*.[68] Recent scholarship has been able to throw entirely new light on the sources of the *Regularis concordia*, largely through the discovery, in a Wolfenbüttel manuscript, of a monastic customary by one Theodoric or Thierry, who was a monk at Fleury until he moved to Amorbach in 1002.[69] So closely does Theodoric's customary correspond to parts of the *Regularis concordia* that there can no longer be any doubt that in his work of compilation Æthelwold was directly influenced by the customs of Fleury.[70] Much of the *Regularis concordia* may be derivative, therefore. However, in the *prohemium* Æthelwold was not following a written source, and this part of the work accordingly allows us to form some opinion of Æthelwold's accomplishments as a writer of Latin prose. We can see at once that his prose is informed by a thorough familiarity with Aldhelm.[71] From Aldhelm, too, Æthelwold probably learned the use of occasional alliteration[72] as well as the use of unusual vocabulary, especially adverbs.[73] The *prohemium* also reveals that Æthelwold was familiar with the diction of Christian-Latin poetry, for he uses a number of words and phrases in his prose which more naturally pertain to verse.[74] It is also interesting that the

---

[67] *Liber Vitae: Register and Martyrology of New Minster and Hyde Abbey, Winchester*, ed. W. de G. Birch (London and Winchester, 1892), p 24: 'Domnus abba Womarus qui olim coenobio Gent prelatus hanc deuotus adiit gentem huiusque se familie precibus humillime commendauit.' Womar's death is recorded in the Anglo-Saxon Chronicle, s.a. 981 C: '₇ on þam ylcan geare forðferde Womær abbot on Gent' (*Two Chronicles* I, p 124). On Womar's abbacy at Ghent (he had been abbot of St Peter's from 953 onwards) see P. Grierson, *Les annales de Saint-Pierre de Gand et de Saint-Amand* (Brussels, 1937), pp xvi, 19 and 21.

[68] Earlier studies which stressed the influence of the reforms of Gerhard of Brogne (e.g. H. Dauphin, 'Le renouveau monastique en Angleterre au Xe siècle et ses rapports avec la réforme de S. Gérard de Brogne', *Revue Bénédictine* 70 (1960), 177-96) and of the Lotharingian customaries (e.g. T. Symons, '*Regularis Concordia*: History and Derivation', *Tenth-Century Studies*, pp 37-59) require correction in light of the discovery and publication of the late tenth-century customary by Theodoric of Fleury: see below.

[69] See, in particular L. Donnat, 'Recherches sur l'influence de Fleury au Xe siècle', in *Études ligériennes d'histoire et d'archéologie médiévales*, ed. R. Louis (Auxerre, 1975), pp 165-74. Theodoric's customary, known as the *Consuetudines Floriacenses antiquiores* (symbol: Th) is edited by A. Davril and L. Donnat, *Consuetudinum saeculi X/XI/XII monumenta non-Cluniacensia*, ed. Hallinger, pp 3-60.

[70] See discussion in *Consuetudinum saeculi X/XI/XII monumenta: Introductiones*, ed. K. Hallinger, Corpus Consuetudinum Monasticarum 7.1 (Siegburg, 1984), pp 331-93.

[71] The following phrases in the *prohemium* derive from Aldhelm's prose *De uirginitate*: *Christi opitulante gratia* (chs 1 [1] and 8 [8]; cf. *Aldhelmi Opera*, ed. Ehwald, p 282); *erectis ad aethera palmis inmensas ... grates* (ch 4 [4]; cf. Ehwald, p 229); *praesago afflatus spiritu* (ch 7 [7]; cf. Ehwald, p 286); and *tyrannidem potentatus* (ch 7 [7]; cf. Ehwald, p 251). The words *conciliabulum* (ch 9 [9]) and *delitesco* (ch 1 [1]) are Aldhelmian, as is the image of bees gathering honey from flowers (ch 5 [5]).

[72] Note, for example, the phrases 'sine ullo suspicionis scrupulo subueniret' (ch 3 [3]) and 'imperitia impediente uel peccatis promerentibus' (ch 9 [9]; cf. also above, p 98).

[73] Note the forms *inconsiderate* (ch 8 [8]), *praesumptuose* (ch 8 [8]), *probrose* (ch 4 [4]) and *suapte* (ch 6 [6]). Curiously, there are very few grecisms in the *prohemium*; but cf. below, n 75.

[74] The phrase *iusto moderamine* (ch 15 [14]) is one used by Juvencus (*Evang.* II.575) and Aldhelm (*CdV* 831); and the phrase *toto mentis conamine* (ch 5 [5]) is a reordered version of Aldhelm's cadence *toto conamine mentis* (*CdV* 89). Note that the same phrase – in the form in which it occurs in the *Regularis concordia* – is found in a poem which originated in Æthelwold's school at Winchester and is possibly the work of Lantfred, namely 'De libero arbitrio', line 171: 'quapropter *toto mentis conamine* poscens' (M. Lapidge, 'Three Latin Poems from Æthelwold's

Latin of the *Regularis concordia* has links with that of Lantfred,[75] as also with the language of Anglo-Saxon diplomatic.[76]

The *prohemium* of the *Regularis concordia*, then, reveals Æthelwold as a proficient Latinist, familiar with the language of Aldhelm and of Christian-Latin poetry, having a flair for flamboyant vocabulary and other stylistic embellishments such as alliteration. Various recognisable features of the style and vocabulary of the *Regularis concordia* are found again in the New Minster foundation charter and in the letter to the unnamed count concerning the stolen gospel-book, which strengthens the suspicion (though it does not constitute proof) that they too are by Æthelwold. From the *Regularis concordia*, too, we discover that Æthelwold's modesty prevented him – on at least one occasion – from claiming the authorship of a work he had composed. It is possible that there are other anonymous Latin writings from this period which remain to be identified as the work of Æthelwold. In this connection it is worth recording that the twelfth-century *Chronicon monasterii de Abingdon* contains a Latin prayer for the protection of Abingdon said to have been composed there by Æthelwold before his departure for Winchester:

> Deus eterne, ante cuius conspectum assistunt angeli et cuius nutu reguntur uniuersa, protege Domine, queso, locum istum qui in nomine tuo et beate Marie constructum est; et per uirtutem nominis tui recedat ab eo uirtus inimicorum umbraque phantasmatum et incursio turbinum, percussio fulminum, lesio tonitruum, calamitas tempestatum omnisque spiritus procellarum. Preterea queso, Domine, ut non ignis domum istam consumat, nec homo inimicus per superbiam eam destruat; sed tu, piissime Deus, conserua eam et guberna, multiplicique fructuum ubertate pinguescat, ut omnes habitantes in ea uoce et corde te hymnizent et suaui modulatione nomen tuum magnificent et super eos descendat benedictio tua et super locum istum maneatque semper. Per Dominum nostrum.[77]

The tradition that Æthelwold composed this prayer at Abingdon is credible enough, although there is nothing particularly striking in its diction which

School at Winchester', *ASE* 1 (1972), 85-137, at 136).
[75] The compound *cuncticreans* (ch 15 [14]) is also used by Lantfred (Praef.), but is otherwise extremely rare. I also suspect that the unusual grecism *cecaumen* ('heat') which is used by Lantfred on one occasion (ch 3; the word probably derives from Martianus Capella, *De nuptiis* I. 17) lies behind the corruption *caumene* in ch 40 [29], and that the passage should be emended so as to read 'locus aptus fratribus designetur, cuius *cecaumenes* refugio hibernalis algor et intemperiei aduersitas leuigetur' ('a place suitable for the monks should be allocated so that through the refuge of its heat the winter cold and inclement weather may be alleviated'). The emendation, if accepted, would constitute a further link between the *Regularis concordia* and Lantfred, and would help to confirm my earlier suggestion that Lantfred was one of the monks 'summoned from Fleury' who advised Æthelwold on monastic customs when he was drawing up the *Regularis concordia*.
[76] The phrase *tam in modicis rebus quam magnis* (ch 15 [14]) seems to be a reflection of a phrase in the New Minster charter, 'possessio in rebus magnis uel modicis' (ch xvii), but such phrasing is not infrequent in tenth-century charters. At the least it suggests that Æthelwold was familiar with the language of diplomatic, which in turn may strengthen the suggestions made earlier that Æthelwold may have had a hand in drafting some of Edgar's charters.
[77] *Chron. Abingdon* I, pp 347-8.

could confirm the attribution on stylistic grounds. Further research on the subject of Æthelwold's Latin writings may perhaps alter this picture.[78]

Latin composition was only one aspect of Æthelwold's literary activity. Wulfstan tells us that 'it was always agreeable to him to teach young people, translating Latin texts into English for them'.[79] That Æthelwold on at least one occasion undertook a substantial project of translation is clear from a passage in the twelfth-century *Liber Eliensis*. There we learn that King Edgar and Queen Ælfthryth granted Æthelwold an estate at Sudbourne 'on the condition that he should translate the *Regula S. Benedicti* from Latin into English'.[80] Now in some eight manuscripts and fragments there survives an Old English translation of the *Regula S. Benedicti*, and although the work is presented anonymously in manuscript, scholars are in agreement that the translation is Æthelwold's.[81] Since the work was commissioned by Edgar and Ælfthryth who were married in 964, and since Edgar died in 975, the dates 964 x 975 probably constitute the outer dating termini for the work of translation. The very great interest of Æthelwold's translation as a piece of scholarship has been established by the important researches of Mechthild Gretsch.[82] As she has demonstrated, Æthelwold for the most part stays very close to the Latin text of the *Regula*, only departing from it occasionally so as to emphasise the importance of the *opus Dei*, the monastic vows or the monks' duties to the poor, or to clarify an ambiguous passage in the Latin.[83] Occasionally these departures incorporate comments from the ninth-century *Expositio in Regulam S. Benedicti* of Smaragdus of Saint-Mihiel, which indicates that Æthelwold had the Smaragdus commentary beside him as he worked through the *Regula*.[84] It is not clear how much Æthelwold relied on such aids to understanding the text; what is clear is that his translation is

---

[78] There is one respect in which the canon of Æthelwold's writings may be clarified. The antiquary John Leland in his *Commentarii de scriptoribus Britannicis* attributed to Æthelwold a treatise on astronomy: 'ipse [*scil.* Æthelwold] vero in mathesi non leviter eruditus, opus elimatum et rotundum de Planetis, Regionibus et Climatibus Mundi, tanquam victurum ingenii monumentum, posteritati reliquit' (ed. A. Hall, 2 vols (Oxford, 1709), I, p 164); and this information is repeated by Pits *et al.* Leland had possibly seen a manuscript containing the well-known letter by Adelbold of Utrecht on the quadrature of the circle addressed to Pope Silvester II (999-1003), and confused the names Æthelwold and Adelbold. Adelbold's Letter is printed by N. Bubnov, *Gerberti postea Silvestri II papae opera mathematica* (Berlin, 1899), pp 299-309 and has nothing to do with our Æthelwold. The point is worth stressing because R. N. Quirk ('Winchester Cathedral in the Tenth Century', *Archaeological Journal* 114 (1957), 26-68, at 30, n 1), having in mind Leland's observation, draws attention to a copy of Adelbold's letter in Oxford, Bodleian Library, Digby 83, and associates it mistakenly with Æthelwold.

[79] *Vita S. Æthelwoldi*, ch 31: 'dulce namque erat ei adolescentes et iuuenes semper docere, et Latinos libros Anglice eis soluere'.

[80] *Liber Eliensis*, p 111: '... eo pacto ut ille regulam sancti Benedicti in Anglicum idioma de Latino transferret'.

[81] Ed. A. Schröer, *Die angelsächsischen Prosabearbeitungen der Benediktinerregel*, 2nd edn rev. with supplement by H. Gneuss (Darmstadt, 1964); for discussion of Æthelwold's authorship, see pp xiii-xviii and 269-72.

[82] *Die Regula Sancti Benedicti in England und ihre altenglische Übersetzung*, Texte und Untersuchungen zur englischen Philologie 2 (Munich, 1973); 'Æthelwold's Translation of the *Regula Sancti Benedicti* and its Latin Exemplar', *ASE* 3 (1974), 125-51; and 'Die Winteney-Version der *Regula Sancti Benedicti*: eine frühmittelenglische Bearbeitung der altenglischen Prosaübersetzung der Benediktinerregel', *Anglia* 96 (1978), 310-48.

[83] *Die Regula*, pp 241-56; 'Æthelwold's Translation', pp 143-4.

[84] *Die Regula*, pp 257-62; 'Æthelwold's Translation', pp 144-6.

nearly impeccable.[85] And although the level of literal accuracy is high, the translation is not *ipso facto* devoid of stylistic embellishment. Often, for example, Æthelwold renders a single Latin word by a pair of Old English words (thus *utilitatis* is rendered 'note and nytwyrðnesse')[86] where the stylistic effect is simply rhetorical emphasis. On the whole, however, such stylistic effects are rare, and it is evident that Æthelwold was principally concerned with clarity of meaning. A reflection of that concern is seen in his consistent preference of certain Old English equivalents for Latin terms, and this preference sets his prose apart from that of other Old English translations. For example, he consistently uses *gedyrstlæcan* (rather than *geþristlæcan*) to render *praesumere*, or *wuldorbeag* (rather than *cynehelm*) to render *corona* in the sense 'crown of life'.[87] The consistent preference of certain English equivalents for common Latin words is a feature which characterises Old English writings produced at Winchester in the late tenth century (see below, pp 108-9); there can be little doubt that it reflects a mental discipline practised and taught by Æthelwold himself.

Before leaving Æthelwold's Old English writings mention should be made of a short prose tract normally referred to as 'King Edgar's Establishment of Monasteries'.[88] The tract is preserved uniquely in BL Cotton Faustina A. x (148r-151v), an early twelfth-century manuscript of unknown origin; it there follows immediately a copy of Æthelwold's translation of the *Regula S. Benedicti*, and there is some presumption that it was originally intended as a preface to that work. The text begins acephalously (probably it lacks only a rubric) and there is a substantial lacuna, of one or three leaves, after fol. 148. Nevertheless it is possible to form a clear impression of the contents. It begins with an account of Pope Gregory's mission to England and the consequent establishment of monasteries (all this drawn from Bede, *Historia ecclesiastica* II.1); there must then have followed an account of the decline of monasticism during the ninth century (now lost by the lacuna), and after the lacuna the text resumes by mentioning Edgar's endowment of Abingdon and the subsequent refoundation of monasteries by Edgar and his wife Ælfthryth. Now there are some significant links – of content and wording – between this Old English tract and the New Minster foundation charter on the one hand, and between it and Æthelwold's translation of the *Regula* on the other, and these links are best explained by the assumption that Æthelwold was the author of all three, as Dorothy Whitelock argued.[89] For

---

[85] Gretsch has noted only two errors in understanding the Latin: see *Die Regula*, pp 279-83 and 'Æthelwold's Translation', p 147. Such a level of accuracy would do credit even to a modern scholar, equipped with dictionaries, concordances, grammars and commentaries (and, often, earlier translations). The implication is that Æthelwold's knowledge of Latin was very sound.

[86] Gretsch, *Die Regula*, pp 263-8; 'Æthelwold's Translation', p 146. Note that in the example cited here (from Schröer's edition, p 11) as often elsewhere the two Old English words form an alliterating pair (cf. p 126, where 'his dædum and domum' renders *iudiciis suis*). We have seen that the occasional use of alliterating pairs was a feature of Æthelwold's Latin prose style.

[87] There is a thorough treatment of Æthelwold's vocabulary in Gretsch, *Die Regula*, pp 308-77 (see pp 332-3 and 362-4 for the examples cited). For *wuldorbeag/corona* cf. also J. Kirschner, *Die Bezeichnungen für Kranz und Krone im Altenglischen* (Munich, 1975), pp 183-4 and 258-9.

[88] *Councils and Synods*, no. 33, pp 142-54.

[89] 'The Authorship of the Account of King Edgar's Establishment of Monasteries' (cited above, n 52).

example, the tract mentions Edgar's commissioning a translation of the *Regula S. Benedicti* ('... he het þisne regul of læden gereorde on englisc geþeodan'); a prohibition on abbesses alienating land to secular lords corresponds precisely to a similar prohibition in the New Minster charter (ch xxi); most importantly, the tract uses a number of words – *canonic, geefenlæcan, gylt, hæfenleast, mærsian, gerihtlæcan* and *þæslic* – which are among those words consciously preferred by Æthelwold in his translation of the *Regula S. Benedicti*.[90] The links between these works, therefore, confirm the impression that Æthelwold was their author.

Taken together these various writings reveal something of Æthelwold as scholar: he had a sound knowledge of Latin and on occasion was given to flamboyant display of his learning; at the same time, his English writings reveal his concern with precision of expression. Unfortunately, however, these writings do not help to answer our original question of what books he had read, and how. From the writings we can be sure that Æthelwold knew the *Regula S. Benedicti* and the commentary by Smaragdus, Bede's *Historia ecclesiastica*, Aldhelm's *De uirginitate* (both prose and verse versions) and some Christian-Latin poets, notably Prudentius and Juvencus. But this is not a very extensive list, and it will not tell us where, for example, Æthelwold learned the various unusual Greek words which are scattered through his writings. Some indirect light on this question comes from a list of twenty-one books which Æthelwold donated to Peterborough, probably at the time of its refoundation.[91] The list includes a book *De litteris grecorum* (presumably a Greek-Latin glossary, but identification is impossible without further specification) and another *Descidia Parisiace polis*, no doubt a copy of the third book of Abbo of Saint-Germain's *Bella Parisiacae urbis*, a masterly confection of Greek-based vocabulary.[92] There are grounds for the suspicion that the list represents the personal collection or selection of Æthelwold; it is at any event a somewhat unrepresentative and mildly eccentric collection with which to stock a new foundation's library.[93] Of patristic texts there is Julian of Toledo's *Prognosticum*, Augustine's *Contra Academicos* and the letters of Cyprian; to these may be added the seventh-century Hiberno-Latin treatise *De duodecim abusiuis seculi* and (probably) Ratramnus of Corbie's *De corpore et sanguine Domini*. Of biblical exegesis there is Bede's commentary on Mark, an unspecified commentary on the Song of Songs, and another on certain psalms. Where, one might ask, are Jerome's numerous biblical commentaries, Augustine, *De ciuitate Dei* or *De trinitate*, Cassiodorus, *Expositio psalmorum*, or Gregory the Great, *Moralia in Iob*, *Homiliae .xl. in euangelia* or *Homiliae in Ezechielem*, to name a few of the most widely studied patristic texts? The somewhat eccentric nature of the list might suggest that the books had belonged to Æthelwold himself, or – as in the

---

[90] See Gretsch, *Die Regula*, p 376.
[91] M. Lapidge, 'Surviving Booklists from Anglo-Saxon England', in *Learning and Literature in Anglo-Saxon England: Studies presented to Peter Clemoes*, ed. M. Lapidge and H. Gneuss (Cambridge, 1985), pp 33-89, at 52-5.
[92] See now P. Lendinara, 'The Third Book of the *Bella Parisiacae Urbis* by Abbo of Saint-Germain-des-Prés and its Old English Gloss', *ASE* 15 (1986), 73-89.
[93] It is interesting to note, nevertheless, that a number of the books on the Peterborough list were known to Ælfric: see below, p 110.

case of *De litteris grecorum* – had been studied by him. But there is no immediate way of proving this conjecture.

A different kind of indirect light on Æthelwold's scholarly achievements is provided by the careers and accomplishments of his pupils. The nature of Æthelwold's relationships with his students is a matter of great interest. We have Wulfstan's observation to the effect that, 'indeed he was terrible as a lion to malefactors and the wayward; but to the humble and obedient he showed himself the meekest of lambs'.[94] Certainly he could be harsh in his treatment of 'malefactors'. His expulsion of the secular clerics from the Old Minster created such a wave of resentment that it led to an attempt on his life,[95] though it is interesting to note that even here one of the 'malefactors' who had been expelled – one Eadsige, a relative of Æthelwold – subsequently repented and as an act of reconciliation Æthelwold showed himself the meekest of lambs and appointed Eadsige to the prestigious position of sacrist in charge of St Swithun's shrine.[96] Æthelwold unquestionably demanded unremittant obedience from his followers, as the gruesome story of Ælfstan and the stew-pot reveals.[97] Yet there may be an inclination among modern scholars to exaggerate this aspect of his character. Lantfred tells a very revealing anecdote about Æthelwold's impatience with 'malefactors'.[98] After the translation of St Swithun, miracles occurred frequently at his tomb, and, on the occurrence of a miracle, the monks were obliged to go to the Old Minster and render appropriate thanks to God. But sometimes miracles occurred three or four times a night. And given that Æthelwold was frequently absent from Winchester, and that human nature is what it is, some of the monks took to staying in bed when the miracles occurred. St Swithun duly reported this malpractice in a dream to a certain lady, who in turn duly informed Æthelwold. Now here is a case where we might have expected an explosion of severity from Æthelwold. Lantfred's comment at this point suggests otherwise: Æthelwold was only '*slightly* disturbed – as befits a learned man' ('commotus *paululum* – ut decet sapientem uirum'). He did not fly back to Winchester in a rage, but sent a calm directive, asking that his commands be obeyed, on the penalty of seven days' bread and water (a penalty which seems to gain severity in light of the Old Minster monks' normal provisions, as we shall see). The point of Lantfred's story seems to be that, in the case of his own *familia* Æthelwold always acted with circumspection and restraint; in other words, his own monks were considered as a class apart and – in spite of their occasional peccadilloes – were given preferential treatment by their abbot and bishop.

---

[94] *Vita S. Æthelwoldi*, ch 28: 'erat namque terribilis ut leo discolis et peruersis, humilibus uero et obedientibus se quasi agnum mitissimum exhibebat'.

[95] Described by Wulfstan, *ibid.*, ch 19.

[96] The principal sources for our knowledge of Eadsige are: Lantfred, *Translatio*, ch 20 (the information that Eadsige was appointed sacrist of Swithun's shrine by Æthelwold); Wulfstan, *Vita S. Æthelwoldi*, ch 18 (Eadsige's expulsion as a secular cleric from the Old Minster and subsequent monastic profession) and *Narratio metrica de S. Swithuno* II.131-50 (an excursus on the holiness of Eadsige which has no correlate in Lantfred); and Ælfric, 'Life of St Swithun', ch 5 (the information that Eadsige and Æthelwold were related: 'þeah ðe se sanct [*scil.* Æthelwold] wære gesib him for worulde').

[97] Wulfstan, *Vita S. Æthelwoldi*, c 14.

[98] *Translatio et miracula S. Swithuni*, ch 10.

There is ample evidence that Æthelwold's own monks were given special treatment by their abbot. In an early twelfth-century manuscript now at Alençon but evidently copied from a (lost) Old Minster exemplar,[99] there is a number of liturgical texts pertaining to the cult of St Æthelwold (see below, pp 114-15), and among these is a brief treatise entitled *De horis peculiaribus* which throws interesting light on the devotional practices of Æthelwold's *familia.*

> Preterea beatus pater Adeluuoldus horas regulares et peculiares sibi ad singulare seruitium instituit quas in tribus cursibus ordinauit, humillima diligentia quosque subiectos ammonens ut hoc secreto famulatu ignitis sathane temptamentis uigilanter resisterent et ea per Dei gratiam resistendo superarent ...[100]

> Moreover, our blessed father Æthelwold instituted regular (supplementary) offices, unique to himself, for our individual observance, and he arranged these offices in three *cursus*, and with the most modest insistence he urged those subject to him to resist the fiery temptations of Satan with this secret observance and, through God's grace, to overcome them by active resistance.

The author of this brief treatise, who was clearly a monk at Winchester under Æthelwold, goes on to specify the three *cursus* in question (all of which consisted largely of psalmody) but, regrettably, does not quote the texts:[101] one to the Virgin Mary, one to SS. Peter and Paul (the patron saints of the Old Minster) and one to All Saints.[102] The point is that the monks of Æthelwold's *familia* were expected to perform a demanding series of private devotions in addition to the normal, communal round of the Benedictine *opus Dei*: and it was the expectation and performance of these additional devotions which distinguished Æthelwold's monks from all others. It is worth remembering that when Æthelwold left Glastonbury to take up his own abbacy at Abingdon, he was accompanied by four loyal monks (Osgar, Foldbriht, Ordbriht and Eadric);[103] when he was subsequently elevated to

---

[99] On the manuscript and its contents, see below, p 115.

[100] PL 137, 107-8.

[101] The author of the treatise simply omitted to copy the three *cursus* because 'copies were available in a number of places' ('que uidelicet hore plerisque in locis habentur adscripte et ideo in hoc codicello sunt pretermisse').

[102] From the point of view of liturgical history, it would be a significant advance in our understanding if the three supplementary offices referred to here could be identified in surviving manuscripts, for it could well reveal that in the sphere of liturgy as in other spheres Æthelwold was a great innovator. Unfortunately it is not possible to identify any of the three with absolute certainty. The Office of All Saints is quite possibly identical to the extra Office of All Saints which is stipulated in the *Regularis concordia* (chs 21 [19], 85 [56] *et passim*); see T. Symons, 'Monastic Observance in the Tenth Century', *Downside Review* n.s. 31 (1932), 446-64, esp. 451-6, and 32 (1933), 137-52. Identification of the supplementary Office of the Virgin is less certain: possibly in question is the brief, unprinted Office for the Virgin in BL Cotton Titus D. xxvii (New Minster, Winchester, s. xi¹), 81v-85r, or the supplementary office known from later Anglo-Saxon sources as the *Horae B.M.V.* (see E.S. Dewick, *Facsimiles of Horae de Beata Maria Virgine from English MSS. of the Eleventh Century*, Henry Bradshaw Society 21 (London, 1902), p ix). No supplementary office of SS. Peter and Paul has yet been identified in an Anglo-Saxon manuscript. I am grateful to Helmut Gneuss for discussion of these supplementary offices.

[103] Wulfstan, *Vita S. Æthelwoldi*, ch 11.

Winchester, several of his Abingdon monks – Osgar again among them – accompanied him once again. Æthelwold's followers were duly rewarded for their loyalty. Monks from Winchester attained to the highest ecclesiastical offices in England.[104] In other respects, too, Æthelwold's *familia* received special treatment. Later Abingdon tradition records that, especially on feast days, Æthelwold's monks were regaled with lavish provisions of food and drink. From a thirteenth-century addition to the (twelfth-century) *Chronicon monasterii de Abingdon*[105] we learn that Æthelwold daily provided each of his monks with a loaf of bread so large that a verse epigram was composed to record its size: 'An Abingdon loaf is equal in weight to five marks.'[106] The daily bread was accompanied by a commensurate amount of cheese, except during Lent, when the cheese was replaced by a large eel.[107] By way of drink each monk was given a flagon of such exceptional size that it was referred to as an 'Æthelwold's Bowl' (*bolla Æthelwoldi*).[108] In fact the provision was so generous that the neighbouring poor were well fed from the leftovers from the monks' table.[109] It is of course difficult to assess how much of the detail of this thirteenth-century report is based on genuine tradition and how much is due to anachronistic exaggeration; but there is no need to doubt the general outline of the report, namely that Æthelwold's monks were treated with lavish generosity.

The close and affectionate relationship between Æthelwold and his monks is reflected in the language used by his pupils to describe this relationship. Thus in a poem by his pupil Godemann (who subsequently became abbot of Thorney), which serves as metrical preface to the famous 'Benedictional of St Æthelwold', Æthelwold is referred to as the shepherd/abbot to whom the lambs are entrusted; more characteristically, the pupils are the *pueri* or 'children' for whose well-being 'father' Æthelwold is responsible.[110] In Godemann's poem Æthelwold is made to pray to Christ that he not lose one 'little lamb' (*agniculum*) entrusted to him, and says, addressing Christ as it were,

> memet ego adsigno ecce tibi pueros quoque quos tu
> seruandos mihi iam dederas ... (20-1)

I myself now consign to You the children whom You have entrusted to me for safe-keeping ...

---

[104] Of Æthelwold's pupils, Æthelgar became archbishop of Canterbury (988-90); Ælfstan (who showed his obedience to Æthelwold by placing his hand in the boiling stew-pot) became bishop of Ramsbury; and Osgar and Godemann became abbots of Abingdon and Thorney respectively.

[105] *Chron. Abingdon* I, pp 343-7 (the text there printed is from Cotton Claudius B. vi of c.1270). Since this information is not found in the earlier of the two manuscripts of the *Chronicon*, doubts have been cast on its authenticity (see Knowles, *Monastic Order*, p 716). Note, however, that the information as transmitted includes a number of Old English words and expressions (e.g. *bolla Æthelwoldi*) which are unlikely to have been fabricated by a thirteenth-century chronicler.

[106] *Ibid.*, p 345: 'Panis Abbendoniae par marcis pondere quinque.'

[107] *Ibid.* p 346.

[108] *Ibid.*

[109] *Ibid.*, p 347: 'Haec uero et his similia tam abundanter tamque circumspecte constituit [*scil.* Æthelwold], ut non solum monachi quoad usum uictus sustentarentur, uerum etiam pauperes ex eorum reliquiis propensius recrearentur.'

[110] The poem is ptd Lapidge, 'The Hermeneutic Style', pp 105-6.

The conventions of describing Æthelwold and his pupils in terms of shepherd/ flock and father/children are frequently found in the Latin writings produced at late tenth-century Winchester, as we shall see.

Given the intimate and affectionate relationship between the abbot and his flock, we should expect that the writing of Æthelwold's pupils would reflect – to some extent at least – the intellectual concerns of their master. In fact the two salient but contradictory features of Æthelwold's own writings – the concern with flamboyant, grecising vocabulary in Latin and with utter clarity of expression in English – are fully seen in the work of his pupils. The aforementioned poem by Godemann provides a fine illustration of the former. This poem, consisting of 38 hexameters, was written to serve as preface to the 'Benedictional of St Æthelwold'; it is copied in Rustic Capitals and gold lettering, and the ornateness of its grecising diction matches that of the book as a whole. Godemann, for example, three times refers to the book as *biblos* (βίβλος) and its illuminations as *agalmata* (ἀγάλματα); Christ the Saviour is twice referred to as *soter* (σωτήρ) and Æthelwold once as *iconomos* (οἰκονόμος, here 'steward of an estate') and once as *boanerges* (βοανηργές).[111] The fact that it was Æthelwold who ordered the book to be written – *iussit qui scribere librum hunc* – suggests strongly that he is the inspiration behind the flamboyant style of the poem. Another aspect of the poem where Æthelwold's influence is to be suspected is its metrical proficiency. We know from Wulfstan that Æthelwold gave his pupils instruction in the rules of metrics.[112] Since there are certain features of Godemann's metrical technique – extensive use of elision, avoidance of end-stopped lines, use of monosyllables in the sixth foot[113] – which recur in Wulfstan's Latin poetry, but which are rare in other tenth-century Anglo-Latin verse, one may suspect that the metrical technique of the pupils reflects the teaching of the master; but since no verse of Æthelwold himself survives, this can be no more than a suspicion.

The other facet of Æthelwold's intellectual complexion – his concern with clarity of expression in English – is reflected in the work of Ælfric.[114] Ælfric desribes himself as a 'student of Winchester'[115] and specifically as a student of Æthelwold.[116] But whatever Ælfric's intellectual debt to his master in other

---

[111] *Boanerges* is a word used in the Greek Gospel of Mark (III.17) to record the name given by Christ to James and John, the sons of Zebedee; the word is simply transliterated in the Vulgate. Godemann mistook it as a singular form.

[112] *Vita S. Æthelwoldi*, ch 31: 'dulce namque erat ei ... regulas grammaticae artis et metricae rationis tradere'.

[113] Examples both of elision and sixth-foot monosyllables in one line: 'memet ego adsigno ecce tibi pueros quoque quos tu' (20) and 'atque patri magno iussit qui scribere librum hunc' (34).

[114] On Ælfric's achievement in general, see P. Clemoes, 'Ælfric', in *Continuations and Beginnings: Studies in Old English Literature*, ed. E. G. Stanley (London, 1966), pp 176-209; idem, 'The Chronology of Ælfric's Works', in *The Anglo-Saxons. Studies ... presented to Bruce Dickins*, ed. P. Clemoes (London, 1959), pp 212-47; and J. Hurt, *Ælfric* (Boston, 1974).

[115] Ælfric, *Vita S. Æthelwoldi*, ch 1 ('Wintoniensis alumnus'). Ælfric is listed as no. lxxv among the Old Minster monks who 'specialiter se deuouerunt' (*Liber Vitae*, ed. Birch, p 26).

[116] *Sermones catholici* I, praef.: 'ego Ælfricus alumnus Aðelwoldi beneuoli et uenerabilis presulis' (*The Homilies of the Anglo-Saxon Church, the First Part containing the Sermones Catholici or Homilies of Ælfric*, ed. B. Thorpe, 2 vols (London, 1844-6), I, p 1); 'Grammar', praef.: 'sicut didicimus in scola Aðelwoldi, uenerabilis praesulis, qui multos ad bonum imbuit' (*Ælfrics Grammatik und Glossar*, ed. J. Zupitza, 2nd edn with foreword by H. Gneuss (Berlin,

respects, there was one respect in which he was entirely independent: he rejected outright Æthelwold's propensity for ostentatious and obscure vocabulary. He states his rejection clearly in his preface to the Second Series of *Sermones catholici*:

> ... festinauimus hunc sequentem librum sicut omnipotentis Dei gratia nobis dictauit interpretare, non garrula uerbositate[117] aut ignotis sermonibus, sed puris et apertis uerbis linguae huius gentis, cupientes plus prodesse auditoribus simplici locutione quam laudari artificiosi sermonis compositione – quam nequaquam didicit nostra simplicitas.[118]

> I hastened to translate the following book as the grace of Almighty God dictated it to me, not in 'garrulous verbosity' or unfamiliar diction, but in the clear and unambiguous words of this people's language, seeking rather to be of benefit to my audience through my straightforward expression than to be praised for the elaboration of an artificial style – which my simple self has in no way mastered.

The concern with unaffected clarity of expression is manifest in the few Latin writings of Ælfric which survive;[119] but it is particularly in his numerous English writings that this stylistic propensity is evident. It is not far-fetched to imagine that this propensity for clarity in translation was learned from Æthelwold. We have seen (above, pp 102-3) that Æthelwold, in his translation of the *Regula S. Benedicti*, established a technique of translation whereby one English equivalent was consistently preferred to others in rendering a Latin word (one example was *gedyrstlæcan*, which was preferred in rendering *praesumere* by Æthelwold to such words as *gebristlæcan*). There are several late tenth-century Old English texts in which lexical

---

Zürich and Dublin, 1966), p 1); and 'Letter to the Monks of Eynsham': 'omnia ... quae in scola eius [*scil*. Æthelwold] degens multis annis ... didici' (*Consuetudinum saeculi X/XI/XII Monumenta non-Cluniacensia*, ed. Hallinger, p 155). It is a pity that Ælfric does not specify *how* many years (*multis annis*) he spent with Æthelwold.

[117] The words *garrula uerbositate* are lifted from Aldhelm, prose *De uirginitate*, ch xix (*Aldhelmi Opera*, ed. Ehwald, p 249) – which shows at least that Ælfric was familiar with the stylistic affectation he was repudiating.

[118] *Ælfric's Catholic Homilies: The Second Series – Text*, ed. M. Godden, EETS, suppl. ser., 5 (London, 1979), p 1. A similar repudiation of *obscura uerba* is found in the preface to the First Series: '... ob edificationem simplicium, qui hanc norunt tantummodo locutionem, siue legendo siue audiendo; ideoque nec obscura posuimus uerba, sed simplicem Anglicam, quo facilius possit ad cor peruenire legentium uel audientium, ad utilitatem animarum suarum, quia alia lingua nesciunt erudiri, quam in qua nati sunt' (*The Homilies*, ed. Thorpe, p 1). On Ælfric's concern with *breuitas*, see A. E. Nichols, 'Ælfric and the Brief Style', *Journal of English and Germanic Philology* 70 (1971), 1-12.

[119] Ælfric's Latin writings include the *Vita S. Æthelwoldi*, the 'Letter to the Monks of Eynsham', Latin prefaces to the two series of *Sermones catholici* as well as to the 'Lives of Saints', the *Colloquium* or scholastic colloquy, the treatise *De ecclesiastica consuetudine* together with three pastoral letters (all ed. B. Fehr, *Die Hirtenbriefe Ælfrics*, with suppl. by P. Clemoes (Darmstadt, 1964), pp 234-49 and 35-57 (*Epist.* 2), 222-7 (*Epist.* 2a) and 58-67 (*Epist.* 3)). To these Latin works may be added the two bilingual works known as Ælfric's 'Grammar' and 'Glossary'. The 'Glossary' includes a substantial amount of exotic vocabulary, some of it Greek-based, some of it derived directly from Lantfred's *Translatio et miracula S. Swithuni*; but the fact that Ælfric provides English equivalents for all these words is clear proof that his pedagogic intention was to demystify them. There is a useful study of the Latin words in the 'Glossary' by R. L. Thomson, 'Ælfric's Latin Vocabulary', *Leeds Studies in English* 12 (1981), 155-61.

preferences like those made by Æthelwold are to be found: the Old English translation of the 'enlarged' *Regula canonicorum* of Chrodegang (a translation almost certainly made at the Old Minster, to judge solely by the names of monks which are inserted by the translator to illustrate Chrodegang's discussion of the hierarchy of authority in a canonry);[120] the interlinear gloss to the 'Lambeth Psalter';[121] and the Old English interlinear gloss to the *Expositio hymnorum*.[122] The most reasonable explanation of the lexical similarities is that all these anonymous translations are the product of one school, that the school was located at Winchester, and Æthelwold was its master. Furthermore, largely because of the preeminence of the Winchester school, the literary language worked out by Æthelwold and his pupils became in effect the standard literary dialect of the late Old English period. The theory of the Winchester origin of 'Standard Old English' was first stated in a pioneering essay by Helmut Gneuss,[123] and although refinements to the theory have been suggested,[124] the most recent research has vindicated the theory in outline and greatly clarified our understanding of the 'Winchester School'.[125] Here, then, is one area where Æthelwold and his pupils left a permanent mark on English learning.

Preeminent among these pupils, from the point of view of Old English literature, was Ælfric. There is no need here to list Ælfric's numerous writings in Old English or to stress his achievements in that field. Our concern is with the way in which Ælfric's Old English writings reflect his study with Æthelwold. These writings are normally adduced – no doubt rightly – as evidence of the standard literary dialect of the 'Winchester school', but it must be said that Ælfric's vocabulary has yet to receive the intensive analysis which has been made of Æthelwold's.[126] It is clear nevertheless that Ælfric frequently shares preferences for certain words as translational equivalents with other translators of the 'Winchester school': thus (to take an example mentioned earlier) Ælfric uses the word *gedyrstlæcan* for Latin *praesumere*, not *geþristlæcan*.[127] Such preferences were no doubt learned from Æthelwold. So, too, the wide range of reading represented by Ælfric's writings may reflect – to some extent at least – texts studied under Æthelwold's direction. Although it is not yet possible to state with precision all the books

[120] *The Old English Version of the Enlarged Rule of Chrodegang*, ed. A. S. Napier, EETS, o.s. 150 (London, 1916); for the list of Old Minster monks, see p 9.
[121] *Der Lambeth-Psalter*, ed. U. Lindelöf, 2 vols (Helsingfors, 1909-14).
[122] H. Gneuss, *Hymnar und Hymnen im englischen Mittelalter* (Tübingen, 1968), pp 265-413.
[123] 'The Origin of Standard Old English and Æthelwold's School at Winchester', *ASE* 1 (1972), 63-83.
[124] See, for example, M. Korhammer, *Die monastischen Cantica im Mittelalter und ihre altenglischen Interlinearversionen*, Texte und Untersuchungen zur englischen Philologie 6 (Munich, 1976), pp 175-245.
[125] W. Hofstetter, *Winchester und der spätaltenglische Sprachgebrauch*, Texte und Untersuchungen zur englischen Philologie 14 (Munich, 1987).
[126] Ælfric's vocabulary: P. Meissner, 'Studien zum Wortschatz Ælfrics', *Archiv für das Studium der neueren Sprachen und Literaturen* 165 (1934), 11-19, and 166 (1935), 30-9 and 205-15; K. Jost, *Wulfstanstudien* (Bern, 1950), pp 159-68 (where the principal focus is not on Ælfric but on Wulfstan the homilist); J. C. Pope, *Homilies of Ælfric: A Supplementary Collection*, 2 vols, EETS, o.s. 259-60 (London, 1967-8), I, pp 99-102; M. R. Godden, 'Ælfric's Changing Vocabulary', *English Studies* 61 (1980), 206-23; and Hofstetter, *Winchester*, pp 38-66.
[127] See Hofstetter, *Winchester*, p 38.

which were known to Ælfric,[128] he was certainly familiar with the following patristic texts: Augustine, *Tractatus in euangelium Ioannis*, *Enarrationes in psalmos*, *De sermone Domini in monte* and various *sermones*; Jerome, *Commentarii in euangelium Matthaei*; Gregory, *Homilia .xl. in euangelia* and *Moralia in Iob*; and Julian of Toledo, *Prognosticum futuri saeculi*.[129] Of Insular Latin writings Ælfric knew many of the works of Bede, including the commentaries on Mark and Luke, the *Homiliae*, the *Historia ecclesiastica*, *De natura rerum* and *De temporum ratione*, as well as the anonymous Hiberno-Latin treatise *De duodecim abusiuis saeculi*. Of Carolingian writings, besides the homiliaries of Paul the Deacon and Haymo of Auxerre, Ælfric evidently knew Alcuin's *De uirtutibus et uitiis* and probably Ratramnus of Corbie, *De corpore et sanguine Domini*.[130] What is striking is that four of these works correspond to titles in the list of books donated by Æthelwold to Peterborough (see above, p 103): Bede's commentary on Mark, Julian of Toledo's *Prognosticum*, the Hiberno-Latin *De duodecim abusiuis saeculi* and (probably) Ratramnus's *De corpore et sanguine Domini*. Can we suppose that these four are books which were studied by Ælfric while he was at Winchester? And did he study them under Æthelwold's supervision? This is perhaps a case where further work on Ælfric's sources may reveal more fully his intellectual debt to Æthelwold.

The student who felt himself to owe the greatest debt to Æthelwold was Wulfstan, the *Cantor* or precentor at the Old Minster in the last part of the tenth century. Wulfstan was one of the most learned and prolific authors of the late Anglo-Saxon period.[131] In addition to the prose *Vita S. Æthelwoldi*, Wulfstan composed the *Narratio metrica de S. Swithuno*, which is the longest and most metrically accomplished surviving Anglo-Latin poem. That he was expert in musical theory is clear from the fact that he composed a work *De*

---

[128] It is Ælfric's major writings – the 'Catholic Homilies' (*sermones catholici*) and 'Lives of Saints' – whose sources await final definition. The sources of the 'Catholic Homilies' were mainly established in two pioneering studies by M. Förster, *Über die Quellen von Ælfrics Homiliae Catholicae* (Berlin, 1892), and 'Über die Quellen von Ælfrics exegetischen Homiliae Catholicae', *Anglia* 16 (1894), 1-61. However, some of Förster's work requires qualification as a result of the demonstration that Ælfric knew some of his sources through the homiliaries of Paul the Deacon and Haymo of Auxerre: see C. L. Smetana, 'Ælfric and the Early Medieval Homiliary', *Traditio* 15 (1959), 163-204, and 'Ælfric and the Homiliary of Haymo of Halberstadt', *Traditio* 17 (1961), 457-69, as well as Pope, *Homilies of Ælfric*, I, pp 154-71. The sources of Ælfric's 'Lives of Saints' also need careful reassessment in the light of P. H. Zettel's recent demonstration that Ælfric made extensive use of the huge hagiographical compilation known as the Cotton-Corpus Legendary: 'Saints' Lives in Old English: Latin Manuscripts and Vernacular Accounts: Ælfric', *Peritia* 1 (1982), 17-37.

[129] Ælfric made excerpts from the *Prognosticum* which are preserved in Boulogne, Bibl. munic. 63, fols 1-10, and are printed and discussed by M. McC. Gatch, *Preaching and Theology in Anglo-Saxon England: Ælfric and Wulfstan* (Toronto, 1977), pp 129-46.

[130] See J. N. Bakhuizen van den Brink, *Ratramnus: De corpore et sanguine Domini* (Amsterdam, 1974), pp 108-31, who notes extensive verbal parallels between Ælfric and Ratramnus (Ælfric, however, does not name Ratramnus as his source); but cf. also J. P. Bouhout, *Ratramne de Corbie: histoire littéraire et controverses doctrinales* (Paris, 1976), pp 145-6, who argues against Ælfric's knowledge of Ratramnus, on the grounds that no English manuscript of *De corpore* is known. The matter could be resolved if it were possible certainly to identify the item *De eucharistia* in the Æthelwold booklist.

[131] There is a full account of his life and writings in the Introduction to Winterbottom and Lapidge, *Wulfstan of Winchester*; see also Gneuss, *Hymnar und Hymnen*, pp 246-8.

harmonia tonorum, now lost. His musical expertise is also to be seen in a number of sequences and tropes which he composed in order to augment the sequence and trope repertories at Winchester as they are preserved in the two 'Winchester Tropers';[132] indeed it is possible that one of the principal scribes of the earlier of the two 'Winchester Tropers' (Cambridge, Corpus Christi College 473, of the beginning of the eleventh century) was Wulfstan himself.[133] Besides the tropes and sequences, Wulfstan was arguably the author of a number of liturgical pieces, including hymns and mass-sets, which originated at Winchester in the late tenth century, as we shall see. But he is not known to have composed any writings in Old English.

It is difficult to estimate the precise nature of the intellectual debt owed by Wulfstan to Æthelwold. Wulfstan entered the Old Minster as a child oblate, possibly during the 960s, for he was still a *pusillus puer* when St Swithun's relics were translated in 971.[134] Some part of Wulfstan's instruction must have been received from Æthelwold in person; but the precise amount is not determinable, for Æthelwold was frequently away from Winchester (above, p 104), and Wulfstan's one personal recollection of time spent in the monastic classroom contains no mention of Æthelwold.[135] As abbot and bishop Æthelwold will have been far too busy to supervise the daily school-exercises of the oblates, and we know in any case that there were monastic teachers specially appointed for that task at Winchester in Æthelwold's day.[136] Nevertheless, Æthelwold took an active interest in the activities of his young monks – as Wulfstan himself tells us[137] – and it is legitimate to ask what aspects of Wulfstan's learning were indebted to Æthelwold's instruction. Æthelwold, for example, was concerned to explain to his monks the rules of metre (*regulas ... grammatice artis*); he was clearly proficient in that skill, and had learned it with Dunstan years earlier at Glastonbury (see above, p 90), even though none of his own verse survives (or has been identified). Now Wulfstan was exceptionally proficient in the skill of metrics. He had studied and digested all the Christian-Latin poets whose poems then constituted the

---

[132] The Winchester trope repertory has been carefully and skilfully analysed by A. E. Planchart, *The Repertory of Tropes at Winchester*, 2 vols (Princeton, 1977); for Wulfstan's role in the composition of tropes in the 'Winchester Tropers', see I, pp 4-16, 25-33 and 145-72. Unfortunately there is no corresponding study of the repertory of sequences in the 'Winchester Tropers', and Wulfstan's contribution here must be a matter of conjecture; see discussion in the Introduction to Winterbottom and Lapidge, *Wulfstan of Winchester*, and in this volume see Berry, ch 6.

[133] See A. Holschneider, *Die Organa von Winchester* (Hildesheim, 1968), pp 11, 19-20 and 76-81, and Planchart, *The Repertory*, I, pp 32-3 and 52-4.

[134] *Narratio metrica de S. Swithuno* I.889: 'nos quoque nos pueri qua tempestate pusilli'.

[135] *Ibid.* II.259-63:

> saepe etiam nobis pueris discentibus una
> quemlibet aut cantum seu qualemcumque libellum
> contigit ut tota penitus nil discere luce
> possemus, signis pro crebrescentibus, omnes
> sed uice continua sacram repetiuimus aedem.

[136] We know, for example, of one *Ioruert* (a Welshman) who was master of the Winchester school at some point during Æthelwold's episcopacy: see Lapidge, 'Three Poems from Æthelwold's School', pp 114-15. It is not clear from the poem whether *Ioruert* was a monk or lay master; he is not listed among the *familia* of the Old Minster in the *Liber uitae* of Hyde (ed. Birch, pp 24-9).

[137] *Vita S. Æthelwoldi*, ch 31 (cited above, n 112).

scholastic curriculum:[138] Juvencus, Caelius Sedulius, Arator, Venantius Fortunatus
and Aldhelm. But he also knew Vergil by heart and, unusually at this date in
England, Horace as well. From attentive study of these poets he learned the
metrical skills which give flexibility and variety to hexameter verse:[139] avoidance of end-stopped lines, use of elision, use of monosyllabic as well as
pentasyllabic words in the fifth and sixth feet of a hexameter, variation of
the metrical patterns of the individual hexameters, and so on.[140] So proficient
a metrician was Wulfstan that he was bold enough on one occasion to essay a
hypermetrical line, a device which was probably learned from Vergil but
which, to my knowledge, was attempted uniquely by Wulfstan among Anglo-
Latin poets.[141] His proficiency is probably also to be seen in his handling of
such complex metrical forms as epanaleptic elegiacs and sapphic stanzas, as
I shall suggest presently.[142] How much of this skill was learned from Æthelwold is
impossible to say, but note that some of the features listed here are also to
be seen in the brief poem of Godemann mentioned above; and Godemann
like Wulfstan was a student of Æthelwold. But Wulfstan will have had other
teachers as well, and from them rather than Æthelwold he will have learned
his skill in musical theory and practice which led to his appointment as
precentor: certainly none of our sources indicate that Æthelwold was a
skilled musician.

In any event, Wulfstan clearly felt a deep personal debt to Æthelwold.
Wulfstan's involvement in the translation of Æthelwold, which took place
on 10 September 996, may arguably be seen as his attempt to discharge that
debt. The circumstances surrounding the translation suggest that Wulfstan
was a principal moving force behind the event. According to his own *Vita
S. Æthelwoldi* (ch 42), before the translation and some twelve years after his
death, Æthelwold appeared in a dream to a blind man named Ælfhelm and
instructed him to go to Winchester:

> Cum festinus Wintoniam perueneris et Veteris Cenobii ecclesiam intra-
> ueris, accersiri fac ad te monachum quendam Wulfstanum, cognomento
> Cantorem. Hic cum ex ore tuo uerba meae legationis audierit, te
> mox indubitanter ad meum perducet tumulum, ibique recipies lumen
> oculorum tuorum.

> When you have made all haste to Winchester and entered the church
> of the Old Minster, get them to fetch you a monk called Wulfstan 'the

---

[138] See M. Lapidge, 'The Study of Latin Texts in Late Anglo-Saxon England: 1. The Evidence
of Latin Glosses', in *Latin and the Vernacular Languages in Early Medieval Britain*, ed.
N. Brooks (Leicester, 1982), pp 99-140.

[139] On the problems faced by Anglo-Latin poets attempting to write quantitative verse, and
Aldhelm's manifest difficulties in overcoming them, see M. Lapidge, 'Aldhelm's Latin Poetry
and Old English Verse', *Comparative Literature* 31 (1979), 209-31.

[140] These features of Wulfstan's verse are analysed in detail in my introduction to the *Narratio
metrica de S. Swithuno* in *The Cult of St Swithun*.

[141] *Narratio* I.182-3: 'lubricus ante fuit, subito mutatur in omne re/ in tantumque Deo se
pectore uouit et ore'.

[142] See discussion in the Introduction to Winterbottom and Lapidge, *Wulfstan of Winchester*,
where it is also suggested that Wulfstan may have been the author of a poem on St Augustine
(inc. 'Aueto placidis praesul amabilis') in a lyric form modelled on Horace (*Carm* I.vi, xv, xxiv,
xxxiii, etc.: each four-line stanza consists of three lesser asclepiads followed by a glyconic), but
unique in Anglo-Saxon England.

Precentor'. When he hears from you the details of my message, he will take you at once and without question to my tomb. There you will get back the sight of your eyes.

The instructions issued here by Æthelwold in the dream prove to be the initial step in the process of translation: the man goes to Winchester, summons Wulfstan and conveys Æthelwold's message; Wulfstan, torn between hope and fear, obediently takes the man to Æthelwold's tomb, where he is duly cured. Thereafter Æthelwold appears to several people in dreams, including Wulfstan (ch 43). Now Wulfstan's account of the events leading to the translation are clearly modelled on Lantfred's account of the translation of St Swithun.[143] There Swithun appeared to a certain smith and instructed him to go to Eadsige (one of the erstwhile canons at the Old Minster, and at that point an estranged relative of Æthelwold), who was in turn asked to communicate Swithun's message to Æthelwold. In due course Æthelwold undertook the translation of Swithun, which proved to be a pretext for reconciliation between Æthelwold and Eadsige. The similarities between Wulfstan's and Lantfred's accounts imply that Wulfstan himself played the cardinal role in Æthelwold's translation that had been played by Eadsige and Æthelwold in the earlier translation of Swithun. Wulfstan will have undertaken this charge as an act of *pietas* to his former master, no doubt; but there is evidence in his *Vita S. Æthelwoldi* that he may also have been fulfilling a promise enjoined on him by Æthelwold while he was still alive. Consider the following passage, an account of a miracle which happened to Æthelwold's mother before Æthelwold was born:

> Quadam namque die cum mater eius stipata ciuibus staret in ecclesia, sacrae missae celebrationi interesse desiderans, sensit animam pueri quem gerebat in utero uenisse et in eum Dei nutu cuncta moderantis intrasse, sicut postea ipse sanctus, qui nasciturus erat, iam episcopus, nobis gaudendo referebat (c. 4).

> Now one day his mother was standing in a crowd of people in church, wanting to take part in the celebration of holy mass, when she felt that the soul of the child whom she bore in her womb had come and entered him at the will of God Who rules all. This is what we were (or: I was) later told by the very saint whose birth was then imminent, when he was a bishop; and joyfully did he tell the tale.

In what circumstances would Æthelwold have conveyed such private information to Wulfstan? It is hardly the matter of a fireside chat. The simplest explanation is that, some time before his death, Æthelwold had conceived the desire to be canonised as a saint — a process which, in tenth-century England, involved no more than a well-publicised translation and a well-circulated *uita*. Accordingly, he enjoined upon Wulfstan the duty of implementing the process after a suitable length of time had passed (in this case twelve years), and, in order to facilitate the task, furnished him with some suitable miracle-stories which could be written up in the eventual *uita*. And Wulfstan duly fulfilled his promise, both by conveying the message of the

---

[143] *Translatio et miracula S. Swithuni*, ch 1.

blind man's dream to the bishop of Winchester (then Ælfheah) and by composing the *Vita S. Æthelwoldi* out of materials supplied by Æthelwold for the task.[144]

Once a saint had been translated, his cult was established by liturgical commemoration on the anniversary or feast of the translation as well as that of his death or *depositio*. The dates of Æthelwold's death (1 August) and translation (10 September) are recorded in a number of Anglo-Saxon liturgical calendars[145] from various parts of the country, which suggests that his cult was fairly widespread (although, as one would suspect, it is principally in Winchester and centres influenced by Winchester that the feasts are recorded). Now a saint could simply be commemorated on his feast day by making use of the standardised prayers for a mass *in natale unius confessoris* which are found in sacramentaries of the time.[146] However, if the saint was thought worthy of special veneration, it was necessary to compose afresh the various pieces used in liturgical celebration: for the mass, mass-sets (consisting of prayers called the *collecta*, *secreta*, *prefatio*, and *postcommunio*) and tropes (especially for the *Introit*); for the office, a hymn would be needed (the liturgical lections which were also needed could be supplied from the saint's *uita*). Given that the precentor carried the overall responsibility for liturgical celebration in his church, and that the tropes and hymns in particular involved musical composition, it will normally have been the precentor's duty to supply the various liturgical pieces needed for the especial veneration of a local saint. We know from later liturgical books from Winchester that tropes and mass-sets for St Æthelwold were in existence by the early eleventh century.[147] There are grounds, therefore, for suspecting that it was Wulfstan – precentor at the Old Minster at the time of Æthelwold's translation – who composed the necessary liturgical pieces for his cult.

The suspicion receives some confirmation from the contents of an early twelfth-century manuscript now Alençon, Bibliothèque municipale 14. Some parts of this manuscript are in the hand of the famous Anglo-Norman historian Orderic Vitalis (1075-1142), among them a copy of Wulfstan's *Vita S. Æthelwoldi* (23r-34v).[148] Now immediately following the end of this

---

[144] Another example of such privileged information is recorded in ch 41: 'sepultus est [*scil.* Æthelwold] in cripta ad australem plagam sancti altaris, ubi eum requiescere debere, *sicut ipse nobis retulit*, olim sibi caelitus ostensum est' (my italics).

[145] Calendars containing feasts of Æthelwold's deposition and translation are ptd F. Wormald, *English Kalendars before A.D. 1100*, Henry Bradshaw Society 72 (London, 1934), nos. 9-13 and 19-20; the deposition only is recorded in no. 16, and the translation only in nos. 6-7.

[146] See, for example, J. Deshusses, *Le sacramentaire grégorien*, 2nd edn (Fribourg, 1979), nos. 1233-5.

[147] *Introit*-tropes for St Æthelwold are found in one of the so-called 'Winchester Tropers', namely Cambridge, Corpus Christi College 473 (see Planchart, *The Repertory*, I, p 145, and II, p 175). Mass-sets for the deposition and translation are found in the late eleventh-century missal from the New Minster, now Le Havre, Bibl. munic. 330 (*The Missal of the New Minster, Winchester*, ed. D. H. Turner, Henry Bradshaw Society 93 (London, 1962), pp 132-3 and 159-60).

[148] This copy of the *Vita S. Æthelwoldi* has been subject to some minor alterations and interpolations by Orderic himself, including the insertion of some seventy lines from the *Narratio metrica de S. Swithuno* into ch 40 of the *Vita S. Æthelwoldi*; this redaction was first ptd by Mabillon and is rptd *PL* 137, 81-104 (see Winterbottom and Lapidge, *Wulfstan of Winchester*, Introduction). On Orderic's autograph manuscripts, including Alençon 14, see M. Chibnall, *The Ecclesiastical History of Orderic Vitalis I: General Introduction* (Oxford, 1980), pp 201-3.

uita is a collection of liturgical materials all pertaining to the cult of St Æthelwold (34v-36r) which may be listed as follows:[149]

(1) an epanaleptic, abecedarian hymn to St Æthelwold beginning 'Alma lucerna micat' (34v-35r);[150]

(2) a *hymnus uespertinalis* (a hymn, that is, for Vespers) for St Æthelwold beginning 'Inclitus pastor populique rector' (35r-v);[151]

(3) an octosyllabic prayer for St Æthelwold, probably intended to be used as a hymn, beginning 'Celi senator inclite' (35v);[152] .

(4) one mass-set, apparently intended for the feast of St Æthelwold's deposition on 1 August (35v);[153]

(5) a second mass-set, this time specifically designated for the translation of St Æthelwold on 10 September (35v-36r);[154]

(6) the brief treatise (mentioned earlier) entitled *De horis peculiaribus*, concerning various private devotional practices instituted by Æthelwold for his own *familia* (36r);[155]

(7) two *Introit*-tropes (with chant-cues) for feasts of St Æthelwold, the first presumably for the deposition, the second for the translation (36r).[156]

At this point the materials pertaining specifically to Æthelwold end, and are followed by various hymns in honour of two other Old Minster saints (Birinus and Swithun: 36r-37v; the remainder of 37v is blank). It seems clear that all these materials were copied from a (now lost) manuscript which originated at the Old Minster, Winchester.

The materials relating to Æthelwold in this manuscript comprise all the various liturgical pieces which would be required for the full celebration of his cult in mass and office. Closer inspection of the individual items reveals that they all emanate from Æthelwold's *familia*. The first item, the epanaleptic, abecedarian hymn in honour of St Æthelwold, refers at one point to Æthelwold as the teacher 'from whose sacred mouth flowed doctrines of eternal life' and from which the poet imbibed everything good; he subsequently beseeches Æthelwold to 'transport to heaven the children (*pueros*) whom he himself nourished':

> Cuius ab ore sacro fluxerunt dogmata uitae
> Hausimus omne bonum cuius ab ore sacro ...
>
> Transfer ad alta poli pueros quos ipse nutristi
> Nos prece continua transfer ad alta poli.

This poem is one of a group of five, all in the same difficult and exacting epanaleptic form and all dedicated to Winchester saints. Because they share

---

[149] All these texts were first ptd from Alençon 14 by Mabillon, whence they are rptd PL 137, 104-8.

[150] PL 137, 104-5; the poem is listed (with bibliography) by D. Schaller and E. Könsgen, *Initia Carminum Latinorum saeculo undecimo Antiquiorum* (Göttingen, 1977), no. 591.

[151] PL 137, 105; see Schaller and Könsgen, *Initia*, no. 8011.

[152] PL 137, 105; see Schaller and Könsgen, *Initia*, no. 1793.

[153] PL 137, 105-6; cf. *The Missal of the New Minster*, ed. Turner, pp 132-3.

[154] PL 137, 106-7; cf. *The Missal of the New Minster*, ed. Turner, pp 159-60.

[155] PL 137, 107-8.

[156] PL 137, 107-8; cf. Planchart, *Repertory*, II, p 175 (nos. 170-1).

many features of style and diction with Wulfstan's *Narratio metrica de S. Swithuno*, it has been thought with fair probability that Wulfstan was their author;[157] in any event they are the work of a member of Æthelwold's own *familia*. The same may be said for the *hymnus uespertinalis*, where the poet once again states explicitly that Æthelwold was his 'father and teacher':

> Inclitus pastor populique rector
> Cuius insignem colimus triumphum
> Nunc Adeluuoldus sine fine letus
>   Regnat in astris.
>
> Qui pater noster fuit et magister ...

The most striking feature of this hymn is its verse form: sapphic stanzas (each stanza consisting of three lesser sapphics followed by a dactylic dimeter acatalectic). To my knowledge the metrical form of this poem is exceedingly rare in pre-Conquest Anglo-Latin; it could only have been attempted by a skilled poet, and we have seen that Wulfstan possessed such skill. A similar reference to Æthelwold's teaching is made in one of the collects for Æthelwold's deposition: the author of this prayer, like the author of the epanaleptic hymn, states that he 'came to know the teaching of all religion through [Æthelwold's] instruction':

> Deus qui preclari sideris sancti pontificis Adeluuoldi illustratione nouam populis Anglorum tribuisti lucem hodierna die clarescere, tuam suppliciter imploramus clementiam, ut cuius magisterio tocius religionis documenta cognouimus, illius et exemplis informemur et patrociniis adiuuemur. Per.

The personal statement concerning Æthelwold's *magisterium* is most unusual in a prayer of this sort, where one normally finds generalised, imprecise statements about the saint's intercessory powers. This prayer too evidently emanated from Æthelwold's *familia*. The brief treatise *De horis peculiaribus* (mentioned earlier) describes private liturgical devotions stipulated by Æthelwold for his *familia*; since these devotions were to be recited as protection against the imminent threat of Antichrist ('instante future persecutionis tempore que iam uicinis Antichristi temporibus ingruit'), one may suspect that they (and the treatise describing them) were composed shortly before A.D.1000 by a member of Æthelwold's *familia*. Finally, the *Introit*-tropes contain several verbal links with the poetry of Wulfstan which are too close to be accidental. For example compare a line from the first of the tropes – 'inter apostolicos stola splendente *ierarchos*' – with a line from Wulfstan's *Narratio metrica de S. Swithuno*:

> *inter apostolicos sed lucet in axe ierarchos.*
>   (*Epistola specialis* 281; my italics)

It is difficult not to think that Wulfstan, the precentor at the Old Minster at the time of Æthelwold's translation, composed all these liturgical pieces

---

[157] See my discussion in P. Dronke, M. Lapidge and P. Stotz, 'Die unveröffentlichte Gedichte der Cambridger Liederhandschrift (CUL Gg. 5. 35)', *Mittellateinisches Jahrbuch* 17 (1982), 54-95, at 59-65; cf. also Gneuss, *Hymnar und Hymnen*, pp 246-7.

which accompany the *Vita S. Æthelwoldi* in Alençon 14. Taken in combination with internal evidence in the *Vita S. Æthelwoldi* itself, one is left with the conclusion that the translation of Æthelwold and the establishment of his cult was a personal undertaking of Wulfstan. It is an excellent illustration of the depth of devotion which Æthelwold inspired in at least one of his pupils.

In spite of Wulfstan's efforts the cult of St Æthelwold remained a local Winchester affair. Few of the liturgical pieces composed specifically for his cult are found in any but Winchester manuscripts (with the exception of Alençon 14 which, as I argued, was probably copied from an Old Minster exemplar). But although the liturgical cult of Æthelwold was of limited extent and duration, his importance for Anglo-Saxon learning can scarcely be overstated. At the very least he trained two of the most prolific and learned authors of the tenth century, Ælfric and Wulfstan *Cantor*. Something of his own exceptional learning may be glimpsed through their writings; but we must hope that future research will bring more of his own to light.[158]

[158] I am very grateful to Robert Deshman, Helmut Gneuss, David Howlett and Simon Keynes for advice on a number of points, and especially to David Dumville for unstinting help at all stages of the preparation of this article.

Chapter 5

THE TEXT OF THE BENEDICTIONAL OF ST ÆTHELWOLD

Andrew Prescott

In Memory of Derek Howard Turner

It has become increasingly apparent that one of the central aims of the ecclesiastical reform in England during the tenth century was the improvement and embellishment of the liturgy of the English church. The achievements of the reformers in this field were numerous and wide-ranging. The latest continental types of hymnal, psalter and other liturgical books were introduced[1] and such imaginative innovations were made as the reenactment during matins on Easter day of the visitation to the sepulchre,[2] which has been described as the 'earliest recorded liturgical music-drama'.[3] Concern for the liturgy is also evident in the artistic products of the reform. The musical innovations of the period were, of course, entirely directed towards the enhancement and beautification of church services.[4] Dunstan and Æthelwold

Work on this paper was begun by D.H.Turner, Deputy Keeper in the Department of Manuscripts, British Library, who was one of the organisers of the exhibition 'The Golden Age of Anglo-Saxon Art', held at the British Museum in 1984 to commemorate the millenium of the death of St Æthelwold. Mr Turner tragically died on St Æthelwold's day 1985. I had been working with Mr Turner in compiling a description of the Benedictional of St Æthelwold for the Department of Manuscripts' *Catalogue of Additions* and so took over the preparation of this article. Mr Turner left detailed notes on the contents of the 'Ramsey' Benedictional and the Sacramentary of Ratoldus, which have been used here. Table Three is based on Mr Turner's transcripts of the incipits of blessings in the Sacramentary of Ratoldus. My conclusions have been deeply influenced by Mr Turner's ideas. In fact, this article is in many respects simply a review of the evidence supporting his statement about the Benedictional in *The Golden Age of Anglo-Saxon Art*, ed. J.Backhouse, D.H.Turner and L.Webster (London, 1984), p 60:

> There are two main textual traditions in benedictionals, the so-called 'Gregorian' and 'Gallican' ... Not the least interesting thing about the Benedictional of St Æthelwold is that it is a conflation of complete benedictionals of both traditions ... This suggests a definite concern for completeness, correctness, by someone, probably Æthelwold himself.

I am grateful to my colleagues Janet Backhouse and Michelle Brown for their assistance in the compilation of this paper.

[1] H.Gneuss, *Hymnar und Hymnen im englischen Mittelalter*, Buchreihe der Anglia 12 (Tubingen, 1968); *The Salisbury Psalter*, ed. C. and K.Sisam, EETS 242 (London, 1959), pp 47-52. Canterbury, however, continued to use the 'Roman' psalter: see further N.Brooks, *The Early History of the Church of Canterbury* (Leicester, 1984), pp 261-5. There are useful general comments on the introduction of new types of liturgical books into England during the tenth century in H.Gneuss, 'Liturgical books in Anglo-Saxon England and their Old English terminology', *Learning and Literature in Anglo-Saxon England: Studies presented to Peter Clemoes*, ed. M.Lapidge and H.Gneuss (Cambridge, 1985), pp 91-142.

[2] *Regularis Concordia*, pp 49-51. On the Easter play, see now G.Bryan, *Æthelwold and Medieval Music-Drama at Winchester* (Berne, 1981).

[3] Bryan, *op. cit.* p 99.

[4] See Berry (ch 6 below).

used their metalworking skills to produce such objects for liturgical use as crosses, bells and chalices.[5] At Winchester, the centre of the most important liturgical reforms, a superb new setting for church services was created by the rebuilding of the Old Minster, 'one of the architectural wonders of the Anglo-Saxon kingdom'.[6]

The outstanding English work of art to have survived from this period is the Benedictional of St Æthelwold (London, British Library, Additional MS 49598).[7] A long Latin poem in golden capital letters at the beginning of the manuscript explains that it was written for Æthelwold by Godeman, a monk, probably at the Old Minster, who afterwards became Abbot of Thorney.[8] It is written in a beautiful caroline minuscule and sumptuously decorated with twenty-eight full-page miniatures (several more are now missing) and nineteen decorated initial pages. It dates from between the translation of St Swithun in 971 and Æthelwold's death in 984.[9] On the basis of iconographical evidence linking the Benedictional with the coronation of King Edgar in 973, R. Deshman has proposed that it was executed in that year.[10] The decoration of the Benedictional has been studied in great detail, but its text has been comparatively neglected. This is unfortunate, since it is a service book of a special and interesting kind which embodies one of the most characteristic of the liturgical reforms associated with Æthelwold. The Benedictional consequently provides a most striking illustration of the link between the artistic achievements of the monastic revival and its concern for the improvement of English liturgical life.

Benedictionals are collections of solemn blessings for the use of bishops.[11] They are closely related to pontificals, a type of liturgical book containing rites which could be celebrated only by a bishop. The distinction between pontificals and benedictionals is not always very clear-cut: benedictionals often occur as part of a pontifical and may include in addition to blessings a

---

[5] See e.g. *Chron. Abingdon*, I, 344-345.

[6] M. Biddle, *Excavations near Winchester Cathedral 1961-1967* [reprint of articles from the *Winchester Cathedral Record*], 3rd edn (Winchester, 1968), p 47.

[7] A black and white facsimile, with a valuable introduction and edition of the text, is G. Warner and H. Wilson, *The Benedictional of St Æthelwold*, Roxburghe Club (Oxford, 1910). For colour reproductions of some of the miniatures, see F. Wormald, *The Benedictional of St Æthelwold* (London, 1959). In addition to the bibliography in E. Temple, *Anglo-Saxon Manuscripts 900-1066* (London, 1976), no. 23, see J. Alexander, 'The Benedictional of St Æthelwold and Anglo-Saxon Illumination of the Reform Period', *Tenth-Century Studies*, pp 169-183, 241-245, pls iii-xiv; F. Wormald, 'The "Winchester School" before St Æthelwold', *England before the Conquest: Studies in Primary Sources presented to Dorothy Whitelock*, ed. P. Clemoes and K. Hughes (Cambridge, 1971), pp 305-312, and reprinted in his *Collected Writings*, I (London and Oxford, 1984), pp 76-84; R. Deshman, 'Christus rex et magi reges: Kingship and Christology in Ottonian and Anglo-Saxon Art', *Frühmittelalterliche Studien* 10 (1976), 367-405, figs. 16, 25, 40, 41; *idem*, 'The Leofric Missal and Tenth-Century English Art', *ASE* 6 (1977), 145-173, pls iii, v.

[8] Warner and Wilson, *Benedictional*, pp xiii-xiv.

[9] *Ibid.*, pp lvi-lvii.

[10] 'Leofric Missal', 154-155; 'Kingship and Christology', 398-404.

[11] This general account of benedictionals is based chiefly on *CBP* pt 3, pp vi-lxv, *The Benedictionals of Freising*, ed. R. Amiet, HBS 78 (1974), pp 3-22, and Warner and Wilson, *Benedictional*, pp xlv-lv. There are also some helpful remarks in G. Dix, *The Shape of the Liturgy*, 2nd edn (London, 1945), pp 511-521, and J. A. Jungmann, *The Mass of the Roman Rite*, trans. F. Brunner (New York, 1951), II, pp 294-297.

few miscellaneous forms for such ceremonies as the reconciliation of penitents and the consecration of chrism on Maundy Thursday. Benedictionals have consequently been described as a 'sub-division of Pontificals'.[12] Blessings are, of course, used in many different church services, but those in benedictionals were mainly intended to be pronounced by the bishop at mass, just before the communion.

Pre-communion blessings first began to appear in the liturgy in the fourth and fifth centuries. Their purpose was, in the words of one early eastern liturgy, that 'we may be made worthy to take communion and share in thy holy mysteries'.[13] They also provided a link between the anaphore, the section of the service containing the eucharistic prayer and other acts preparatory to communion, and the communion itself. Moreover, at this time those attending mass were not obliged to take communion and people often left the service at the conclusion of the anaphore. A blessing at this point was a convenient way of dismissing those not staying for communion.

Pre-communion blessings were used widely in eastern churches and many early eastern liturgies make provision for them.[14] They also appeared in North Africa, as is shown by a passage of St Optatus of Mela in which he refers to the laying on of hands before receiving communion.[15] St Augustine of Hippo also mentions the use of blessings, which in the light of Optatus's comments would seem likely to be pre-communion blessings, and even gives the texts of some of them.[16] Pre-communion blessings were not, however, used in Rome. It has been suggested that such features of the Roman mass as the post-communion *oratio super populum* and the declaration *pax vobiscum* before the kiss of peace may have had their origins in a blessing before the communion, but such theories are difficult to substantiate.[17] It was in Spain and France that pre-communion blessings reached their most highly-developed form and became a particularly popular part of the mass.

They were used in Spain from an early date. The decrees of the fourth Council of Toledo in 633 condemned those celebrants who moved the blessing from before to after the communion,[18] while the second Council of Seville in 619 ordered that mere priests should not give solemn blessings.[19]

---

[12] *The Claudius Pontificals*, ed. D. H. Turner, HBS 97 (1971), p xi.

[13] The 'Liturgy of St James', cited by Jungmann, *Mass of the Roman Rite*, II, p 294.

[14] Examples include the *Euchologium* attributed to Sarapion, Bishop of Thmuis in Egypt about 339-63, the Coptic and Ethiopic versions of the *Apostolic Tradition* ascribed to Hippolytus, the schismatic Bishop of Rome, who died in 236 or 237, as well as the liturgies of St James, St Basil and St Mark: see further *CBP* pt 3, pp ix-xi. Amiet sees the blessing before the communion as a purely Gallican practice and does not mention its appearance in the East.

[15] *De Schismate Donatistarum*, ii, 20: *PL* 11, col. 975. Amiet, *Freising Benedictionals*, pp 11-12, argues that the pre-communion blessing was probably not known in North Africa, but does not mention this passage.

[16] *Letter* 149, 16; *Letter* 179, 4; *Ex Sermone contra Pelagianos*, 3: *PL* 33, col. 637, 775; *PL* 39, col. 1721.

[17] On the *oratio super populum*, see G. Morin, 'Un recueil gallican inédit de Benedictiones episcopales en usage à Freising aux VIIe-IXe siècles', *Revue Bénédictine* 29 (1912), 170, Amiet, *Freising Benedictionals*, pp 10-11, and Dix, *Shape of the Liturgy*, p 518. On the *pax vobiscum*, see D. Buenner, *L'Ancienne Liturgie Romaine: le Rite Lyonnais* (Lyons and Paris, 1934), pp 279-280 and *CBP* pt 3, pp xvi-xvii.

[18] Canon 18: *PL* 84, col. 372.

[19] Canon 7: *PL* 84, col. 596-7.

St Isidore stated that such blessings should follow the three-fold form which Moses had been told to use:[20]

> The Lord said to Moses, 'Say to Aaron and his sons, Thus you shall
> bless the people of Israel: you shall say to them,
> The Lord bless you and keep you:
> The Lord make his face to shine upon you, and be gracious to you:
> The Lord lift up his countenance upon you, and give you peace.'[21]

A number of Spanish liturgical books dating from before the romanisation of the Spanish rite in the eleventh century contain collections of pre-communion blessings.[22] These are in three short clauses, as prescribed by St Isidore, and are written in an economic rhythmic prose, with rhymes between the middle and end of each clause.[23] Many of these forms probably predate the Muslim conquest and are interesting specimens of Visigothic literature.

Early church councils in France also made decrees relating to pre-communion blessings. The Council of Agde in 506 followed by the first and third Councils of Orleans in 511 and 538 ordered that no one should leave mass until the blessing had been pronounced.[24] St Caesar of Arles (470-540) stressed the importance of making proper preparation for communion by receiving the blessing in a humble fashion, with a bowed head. He also denounced the habit of leaving mass before the blessing.[25] The Council of Agde further decreed that priests should not give the blessing.[26] The *Expositio Antiquae Liturgiae Gallicanae* provides a short set form of blessing which priests could use.[27] The more elaborate forms varying according to the season were reserved to bishops. The *Expositio* also repeats St Isidore's statement that the solemn episcopal blessing should follow the form given in the Book of Numbers.

No complete early Gallican benedictional survives. There are, however, a few fragmentary collections, the most substantial of which are in the *Missale Gothicum* (Rome, Vatican Library, MS Reg. lat. 317), compiled towards the end of the seventh century in the diocese of Autun,[28] and the *Missale Gallicanum Vetus* (Rome, Vatican Library, MS Palat. lat. 493), written in the middle of the eighth century.[29] It is not possible to establish the relationship

---

[20] *De Ecclesiasticis Officiis*, i, 17: PL 83, col. 754.
[21] Numbers 6, 22-26 (RSV).
[22] Listed in *CBP* pt 3, pp xxi-xxii.
[23] E.g. *CBP* no. 1421, analysed in pt 3, p xxii.
[24] C. Munier, *Concilia Galliae A. 314-A. 506*, Corpus Christianorum, Series Latina, 148 (1963), p 212; C. de Clercq, *Concilia Galliae A. 511-A. 695*, Corpus Christianorum, Series Latina, 148A (1963), pp 11, 125-6.
[25] *PL* 39, col. 2276-2282; see also *CBP* pt 3, p xiii.
[26] Munier, *Concilia Galliae*, p 211.
[27] I. 26a-26b: *Expositio Antiquae Liturgiae Gallicanae*, ed. E. C. Ratcliff, HBS 98 (1971), pp 15-16.
[28] Edited by L. C. Mohlberg, *Missale Gothicum*, Rerum Ecclesiasticarum Documenta, series maior, Fontes 5 (1961). The blessings are listed in *CPB* pt 3, pp 75-6.
[29] Edited by L. C. Mohlberg, L. Eizenhöfer and P. Siffrin, *Missale Gallicanum Vetus*, Rerum Ecclesiasticarum Documenta, series maior, Fontes 3 (1958). The blessings are listed in *CBP* pt 3, pp 74-5. Three other fragments of eighth-century Gallican benedictionals also survive, containing altogether four blessings (*CBP* nos. 101, 240, 1162, 1857). They are printed in an appendix to this edition of *Gallicanum Vetus*.

between these collections. They only contain a handful of blessings and none of the forms are common to both manuscripts. The blessings are in a variety of styles and are apparently taken from more than one source. They are more prolix and elaborate than the Visigothic blessings, often assuming the character of general prayers and containing more than three clauses.[30] Some, however, use internal rhyme in a way which suggests that they were influenced by Visigothic forms.[31]

During the eighth century, the Gallican liturgy became increasingly subject to Roman influence, chiefly as a result of the introduction of two famous types of service book. The first were the so-called Gelasian sacramentaries of the eighth century, a misleading name which refers to a tradition that a service-book was compiled by the fifth-century pope, Gelasius I. In fact, the Gelasian sacramentaries of the eighth century consist of material taken from prayer collections used by Roman priests combined with some Gallican elements.[32] They probably first appeared in France in the third quarter of the eighth century. The other vehicle of Roman influence was the *Hadrianum*, a service book sent by Pope Hadrian I in response to a request of Charlemagne following his visit to Rome in 781. This sacramentary was said by the Pope to contain the pure Roman use, uncontaminated by other traditions. Charlemagne commanded that the *Hadrianum* should be used throughout his dominions, but it lacked many of the most familiar features of services in the Frankish church. The eighth-century Gelasian sacramentary consequently continued in use as a supplement to the *Hadrianum*, a practice which seems to have had official sanction, perhaps from Alcuin himself.[33] This was a very cumbersome arrangement and eventually an appendix to the *Hadrianum* was produced which contained a digest of the additional material in the eighth-century Gelasian.[34]

None of these Roman books made provision for pre-communion blessings. Various attempts were made to produce collections of blessings for use with them, so that the pattern of development of the Gallican benedictional was extremely complex. Different types of benedictional appeared and almost all the surviving manuscripts differ from one another in important respects. The most convincing attempt so far to establish the relationship between these texts occurs in a series of remarkable studies by the great liturgical scholar, Dom Jean Deshusses.[35]

---

[30] E.g. *CBP* no. 781 (from *Missale Gothicum*: no. 22 in Mohlberg's edition).

[31] E.g. *CBP* nos. 9, 605 (from *Missale Gothicum*: nos. 122 and 169 in Mohlberg's edition), analysed in *CBP* pt 3, pp xxiii–xxiv.

[32] B. Moreton, *The Eighth-Century Gelasian Sacramentary* (Oxford, 1976), particularly pp 168-174.

[33] J. Deshusses, 'Le "Supplement" au Sacramentaire Grégorien: Alcuin ou saint Benoît d'Aniane?', *Archiv für Liturgiewissenschaft* 9 (1965), 58-59.

[34] For an analysis of its contents, see Deshusses 'Le "Supplement" au Sacramentaire Grégorien', 48-58, 60-63. It has been printed frequently. The latest edition is J. Deshusses, *Le Sacramentaire Grégorien*, Spicilegium Friburgense, 16, 24, 28 (1971-1982), nos. 1019-1805.

[35] In addition to the works by him already cited, see 'Le benedictionnaire gallican du VIIIe siècle', *Ephemerides Liturgicae* 77 (1963), 169-187. There is also a useful discussion of the Gallican benedictional in Amiet, *Freising Benedictionals*, pp 23-63, but this does not consider a number of important issues, such as the relationship between the short and long benedictionals, so Deshusses's interpretation is followed here.

Two main types of Gallican benedictional emerged in the eighth century.[36] One consisted in its original version of perhaps about seventy-five blessings, while the other was much shorter, probably containing at first about twenty-five blessings, many of which are also found in the long benedictional. Deshusses has shown that the long benedictional was produced first, being perhaps compiled in the diocese of Autun towards the end of the seventh century from a variety of sources, including the collections in the *Missale Gothicum* and *Gallicanum Vetus*. The short benedictional, which seems to date from the middle of the eighth century, was essentially an abridgement of the long version, with the addition of a few other forms such as three blessings in *Gallicanum Vetus* which do not appear in the long version.[37] It was probably intended for use in monasteries, where, since bishops were not regularly present, service books did not need to offer a wide variety of blessings covering many different sorts of occasions.

The eighth-century Gelasian Sacramentary only began to appear widely in cathedrals towards the end of the century, when it was used as a supplement to the *Hadrianum*. In cathedrals, a larger range of blessings was required than was available in the short benedictional and the longer version was preferred. The most important surviving copies of the long benedictional all date from this period and mainly occur as additions to Gelasian sacramentaries. They show great textual variety. They are all further removed from the original archetype than the recension used in compiling the short benedictional. The version which appears to be closest to the original is that in the Sacramentary of Angoulême (Paris, Bibliothèque Nationale, MS lat. 816),[38] but even here the order of the blessings has been changed, apparently under the influence of the short benedictional, so that they begin at Advent. A manuscript from Freising (Munich, Bayerische Staatsbibliothek, Cod. lat. 6430) contains versions of both the short and long benedictionals.[39] In this manuscript, a recension of the long benedictional was used in which not only had the order of the blessings for general Sunday use been radically altered, but blessings inserted from another source and new blessings created by running together groups of three post-communion prayers. In the long benedictional in the Sacramentary of Gellone (Paris, BN, MS lat. 12048),[40] special blessings were provided for all the Sundays after Easter and Pentecost. The extra blessings were obtained by splitting in half forms intended for general Sunday use, as well as by borrowing material from the short benedictional and the source of the long benedictional in the Freising manuscript.

During this transitional period when the eighth-century Gelasian sacramentary and the *Hadrianum* were used together, a completely new benedictional

---

[36] The next two paragraphs are based on Deshusses, 'Le benedictionnaire gallican'.

[37] *CBP* 81, 245, 341 (nos. 222, 228, 234 in the edition of Mohlberg *et al.*); cf. Deshusses, 'Le benedictionnaire gallican', 180.

[38] Edited by P. Cagin, *Le Sacramentaire Gélasian d'Angoulême* (Angoulême, 1919). The blessings are nos. 1799-1872 and 2317-2318.

[39] Both benedictionals have been edited by Amiet, *Freising Benedictionals*, and the shorter benedictional also by W. Dürig, 'Das Benedictionale Frisingense vetus', *Archiv für Liturgie-wissenschaft* 4 (1955), 223-244.

[40] P. de Puniet, *Le Sacramentaire romain de Gellone* (Rome, 1938) [reprint from *Ephemerides Liturgicae* 52 (1938)]. The long benedictional is nos. 1987-2100. This manuscript also contains a version of the short benedictional: nos. 1974-1985.

was composed in the Visigothic style, using rhythmic prose with internal rhymes.[41] This benedictional was accompanied by a collection of prefaces, mostly drawn from the eighth-century Gelasian sacramentary, but also including some new pieces which were reworkings of Gelasian prayers, again in the Visigothic style. This collection of blessings and prefaces seems originally to have been produced for local use as an appendix to the Gelasian sacramentary, but subsequently enjoyed an illustrious career. When a digest of material from the Gelasian sacramentary was produced for use as a supplement to the *Hadrianum*, these prefaces and blessings were added as an appendix. The supplement contained some new prayers in the same style as the blessings and prefaces, which shows that they are all the work of the same person. This compilation was issued with an explanatory preface and became a standard addition to the Gregorian sacramentary.

This supplement was long thought to have been the work of Alcuin, but this is extremely unlikely, since, as Deshusses has stressed, it was produced by someone steeped in Visigothic traditions. Deshusses has argued that the author was more probably the Visigoth Witiza, who, as Benedict of Aniane, became the spiritual leader of the Empire under Louis the Pious.[42] This theory is supported by stylistic parallels between the preface to the supplement and known works of Benedict.[43] Aniane's benedictional seems originally to have been composed for use in a monastery and is quite short, containing fifty-two blessings. It makes provision only for the most important feasts and contains a large selection of forms for general daily use. As its use spread, additional blessings were inserted and the general forms were assigned to specific occasions. A number of expanded versions of Aniane's benedictional appeared. The most common is found in a group of manuscripts associated with the monasteries of St Amand near Tournai and Corbie in Amiens.[44] This contains about thirty-six extra blessings, most of which are in the same style as those of Aniane, making use of internal rhyme,[45] and sometimes even borrowing old Visigothic forms.[46] This version of Aniane's benedictional is familiar from the *Missale Sancti Eligii* (Paris, BN, MS lat. 12051), the basis of Ménard's edition of the Gregorian sacramentary, which was reprinted by Migne.[47] This form of benedictional has been called 'Gregorian',[48] because of its association with the version of the Gregorian sacramentary in the *Hadrianum*.

Pre-communion blessings provide one of the most striking examples of the occasional triumph of Gallican over Roman practice. With the spread of the *Hadrianum* and its supplement, they passed from France to many other

---

[41] See the analysis of the contents of this supplement in Deshusses, 'Le "Supplement" au Sacramentaire Grégorien', 48-58, 60-3.

[42] *Ibid.*, 60-5. Reiterated by Deshusses in *Sacramentaire Grégorien*, III, 67-75. For a different view, see L. Wallach, *Diplomatic Studies in Latin and Greek Documents from the Carolingian Age* (New York, 1977), pp 252-255, and K. Gamber, 'Der fränkische Anhang zum Gregorianum im Licht eines Fragments aus dem Anfang des ix. Jhts.', *Sacris Erudiri* 21 (1972-3), 267-289.

[43] Deshusses, 'Le "Supplement" au Sacramentaire Grégorien', 65-9, and *Sacramentaire Grégorien*, III, pp 71-4.

[44] Listed and discussed in Deshusses, *Sacramentaire Grégorien*, I, pp 72-5, and II, p 29.

[45] E.g. *CBP* nos. 1337, 1804.

[46] E.g. *CBP* nos. 149, 169, 360, 380, 1388, 1523, 1745, 1815, 1880.

[47] *PL* 78, cols 25-240. See also Deshusses, *Sacramentaire Grégorien*, nos. 3811-3847 and 3872-3892, which prints similar collections in Cambrai, Bibliothèque Municipale, MSS 162-164.

[48] Turner, *Claudius Pontificals*, pp xi-xii.

countries and remained in use throughout most of western Europe until the sixteenth century.[49] As has been seen, two main forms of benedictional had been established: the 'Gallican', with its short and long versions, and the 'Gregorian', based on the benedictional of Benedict of Aniane. Later benedictionals drew extensively on these traditions, but combined, reworked and developed them in many different ways. The order of blessings was altered and they were assigned to different feasts. Extra blessings were added to suit local circumstances and to give celebrants a greater choice of forms. Old blessings were dropped and replaced with material from other sources. Moreover, the composition of new forms of blessing was a popular form of literary activity and almost every benedictional contains at least one or two pieces which are apparently new works. As the use of pre-communion blessings spread and more benedictionals were produced, the cumulative effects of this continual transposition, substitution and addition became increasingly complex. It is consequently rare to find that the text of any two benedictionals is exactly the same, and it is perhaps more difficult to establish the sources and interrelationship of benedictionals than any other type of liturgical manuscript.

Since the forms of service brought to England by St Augustine were Roman, they did not include pre-communion blessings. St Boniface was evidently surprised by the practice when he encountered it on the continent and he wrote to Pope Zacharias asking whether it was permissible. In his reply, dated 4 November 751, the Pope roundly condemned such blessings as foreign to apostolic tradition.[50] They nevertheless spread to England with the importation of Frankish service books in the ninth century. One of the decrees of the Council of Chelsea in 816 refers to a *liber ministerialis* containing a rite for the consecration of churches, of which all the bishops in the province of Canterbury needed to have a copy. This was probably a pontifical which may perhaps have included a benedictional.[51]

The oldest complete English benedictional to have survived is in the Leofric Missal (Oxford, Bodleian Library, MS Bodley 579).[52] This manuscript is

---

[49] On the later history of the pre-communion blessing, see *CBP* pt 3, pp xviii-xx and Amiet, *Freising Benedictionals*, pp 15-22. The practice disappeared from general use in the sixteenth centurq but persisted in France until the campaign to secure greater uniformity with the Roman rite in the nineteenth century, when it was suppressed except as a local custom in the cathedrals of Lyons and Autun. In 1970, however, a new Roman missal appeared which included twenty blessings to be used 'at the discretion of the priest, at the end of the Mass, or after the liturgy of the word, the office, and the celebration of the sacraments'. Most of these forms were based on blessings composed by Aniane: *Roman Missal Revised By Decree of the Second Vatican Council* [Official English Text] (London, 1974), pp 364-377. See also *CBP* nos. 2068-2093 and T. Krosnicki, 'New Blessings in the Missal of Paul VI', *Worship* 4 (1971), 199-205.

[50] *PL* 89, col. 951.

[51] Canon 2: A. Haddan and W. Stubbs, *Councils and Ecclesiastical Documents relating to Great Britain and Ireland* (Oxford, 1869-71), III, 580. Brooks, *Church of Canterbury*, pp 164-5 suggests that this service book may correspond to the pontifical in the Sacramentary of Ratoldus (Paris, Bibliothèque Nationale, MS lat. 12052). On the Sacramentary of Ratoldus, however, see further below, pp 135-42.

[52] Edited by F. Warren, *The Leofric Missal* (Oxford, 1883). See also C. Hohler, 'Some Service Books of the Later Saxon Church', *Tenth-Century Studies*, pp 69-70, 78-80, and N. Ker, *Catalogue of Manuscripts containing Anglo-Saxon* (Oxford, 1957), no. 315. H. Gneuss, 'Manuscripts written or owned in England up to 1100', *ASE* 9 (1981), 15 (no. 202) notes a fragment of a benedictional in Cambridge, Trinity Hall, MS 24, ff 78-83, which he tentatively

basically a copy of an English service book made by a foreign scribe in about 900. A Glastonbury calendar of about 970-980 was later inserted in it, indicating that it was probably at Glastonbury about this time. It subsequently found its way to Exeter, where further prayers and other material were added to it in the tenth and eleventh centuries. In the main text, the blessings have been placed in the order of service rather than in an appendix. They were all drawn from the benedictional of Benedict of Aniane, omitting only one form, the alternative blessing for Easter Day. This suggests that the earliest form of benedictional known in England was that found in the supplement to the *Hadrianum*.

The Benedictional of St Æthelwold provides a striking contrast to the benedictional in the Leofric Missal.[53] Æthelwold is very much longer, containing more than three times as many blessings as the Leofric Missal. It not only provides blessings for a more extensive range of occasions, but also gives alternative forms for major feasts. It in fact combines together two almost complete benedictionals: a Gregorian benedictional similar to that in the *Missale Sancti Eligii* and a version of the long Gallican benedictional. The text of the Gallican benedictional which was used was closely related to that in the Sacramentary of Angoulême but also contained a few additional forms which are found in the Freising manuscript.[54] For major feasts Æthelwold usually gives a Gregorian blessing first then a Gallican alternative. In addition to this continental material, Æthelwold also includes a number of blessings which occur only in English manuscripts or those closely related to English traditions.

The systematic and skilful fashion in which these different types of blessing were combined together in the Benedictional of St Æthelwold is apparent from the following table, which shows the sources of all the blessings in Æthelwold. It is based on the edition of the text by H. Wilson included in the 1910 facsimile. Some blessings are missing because of the removal of leaves from the manuscript, but the lost text was reconstructed by Wilson. These blessings are shown in square brackets. The figures preceded by the letters CBP give the number of the blessing in the monumental collection of episcopal blessings compiled by Dom Edmond Moeller, which contains detailed collations with a wide range of other manuscripts. For Gregorian blessings, references are also given to Deshusses's edition of the Gregorian sacramentary. They relate either to the supplement of Aniane (S),[55] which Deshusses prints from Cambrai, Bibliothèque Municipale, MS 164, or to the blessings added to Aniane's benedictional in the St Amand group of manuscripts, which Deshusses prints as 'Textes Complémentaires' (TC) from Cambrai MSS 162, 163 and 164.[56] References are also given to the column numbers of Ménard's edition of the *Missale Sancti Eligii* as reprinted in the

---

dates as eighth century.

[53] The text of the Benedictional of St Æthelwold is printed in Warner and Wilson, *Benedictional*, pp 1-47.

[54] Cf. Amiet, *Freising Benedictionals*, pp 54-5 and Deshusses, 'Le benedictionnaire gallican', 176. Neither mentions the appearance of Gregorian and English forms in Æthelwold and other English texts.

[55] Deshusses, *Sacramentaire Grégorien*, nos. 1738-1789.

[56] *Ibid.*, nos. 3811-3847 and 3872-3892.

Patrologia Latina, volume 78 (EL). For Gallican blessings, the number of the blessing in P. Cagin's edition of the Sacramentary of Angoulême[57] is given (A) or, if it does not appear in this source, its number in R. Amiet's edition of the Benedictionals of Freising (F).[58]

TABLE ONE   The sources of the blessings in the benedictional of St Æthelwold

1.	Advent 1	Gregorian:	CBP 1544; S 1768; EL 191
2.	Alia	Gallican:	CBP 37; A 1802
3.	Advent 2	Gregorian:	CBP 663; TC 3845; EL 191
4.	Alia	Gallican:	CBP 1352; A 1803
5.	Advent 3	Gregorian:	CBP 1722; S 1769; EL 192
6.	Alia	Gallican:	CBP 1307; A 1799
7.	Advent 4	Gregorian:	CBP 1200; TC 3847; EL 194-195
8.	Feria IV	Gallican:	CBP 1072; A 1804
9.	Feria VI	Gallican:	CBP 909; A 1818
10.	Sabbato in XII Lectionibus	Gallican:	CBP 286; A 1819
11.	Christmas Eve	Gregorian:	CBP 1643; S 1738; EL 30
12.	In Gallicantu	Gallican:	CBP 1857; A 1805
13.	Primo Mane	Gallican:	CBP 1021; A 1808
14.	Christmas Day	Gregorian:	CBP 321; S 1739; EL 31-32
15.	Alia	Gallican:	CBP 932; A 1806
16.	St Stephen	Gregorian:	CBP 854; S 1740; EL 33
17.	Alia	Gallican:	CBP 38; A 1809
18.	St John the Evangelist	Gregorian:	CBP 1566; S 1741; EL 34
19.	[Alia	Gallican:	CBP 1161; A 1811]
20.	Holy Innocents	Gregorian:	CBP 1600; S 1742; EL 35-36
21.	Alia	Gallican:	CBP 579; A 1812
22.	Octave of Christmas	Gregorian:	CBP 1545; S 1743; EL 37
23.	Christmas 1	Gregorian:	CBP 1168; TC 3824; EL 38
24.	Epiphany	Gregorian:	CBP 732; S 1744; EL 39
25.	Alia	Gallican:	CBP 1087; A 1815
26.	Epiphany 1	Gregorian:	CBP 926; TC 3825; EL 40
27.	Epiphany 2	Gregorian:	CBP 1143; TC 3826; EL 41
28.	Epiphany 3	Gregorian:	CBP 1711; TC 3827; EL 47
29.	Epiphany 4	Gregorian:	CBP 2019; TC 3828; EL 48
30.	Epiphany 5	Gregorian:	CBP 855; TC 3829; EL 49
31.	Epiphany 6	Gregorian:	CBP 1005; TC 3830; EL 49
32.	Alia	Gallican:	CBP 42; A 1868
33.	St Sebastian	Gallican:	CBP 1160; A 1840
34.	St Agnes	Gregorian:	CBP 175; S 1775; EL 172
35.	St Vincent	English:	CBP 156

---

[57] *Le Sacramentaire Gélasien d'Angoulême* (Angoulême, 1919).
[58] *The Benedictionals of Freising*, HBS 88 (1974), pp 76-120.

36. Conversion of St Paul	Gregorian:	CBP 940; TC 3811; EL 44
37. St Agnes (alia)	Gregorian:	CBP 149, 169; TC 3833; EL 176
38. Form of blessing of candles on Feast of the Purification		
39. Purification	Gregorian:	CBP 1674; S 1745; EL 46
40. St Agatha	Gallican:	CBP 1956; A 1846
41. St Vedast	Gallican:	CBP 704, 910; F XV
42. St Peter in Cathedra	Gallican:	CBP 851; F XVIII
43. St Gregory	Gallican:	CBP 807; A 1843
44. Annunciation	Gallican:	CBP 874; A 1834
45. St Ambrose	Gallican:	CBP 1254; A 1842
46. Septuagesima	Gregorian:	CBP 1584; TC 3813; EL 53
47. Alia	Gallican:	CBP 1913; A 1800, 1859
48. Sexagesima	Gregorian:	CBP 632; TC 3814; EL 54
49. Alia	Gallican:	CBP 42; A 1868
50. Quinquagesima	Gregorian:	CBP 1694; TC 3815; EL 55
51. Feria IV	Gallican:	CBP 82; F CXXXVII
52. Beginning of Lent	Gallican:	CBP 247; A 1816
53. Lent 1	Gregorian:	CBP 192; S 1746; EL 58
54. Lent 2	Gallican:	CBP 101; A 1870
55. Alia	Gallican:	CBP 1924; A 1817
56. Lent 3	Gregorian:	CBP 702; EL 142
57. Alia	Gregorian:	CBP 1576; S 1747; EL 62
58. Lent 4	Gallican:	CBP 909; A 1818
59. Alia or Lent 5	Gallican:	CBP 286; A 1819
60. Palm Sunday	Gregorian:	CBP 180; S 1751; EL 77
61. Alia … in passione Domini	Gregorian:	CBP 1671; S 1752; EL 81
62. Alia	Gallican:	CBP 13; A 1820
63. Alia	Gallican:	CBP 1097; A 1821
64. Maundy Thursday	Gregorian:	CBP 233; S 1753; EL 83-84
65. Alia	Gallican:	CBP 113; A 1822
66. Holy Saturday	Gregorian:	CBP 879; S 1754; EL 91
67. Alia	Gallican:	CBP 1010; A 1823
68. Easter Day	Gregorian:	CBP 292; S 1755; EL 92
69. Alia	Gallican:	CBP 858; A 1824
70. Feria II	Gregorian:	CBP 1106, 510; TC 3879; EL 93
71. Feria III	Gregorian:	CBP 1207; TC 3816; EL 94
72. Feria IV	Gregorian:	CBP 1268; TC 3817; EL 94
73. Feria V	Gregorian:	CBP 1815; TC 3818; EL 95
74. Feria VI	Gregorian:	CBP 216; TC 3819; EL 96
75. Saturday after Easter	Gallican:	CBP 995; A 1825
76. Octave of Easter	Gregorian:	CBP 679; S 1756; EL 97
77. Easter 1	Gregorian:	CBP 314; S 1757; EL 104
78. Alia	Gregorian:	CBP 1070; S 1758; EL 104-105
79. Easter 2	Gallican:	CBP 576; A 1826

80. Alia	Gallican:	CBP 884; A 1827
81. Alia	Gallican:	CBP 877; A 1828
82. Alia	Gallican:	CBP 1799; F XLVIII
83. SS Tibertius & Valerian	Gregorian:	CBP 153; S 1772; EL 166
84. Invention of Holy Cross	Gregorian:	CBP 310, 190; S 1764; EL 102
85. In Laetania maiore	Gregorian:	CBP 1560; S 1759; EL 106
86. Alia ... de Ieiunio	Gallican:	CBP 1919; A 1829
87. Eve of Ascension	Gregorian:	CBP 380; TC 3831; EL 110
88. Ascension Day	Gregorian:	CBP 281; S 1760; EL 109
89. Sunday after Ascension	Gallican:	CBP 1152; A 1830
90. Eve of Pentecost	Gregorian:	CBP 186, 294; S 1761; EL 111
91. Pentecost	Gregorian:	CBP 948; S 1762; EL 112
92. Alia	Gallican:	CBP 1086; A 1831
93. Saturday after Pentecost	Gregorian:	CBP 301, 187; TC 3821; EL 115
94. Octave of Pentecost	Gregorian:	CBP 1804; TC 3822; EL 116
95. Alia	Gallican:	CBP 1258; A 1832
96. Pentecost 1	Gregorian:	CBP 159; S 1777; EL 175
97. Alia	Gallican:	CBP 1913; A 1800, 1859
98. Pentecost 2	Gregorian:	CBP 1880; TC 3832; EL 175
99. Alia	Gallican:	CBP 22; A 1860
100. Pentecost 3	English:	CBP 287
101. Pentecost 4	Gregorian:	CBP 1337; TC 3834; EL 177
102. Alia	English:	CBP 120
103. Pentecost 5	Gregorian:	CBP 1696; S 1778; EL 177
104. Alia	Gallican:	CBP 220; A 1863
105. Pentecost 6	Gregorian:	CBP 31; TC 3835; EL 178
106. Alia	Gallican:	CBP 1251; A 1865
107. Pentecost 7	Gregorian:	CBP 1433; S 1779; EL 179
108. Alia	Gallican:	CBP 1256; A 1866
109. Pentecost 8	Gregorian:	CBP 1962; TC 3836; EL 179
110. Alia	English:	CBP 128
111. Pentecost 9	Gregorian:	CBP 1499; S 1780; EL 180
112. Alia	English:	CBP 381
113. Pentecost 10	Gregorian:	CBP 921; TC 3837; EL 180
114. Alia	Gallican:	CBP 42; A 1868
115. Pentecost 11	Gregorian:	CBP 1236; S 1781; EL 181
116. Alia	English:	CBP 128
117. Pentecost 12	Gregorian:	CBP 1388; TC 3838; EL 181-182
118. Alia	English:	CBP 1935
119. Pentecost 13	Gregorian:	CBP 631; S 1782; EL 182
120. Alia	English:	CBP 218
121. Pentecost 14	Gregorian:	CBP 360; TC 3839; EL 183
122. Alia	English:	CBP 129
123. Pentecost 15	Gregorian:	CBP 571; S 1783; EL 183
124. Alia	English:	CBP 901

125.	Pentecost 16	Gregorian:	CBP 1745; TC 3840; EL 184
126.	Alia	English:	CBP 1920
127.	Pentecost 17	Gregorian:	CBP 1528; S 1784; EL 184
128.	Alia	Gallican:	CBP 108; F CXXXI
129.	Pentecost 18	Gregorian:	CBP 1562; S 1785; EL 185
130.	Alia	English:	CBP 1912
131.	Pentecost 19	Gregorian:	CBP 1886; S 1786; EL 185
132.	Alia	English:	CBP 1432
133.	Pentecost 20	Gregorian:	CBP 1703; S 1787; EL 186
134.	Alia	English:	CBP 707
135.	Pentecost 21	Gregorian:	CBP 1563; S 1788; EL 187
136.	Alia	English:	CBP 742
137.	Pentecost 22	Gregorian:	CBP 365; TC 3841; EL 187
138.	Pentecost 23	Gregorian:	CBP 1523; TC 3842; EL 188
139.	Alia	Gallican:	CBP 98; A 1871
140.	St Ætheldreda	English:	CBP 1805
141.	Nat. St John the Baptist	Gregorian:	CBP 179; S 1763; EL 122
142.	Alia	Gallican:	CBP 835; A 1836
143.	SS Peter and Paul	Gregorian:	CBP 193; S 1765; EL 123
144.	Alia	Gallican:	CBP 981; A 1837
145.	St Swithun	English:	CBP 1088
146.	St Benedict	English:	CBP 1770
147.	St Laurence	English(?):	CBP 1948
148.	Assumption BVM	Gregorian:	CBP 1053; S 1766; EL 134
149.	St Bartholomew	Gallican:	CBP 905; A 1839
150.	Decoll. St John the Baptist	Gregorian:	CBP 1194; S 1767; EL 136
151.	Alia	Gallican:	CBP 1264, 1900; F LXVIII
152.	[Nativity BVM	English(?):	CBP 1697]
153.	Alia	English:	CBP 1654
154.	Exaltation of Holy Cross	Gallican:	CBP 792; A 1833
155.	St Matthew	Gallican:	CBP 101; A 1870
156.	Sabbato mense septimi	English:	CBP 381
157.	Michaelmas	English:	CBP 1501
158.	Alia	English:	CBP 342, 227
159.	All Saints	English:	CBP 1743
160.	Alia	English(?):	CBP 297
161.	St Martin	Gallican:	CBP 1090; A 1844
162.	Alia	Gallican:	CBP 807; A 1843
163.	St Cecilia	English(?):	CBP 1948
164.	St Clement	English:	CBP 1706
165.	Eve of St Andrew	English:	CBP 1695
166.	St Andrew	English:	CBP 817
167.	Alia	English:	CBP 1252
168.	St Thomas	English:	CBP 602
169.	One Apostle	Gregorian:	CBP 1203; S 1770; EL 51

170. One Martyr	Gregorian:	CBP 57; S 1771; EL 164-165
171. Many Martyrs	Gregorian:	CBP 153; S 1772; EL 166
172. One Bishop Confessor	Gregorian:	CBP 1733; S 1773; EL 168
173. Many Confessors	Gregorian:	CBP 1968; S 1774; EL 147, 170
174. One Virgin	Gregorian:	CBP 149, 148, 169; TC 3833; EL 176
175. One Virgin Martyr	Gregorian:	CBP 175; S 1775; EL 172
176. Many Virgins	Gregorian:	CBP 1742; S 1776; EL 172
177. Dedication of a church	Gregorian:	CBP 123; EL 161

The systematic fusing together in the Benedictional of St Æthelwold of two virtually complete texts representing the main traditions then current on the continent is a remarkable achievement. In most benedictionals, the borrowing of blessings from other sources is a more haphazard process. Moreover, Æthelwold does not extensively rearrange the blessings and remains very close to its original sources. Where the position of blessings is changed, they are usually assigned to related feasts, so that, for example, two Gallican blessings given for the beginning of Lent in the Sacramentary of Angoulême are allocated in Æthelwold to two Ember Days in Advent (nos. 9, 10). Sometimes, blessings are moved to different places in the same season, as during Easter, where four blessings provided in the Sacramentary of Angoulême as alternatives for Easter Day are used for the Saturday after Easter and as alternatives for Easter 2 (nos. 75, 80-82). Blessings for the common of saints are also occasionally assigned to the feasts of particular individuals[59] and forms for general use may be allocated to set days.[60] On the whole, however, blessings are still used in Æthelwold for the same feasts as in the *Missale Sancti Eligii* and the Sacramentary of Angoulême. The only place in Æthelwold where the alternation of Gregorian and Gallican forms breaks down so that there is a radical departure from the original sources is in Lent. Here, Æthelwold omits the forms given in Aniane's supplement for the third, fourth and fifth Sundays in Lent and Aniane's blessing for the second Sunday in Lent is used only as an alternative for the following week (no. 57). The Gregorian form given as a first blessing for the third Sunday in Lent (no. 56) is used in the *Missale Sancti Eligii* for an Ember Day in September. The rest of the blessings in Lent are Gallican.[61]

The immediate question raised by this analysis of the text of the Benedictional of St Æthelwold is whether it was compiled at Winchester or imported from elsewhere. The splendid appearance of the manuscript certainly suggests that it was a de-luxe copy of a special text and a Winchester compilation is more likely to have received such treatment than one from elsewhere. Moreover, the systematic arrangement of the text and its proximity to the original sources all suggest that it was a recent production which had not been subjected to extensive recopying. The appearance of a Gallican blessing for the feast of St Vedast (no. 41) might be taken as an indication that the text originated in northern France, but it may simply

---

[59] E.g. nos. 34, 40, 41, 83.
[60] E.g. the Gallican blessings used for Sundays after Pentecost.
[61] This was first pointed out by Turner, *Claudius Pontificals*, pp xvi-xvii.

mean that the version of the Gallican benedictional used by the compiler of Æthelwold came from that area.

The English blessings do not greatly assist in determining where the main text was compiled. They are in a variety of styles and are apparently drawn from a number of different sources. The English blessings for Sundays after Pentecost, for example, consist of short, simple clauses, varying in number, while on the other hand the blessing for the feast of St Ætheldreda (no. 140) is in three lengthy sections written in extremely high-flown language. Some of the English blessings are probably entirely native compositions,[62] while others are adaptations of continental forms.[63] A few were undoubtedly composed at Winchester in St Æthelwold's time, the most obvious example being the blessing for St Swithun's Day (no. 145), with its reference to recent miracles at the saint's shrine, but this is not sufficient to establish that the whole text was compiled there. Moreover, some of the English forms are taken from sources outside Winchester, such as the first blessing for St Andrew's Day (no. 166), which, since it describes Andrew as a special patron, was probably written at Wells sometime after it became an episcopal see in 908.[64]

In attempting to determine whether the text of the Benedictional of St Æthelwold originated at Winchester, an obvious starting point is a comparison with the 'Ramsey' Benedictional (Paris, BN, MS lat. 987).[65] This was at one time thought to be the benedictional sent from Ramsey Abbey to Gauzlin, Abbot of Fleury (1004-1029),[66] but it contains at the end an additional group of blessings clearly intended for use at Canterbury which were inserted in the manuscript sometime after the Translation of St Ælfheah in 1023.[67] It seems more likely that it was produced at Winchester rather than Ramsey and sent to Canterbury not Fleury. Apart from where leaves have been physically removed from one or other of the manuscripts, 'Ramsey' contains the same blessings as Æthelwold in precisely the same order, with three exceptions. It omits the blessings for the feasts of SS Ætheldreda and Swithun (nos. 140, 145), which were perhaps not needed at Canterbury, and the alternative blessing for the feast of SS Peter and Paul (no. 144). However, the headings given for particular blessings in 'Ramsey' sometimes differ from those in Æthelwold, so that the blessings are assigned to different feasts.

For example, 'Ramsey' occasionally gives a long series of alternative blessings which in Æthelwold are allotted to specific occasions, producing a neater arrangement. Thus, in 'Ramsey', after the blessing for the last Sunday in Advent, there are three blessings described as 'alia de adventu domini',

---

[62] E.g. nos. 124, 134, 157, 164 are all considered by Moeller to be 'probablement d'origine anglaise'.

[63] E.g. nos. 35 (based on a blessing in the Sacramentary of Gellone: *CBP* no. 239); 100 (based on a blessing in the Sacramentary of Angoulême: *CBP* no. 288); 167 (based on a blessing in the *Missale Gothicum: CBP* no. 1252).

[64] See Hohler, 'Service Books', p 66, and Turner, *Claudius Pontificals*, p ix.

[65] Not published, but fully collated with the text of Æthelwold in Warner and Wilson, *Benedictional*, pp 1-56, and *CBP*. Extensive use has also been made of notes on the contents of 'Ramsey' left by D. H. Turner.

[66] L. Delisle, 'Mémoire sur d'Anciens Sacramentaires', *Mémoires de l'Académie des Inscriptions et Belles-Lettres*, 32 pt 1 (1886), 215-16.

[67] *The Canterbury Benedictional*, ed. R. M. Woolley, HBS 51 (1917), pp xix-xxv.

intended for general use in Advent. In Æthelwold, these are assigned to the three Ember Days in Advent (nos. 8-10). It seems that the confusion in Æthelwold over the arrangement of the blessings in Lent was the result of a similar process. 'Ramsey' does not give blessings for the last three Sundays in Lent, but includes three alternative Gallican blessings for the beginning of Lent, together with other blessings for Ember days and weekdays. In Æthelwold, these have been reallocated to provide blessings for all the Sundays in Lent, but, since the original sequence in 'Ramsey' has been retained, the Gregorian and Gallican forms do not alternate in the same way as elsewhere. This table shows what happened:

TABLE TWO   Blessings for Lent in the 'Ramsey' Benedictional and the Benedictional of St Æthelwold

'RAMSEY'		ÆTHELWOLD
Beginning of Lent (Gallican)	=	52: Beginning of Lent
Alia (Gregorian)	=	53: Lent 1
Alia (Gallican)	=	54: Lent 2
Alia (Gallican)	=	55: Alia
Sabbato in xii lectionibus (Gregorian)	=	56: Lent 3
Lent 2 (Gregorian)	=	57: Alia
Feria (Gallican)	=	58: Lent 4
Alia (Gallican)	=	59: Alia or Lent 5

The overall arrangement of the text has also been improved in Æthelwold. For example, in 'Ramsey' the blessings for Septuagesima come straight after those for the Sundays after Epiphany. There then follows a group of blessings for saints' days and after that the blessings for the rest of the Sundays before Lent. In Æthelwold, the headings have been slightly altered, so that the blessings for Septuagesima immediately precede those for Sexagesima and Quinquagesima (nos. 46-50). Another interesting difference between 'Ramsey' and Æthelwold is that forms for blessing palms on Palm Sundays are included in 'Ramsey' but not in Æthelwold. 'Ramsey' also gives a blessing for use at vespers on Easter Day, which in Æthelwold becomes the alternative blessing for mass on Easter Day (no. 69). This suggests that a deliberate attempt was made in Æthelwold to remove extraneous material and ensure that the text consisted entirely of blessings for use at mass before the communion. This seems to reflect the influence of someone who liked clear-cut, neat distinctions between service books.

The differences between the texts of the 'Ramsey' Benedictional and the Benedictional of St Æthelwold suggest that 'Ramsey' provided the immediate source of Æthelwold. The changes in the headings in Æthelwold represent attempts to produce a tidier and more rational structure. 'Ramsey' does not, however, provide any further clues as to the ultimate origins of this hybrid form of benedictional. It is also a Winchester manuscript and appears to be not much older than Æthelwold. Indeed, its hand is very similar to that in Æthelwold and, in view of the close relationship between the two texts, it seems almost certain that both manuscripts are the work of the same scribe, Godeman.[68]

The two leading students of benedictionals, Dom Jean Laporte and Dom Edmond Moeller, have both placed the Benedictional of St Æthelwold in a group of French manuscripts which they call the family of St Vedast in Arras.[69] The basis on which they arrived at this classification is not entirely clear. They include in this group, for example, the benedictional in an eleventh-century pontifical of Trèves adapted to the use of Cambrai (Paris, BN, MS lat. 13313), which is a copy of the blessings in the supplement to the *Hadrianum*, with just eight additional forms, all except one of which are drawn from German sources. This manuscript displays none of the characteristics of the Benedictional of St Æthelwold and seems to bear no relationship to it.

Dom Laporte and Dom Moeller consider the chief source of this group to be Paris, BN, MS lat. 12052, the well-known Sacramentary of Ratoldus, which has been the subject of a penetrating discussion by Christopher Hohler.[70] This manuscript was owned by Ratoldus, abbot of Corbie in Amiens from 972 until his death in 986. Corbie was, of course, the house from which Æthelwold requested monks to teach his community at Abingdon the proper singing of the chants and which exercised an important influence on liturgical development in England during the tenth century.[71] The Sacramentary of Ratoldus was not, however, compiled at Corbie. New leaves had to be inserted to make it suitable for use there. Since it contains a calendar of the monastery of St Vedast in Arras, it has been assumed that the text was put together there, but Hohler has shown that its origins lie much further back. It appears to be a Saint Denis sacramentary adapted for use by the Bishop of Dol in Brittany in the 920s and further modified by the Breton and Norman clergy who took refuge from the Vikings in the church of Saint Symphorien at Orleans.

At some stage, an English pontifical was incorporated into the text. The origins of this pontifical are apparent from the inclusion of an English coronation service, which has been imperfectly adapted for use in France. The blessings in Ratoldus, which have been placed in the order of service, would have been part of the pontifical and so are English in origin, rather than French. This is confirmed by the appearance of the Wells blessing for St Andrew's day which describes the saint as a special patron. If Ratoldus is indeed the source of a group of benedictionals which includes Æthelwold, this group would be of English origin, not, as Laporte and Moeller suggest,

---

[68] On the hand of 'Ramsey', see T.A.M.Bishop, *English Caroline Minuscule* (Oxford, 1971), p 10; Wormald, *Benedictional*, p 10; *New Palaeographical Society*, 1st ser., pl 83.

[69] J.Laporte, 'Quelques Particularités de Recueil des "Benedictiones Pontificales" de Durand de Mende', *Mélanges en l'Honneur de Monseigneur Michel Andrieu*, Revue des Sciences Religieuses, vol. hors série (1956), 282; *CBP* pt 3, p xxxviii.

[70] Hohler, 'Service Books', pp 64-9. See also Turner, *Claudius Pontificals*, pp xxx-xxxiii. This account of the blessings in Ratoldus is based on notes of their incipits left by D.H.Turner.

[71] *Chron. Abingdon* I, 129. On Corbie, see further *The Missal of the New Minster, Winchester*, ed. D.H.Turner, HBS 93 (1962), pp xiii-xviii, and C.A.Gordon in London, British Library, Additional MS 44920, ff 20-26.

north French. Although Hohler disagrees with Laporte and Moeller as to the provenance of this collection, he concurs in their view that it predates Æthelwold, since he argues that the pontifical was incorporated in Ratoldus in the 930s.

The following table shows the sources of the blessings in the Sacramentary of Ratoldus. If a blessing is also found in Æthelwold, its number in Table One is given, preceded by the dipthong Æ. Where Ratoldus uses a blessing for a different feast to Æthelwold, this is noted in round brackets, except for the Sundays after Pentecost, which are numbered in Ratoldus from Pentecost and in Æthelwold from the Octave. Otherwise references are in the same form as in Table One.

TABLE THREE   Sources of the blessings in the Sacramentary of Ratoldus

1.	Dedication of a church	Æ 177: Gregorian
2.	Consecration of a bishop	CBP 1081; A 1852: Gallican
3.	For kings	Not in CBP: beg. Omnipotens pater et genitus sanctus
4.	Daily for kings	Not in CBP: beg. Christus rex regum
5.	Christmas Eve	Æ 11: Gregorian
6.	De Nocte	Æ 12: Gallican (In gallicantu)
7.	Mane Primo	Æ 13: Gallican
8.	Christmas Day	Æ 14: Gregorian
9.	Alia	Æ 15: Gallican
10.	St Stephen	Æ 16: Gregorian
11.	St John the Evangelist	Æ 18: Gregorian
12.	Holy Innocents	Æ 20: Gregorian
13.	Christmas 1	Æ 138: Gregorian (Pentecost 23)
14.	Eve of Octave of Christmas	CBP 1797; A 1813: Gallican
15.	Octave of Christmas	Æ 22: Gregorian
16.	1st Sunday after Octave	Æ 23: Gregorian (Christmas 1)
17.	Epiphany	Æ 24: Gregorian
18.	Epiphany 1	Æ 26: Gregorian
19.	St Hilary	Æ 25: Gallican (Epiphany, *alia*)
20.	Epiphany 2	Æ 27: Gregorian
21.	SS Sebastian & Fabian	Æ 33: Gallican (St Sebastian)
22.	St Agnes	Æ 34: Gregorian
23.	St Vincent	Æ 35: English
24.	Epiphany 3	Æ 28: Gregorian
25.	Conversion of St Paul	Æ 36: Gregorian
26.	Purification	Æ 39: Gregorian
27.	Epiphany 4	Æ 29: Gregorian
28.	St Agatha	Æ 40: Gallican
29.	St Vedast	Æ 41: Gallican
30.	Epiphany 5	Æ 30: Gregorian
31.	St Valentine	Æ 43: Gallican (St Gregory)

32. St Peter in Cathedra	Æ 42: Gallican
33. Epiphany 6	Æ 31: Gregorian
34. St Gregory	Æ 43: Gallican
35. St Cuthbert	Æ 45: Gallican (St Ambrose)
36. St Benedict	Æ 45: Gallican (St Ambrose)
37. Annunciation	Æ 44: Gallican
38. Septuagesima	Æ 46: Gregorian
39. Sexagesima	Æ 48: Gregorian
40. Quinquagesima	Æ 50: Gregorian
41. Feria IV	Æ 52: Gallican (Beginning of Lent)
42. Lent 1	Æ 53: Gregorian
43. Feria II	Æ 54: Gallican (Lent 2)
44. Feria IV	Æ 55: Gallican (Lent 2, *alia*)
45. Ordination of Deacons	CBP 218, 138: only otherwise occurs in English MSS. Probably adaptation of Æ 120 (Pentecost 13, *alia*)
46. Ordination of priests	Æ 56: Gregorian (Lent 3)
47. Alia	CBP 1803: only otherwise occurs in English MSS
48. Lent 2	Æ 57: Gregorian (Lent 3, *alia*)
49. Feria II	Æ 58: Gallican (Lent 4)
50. Feria IV	Æ 59: Gallican (Lent 4, *alia*, or Lent 5).
51. Feria VI	Æ 37: Gregorian (St Agnes, *alia*)
52. Lent 3	CBP 1577; S 1748: Gregorian
53. Feria II	CBP 1554: only otherwise occurs in a sacramentary of St Thierry in Rheims, on which see pp 142-3, below
54. Feria IV	Æ 47: Gallican (Septuagesima, *alia*)
55. Feria VI	Not in CBP: beg. Omnipotens Deus qui a muliere
56. Lent 4	CBP 1193; S 1749: Gregorian
57. Feria II	Æ 59: Gallican (Lent 4, *alia*, or Lent 5)
58. Feria IV	Not in CBP: beg. Deus qui genus humanum
59. Feria VI	Not in CBP: beg. Benedicat vos omnipotens Deus qui per humilitatem
60. Lent 5	CBP 8; S 1750: Gregorian
61. Feria IV	Æ 62: Gallican (Passion, *alia*)
62. Feria VI	CBP 288; A 1864: Gallican
63. Palm Sunday	Æ 60: Gregorian
64. Feria II	Æ 61: Gregorian (*Alia ... in passione domini*)
65. Feria IV	Æ 63: Gallican (Passion, *alia*)

66. Feria V	—Æ 64: Gallican
67. Feria VII	Æ 66: Gregorian
68. Easter Day	Æ 68: Gregorian
69. Feria II	Æ 70: Gregorian
70. Feria III	Æ 71: Gregorian
71. Feria IV	Æ 72: Gregorian
72. Feria V	Æ 75: Gallican (Sat. after Easter)
73. Feria VI	Æ 79: Gallican (Easter 2)
74. Feria VII	CBP 1076, F XLVI: Gallican
75. Octave of Easter	Æ 76: Gregorian
76. Easter 1	Æ 73: Gregorian (Easter, feria v)
77. Easter 2	Æ 74: Gregorian (Easter, feria vi)
78. SS Tibertius & Valerian	Æ 83: Gregorian
79. St George	Æ 170: Gregorian (One martyr)
80. Easter 3	Æ 69: Gallican (Easter Day, *alia*)
81. Easter 4	Æ 77: Gregorian (Easter 1)
82. In Litania Maiore	CBP 112; F CXLVII: Gallican
83. Die Secundo	Æ 85: Gregorian (*In laetania maiore*)
84. Die Tertio	Æ 86: Gallican (*Alia … de ieiunio*)
85. Ascension Day	Æ 88: Gregorian
86. Sunday after Ascension	Æ 87: Gregorian (Eve of Ascension)
87. Ascension (alia)	Æ 89: Gallican (Sun. after Ascension)
88. SS Philip & James	Æ 169: Gregorian (One apostle)
89. Invention of Holy Cross	Æ 84: Gregorian
90. SS Nereus & Achilleus	CBP 1916: only otherwise occurs in English MSS
91. Eve of Pentecost	Æ 90: Gregorian
92. Pentecost	Æ 91: Gregorian
93. Feria II	Æ 92: Gallican (Pentecost, *alia*)
94. Feria III	Æ 93: Gregorian (Sat. after Pentecost)
95. Feria IV	Æ 94: Gregorian (Octave of Pentecost)
96. Feria VII	Æ 95: Gallican (Octave of Pentecost, *alia*)
97. Octave of Pentecost	CBP 351, F CIV: Gallican
98. Pentecost 2	Æ 139: Gallican (Pentecost 23, *alia*)
99. St Medard	Not in CBP: beg. Domine Iesu Christe pastor bone. Perhaps adapted from Æ 108 (Pentecost 7, *alia*)
100. Feria VI	Æ 139: Gallican (Pentecost 23, *alia*)
101. Pentecost 3	Æ 98: Gregorian
102. SS Basilides, Cyrinus, Nabor & Nazarius	Not in CBP: beg. Enutri quaesumus domine plebem tuam. Occurs in an English MS not collated in CBP[72]

---

[72] Turner, *Claudius Pontificals*, p 76 (SS Alexander and Eventius).

103. Pentecost 4	Æ 37, 174: Gregorian (St Agnes; One virgin)
104. SS Gervase & Protase	CBP 1266: only otherwise occurs in English MSS
105. Pentecost 5	Æ 101: Gregorian
106. Eve of Nat. St John the Baptist	Æ 142: Gallican (Nat. St John the Baptist, *alia*)
107. Nat. St John the Baptist	Æ 141: Gregorian
108. Pentecost 6	Æ 99: Gallican (Pentecost 2, *alia*)
109. SS Peter & Paul	Æ 143: Gregorian
110. St Paul	Æ 144: Gallican (SS Peter & Paul, *alia*)
111. Pentecost 7	Æ 105: Gregorian
112. SS Processus & Martinian	CBP 1916: only otherwise occurs in English MSS
113. Pentecost 8	CBP 171; F CXXV: Gallican
114. Pentecost 9	Æ 109: Gregorian
115. Pentecost 10	CBP 1855, F CXIIIa: Gallican
116. Pentecost 11	Æ 113: Gregorian
117. Pentecost 12	CBP 2024, F CXXXb: Gallican
118. St Laurence	CBP 597; F XVII, LXVI: Gallican
119. Pentecost 13	Æ 117: Gregorian
120. Assumption BVM	Æ 148: Gregorian
121. Pentecost 14	CBP 239: Gallican (from the Sacramentary of Gellone)
122. St Bartholomew	Æ 149: Gallican
123. Pentecost 15	Æ 121: Gregorian
124. Decoll. St John the Baptist	Æ 150: Gregorian
125. Nativity BVM	Æ 152: English(?)
126. Pentecost 16	CBP 77; A 1869: Gallican
127. SS Protus & Hyacinth	CBP 1916: only otherwise occurs in English MSS
128. Exaltation of Holy Cross	Æ 154: Gallican
129. Pentecost 17	Æ 125: Gregorian
130. Pentecost 18	CBP 340, 220; F CV: Gallican
131. Feria VII	Æ 112, 156: English (Pentecost 9, *alia*; *Sabbato Mense Septimi*)
132. Pentecost 19	CBP 288; A 1864: Gallican
133. St Matthew	Æ 155: Gallican
134. Pentecost 20	Not in CBP: beg. Adesto domine propitius
135. Michaelmas	CBP 14; F LXX: Gallican
136. Pentecost 21	CBP 1852: only otherwise occurs in English MSS
137. SS Denys, Rusticus & Eleutherius	CBP 1347; F LXV: Gallican

138. Pentecost 22	Æ 31, 113: Gregorian (Epiphany 6; Pentecost 10)
139. Pentecost 23	Not in CBP: beg. Dirigat vos dominus
140. All Saints	CBP 1925; A 1841: Gallican
141. Pentecost 24	Not in CBP: beg. Benedicat vos dominus caelorum
142. Pentecost 25	Æ 54: Gallican (Lent 2)
143. St Martin	Æ 161: Gallican
144. Pentecost 26	Æ 104: Gallican (Pentecost 5, *alia*)
145. St Cecilia	Æ 163: English(?)
146. St Clement	Æ 164: English
147. St Chrysogonus	CBP 1561: only otherwise occurs in English MSS
148. Pentecost 27	CBP 725; F CXXXVIII: Gallican
149. Eve of St Andrew	Æ 165: English
150. St Andrew	Æ 166: English
151. Advent 1	Æ 1: Gregorian
152. Advent 2	Æ 3: Gregorian
153. St Lucy	Æ 10: Gallican (*Sabbato in xii lectionibus*)
154. St Thomas	Æ 2: Gallican (Advent 1, *alia*)
155. Advent 3	Æ 5: Gregorian
156. Feria IV	Æ 9: Gallican (Advent 4, fer. vi)
157. Feria VI	Æ 6: Gallican (Advent 3, *alia*)
158. Feria VII	Æ 8: Gallican (Advent 4, fer. iv)
159. Advent 4	Æ 7: Gregorian
160. De Sancta Trinitate	Æ 94: Gregorian (Octave of Pentecost)
161. Ad Poscendam Suffragia Sanctorum	Æ 153: English (Nativity BVM, *alia*)
162. Ad Suffragia Angelorum	CBP 779; TC 3823; EL 143: Gregorian
163. De Sapentia	Æ 103: Gregorian (Pentecost 5)

This analysis confirms the English origins of the benedictional in the Sacramentary of Ratoldus. For example, the blessing given for the feast of St Ambrose in Æthelwold (Æ no. 45) is assigned in Ratoldus to St Cuthbert (Rat. no. 35), a change which would be unlikely in a French manuscript. A number of forms are otherwise found only in English manuscripts. Indeed, there appear to be some strong parallels between the blessings in Ratoldus and those in the 'Lanalet' Pontifical (Rouen, Bibliothèque Municipale, MS A. 27),[73] probably compiled in the first half of the eleventh century for the bishop of Crediton. 'Lanalet' is the only other manuscript in which the English forms used in Ratoldus for the feasts of SS Gervase and Protase,

---

[73] Edited by G. H. Doble, *Pontificale Lanaletense*, HBS 74 (1937).

Protus and Hyacinth and Chrysogonus (Rat. nos. 104, 127 and 147) are assigned to exactly the same feasts.[74]

Like Æthelwold, Ratoldus contains a mixture of Gregorian and Gallican blessings. Ratoldus does not, however, combine the two traditions as systematically as Æthelwold. Alternative forms for particular feasts are generally not given. Gallican and other non-Gregorian forms appear haphazardly in no obvious pattern. The only point at which there is alternation between Gregorian and Gallican blessings like that in Æthelwold is in the Sundays after Pentecost, where a Gregorian form is given for one Sunday, then a Gallican form for the next and so on. Most of these Gallican blessings do not, however, appear in Æthelwold and there does not appear to be any direct relationship between the two manuscripts at this point. Since Ratoldus does not usually give alternative blessings, it does not contain many of the Gallican forms which appear in Æthelwold. Ratoldus cannot, therefore, have been the direct source of the hybrid benedictional in 'Ramsey' and Æthelwold.

The benedictional in Ratoldus draws on a wider range of sources than Æthelwold. It includes a number of extra Gallican blessings which are not found in the Sacramentary of Angoulême. This suggests that Ratoldus either used a different version of the Gallican benedictional to Æthelwold or that additional Gallican blessings were borrowed from another source. Whatever the explanation, it seems that the process by which the text of the benedictional in Ratoldus was put together was more complex than with Æthelwold. Ratoldus is not so close to the original Gregorian and Gallican sources, often assigning blessings to completely different feasts. In order to accommodate a new blessing for the twenty-third Sunday in Pentecost (Rat. no. 139), for example, the Gregorian blessing for that Sunday was moved to the first Sunday after Christmas (Rat. no. 13). Perhaps the most insensitive rearrangement is the use of a Gallican blessing for Epiphany at the feast of St Hilary (Rat. no. 19).

It sometimes seems in Ratoldus that spare alternative blessings from a compilation similar to Æthelwold have been used to fill up gaps. For example, the alternative blessing for Advent Sunday in Æthelwold and the blessing for one of the Ember Days (Æ nos. 2, 10) in Advent are used in Ratoldus for two saints' days which fall in Advent (Rat. nos. 153, 154). Indeed, occasionally the impression is given that Ratoldus was dependent on Æthelwold. The blessing in Ratoldus for St Medard (Rat. no. 99) is, for instance, perhaps based on the alternative blessing in Æthelwold for the seventh Sunday after Pentecost (Æ no. 108), while the blessing for use at the ordination of deacons (Rat. no. 45) is probably an adaptation of Æthelwold's alternative blessing for the thirteenth Sunday after Pentecost (Æ no. 120). Although Ratoldus includes the Gregorian blessings for Lent omitted from Æthelwold, it nevertheless gives the blessings used by Æthelwold for Lent in exactly the same sequence, using them for different occasions (Rat. nos. 41-44, 46, 48-50). As has been seen, this arrangement of blessings is a very unusual one. Ratoldus only preserves this order by assigning one of the Lent blessings to the ordination of priests, a choice which perhaps reflects reliance on a source similar to Æthelwold.

[74] *Ibid.*, pp 95, 97, 100.

If it was not for the fact that Hohler argues that the benedictional in Ratoldus is about forty years older than either 'Ramsey' or Æthelwold, one might be inclined to think that Ratoldus was derived from these Winchester texts. Hohler's dating is dependent upon the assumption that, because the blessings are incorporated in the order of service, they were inserted there at roughly the same time that the rest of the main text was put together.[75] However, since it is clear that the basic text of Ratoldus went through a number of copies, there is no reason to suppose that the material from the English pontifical could not have been added to the sacramentary at almost any time up until shortly before the death of Ratoldus. It is consequently reasonable to conclude that the benedictional in Ratoldus is a compressed and amended version of a text which was derived from either 'Ramsey' or Æthelwold but probably already contained some substantial additions and alterations. If it is assumed that the text of 'Ramsey' is a few years older than Æthelwold, this would mean that the pontifical in Ratoldus dates from between about 965 and 980.

Another continental manuscript which shows some similarities to 'Ramsey' and Æthelwold is a sacramentary of the abbey of St Thierry in Rheims (Rheims, Bibliothèque Municipale, MS 214), which dates from the end of the tenth century. The blessings in this manuscript were edited by Ménard as an appendix to his edition of the Gregorian Sacramentary and reprinted by Migne.[76] The parallels between this compilation and the Winchester benedictionals are evident from the collation table by H. Wilson included in the facsimile edition of the Benedictional of St Æthelwold.[77] The St Thierry benedictional, however, makes use of material which does not appear in the Winchester texts. Like Ratoldus, it contains some Gallican blessings from a different version of the long benedictional to that used in Æthelwold.[78] Some only otherwise occur in later benedictionals from Sens and Nevers.[79] These may perhaps be new forms composed at St Thierry which were afterwards borrowed for use elsewhere. Alternatively, they may indicate that the compiler of the St Thierry text drew some material from another completely different tradition.

---

[75] Hohler, 'Service Books', p 68: '... the putting together of Ratoldus's text was certainly not done in the 970s, it was done in the 920s; and the coronations for which it was successively modified are manifestly those of Athelstan in 925 and Louis d'Outremer in 936'. This would presumably mean that, in Hohler's view, the pontifical was incorporated in Ratoldus shortly after 936. The appearance of a coronation service of this date in the pontifical does not necessarily mean that the pontifical itself dates from this period. There is no reason why a later compilation could not include a version of a particular rite which was put together slightly earlier. Brooks, 'Church of Canterbury', pp 164-5, notes that Ratoldus also contains a bishop's profession of faith and obedience in use in the early ninth century, which confirms that the pontifical in Ratoldus does include some much earlier material. Ratoldus also contains an unusual mass for St Cuthbert (Hohler, 'Service Books', pp 66-7), but this was presumably part of the pontifical – the other copy noted by Hohler is also in a pontifical.
[76] *PL*, 78, cols 605-628. This edition may be defective: it is surprising that there are no blessings for Hoiy Week. However, I have not been able to check the printed version against the MS. For a description of this MS, see *CBP* pt 3, pp 68-9, and V. Leroquais, *Les Sacramentaires et les Missels manuscrits des Bibliothèques publiques de France* (Paris, 1924), I, pp 91-94.
[77] Warner and Wilson, *Benedictional*, pp 52-5. See also pp lviii-lix.
[78] E.g. blessings nos. 74, 82, 97 ic tpe Sacramentary of Ratoldus and *CBP* nos. 341, 351, 1855.
[79] E.g. *CBP* nos. 352, 970.

Although the St Thierry collection is more eclectic than Æthelwold, it seems at first sight to bear a closer relationship than Ratoldus to the Winchester texts. Unlike Ratoldus, the St Thierry benedictional gives alternative Gregorian and Gallican blessings in a number of places such as during Advent and for the Sundays preceding Lent. However, this is not done as consistently as in Æthelwold and only one form is given for such important feasts as Christmas and Easter. The St Thierry text differs completely from Æthelwold in the blessings for the Sundays after Pentecost. Like Ratoldus, it gives only one blessing for each Sunday, which is alternately Gregorian and Gallican. Indeed, detailed examination suggests that the St Thierry manuscript is more closely related to Ratoldus than Æthelwold. About three-quarters of the blessings in the *temporale* of the St Thierry text are common to both collections. In the *sanctorale* they share some unusual forms such as the Gallican inspired blessings for the feasts of St Laurence and SS Denys, Rusticus and Eleutherius (the latter used in the St Thierry benedictional for the feast of SS Cornelius and Cyprianus) which are otherwise only found in English manuscripts (Rat. nos. 118, 137). Indeed, one blessing (Rat. no 53) occurs only in these two manuscripts.

Since it is apparent from Ratoldus that a benedictional derived from 'Ramsey' or Æthelwold was known in France in the third quarter of the tenth century, it seems likely that the St Thierry benedictional also made use of this source. In the St Thierry text, the Winchester inspired exemplar has not been shortened, as it has in Ratoldus, but some forms have been omitted and a considerable amount of other material inserted.

This analysis of the Sacramentary of Ratoldus and the St Thierry sacramentary emphasises how, as the texts of benedictionals passed from place to place, they changed very rapidly in structure and content. Every time a text was copied, blessings were reworked, moved to other feasts or omitted, while new material was added from other sources. This makes the clearly defined structure and proximity to the original sources of the Winchester benedictionals all the more striking. Since benedictionals are such a fluid type of text, it is inconceivable that such a carefully organised collection as that found in 'Ramsey' and Æthelwold could be anything other than an original compilation made in Winchester during the episcopate of St Æthelwold which drew together the Gregorian and Gallican traditions and mixed them with a considerable quantity of English material.

This hybrid benedictional was extremely influential. Ratoldus and the St Thierry sacramentary indicate that it was known abroad within a short time of its compilation, but it also lies at the root of most later English benedictionals. It is not possible here to do more than sketch the broad outline of the development of English benedictionals up to the end of the eleventh century.[80] It seems that within a short time of the appearance of the 'Ramsey'/Æthelwold text an abridged version was produced which omitted most of the alternative blessings. An example of this form of benedictional occurs in the first of the pontificals in London, BL, Cotton MS Claudius A. iii

---

[80] A detailed account of the development of later English benedictionals with full references will be given in an article I am currently preparing for the *British Library Journal*. For a list of English benedictionals dating from before 1100, see Gneuss, 'Liturgical Books', pp 133-4.

(ff 106-132v).[81] At the same time, the full text of the benedictional was being modified. The Anderson Pontifical (London, BL, Additional MS 57337) contains a version of Æthelwold in which, for instance, the Gregorian blessings for the third to fifth Sundays in Lent have been reinstated, extra Gallican blessings inserted to provide alternatives in a few places where Æthelwold does not give them and some blessings moved to different feasts. A shortened version of such a modified copy of Æthelwold then seems to have developed. This was in turn expanded by the addition of blessings for votive masses, masses on weekdays and such daily offices as vespers and matins. This appears to have been the most common type of English benedictional in the late tenth and eleventh centuries. Examples are the Benedictional of Archbishop Robert (Rouen, Bibl. Mun., MS Y. 7)[82] and the closely related benedictional in the Sherborne Pontifical (Paris, BN, MS lat. 943).[83]

The Benedictional of St Æthelwold appears to have inspired a tradition of composing new forms of episcopal blessings in England, the most remarkable product of which was the eleventh-century benedictional in London, BL, Additional MS 28188.[84] This is a copy, apparently made for use at Exeter, of a text which originated at Winchester.[85] It contains more than 170 blessings. All but a handful are new compositions or substantial reworkings of older pieces. There are more new blessings than in any previous benedictional, a notable literary *tour de force*. Some of these blessings were incorporated in the mainstream English tradition. The first attempt to do so was in the Winchester pontifical subsequently owned by Bishop Sampson of Worcester (Cambridge, Corpus Christi College, MS 146).[86] This is basically a modified version of the full text of Æthelwold also containing some of the additional material which appears in such compilations as the Benedictional of Archbishop Robert. However, a few of the forms from Additional MS 28188 have also been included together with some new blessings. The appearance of the new blessings suggests that the compiler of this benedictional may have been the author of Additional MS 28188. The benedictional in Bishop Sampson's pontifical was subsequently expanded and developed, with further new forms being inserted, to produce the Canterbury Benedictional (London, BL, Harley MS 2892).[87] The Canterbury Benedictional is a huge compilation, containing nearly twice as many blessings as Æthelwold, and may perhaps be regarded as the climax of the tradition of compiling benedictionals started by the 'Ramsey' Benedictional and the Benedictional of St Æthelwold.

The characteristic structure of the Winchester benedictionals, with the combination of different continental traditions as well as the inclusion of a

---

[81] Edited by Turner, *Claudius Pontificals*, pp 1-28.

[82] Edited by H. Wilson, *The Benedictional of Archbishop Robert*, HBS 24 (1903).

[83] Not published, but all the blessings from it are included in *CBP*.

[84] Not published, but the blessing for the feast of the Conception of the BVM is printed in E. Bishop, *Liturgica Historica* (Oxford, 1918), p 240 (reprinted in *CBP* no. 1987).

[85] Bishop, *op. cit.*, pp 239-240; M. Clayton, 'Feasts of the Virgin in the liturgy of the Anglo-Saxon Church', *ASE* 13 (1984), 227-9.

[86] M. R. James, *Catalogue of the Manuscripts in the Library of Corpus Christi College, Cambridge* (Cambridge, 1912), I, pp 332-335. This work was extensively used by Wilson in the notes to his *Benedictional of Archbishop Robert* (see n 82).

[87] See n 67.

substantial amount of English material, is echoed in other products of the tenth-century monastic revival in England. A parallel which immediately springs to mind is the *Regularis Concordia*, which was the work of Æthelwold himself. This not only draws together different practices associated with the two great continental reform movements, one inspired by St Gerard of Brogne and based in Lotharingia and the other centred on Cluny, but also contains a significant English element. It has been suggested that this mixed customary was a local product,[88] in which case its similarities to the benedictionals would be very striking. However, it has also been argued that it is basically a continental compilation, transmitted to England by way of Fleury.[89] This view is supported by a description of the customs of Fleury written in about 1010 by a monk called Thierry of Amorbach, from which it seems that the practices of Fleury closely resembled those in the *Regularis Concordia*.[90] Whatever the ultimate origins of the *Regularis Concordia*, it is nevertheless clear from the preface that Æthelwold was conscious that this text brought together different practices 'even as honey is gathered together by bees from all manner of wild flowers and collected together into one hive'.[91] A similar approach is evident in his Benedictional.

Other interesting parallels to the 'Ramsey' Benedictional and the Benedictional of St Æthelwold occur in the famous Winchester tropers,[92] which, although they were produced after Æthelwold's death, are nevertheless based on the repertory established during his episcopate. These two manuscripts have recently been analysed in great detail by Alejandro Planchart.[93] Like benedictionals, the contents of tropers are extremely eclectic and varied, and no two tropers ever include exactly the same forms. They are often confusing in their arrangement, but the Winchester tropers are notable for their extremely clear and rational structure,[94] a quality shared by the benedictionals. Again, the Winchester tropers consist essentially of a combination of two different continental traditions, this time French and German.[95] Planchart considers that this reflects the use of a source from northern France, where such mixed compilations were common. The tropers also include, like the benedictionals, a substantial number of English forms.[96] This led Planchart to emphasise that the importation of continental practice during the monastic

[88] T. Symons, 'Sources of the Regularis Concordia', *Downside Review* 54 (1941), 14-36, 143-170, 264-289, and 'Regularis Concordia: History and Derivation', *Tenth-Century Studies*, pp 43-59.
[89] E. John, 'The Sources of the English Monastic Reformation: a comment', *Revue Bénédictine* 70 (1960), 201-203.
[90] A. Davril, 'Un Coutumier de Fleury du début du XIe siècle', *Revue Bénédictine* 76 (1966), 351-354, and 'Un moine de Fleury aux environs de l'an mil: Thierry dit d'Amorbach', *Études Ligériennes d'histoire et d'archéologie médiévales*, ed. R. Louis (Auxerre, 1975), pp 97-104; L. Donnat, 'Recherches sur l'influence de Fleury au Xe siècle', *Études Ligériennes*, pp 165-174. See also the comment by M. McC. Gatch, 'The Office in Anglo-Saxon Monasticism', *Learning and Literature in Anglo-Saxon England*, p 347, n 26, and in Lapidge ch 4, pp 98-9.
[91] *Regularis Concordia*, p 3.
[92] Cambridge, Corpus Christi College, MS 473, and Oxford, Bodleian Library, MS Bodley 775. Also discussed in this volume by Lapidge (ch 4, p 111) and Berry (ch 6, pp 155-7).
[93] *The Repertory of Tropes at Winchester* (Princeton, 1977).
[94] Ibid., pp 33, 72-95, 391-2.
[95] Ibid., pp 131-141.
[96] Ibid., pp 145-172.

revival was intended 'not to supplant an English practice but to strengthen and confirm a reform that had its origin within the English church and retained its English character until the first quarter of the 11th century'.[97] The benedictionals confirm this judgement by showing how, although continental traditions were imported and developed, the production of new local forms was encouraged and older English compositions retained.

It appears then that a characteristic of the tenth-century monastic revival in England was a self-conscious attempt to synthesise different continental traditions, whilst at the same time confirming and strengthening local practice. The two Winchester benedictionals provide perhaps the most clear-cut testimony to this outlook. It has been suggested, in connection with the *Regularis Concordia*, that this may reflect a concern to reconcile the practices of the different continental reform movements.[98] This is not a convincing explanation of the mixed character of the benedictionals, since there is no reason to connect the use of one or the other type of benedictional with a particular school of monasticism. The production of such hybrid texts in England perhaps rather reflects a determination to ensure that English practice represented the best available. It may also have been due to an attempt to embellish Roman rites by incorporating material from the Gallican liturgy. It was perhaps mistakenly assumed that the Gregorian benedictionals represented Roman use because of their association with the Gregorian sacramentary. The compiler of the Winchester benedictionals seems, like Æthelwold in the *Regularis Concordia*, to have had in mind 'the letters in which our holy patron Gregory instructed the blessed Augustine that, for the advancement of the rude English church, he should establish there the seemly customs of the Gallic Churches as well as those of Rome'.[99]

The text of the Benedictional of St Æthelwold provides insights into many other aspects of the tenth-century monastic revival in England. For example, the elaboration of the ceremony of the episcopal blessing before communion evident in the Winchester benedictionals is a reminder of the important role played by the office of bishop in the reform. The early vocations of both Dunstan and Æthelwold were encouraged by Bishop Ælfheah of Winchester, while Oswald's mentors were Archbishops Oda of Canterbury and Osketel of York. Moreover, it was only when Æthelwold and the others themselves became bishops that they were able to implement effectively a thorough-going policy of reform. They did not, however, use their office simply as a platform to conduct a campaign of monastic plantation, but took their general responsibilities very seriously. Æthelwold's concern for his pastoral duties and the importance he attached to the episcopal blessing as a means of helping him to discharge them is apparent from Godeman's poem at the beginning of the Benedictional: 'This book the Boanerges aforesaid caused to be indited for himself in order that he might be able to sanctify the people of the Saviour by means of it and to pour forth holy prayers to God for the flock committed to him, and that he may lose no little lambkin of the fold.'[100]

---

[97] *Ibid.*, p 391.
[98] E.g. Symons in *Regularis Concordia*, pp xlv-lii, and 'Regularis Concordia: History and Derivation', pp 43-59.
[99] *Regularis Concordia*, p 3.
[100] The quotation is from the translation of the prefatory poem by Warner and Wilson,

The leaders of the reform in England were anxious not only to revive monasticism in England, but also to make English church life in general more progressive and vigorous. The development of more elaborate benedictionals was one expression of this concern. The benedictional texts are not, however, only of interest as indirectly illustrating different aspects of the monastic revival. The 'Ramsey' Benedictional and the Benedictional of St Æthelwold, together with the later benedictionals inspired by them, contain a large number of English Latin compositions of the period, which deserve greater attention as one of the most characteristic literary products of the reform.

There is, however, one final question to be considered, and that is whether Æthelwold or Godeman was primarily responsible for the compilation of the hybrid benedictional which appears in the 'Ramsey' Benedictional and the Benedictional of St Æthelwold. It would be surprising if Æthelwold, who produced such important texts as the *Regularis Concordia* and the translation of the Rule of St Benedict, took no part in the preparation of a liturgical collection for his own use. Moreover, as has been seen, the benedictionals show a concern for order and completeness which would seem to reflect the influence of a personality like Æthelwold's. However, since Godeman's prefatory poem is to a large extent a panegyric on 'the Boanerges aforesaid', one might expect that, if Æthelwold had taken any direct part in the preparation of the text, Godeman would have mentioned it. The involvement of Godeman in the preparation of both benedictionals is very striking. It was probably Godeman who, as the scribe of both manuscripts, was responsible for tidying up the 'Ramsey' text to produce the Benedictional of St Æthelwold. Perhaps the most likely explanation is that Godeman produced 'Ramsey' in accordance with general instructions given by Æthelwold to be sent to Canterbury, perhaps to Dunstan. Æthelwold, pleased with the results of Godeman's work, then instructed him to prepare a further copy, splendidly illuminated and decorated, for his personal use.

Benedictional, pp xii-xiii. The original poem is printed in full by Warner and Wilson, *Benedictional*, p 1, and M. Lapidge, 'The hermeneutic style in tenth-century Anglo-Latin literature', *ASE* 4 (1975), 105-7.

Chapter 6

WHAT THE SAXON MONKS SANG:
MUSIC IN WINCHESTER IN THE LATE TENTH CENTURY

Mary Berry

Thanks to the work of many scholars, including the contributors to this volume, we now know a considerable amount about Winchester in the time of Æthelwold and about the culture that flourished there. We know a good deal about the appearance of the Old Minster after it was rebuilt by Æthelwold and his successors, and something of the other great buildings in Winchester that grew up around it – New Minster, Nunnaminster and the royal palace.[1] Much is also known about Æthelwold himself and the art and learning which he encouraged.[2] All of it adds up to a fuller understanding of a culture in itself immensely creative, full of vigour, ingenious, experimental, self-confident; a culture that was above all a Christian culture – Christian in a way people living in the twentieth century have never had the remotest opportunity of experiencing. We can only try to recreate as much of it as we can and in as many different dimensions as possible. The tenth-century reform can still be a visual experience for us, but what was the *sound* of it? What did people *hear* inside those great buildings? What was going on, day by day, and on the major feast days, in the three great monastic churches of Winchester?

Supposing, for example, that one of the Saxon kings had been staying in his palace in Winchester towards the end of the tenth century, and had walked across with all ceremony, to the Old Minster to hear Mass on Easter Day: what might he have heard on such an occasion? One must imagine what it would have been like to find oneself inside that venerable church, the scene of so much of Æthelwold's toil. The king would have surveyed the scene from his special seat. He would have heard the sound of the clergy processing into the church during the singing of the great troped Introit, *Psallite regi magno / Resurrexi*. Between the chanting of the Epistle and the solemn proclamation of the Gospel he would have heard the florid *Alleluia, Pascha nostrum*, an elaborate chant that had been sung on Easter Day for generations, but at Winchester it was sung in *organum*, an early form of two-part harmony. This would have been followed by a splendid and fully developed Easter sequence: *Fulgens preclara*.[3] These few items, in themselves,

---

[1] M. Biddle, '*Felix Urbs Winthonia*: Winchester in the Age of Monastic Reform', *Tenth-Century Studies*, pp 123-40.
[2] See Introduction pp 1-12.
[3] Cambridge, MS Corpus Christi College 473, fol. 96r, is the Winchester source of this famous sequence, text and melody (see plate II). The second part, or *vox organalis*, is on fol. 154v. See also *Regularis Concordia*, p 51, n 18.

illustrate some of the extraordinary achievements of tenth-century monastic musicians. In the first place, the tenth century saw the full flowering of the art of *troping*: this is the art by which the traditional chants of the Proper and of the Ordinary of the Mass were introduced, followed by, or interlaced with newly-composed passages, expanding and interpreting the meaning of the texts, and heightening their dramatic content. The second was the adoption and further development of two early systems of musical notation, so that from now on, the music they were performing in Winchester could be recorded by scribes on parchment for fellow-monks to read and sing from and pass on to future generations. The third achievement was the momentous discovery of the art of harmony, the adding of a second part to be performed simultaneously with the existing chant. There is even a hint, in the last of these three pieces, of a fourth achievement, involving some use of instruments other than the human voice, to add to the general magnificence of a solemn celebration.

Before attempting to assess any of these achievements, however, we must take a brief look at the everyday musical life of the Saxon monks. It is a fairly simple matter to reconstruct the monastic timetable from the pages of the *Regularis Concordia*, the monastic agreement drawn up in Winchester as a result of the Council held there shortly before the end of Edgar's reign, for the guidance of the English houses of monks and nuns.[4] During the summer the monks rose at 1.30a.m., and went into the church to recite, on their knees, the first prayers of the day: the *Trina Oratio*, sets of prayers and psalms for the monks themselves, for the Royal House, and for the Faithful Departed. Then they chanted a group of psalms known as the *Gradual Psalms* (Ps 120-134), and finally the long night Office of Nocturns, made up chiefly of twelve psalms, three canticles, twelve readings and twelve responsories. More psalms followed for the Royal House, after which there was a short break. Towards dawn they sang the Office which is known today as Lauds, but was then called Matins, an office made up of seven psalms. This was followed by the *Miserere* (Ps 51) and further psalms and prayers for the Royal House. Then came a succession of antiphons, memorials of the Holy Cross, of the Blessed Virgin Mary, and of the saint who was the Patron of the House, after those the Office of Matins of All Saints, preceded by an antiphon sung in honour of the saint before whose altar the office was to be recited, and this was followed by Matins of the Dead. Next came a well-earned break, during which the monks washed and changed their shoes. By this time they had been singing for about three hours.

At 5.00a.m. they returned to the church and again recited the *Trina Oratio*. This was followed by a period of reading, the *lectio divina*. At about 6.00a.m. they chanted Prime, followed by the further recitation of psalms, including the seven *Penitential Psalms* (Ps 6, 32, 38, 51, 102, 130 and 143), and the *Litany of the Saints*. The Morrow, or Morning, Mass came next, followed by the short capitular Office, and five psalms for the Departed. The day's work was distributed during the Chapter meeting and a work period followed. Then, at 8.00a.m., came Terce, more prayers for the Royal

---

[4] *Regularis Concordia*, ch 1, and Introduction, pp xliii-xliv. See also D. Knowles, *The Monastic Order in England*, 2nd edn (Cambridge, 1966), ch 26 and appendix 18.

House, and the Principal Mass. At 9.30a.m. there was a further period of *lectio divina* and at 11.30 the Hour of Sext, followed by prayers for the Royal House. Towards midday they ate their first meal of the day: *prandium*. By now they had been singing for nearly seven hours. The monks were then granted what was no doubt a much-needed siesta of about an hour and a half, from 1.00p.m. to 2.30p.m., after which they rose for the Hour of None, which was followed, like the other hours, by psalms and prayers for the Royal House. Then came, not exactly our afternoon tea-break, but some kind of drink allowance, before the monks went off to resume their work at about 3.00p.m. Towards sunset they sang Vespers of the day in choir, followed by the *Miserere* and the usual prayers for the Royal House. Then came two further Offices of Vespers, corresponding to the two extra morning Offices: Vespers of All Saints and Vespers of the Dead, both of which were made up of psalmody, antiphons, short readings and responsories. *Cena*, the evening meal, followed, and then the monks changed into their night shoes ready for Compline, which was followed by the *Miserere*, further prayers and psalms for the Royal House, and the *Trina Oratio*. They retired to bed at about 8.30p.m. They had been up for about nineteen hours and of these about eleven had been spent in singing. There can hardly have been many moments of the day when the three monastic churches of Winchester were not ringing with song.

That was the summer timetable. The winter one was similar, with account taken of the longer nights and shorter days. The monks rose an hour later and retired to bed two hours earlier, but no provision was made in winter for a siesta in the middle of the day, and there was only one meal: *cena*.

The point that leaps to mind as one looks through that timetable is the extensive use of psalmody throughout the Anglo-Saxon monk's day. I might add that the texts sung at the two daily Masses were themselves very largely drawn from the Psalms. Monks and nuns, and indeed the children they were educating under their roofs, had all to start by learning the entire Psalter by heart. Up to about the year 1050 the version of the psalms familiar to the Saxon monks would have been the so-called 'Roman' Psalter, St Jerome's first Latin version. Gallican psalters were beginning to be copied in England from about 1050, notably at Winchester. But A.P.Campbell, in the Introduction to his edition of the *Tiberius Psalter* stresses the predominance of the 'Roman' Psalter in England until the late tenth century.[5] Singing the psalms day and night was the very bread and butter of their musical diet. Even without the additions mentioned in the *Regularis Concordia* (the *Gradual Psalms*, the seven *Penitential Psalms*, the *Miserere* and the psalms appointed to be chanted for the Royal House or for the Departed), the *Rule of St Benedict* stipulated that the entire Psalter was to be sung through each week.[6] Benedict suggested in his Rule a way of dividing up the Psalter over

[5] A.P.Campbell, *The Tiberius Psalter* (Ottowa, 1974). See also J.B.L.Tolhurst (ed.), *The Monastic Breviary of Hyde Abbey, Winchester*, 6 (London, 1942), 13-14: 'It should be pointed out that in England previously to about the year 1050, St Jerome's first version was generally used and that this was subsequently changed for the Gallican psalter, his second version, though the nuns of Barking still retained the older version in the fifteenth century.'
[6] *The Rule of St Benedict in Latin and English with Notes*, ed. T.Fry (Minnesota, 1980), ch xviii, 'Quo ordine ipsi psalmi dicendi sunt', pp 212-14.

the seven days of the week, apportioning groups of psalms to each of the Hour services. This division of the Psalter was followed by the Saxon monks and nuns, and it is what many monasteries of monks and nuns still follow today.

The basic choice of texts for the yearly cycle of Masses was firmly established well before the tenth century, and it agrees, in the main, with what is still sung today. An anecdote from the lives of St Æthelwold illustrates this in an interesting way.[7] The event took place on Saturday, 19 February 964. It is well-known that one of Æthelwold's reforms involved bringing Benedictine monks from Abingdon to replace the secular canons who were at that time serving the Old Minster. When the monks arrived, they heard the canons singing the Communion Antiphon at the end of Mass. It is no surprise to hear that they were singing the antiphon 'Servite Domino ...' on that particular day, 'Serve ye the Lord with fear ...' The text comes from Psalm 2, which was appointed to be sung on the Friday following Ash Wednesday, and all the music of this Mass was repeated on the following day, the 'Saturday in the beginning of Lent', as specified in Wulfstan's account.[8] Since it was sung two days running, it was an antiphon the monks and canons would have known very well. And this particular antiphon is still to be found today in its old place, even in the modern *Graduale*, after all the changes of Vatican II. Æthelwold's monks took the text of that antiphon to be an open invitation for them to take over the church. This is how Ælfric describes the scene:

> Now it happened ... that while the monks who had come from Abingdon were standing at the entrance of the church, the clerics inside were finishing Mass, singing for the Communion: 'Serve ye the Lord with fear, and rejoice unto him with trembling; embrace discipline, lest you perish from the just way'. As if they were saying: 'We could not serve God, nor observe his discipline; do you at least act so that you may not perish like us'. And the monks, hearing their singing, said one to another: 'Why do we linger outside? Behold, we are exhorted to enter.'[9]

That incident highlights the immediacy of the sung liturgy to those for whom it was more than a daily routine. The psalms were an integral part of the life of the Saxon monks, and could be applied to any and every situation.

The liturgy itself did something similar, but at a deeper level. Psalm verses were applied to the birth, death and resurrection of Christ, so that in singing the inspired texts and reliving their prophetic content the monk might experience an encounter with the Master through a re-enactment of a gospel event. The liturgy, seen in this light, was more than a celebration: it was also exegesis and, in a very real sense, representation, that is, 're-presentation', something akin to but more vital than drama. A case in point is the Introit for Midnight Mass, in which the Hebrew Psalmist's words, taken again from Psalm 2 (verse 7), are placed in the mouth of Christ as he reflects upon his eternal relationship with his Father: 'The Lord said to me: "Thou art my Son: this day have I begotten thee."'

---

[7] Ælfric ch 12-14, and Wulfstan ch 16-18.
[8] Wulfstan ch 17.
[9] Ælfric ch 13, trans. *EHD*, p 903.

This custom of using boldly chosen and strikingly apt Old Testament texts with a well-defined Christological application is even more impressive in the Introit *Resurrexi* for Easter Day. Once again the words of a psalm verse are placed in the mouth of Christ, this time at the moment of his rising from the dead. The psalm chosen is Psalm 139, verse 18 and other verses from the same psalm: 'When I wake up I am present with thee ... Thou hast laid thine hand upon me ... Such knowledge is too wonderful and excellent for me.' The Saxon monks sang those words each year as Easter came round; they sang it with the whole of Western Christianity, then as now. The first word of the Introit, in Jerome's translation, is 'Resurrexi', 'I am risen', which is, of course, much stronger than 'When I wake up'. Moreover, from at least the time of Amalar of Metz (c.830) and probably several centuries before him, Christian tradition has applied this verse to the person of Christ at the moment of the Resurrexion, and the bare text, with no additions, is highly eloquent when used in the context of Easter.[10] But that was not enough for the new fervour, the new creative spirit of the period we are studying: newly composed words and music – that is, tropes – were introduced before or after each phrase of the original text, deepening and enhancing its meaning. Without the tropes the text appears as follows, the only addition being the *alleluias* at the conclusion of each phrase:[11]

> Resurrexi, et adhuc tecum sum, Alleluia.
> Posuisti super me manum tuam, Alleluia.
> Mirabilis facta est scientia tua, Alleluia, alleluia.
>> Domine, probasti me et cognovisti me:
>> Tu cognovisti sessionem meam et resurrectionem meam.

> I am risen, and am present with you, Alleluia.
> You have laid your hand upon me, Alleluia.
> Such knowledge is too wonderful and excellent for me, Alleluia, alleluia.
>> Lord, you have searched me out and known me:
>> You know my down-sitting and my up-rising.

Expanded and enriched with tropes the Christological implications of the text are highlighted: the Introit becomes an extended monologue sung by the risen Christ: [The text of the Introit is shown in plate I]:

Trope
> Sing to the great King, who has overcome the power of death, EYA!

1st phrase of Introit
> I am risen, and am present with you, Alleluia.

Trope
> I slept, Father; I shall rise again at dawn and my sleep is sweet.

2nd phrase of Introit
> You have laid your hand upon me, Alleluia.

---

[10] 'Die sancto paschae in introitu per ora prophetarum praesentat se Christus ex resurrectione Patri suo in ecclesia sua, dicens: "Resurrexi et adhuc tecum sum"', *Amalarius Episcopi opera liturgica omnia*, ed. J. M. Hanssens, II: *Liber Officialis*, Libellus I, xxxiii, De die sancto paschae: *Studie Teste*, 139 (Rome, 1948), 167.

[11] For the early standard text of the Easter Introit, see *Antiphonale Missarum Sextuplex*, ed. R.-J. Hesbert (Rome, 1935), 100-101. All translations are my own, unless otherwise stated.

Trope
    Yea, Father, even as it pleased you that in dying I should become
    the death of Death, the death-bite of Hell, and life for the World.
3rd phrase of Introit
    Such knowledge is too wonderful and excellent for me.
Trope
    You concealed this knowledge from the wise and revealed it to children,
                                          Alleluia.

Final phase of Introit
    Alleluia, alleluia.
Introductory trope to the Verse
    Behold, I, the true Sun, have known my setting;
    And I alone have risen above it.
Verse
    Lord, you have searched me out and known me:
    You know my down-sitting and my uprising.

And so it goes on, as the Introit is repeated, phrase by phrase, with its
tropes, during the solemn procession of the clergy as they enter the church.
This continues until a dramatic moment is reached in the music: The Father
himself enters, as it were, into dialogue with his Son:

Trope
    'Arise, my Glory, my Son'

and the Son replies:

    'I shall arise at dawn, O my Father.'[12]

From a dialogue such as this, it is only a step to the creation of an original
and self-contained liturgical drama. Winchester had its own version of the
celebrated *Quem queritis* trope,[13] similar to but not identical with the text
and rubrics as they appear in the *Regularis Concordia*.[14] The dialogue this
time takes place between the Angel at the tomb of Christ and the Marys,
who have come to prepare the body of Christ for burial.

    'Whom do you seek?'

asks the Angelic voice;

    'Jesus of Nazareth, the Crucified'

they reply.

The high point in the dialogue is reached as the Angel exclaims:

    'He is not here, he is risen, as he foretold ...'[15]

---

[12] MS CCC 473, fol. 27rv; Oxford, MS Bodley 775, fol. 19v and 20r. See also A.E.Planchart, *The Repertory of Tropes at Winchester*, 2 vols (Princeton, 1977), I, 146-154.
[13] MS CCC 473, fol. 26v and MS Bod. 775, fol. 17r. For a summary of recent research into the origin, nature and development of the 'Quem queritis', see J.Stevens, *Words and Music in the Middle Ages, Song, Narrative, Dance and Drama, 1050-1350* (Cambridge, 1986), p 330, n 53.
[14] *Regularis Concordia*, ch 5, para 51.
[15] Susan Rankin has kindly allowed me to use her musical transcription of the 'Quem queritis' trope from MS Bod. 775, fol. 17v for the recording *Anglo-Saxon Easter* (see below, n 27).

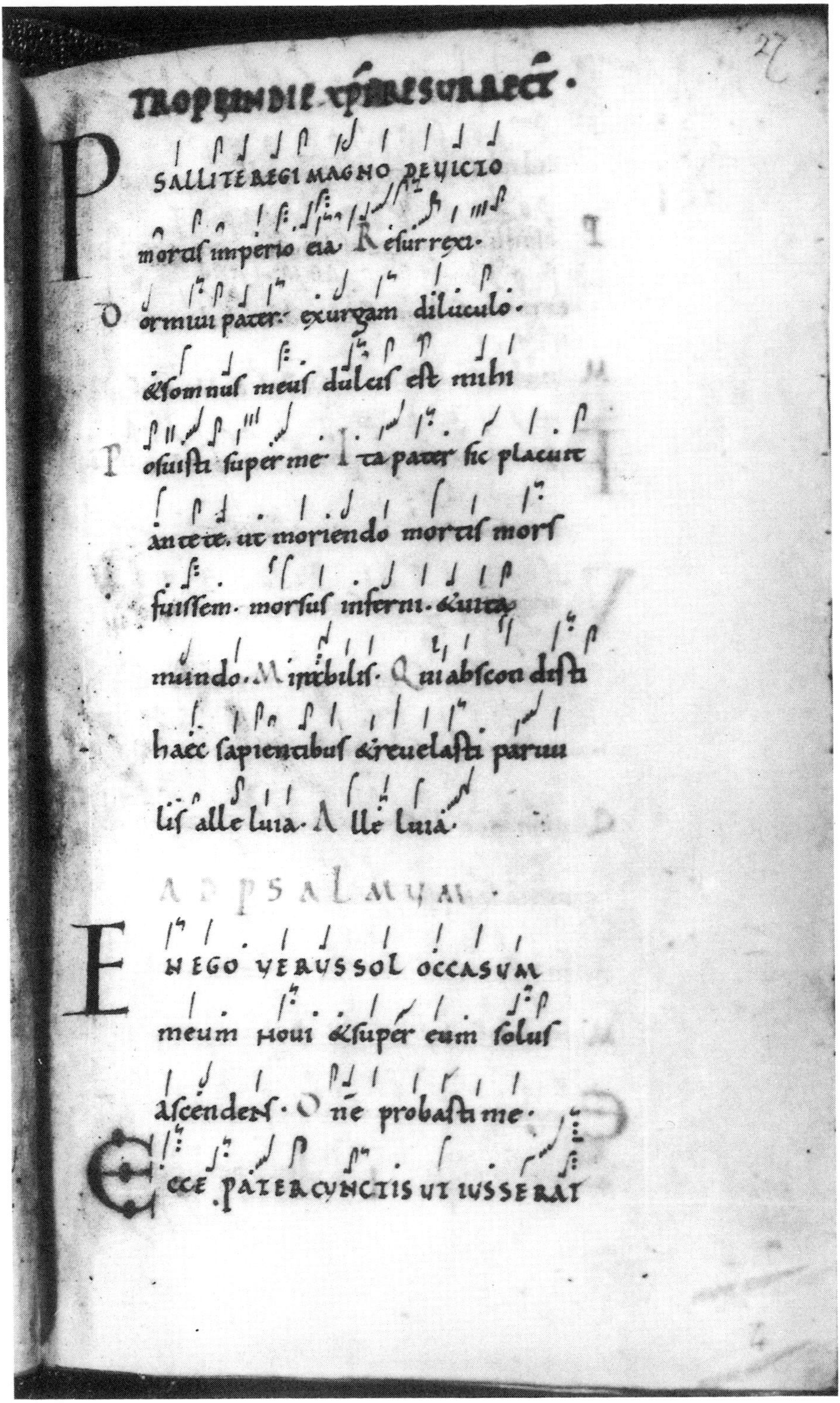

Plate I Troped Introit for Easter Day: *Psallite regi magno*/*Resurrexi*, CCC MS 473, fol. 27r, by courtesy of the Master and Fellows of Corpus Christi College, Cambridge

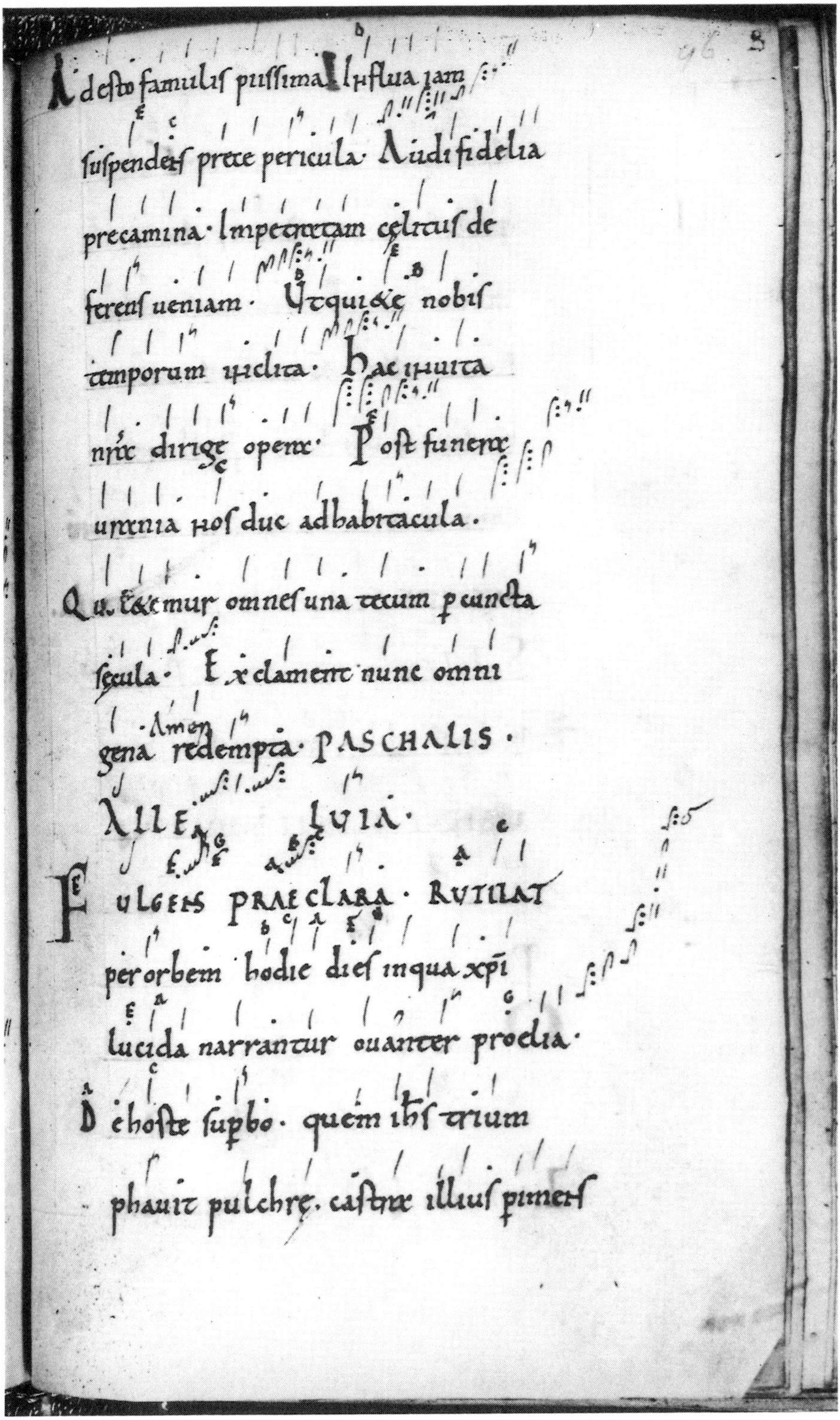

Plate II   Easter Sequence: *Fulgens preclara*, showing dual notation,
neums and letters, CCC MS 473, fol. 96r, by courtesy of
the Master and Fellows of Corpus Christi College, Cambridge

Tropes were added on major feast days to all the items of the Proper, with the exception of the Gradual, and to most items of the Ordinary. The tropes just mentioned are but isolated examples of the vast repertoire compiled for use at the Old Minster in the time of St Æthelwold. We are fortunate in having two important manuscript sources for this repertoire, one in Oxford, MS Bodley 775, and one in Cambridge, Corpus Christi College, MS 473 (see plates I-III). Both contain full musical notation. The Oxford manuscript is thought to be a mid-eleventh-century copy of an earlier prototype, now lost but originally copied piecemeal between c.978 and c.985, a few months after the death of Æthelwold.[16] So although this Bodleian manuscript was only copied in the eleventh century, it actually represents the state of the liturgy at Winchester between 978, the date of Æthelred's coronation, and 980, the year of the rededication of the Old Minster, when the date of the festival of dedication was changed from 24 November to 20 October.[17] The Oxford manuscript is a largish book: the pages measure 273mm x 167mm; it has been rather carelessly copied and clumsily revised. By contrast the Cambridge manuscript is a tiny book, about half the size of the Oxford one, its pages measuring 146mm x 92mm. Planchart dates it between 996, the date of Æthelwold's translation, and 1006, the date of the death of Bishop Cenwulf to whom Ælfric's *Life of St Æthelwold* was dedicated.[18]

Wulfstan is the first singer we encounter at Winchester whose name we actually know. And not only is his name an important one, but it is central to the whole scene of monastic musical activity. The two principal scholars who have worked on the Winchester Tropers, Andreas Holschneider and Alejandro Planchart, both identify him as the main scribe of CCC 473, a scribe who is meticulously careful and accurate;[19] and it is probable that the book was written for Wulfstan's own personal use. It is an orderly book, intended for practical use in the services, not merely an anthology or a book of reference.

Both manuscripts have musical notation represented by staffless neums, which means that the music can only be transcribed with the aid of later sources with music on lines to indicate precise pitches.[20] The Winchester neums are characteristic of Anglo-Saxon notation: almost vertical, sloping slightly to the right. The fine musical notation of CCC 473 is remarkably elegant and beautiful. This manuscript, too, has an added bonus: certain pieces, in addition to the neum notation, use a form of notation made up of letters of the alphabet. This alphabetic notation may be seen in certain parts of the Easter sequence in plate II: *Fulgens preclara*. The placing of the semitones shows that the Winchester musicians started what we know as the major scale with the first letter of the alphabet: A, which seems entirely logical! We will return to this point later. Pieces written with this dual notation, can, of course, be transcribed without the aid of later manuscripts.

[16] Planchart, *Repertory of Tropes*, I, 40-42.
[17] *Ibid.*, I, 26-7.
[18] *Ibid.*, I, 26-32.
[19] A. Holschneider, *Die Organa von Winchester* (Hildesheim, 1968), pp 11, 19-20 and 76-81, and Planchart, *op. cit.*, I, 32-3 and 52-4.
[20] One such source is the *Downpatrick Gradual* (Oxford, MS Bodley Rawlinson, C 892). See David Hiley's note 'The Transcriptions' on the sleeve of *Anglo-Saxon Easter* (n 27).

Both Planchart and Holschneider have surmised that Wulfstan was not only a scribe but also a composer. They, and other scholars, think he was responsible for the composition of many of the tropes in the Winchester repertoire,[21] more especially, though not exclusively, those for English saints which would not normally be found in the Continental sources. It would be reasonable to suggest that Wulfstan, the disciple and fervent admirer of Æthelwold, may have composed the tropes in honour of his revered master when the latter was officially canonised and recognised as a Confessor and his bones translated from the crypt to the cathedral itself (in the year 996).[22] These particular tropes are also found, together with other poems by Wulfstan, in a revision of Wulfstan's *Life* of the saint copied by Ordericus Vitalis in MS Alençon 14.[23]

The Cambridge book is of particular interest because, in addition to the tropes, it contains a large collection of *organa*, the most important collection of early two-part settings, in fact, that exists. Plate III illustrates one example. For centuries these little pieces – and there are close on two hundred of them – have remained unsung, because it was thought transcription was impossible. Recent attempts, however, and in particular those of Holschneider, have shown that plausible transcriptions are within our grasp.[24] Holschneider attributes the composition of the majority of these little polyphonic settings to Wulfstan the Cantor.[25] If they are his, one can understand the excitement and enthusiasm expressed in the titles he gave to the various groups of pieces with *organa*: one can sense the delight and pride of the composer in his newly-discovered art. He introduces the *organa* in the Kyriale section with these words: 'Incipiunt melliflua organorum modulamina super dulcissima celeste preconia.' The 'mellifluous harmonies' clearly delighted the ears of the Saxon monks: they were added not only to Kyries, but also to the Glorias, the Tracts, the Sequences, the Alleluias as well as to certain Responsories and processional chants. Epithets abound to describe the novel sound of these harmonies: *amoenissima* 'most charming'; *jocunda* 'delightful'; *pulchra* 'lovely'; *dulcisono* 'sweet-sounding'; *pulcherrima* 'most beautiful'.[26] To our ears, the sound of these pieces is surprisingly vigorous and modern. Some singers who recently made a recording of the Easter music in the Winchester Tropers were full of enthusiasm: they found that the harshness of the rows of consecutive fourths, and the seconds merging into unison, far from being ugly, had a strange and exciting attractiveness.[27]

[21] Planchart, *Repertory of Tropes*, I, 25; Holschneider, *Die Organa*, 76-81; L. Gushee, 'Wulfstan of Winchester', *The New Grove Dictionary of Music and Musicians* (London, 1980), XX, 546.
[22] See also Lapidge, 'Æthelwold as scholar and teacher', ch 4, espec. pp 111-17.
[23] Planchart, *Repertory of Tropes*, I, 30. The contents of this manuscript were edited by Mabillon and have been reprinted in *PL* 137, 104-8.
[24] Holschneider, *Die Organa von Winchester*, pp 156-181.
[25] *Ibid.*, pp 76-81.
[26] 'Melliflua', CCC 473, fol. 135r; 'amoenissima', 'jocunda', *ibid.*, fol. 135v; 'pulchra', *ibid.*, fol. 136r; 'Organa dulcisono docto modulamine compta ut petat altare resonat laus ista sacerdos', *ibid.*, fol. 138v; 'organa pulcherrima', *ibid.*, fol. 180v.
[27] *Anglo-Saxon Easter* – Chants and Tropes for the Mass on Easter Day from the Winchester Troper: The Schola Gregoriana of Cambridge/Mary Berry, DG Archiv Produktion Digital-Stereo 413 546-1. The recording was made in the priory church of St Mary, at Deerhurst in Gloucestershire. The *Kyrie*, *Gloria*, *Alleluia* and *Sequence* show examples of two-part organum.

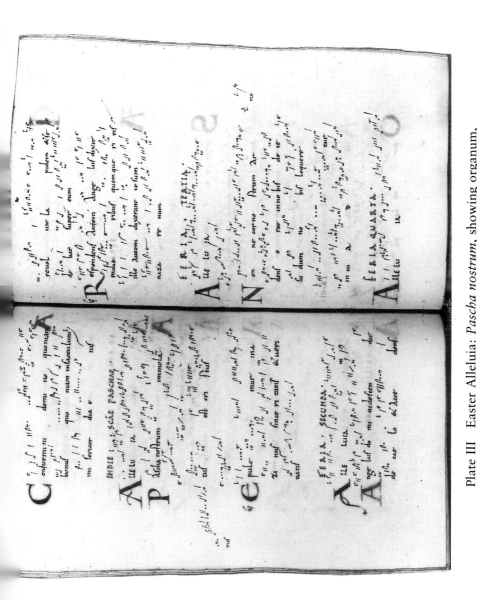

Plate III   Easter Alleluia: *Pascha nostrum*, showing organum,
CCC MS 473, fols 164v–165r, by courtesy of the Master and Fellows of
Corpus Christi College, Cambridge

Plate IV   Group of cantors at the funeral of Edward the Confessor
from the Bayeux Tapestry

The question must now be asked: how were these tropes and the *organa* actually performed by the Saxon monks? A distinction seems always to have been made between performance by a solo cantor and that of the main body of singers. In the standard chants florid virtuosic passages had always been the province of the solo cantor: he is the one who holds a book in his hand, a book such as the *Cantatorium* of St Gall,[28] often a small slim volume, easy to hold, a book containing all the melismatic chants, but only cues for the others. The Bayeux Tapestry shows Saxon singers at the funeral of Edward the Confessor, and two of them are holding in their hands books of small dimensions (see plate IV).[29]

The two Winchester Tropers belong properly to this category of book: the tropes were intended to be sung by soloists, in alternation with the choir. There was plenty of scope for alternation too in other parts of the liturgy, in hymns and sequences, for example; and it is significant that the instrumental letters noticed in the sequence *Fulgens preclara* (see plate II) occur in the first half only of each double verse of the structure, as well as in all the single verses, but not throughout the whole piece. It has been suggested that these sections with letters were intended to be accompanied by an instrument, and in that case the instrument may have been one requiring keyboard tablature such as an organ. If so, the letters in the Cambridge manuscript may well represent the earliest keyboard tablature yet discovered. For the alphabetic notation which makes the major scale begin on A rather than on C was commonly used only in connection with the calculation and measurement of organ pipes.[30]

It cannot be mere coincidence that it is the same Wulfstan the Cantor who wrote the famous description of the fantastic organ that was reputedly installed at the Old Minster some time after 990. It appears in the prologue of his verse *Life of St Swithun*.[31] Wulfstan is addressing Bishop Ælfheah II (984-1005), Æthelwold's successor, and he was praising his many achievements. Not only had he added to Æthelwold's crypt, but he had enlarged the organ originally installed by Æthelwold, making it one of the wonders of the world:

Such as are nowhere seen, fixed on a double floor,

he says – presumably a platform, or a special gallery, perhaps –

twice six bellows are joined above in order, and below it lie four and ten. With alternating breaths they render a great amount of air. Which bellows seventy strong men work, moving their arms and dripping with much sweat, each eagerly encouraging his companions to drive the air upwards with all strength and cause to roar the full chest of ample curve, which alone supports 400 pipes in order, which the hand controls with organistic skill: it opens the closed and in turn closes the

[28] Saint-Gall, Stiftsbibliothek, MS 359, which dates from the end of the ninth century.
[29] The singers can be seen in colour in plate 30 of *The Bayeux Tapestry*, ed. D. Wilson (London, 1985).
[30] Planchart, *Repertory of Tropes* I, 52; Holschneider, *Die Organa von Winchester*, pp 89-92; A. Holschneider, 'Die instrumentalen Tonbuchstaben im Winchester Troper', *Festschrift Georg von Dadelsen* (Stuttgart, 1978), p 159. See also C. Page, 'The earliest English keyboard', *Early Music* 7 (1979), 309-14.
[31] Wulfstan, *Narratio*, pp 69-70, lines 141-70.

opened as the fixed song of various notes requires. And two brethren
of concordant spirit sit, and each, responsible, manages his own
alphabet; and there are hidden holes in four times ten tongues, and
each holds ten in its own order. Hither some tongues run, thence some
return, maintaining the individual holes for the proper pitches; and
they strike the seven separate joyful notes of the scale mixed with the
song of the lyric semitone

– the Bb, presumably –

and in the manner of thunder the iron voice beats upon the ears that
they may receive no sound but this alone; the sound makes so much
clamour, echoing here and there, that men stop their ears with their
hands, hardly able to bear the roar as they draw near, the roar which
the various sounds make as they burst forth. And the melody of the
pipes is heard all over the city, and the flying fame of it spreads
through the land.

Most modern writers on the medieval organ appear to take Wulfstan's
description with rather more than a pinch of salt. James McKinnon, whose
translation (with a few adjustments) I have borrowed, does however make
out a case for its physical existence and speculates on the most likely position
for such a massive instrument. He opts for the newly extended east end,
where the organ would be conveniently – though perhaps that is hardly the
word – close to the singers.[32] Another possibility might have been up aloft in
the westworks, where, open to the winds, the instrument would indeed be
heard 'all over the city'.

Illustrations exist of early organs containing some of the features of
Wulfstan's description, notably in the ninth-/tenth-century Utrecht Psalter,[33]
and the Psalter of Ædwine.[34] These two sketches, which are almost identical,
show several men working the 'bellows', though many fewer than 'seventy',
which may well be poetic hyperbole, unless perhaps the monks pumped in
relays. But the interesting fact, to my mind, is that in both sketches there are
two players seated side by side, reminiscent of Wulfstan's 'two brethren of
concordant spirit, each managing his own alphabet'. This has been interpreted
in various ways: Holschneider thinks the instrument may have been some
kind of double organ.[35]

Was the tenth-century Winchester organ truth or fiction? One of the chief

[32] J.W. McKinnon, 'The Tenth-Century Organ at Winchester', *The Organ Yearbook* 5
(1974), 4-19.
[33] Nordlingen, BRD, Stadtarchiv, Stadtbibliothek und Volksbucherei, MS Uu 32, fol. 83r. See
New Grove Dictionary XIII, 728 for an illustration of the organ from the Utrecht Psalter.
[34] Cambridge, Trinity College, MS R.17.I. This is a copy of the Utrecht Psalter, text and illustrations, dating from the mid-twelfth century. It comes from the scriptorium of Christchurch,
Canterbury. On fol. 261v there is a picture of an organ similar, though not identical in every
detail, to the one in the Utrecht Psalter. In both illustrations there are two players, and as in
Wulfstan's poem, each is 'managing his own alphabet'. In the Canterbury picture the player on
the left faces a set of six brown pipes, and his companion a set of four blue ones. They are
assisted by a team of four blowers.
[35] Holschneider, *Die Organa von Winchester*, pp 140-1. He bases his theory on Wulfstan's
assertion that two players are needed, each with his own set of keys, 20 + 20, making a total of
40: 'four times ten tongues'.

arguments often used by scholars to disprove its physical existence is that it appears to be unique; scholars would be less inclined to disbelief if some evidence could be found of other contemporary instruments of like proportions: nothing of such a vast size would appear to be forthcoming. Yet the Winchester organ may not have been unique. There is a colourful account in a reliable contemporary source of the elaborate celebrations that took place at Ramsey Abbey on 8 November 991, on the occasion of the rededication of the church by St Oswald, then Archbishop of York, together with Bishop Æscio of Dorchester.[36] This was the last of Oswald's annual visits to Ramsey: he died a few months later, the last of the three great monastic reformers. The date of the event in Ramsey is significant in itself: 991, almost the very year of the supposed installation of Bishop Ælfheah's great organ at Winchester. Accounts such as this Ramsey description of a great liturgico-musical event are frequently found in the later Middle Ages and such a celebration would have been almost commonplace if it had taken place, exactly as described in the manuscript, in about 1491, not 991, five hundred years before the full medieval flowering of complex patterns of *alternatim* performance. For these tenth-century Ramsey celebrations involved the alternation of cantors and choir, of the two sides of the choir, and most probably too, of two pairs of polyphonic singers and of the organ. It is quite astonishing to find all this happening so early in a monastery of Anglo-Saxon monks in the depths of the fens. We are told that the church had been splendidly adorned for the occasion, with curtains and tapestries and vast numbers of blazing candles. After the solemn Mass of Dedication, Æthelwine, the princely founder of the Abbey, gave a sumptuous banquet. Then, as evening fell, everyone was again summoned into the church for Vespers. The author, himself a monk of Ramsey and an eye-witness, describes the scene in these terms:

> As the Bishops, the Princes, the Abbots and the Soldiers entered (the church) a huge crowd of people gathered, who, on beholding the splendour of the holy building burst out into the praises of the God of Heaven with serene minds and sincere hearts. The monks' choir then began to sing the service, with the Precentor and three of his fellow cantors ruling the choir. When they had finished the solemn florid responsory, there followed a whole series of chants, praise upon praise, hymn after hymn. Whereupon the Organist climbed up aloft to his seat *with a great troop of people*, and with thunderous clamour incited the hearts of the faithful to praise the Name of the Lord. The joyful choir, on hearing this with willing ears, began to sing their chants to Christ who is the glory of the holy Angels, singing the sweet praises *in alternation*. When the right-hand side of the choir finished singing the well-known notes of the chant, then the left-hand side gave praise to God, *jubilating with the organs. Alternating thus* among the brethren, together with the five voices,

– this presumably means the four cantors and the organ –

that evening presented a magnificent spectacle to the assembled people.[37]

[36] 'Vita Sancti Oswaldi', *Hist. York* I, 464-5.
[37] Translation and italics are the author's own.

The chronicler was clearly impressed and moved by the liturgical and musical splendour, and he goes on to describe in joyful detail the feasting and drinking that followed!

That eye-witness – and ear-witness – account of a great monastic and princely event comes as a fitting conclusion to this brief introduction to what the Saxon monks sang. It highlights the splendour and magnificence of sound and spectacle to be found in the rich liturgical life of the great reformed monastic houses of Anglo-Saxon England towards the close of the tenth century. This was certainly more especially true of Winchester, the great royal and monastic heart of England, where Æthelwold's influence had established a tradition of sumptuous liturgy in a building worthy of it. The city of Winchester was a centre of astonishing musical creativity and innovation, but at the same time it was a centre of musical continuity, where the majority of chants sung there so faithfully from day to day had been handed down to the monks and nuns from their English and European predecessors of earlier centuries. Wulfstan the Cantor, poet, biographer, superb music calligrapher and almost certainly a composer of genius worked and sang there. But he was not alone. There were also generations of ordinary monks, whose day began at 1.30a.m., and who chanted the praises of God day in, day out over many centuries. There were also generations of nuns in their monastery of Nunnaminster following the same daily round of sung praise. Thanks to the wisdom and guidance of Æthelwold, bishop of Winchester, himself a monk participating in the daily chanting, those lives of men and women were moulded by an unceasing rhythm of sung prayer. One often hears people say of ancient buildings: 'Ah! if only these stones could speak!' In Winchester perhaps the stones might sing?

Chapter 7

LATE PRE-CONQUEST SCULPTURES WITH THE CRUCIFIXION SOUTH OF THE HUMBER

Elizabeth Coatsworth

The life of St Æthelwold is well documented, compared to the lives of many of his contemporaries,[1] and in particular, we are well informed about his involvement in the monastic reforms of the tenth century and in the consequences that flowed from these. These included the foundation and revival of monasteries and nunneries in his own diocese of Winchester and in the East Midlands. We know that the reforms in many cases were associated with major programmes of church building and rebuilding,[2] and with the enrichment of the churches through gifts of objects in gold and silver.[3] His contemporaries, Dunstan and Oswald, the other leaders of the reform movement, patronised similar developments elsewhere in southern England.[4] Sculpture of the period is rarely mentioned, however, and never for its own sake.[5] The use of sculptures in liturgical contexts is now accepted for this period,[6] but it is much more difficult, in practice, to assign particular remains to within Æthelwold's lifetime, or even to the period immediately after. If there is any chance, however, of showing developments in sculpture, and particularly in architectural sculpture, in southern England in connection with the reform then it must be through a study of the surviving sculptures of the Crucifixion: both because of the numbers with this theme, and because its central importance in Christian thought and liturgy mean that references to it occur across a wide range of contemporary literature. There

---

[1] See Introduction, esp. pp 1-6.

[2] M. Biddle, '*Felix Urbs Winthonia*: Winchester in the Age of Monastic Reform', *Tenth-Century Studies*, pp 123-40, esp. pp 132-9.

[3] See, for example, his gifts to Peterborough, Robertson no. 39, which included three silver crosses.

[4] The main sources are, for Dunstan: *Epistola Adelardi ... de vita S. Dunstani* and *S. Dunstani vita auctor B*, in *Memorials*, pp 53-68 and 3-52; and Oswald: *Vita Oswaldi auctore anonymo*, in *Hist. York*, I, 399-475. For references to the continuing arguments about the relative importance of the roles of these figures, especially Dunstan and Æthelwold, see Introduction, pp 9-10.

[5] See C. Dodwell, *Anglo-Saxon Art. A New Perspective* (Manchester, 1982), chap. IV, esp. pp 109-19. Sculptures are usually only mentioned because of a connection with a venerated or important figure; most references are post-Conquest and are often of doubtful value to the art historian.

[6] Brieger argued that roods were actually an Anglo-Saxon development: see P. H. Brieger, 'England's Contribution to the Origin and Development of the Triumphal Cross', *Medieval Studies* 4 (1942), 85-91. More is now known about the use of sculptures in continental churches, both from documentary sources and from studies of their remains: H. Keller, 'Zur Entstehung der sakralen Vollskulptur in der ottonischen Zeit', *Festschrift für Hans Jantzen* (Berlin, 1951), pp 71-91; H. M. Taylor, 'Tenth-Century Church Building in England and on the

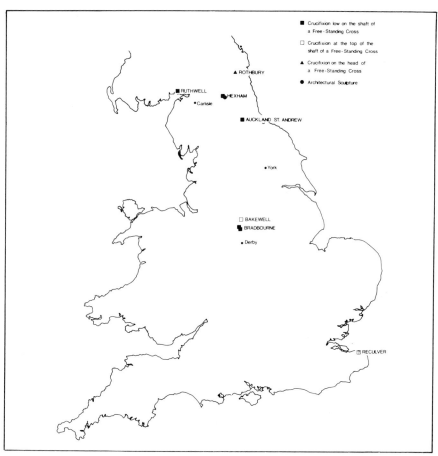

Fig. 1   Map showing sculptures with Christ on the Cross from mid ninth or
earlier centuries

are twenty-five surviving sculptures probably or certainly with the Crucifixion
scene, which are arguably of pre-Conquest date, in the area south and east
of a line drawn between Humber and Severn.[7] I have restricted my study to

---

Continent', in *Tenth-Century Studies*, pp 141-68; R. Haussherr, *Der Tote Christus am Kreuz.
Zur Ikonographie des Gerokreuzes* (unpubl. diss. Bonn, 1963).

[7] Appendix 1 (below, p 188), gives details of twenty-three sculptures certainly or probably with
the Crucifixion theme from southern and eastern England; Appendix 2 (below, p 193), lists a
further seven published as examples of this theme or of the pre-Conquest period, but either not
certainly of this date, or not certainly representations of the Crucifixion. The two most important
sculptures from this group, both from Daglingworth, are however discussed in the text as they
provide interesting points of comparison with other sculptures. Inclusion in Appendix 1 does
not mean that attribution to either the iconography of the Crucifixion or a pre-Conquest date is
unarguable, and some of the problems are rehearsed in the text. There are in addition a small
number of sculptures from these areas with related themes (see for example, the grave-marker
in n 10, below) but these have been omitted as irrelevant to the present discussion. These
numbers should be set against those for England (excluding the South-West peninsula) as a

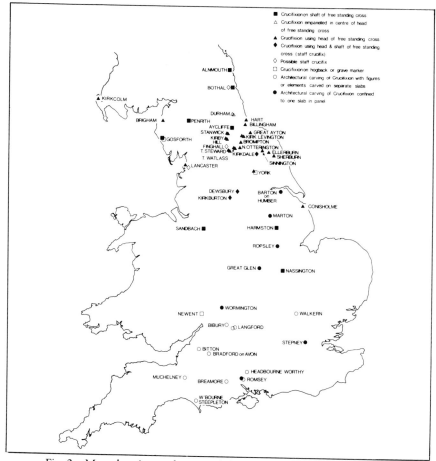

Fig. 2 Map showing sculptures of the Crucifixion from late ninth to
eleventh centuries

the majority of these in which Christ is shown (where he has survived)
wearing a loincloth, since it is within this group that the most characteristically southern variants in iconography appear.[8] However, there are no
absolute criteria for placing these in series. Evidence for dating consists
mainly of comparisons of style and iconography with works in other media.
I have used architectural evidence where possible, but this is often inconclus-
ive, and in most cases does not lead to close dating within a decade or even
a quarter century. I have tried a new approach, looking first at the development

whole: seventy-two sculptures from fifty-six different sites, not counting those with related or
dependent themes: E. Coatsworth, *The Iconography of the Crucifixion in pre-Conquest
Sculpture in England* (Ph.D., 2 vols Durham, 1979). One of this number, from Kirby Grindalythe
in Yorkshire was found after 1979.

[8] I intend to discuss the three robed examples from Langford, Bitton and Walkern, and the
cross-head from Conisholme, in a forthcoming article devoted to this iconography through the
whole pre-Conquest period.

of monuments appropriate to the Crucifixion; then discussing the surviving material by diocese (using those established in the reform period), to see if any regional or period groups emerge, especially in association with the evidence from manuscript painting; and finally attempting to set the monumental remains in their contemporary context.

Crucifixion sculptures: monument types

The archaeological and architectural information provided by the monuments has some interesting features, although the small size of the sample must always be borne in mind. Among the free-standing monuments, for example, only the small carving from Newent (Gloucs) (plate Vd) is clearly a grave-marker, though it may have been found in rather than on a grave.[9] It is identified as a personal monument by the inscription EDRED, which appears twice. The extraordinarily crowded iconography, unique in all pre-Conquest sculpture, and indeed in depictions of this scene in any medium, could indicate an individual as much as a period taste.[10]

There are only three other free standing monuments with the Crucifixion in the whole area, including Reculver (Kent), where the Crucifixion if not the whole cross is missing. Leland described a cross with a Crucifixion scene apparently at the top of the shaft immediately below the cross-head 'in the enteryng of the qyer' of the church there.[11] Peers found further documentary evidence that there was a cross in this position in the thirteenth century, and believed that in excavation he had found a base for this cross contemporary with a seventh-century floor.[12] H. M. Taylor's re-examination of this evidence showed that the base was more likely that of an altar before the chancel arch, perhaps comparable to an altar in this position at St Riquier before 799 which was dedicated to the Holy Cross.[13] There is therefore no archaeological evidence for the date of the cross, and it could have been a later addition.

The evidence of the earliest Northumbrian and Mercian crosses suggests that the earliest sculptural setting for the scene on a cross was on the shaft: at the base of the carved area and in effect at about eye level. This conservative tradition was carried on in northern areas until very late in the pre-Conquest period.[14] The cross-shaft at Nassington (Northants), and even that

[9] E. Conder *et al.*, 'Proceedings 13 June 1912', *Proceedings of the Society of Antiquaries of London*, 2nd ser. 24 (1911-12), 323-6.

[10] There are other grave-covers with a similarly 'one off' character, as on a grave-cover with a seated lamb at the centre of a cross and an unusual combination of other figures and elements from Ramsbury in Wiltshire. See G. B. Brown, *Anglo-Saxon Sculpture*, The Arts in Early England VI, ii, ed. E. H. L. Sexton (London, 1937), pp 290-1.

[11] J. Leland, *The Itinerary … in or about the Years 1535-1543*, ed. L. Toulmin-Smith (London, 1906-10), pp 59-60.

[12] C. R. Peers, 'Reculver, its Saxon Church and Cross', *Archaeologia* 76 (1928), 241-56, esp. 250.

[13] H. M. Taylor, 'Reculver Reconsidered', *Archaeological Journal* 125 (1968), 291-6. Excavations by B. J. Philp in 1969 in any case established that the floor was not seventh century: D. M. Wilson and D. G. Hurst, 'Medieval Britain in 1969', *Medieval Archaeology* 14, 161.

[14] See E. Coatsworth, 'Two Examples of the Crucifixion at Hexham', *St Wilfrid at Hexham*, ed. D. P. Kirby (Newcastle-upon-Tyne, 1974), pp 180-4; *ibid.*, 'The Crucifixion Scenes on a Cross at Aycliffe, Co. Durham', *Anglo-Saxon and Viking Age Sculpture*, ed. J. T. Lang, BAR British Series 49 (Oxford, 1978), pp 114-16. The scene seems initially to have been viewed as part of a cycle, and was probably copied from cycles of paintings on rectangular panels of

at Harmston (Lincs), seem to suggest that areas outside Northumbria could be similarly conservative. However at Bakewell (Derbys), on a cross of c.800 or a little later, the scene is at the top of the shaft with the width of the cross accommodated in the lower arm of the cross-head.[15] What seems to be the earliest example of a sculptured crucifix is at Rothbury in Northumberland. This cross has been dated to the ninth century, and its Crucifixion iconography in particular shows influence from ninth-century Carolingian court art.[16] As the Carolingian parallels suggest that the immediate source of influence could have been ivory panels on book-covers, for example, rather than crucifixes, there is room to speculate that the development of the stone crucifix may have been an aesthetic as well as a liturgically useful development. Leland's description of the cross at Reculver suggests a development close to the Bakewell type rather than a crucifix. Fragments of a round-shafted cross now at Canterbury Cathedral have commonly been identified with that described by Leland, but they may represent more than one cross, possibly as late as c.900. The surviving scenes do not include the Crucifixion.[17]

Most of the remaining sculptures are clearly architectural, although this has to be deduced from the form of the surviving monuments because most of them are not *in situ*. There are two main monument types. The first consists of multiple slabs each with elements of the design, and sometimes shaped to accommodate the outline of a figure: most of the larger roods are of this type. The second consists of a single panel, with or without a border. It is not, however, possible to be certain that some panels are not in fact separated from other slabs with other elements of the Crucifixion scene: the handless Crucifixion at Wormington suggests this possibility. The distinction is neither merely size, for Langford I belongs to the first group but is much smaller than Breamore or Headbourne Worthy; nor is it presumed original position, for the panel above the chancel arch at Barton-on-Humber is on a much smaller scale than is suggested by other remains in the same position or at a similar height above ground. Evidence *in situ* suggests three possible positions. First is above the chancel arch as at Barton-on-Humber, Bibury, Bitton, and Bradford-on-Avon, although in three of these cases there is no surviving Christ figure, and at Bradford-on-Avon the angels were removed and replaced, apparently in the same wall, in the nineteenth century.[18] The sculptures at Daglingworth, which may in any case be post-Conquest are more difficult to assess. One of the Crucifixion scenes, and the panels with

---

canvas or wood. Cross-shaft panels tend to be narrow in proportion to height, and the cross to dominate the scene, with the result that the remaining space was not usually wide enough to accommodate either a correctly proportioned cross and Christ figure, or more than one figure beneath each arm.

[15] E. Routh, 'A Corpus of the pre-Conquest Carved Stones in Derbyshire', *Archaeological Journal* 94 (1937), 1-42, esp. 5-7; Coatsworth, *The Iconography of the Crucifixion*, I, 198-200.

[16] Coatsworth, *Iconography of the Crucifixion*, I, 200-7; R. Cramp, *Corpus of Anglo-Saxon Stone Sculpture, I, County Durham and Northumberland* (Oxford, 1984), pp 217-21.

[17] *The Golden Age of Anglo-Saxon Art 966-1066*, ed. J. Backhouse, D. H. Turner, and L. Webster (London, 1984), no. 22, pp 40-41.

[18] The best evidence is for Bitton, where a pair of feet on a *suppedaneum*, an open-jawed snake below, are *in situ*. This sculpture is not further discussed in the present paper because other evidence suggests it was part of a robed figure. The panel at Barton-on-Humber has only a head, presumably of Christ; and at Bibury and Bradford-on-Avon there is no cross or Christ figure.

St Peter and Christ in Majesty belonging to the same series, were found built into the chancel arch, face inwards. Their position relative to the arch is by no means clear, however, and it is of course possible that they were reused as building stones at some later period.[19] The second position for which there is architectural evidence is above an exterior door: the south door if the robed figure at Walkern is a rood and is pre-Conquest;[20] and the west door at Headbourne Worthy.[21] Finally, a Crucifixion could have been part of a larger exterior programme of decoration: the only trace of this, however, is the crude little figure from Ropsley, which is carved on one of the original quoin stones of the possibly pre-Conquest church. The second Crucifixion at Daglingworth, which must be dated with the first on stylistic grounds (and so is probably post-Conquest), was removed from the outside of the east wall of the chancel in 1972, but was said to have occupied the same position in that wall, high in the gable, as before its rebuilding in 1845.[22] All the architectural evidence above is, of course, dependent on the dating of the church fabric, and this cannot often be dated at all closely,[23] while the reuse of sculptures in new positions by mediaeval builders is well attested, for example, at Breamore,[24] Langford,[25] and Romsey.[26]

The Sculptures

In this analysis, I have started with the two dioceses (Winchester and Dorchester-on-Thames) with which Æthelwold was chiefly associated, and which between them account for half the surviving Crucifixion sculptures. The evidence from other dioceses is very scanty, with one or even no examples from most. The majority are from areas west of Winchester, and it is for this reason that these are considered next. Looking at the material on a regional basis throws up some interesting connections, but also emphasises the scarcity of the surviving remains.

[19] They seem to have been found face inward in the jambs. See H. M. Taylor and J. Taylor, *Anglo-Saxon Architecture*, 2 vols (Cambridge, 1965), pp 188-9; *ibid.*, 'Architectural Sculpture in pre-Norman England', *Journal of the British Archaeological Association*, 3rd ser. 29 (1966), 15-16, where they are used to support a pre-Conquest date for the arch.
[20] A robed figure not further discussed in this paper. See Taylor and Taylor, *Anglo-Saxon Architecture*, pp 628-30; and *ibid.*, 'Architectural Sculpture', 9-11.
[21] Accepted as *in situ* by Taylor and Taylor, 'Architectural Sculpture', 4-6.
[22] W. Bazeley, 'Notes on the Manor, Advowson, and Church of Daglingworth', *Transactions of the Bristol and Gloucestershire Archaeological Society* 12 (1887-8), 54-69, esp. 66-7. Taylor and Taylor, *Anglo-Saxon Architecture*, p 188. For the surviving evidence for a major programme of sculpture including the Crucifixion, in comparison with what has been deduced from literary sources, see R. N. Quirk, 'Winchester New Minster and its Tenth-Century Tower', *Journal of the British Archaeological Association* 3rd ser. 24 (1961), 16-54.
[23] The period brackets A, B, and C used by Taylor and Taylor, *Anglo-Saxon Architecture*, *passim*, are extremely wide, and even so are sometimes disputed. See, for example, the discussion on Bradford-on-Avon, p 176 below, and n 79.
[24] W. Rodwell and E. C. Rouse, 'The Anglo-Saxon Rood and other Features in the South Porch of St Mary's Church, Breamore, Hampshire', *Antiquaries Journal* 64 (1984), 298-325. The rood seems to have been moved to its present position in the fifteenth century.
[25] See Langford I and II, Appendix 1, p 190.
[26] Both sculptures from this site are out of their original position: see Appendix 1, p 191 below. Romsey II is also in a different stone to the wall in which it is now set: see Quirk, 'Winchester New Minster and its Tenth-Century Tower', 29.

Winchester Diocese

No sculpture of the Crucifixion has survived from Winchester itself, but there are four in the diocese, all from a relatively small geographical area. Two are from Romsey Abbey, which had been founded in the reign of Edward the Elder, but was reformed or refounded in 967, presumably under Æthelwold's influence. King Edgar was a major patron of the nunnery, and his infant son, Edmund, was buried there in 971.[27] The evidence suggests it was a very important foundation, but no evidence of its fabric now survives above ground.[28] The two Crucifixion sculptures from this site are in marked contrast to each other. Romsey I (plate Ia) is a small unframed panel, on which a full group composition is represented in delicate detail. The background is cut away, leaving figures and plant motifs in sharp outline, though shallow relief. The figure of Christ (type 1)[29] is set high on a tall Latin cross with a tall stem and T-shaped terminals.

Kendrick compared the plant ornament and energetic postures of the minor figures on this panel to manuscripts and ivories of the Winchester school, but considered its iconography Byzantine in origin, comparing it with the central panel of an eleventh-century ivory triptych in Berlin.[30] This indeed has a similar layout, but the differences are quite significant. In the Berlin example Christ is bearded; the cross is plain; the angels are empty-handed; Mary and John both appear in groups of three figures, and Mary's hands are veiled and her head is bowed; there is no plant ornament; the spear- and sponge-bearers both turn their backs, and this and other touches produce a more static effect. In fact, the Berlin panel is unusual in Byzantine art, and seems to have been influenced, like the Romsey panel, by a very distinctive iconography characteristic of work of the Metz school of the tenth century: this is seen particularly in the tall-stemmed decorated cross and in the figures in two registers on either side of the cross below. The same iconography is also recognisable on a tenth-century cross at Alnmouth (Northumberland), an indication that models of this type had a wide circulation.[31] Some of the features at Romsey are found not only in work of the Metz school, but were well established in the Carolingian iconography of

[27] S813; D. Knowles and R. N. Hadcock, *Mediaeval Religious Houses, England and Wales* (Bristol, 1971), p 480; M. A. Meyer, 'Patronage of the West Saxon Royal Nunneries in Late Anglo-Saxon England', *Revue Bénédictine* 91 (1981), 332-58.

[28] J. C. Cox, 'Abbey of Romsey', *VCH Hampshire and the Isle of Wight*, II (London, 1903), pp 126-32. The Domesday valuations of the monsteries are listed in D. Hill, *An Atlas of Anglo-Saxon England* (Oxford, 1981), figs 248-9.

[29] The typology used in this analysis is based on the position of the trunk and legs of Christ only, since the head and arms are most likely to be missing or damaged; or to have been determined with regard to the available space. Type 1 is a completely upright, frontal figure, with straight legs. In type 2 the trunk sags to one side so that one hip is lower than the other, but the legs are not bent at the knee, and frontality is preserved. In type 3, the legs are bent and drawn to one side, and the body sags and turns at least slightly from the frontal position.

[30] T. D. Kendrick, *Late Saxon and Viking Art* (London, 1949), p 48. See also D. Talbot Rice, *English Art 871-1100*, The Oxford History of English Art, II (Oxford, 1952), p 108. The triptych is illustrated in O. M. Dalton, *Byzantine Art and Archaeology* (Oxford, 1911), fig. 40.

[31] See A. Goldschmidt, *Die Elfenbeinskulpturen aus der Zeit der Karolingischen und Sächsischen Kaiser VIII-IX Jahrhundert*, I (Berlin, 1914; repr. 1969), pl XXXII, no. 78. For the Alnmouth cross, see E. Coatsworth, 'The Crucifixion on the Alnmouth Cross', *Archaeologia Aeliana*, 5th ser. 5 (1977), 198-201.

the Crucifixion from which this derived: the foliage growing from the cross, for example; the wand-carrying angels; and the distinctive posture of the sponge-bearer.[32] The hooked ends of the cross bear comparison with Stepney and Langford I, discussed below, and with two Anglo-Saxon ivory crucifixes dated to the late tenth/ early eleventh century, one of which has figures of John and Mary in very similar poses to Romsey.[33] As Kendrick saw, Mary's fluttering drapery and the form of the plant ornament also relate this sculpture to Winchester art of the tenth century. It is possible, therefore, to suggest that this sculpture too dates from the last quarter of the tenth century, and shows a considerable dependence on imported models.

The larger rood, Romsey II (plate Ib), is carved on three separate slabs: one consisting of the cross-shaft with the *Manus Dei*, head and trunk of Christ; and one for each arm. This is one case where it cannot be certain that the rood originally stood alone, without other elements or accompanying figures. The cross is a plain Latin cross, with a sloping *suppedaneum* of triangular section. Christ (type 1) has a flat top to his head, and there is a hole drilled into one side: the other side is damaged. The figure is in deep relief, and one of its most interesting features is the modelling of the breast, upper legs and arms, and even of details such as the fleshy part of the hands. This naturalism fails at the feet, which are oddly flat and conformed to the ledge beneath.

Dating of this rood to the pre-Conquest period has relied heavily on the presence of the *Manus Dei*.[34] This feature derives ultimately from Carolingian court art, and was indeed popular in southern English manuscripts of the tenth and eleventh centuries,[35] but it is also found, though more rarely, as late as the twelfth century.[36] There is, however, other evidence for a tenth-century date which is partly stylistic and partly iconographical. In dress and in its heavy monumentality the Romsey rood compares closely with large wooden crucifixes from continental centres, such as the cross of Gero at Cologne, which has been dated to the tenth century, and, in particular, an example from Ringelheim of the early eleventh century.[37] The smooth moulding of fabric over limbs is as characteristic of this style as are the clinging dampened folds of the twelfth-century.[38] Moreover the same features of style and

[32] See for example the Crucifixion miniature in the Coronation Sacramentary of Charles the Bald: G. Schiller, trans. J. Seligman, *The Iconography of Christian Art. II. The Passion of Jesus Christ* (Gutersloh and London, 1972), pl 362. See also the fresco from St Pierre-les-Eglises (Vienne) and the gold altar in S. Ambrogio, Milan, both ninth-century, for comparable treatment of the spear- and sponge-bearers and half-figures of angels carrying wands: P. Thoby, *Le Crucifix des Origines au Concile de Trente. I. Etude Iconographique* (Nantes, 1959), pl XXXIX, no. 88; J. Reil, *Christus am Kreuz in der Bildkunst der Karolingerzeit* (Leipzig, 1930), pl VI.
[33] J. Beckwith, *Ivory Carvings in Early Medieval England* (London, 1972), pls 69 and 72.
[34] Dated to 1000-20: Talbot Rice, *English Art 871-1100*, p 98; Quirk, 'Winchester New Minster', p 29. But dated to the twelfth century in Kendrick, *Late Saxon and Viking Art*, pp 49-50.
[35] E. Temple, *Anglo-Saxon Manuscripts 900-1066* (London, 1976), pls 134, 171, 246, 256, 261, 289, and 312; Beckwith, *Ivory Carvings*, pls 67-74.
[36] C. Väterlein, ed., *Die Zeit der Staufer. Katalog der Ausstellung*, II (Stuttgart, 1977), pl 426.
[37] R. Wesenberg, *Frühe mittelälterliche Bildwerke. Die Schulen Rheinischer Skulptur und ihre Ausstrahlung* (Düsseldorf, 1972), pl 1; Thoby, *Le Crucifix*, pl XXXVII, no. 84.
[38] Kendrick, *Late Saxon and Viking Art*, pp 49-50. He saw the moulded drapery style as a continuing and progressively hardening feature of the developing Romanesque style, with the Romsey rood at the end of the tradition, but see the Sherborne Pontifical, n 39, below.

Plate I   a. Romsey I (Hants)

Plate I   b. Romsey II (Hants)

iconography are reflected in manuscripts: for example in the late-tenth-century Sherborne Pontifical there is the *Manus Dei*, and the same interest in modelling and monumentality. This manuscript may have been made in Canterbury, or at Sherborne, but it is strongly influenced by Winchester art of this period.[39] A psalter, which was made at Winchester in the mid eleventh century, has a more stylised version of the same iconography.[40] There is also a clear implication that the figure once had something attached to its head. If it was a crown this was also a feature of Winchester art, influenced, it has been suggested, by Æthelwold's ideas of kingship.[41] There is some evidence in the run of the walling, and in the fact that, although built up in masonry blocks it is not in the same stone, that the cross is not in its original position, but was moved to its present one in a major rebuilding programme in the twelfth century.[42] There are therefore a number of grounds for believing that this great sculpture is pre-Conquest and of the late tenth/ early eleventh century. The rich convent, with its royal associations, established or re-established by Edgar in 967, seems an appropriate *milieu* for the two sculptures with their associations with Ottonian court art.

At Breamore (plate Ic), a full group composition has been cut back flush with the wall, except for the clouds, but the outline of each figure and element has survived, and a number of details can be distinguished. Christ (type 3) is shown hanging from the cross. He is nimbed, and there is new evidence for a metal trimming, perhaps a crown of bronze fixed to wooden dowels.[43] His body seems to hang in a tense curve, with his hips pushed far out to his left, but missing detail may have created a more sagging effect. As the figure is constructed at present, Christ's arms appear to stretch upwards and outwards, with the hands raised from the wrist rather than drooping. Kendrick accepted this as a feature of an exaggerated period style,[44] but A. R. and P. M. Green believed the arms were reversed and upside down, and believed that this was evidence that the sculpture had been moved and incorrectly reassembled.[45] Rodwell, after a recent and very detailed study, although agreeing that the sculpture has been moved, has returned to Kendrick's position, on the grounds that the arms of the cross would not fit if they were reversed from their present position, and that the nimbus impinges on to one cross-arm.[46] If

[39] Paris, Bibliothèque Nationale Lat. 943, fol. 4v: Temple, *Anglo-Saxon Manuscripts*, pp 60-1 and pl 134; *Golden Age*, no. 34, p 55.
[40] London, British Library MS Arundel 60, fol. 12v: Temple, *Anglo-Saxon Manuscripts*, p 120 and pl 312. It is not certain at which Winchester scriptorium this was made: *Golden Age*, no. 67, p 83.
[41] See for example the mid-eleventh-century Winchester Psalter, London, British Library MS Cotton Tiberius CVI, fol. 13, where the crown is represented as a dotted outline to distinguish it from the cruciferous halo: Temple *Anglo-Saxon Manuscripts*, pp 115-17 and pl 311. See also BL Arundel 60 (n 40, above). For the association of attributes of kingship with the figure of Christ and the importance of Æthelwold in the development of these ideas, see R. Deshman, 'Christus rex et magi reges': Kingship and Christology in Ottonian and Anglo-Saxon Art', *Frühmittelälterliche Studien* 10 (1976), 367-405.
[42] See nn 26 and 28 above. The main evidence for earlier foundations is in C. R. Peers, 'Recent Discoveries in Romsey Abbey Church', *Archaeologia* 57 (1901), 317-20.
[43] Rodwell, 'The Anglo-Saxon Rood ... Breamore', 309, and pls.
[44] Kendrick, *Late Saxon and Viking Art*, p 46.
[45] A. R. and P. M. Green, *Saxon Architecture and Sculpture in Hampshire* (Winchester, 1951), pp 37-9.
[46] Rodwell, 'The Anglo-Saxon Rood ... Breamore', 309.

he and Kendrick are right, however, the position of the hands is inexplicable, and the cross-arm on the spectator's right continues to look as if it does not fit. All details of clothing are now missing. The *Manus Dei* appears out of clouds represented as waves in relief, and reaches down to touch Christ's nimbus. The sun and moon, in framed panels at the end of the cross-arms, were carved in high relief, but all detail has been hacked away.

Some features of the figures of John and Mary can be distinguished: both are nimbed, with hands and arms held close to the face and body. John, on Christ's left, has a shorter dress than Mary, and is in the act of taking a step forward towards the cross. Beneath his feet is a patch with an irregular outline which seems to represent the ground on which he stands. It is difficult indeed to distinguish features of style, but the postures of these figures were well established in Western art from the ninth century, together with conventional indications of landscape beneath their feet: for example, in a ninth-century wall-painting at Trier,[47] in the Sherborne Pontifical,[48] the Ramsey Psalter,[49] and in English ivories of the late tenth/ early eleventh century.[50] The Breamore figures may have been more restrained, but the absence of detail makes this difficult to assess. Apart from the arms, the sagging figure of Christ is that of the late-tenth-century Arenberg Gospels, with which the manner of representing the *Manus Dei* also bears comparison.[51]

The rood at Headbourne Worthy (plate Id) has also been cut back and whitewashed, but in many details it seems to have been close to Breamore: the shaft of the cross (which, however, narrows towards the foot) has a similar square cut moulding, and the *Manus Dei* issues from a cloud represented by wavy lines. The figure of Christ sags less heavily (type 2), and more detail is missing: his head is nimbed but has been cut back to form a deep cavity; and little has survived of his arms. The figures of John and Mary also seem to have similar restrained gestures: both are nimbed, broader at the shoulder than at the foot, and enough detail of the dress survives to indicate close packed, even fluttering draperies. The narrow, fluted folds in John's dress, for example, compare closely with those in Mary's veil in the Ramsey Psalter, and the 'hobble' effect of the sharply tapering garments is also very close to this manuscript.[52] The Crucifixion in the 'Missal' of Robert of Jumièges seems also to have been close in iconography and style to the sculpture: similar folds forming a narrow zigzagging line appear in the dress of both Mary and John. This manuscript was made before 1023, and the immediate source, of its text at least, is believed to be a Peterborough manuscript, that is, from a monastery revived by St Æthelwold.[53] There is

[47] Schiller, *Iconography of Christian Art*, II, pl 347.
[48] See n 39 above.
[49] London, British Library Harley 2904, fol. 3v. Temple, *Anglo-Saxon Manuscripts*, pp 64-5 and pl 142. This is late tenth century and was probably made in Winchester apparently for the use of Ramsey Abbey, Huntingdonshire: *Golden Age*, no. 41, p 60.
[50] Beckwith, *English Ivories*, pl 72.
[51] New York, Pierpont Morgan Library MS 869, fol. 9v: Temple, *Anglo-Saxon Manuscripts*, pp 74-5 and pl 171; The Gospels date to the late tenth century, and were probably made at Christ Church, Canterbury: *Golden Age*, no. 47, p 68.
[52] See above, n 49.
[53] The 'Missal' (Sacramentary) of Robert of Jumièges: Rouen, Bibliothèque Municipale MS Y. 6, fol. 71v. See Temple, *Anglo-Saxon Manuscripts*, pp 89-91; *Golden Age*, no. 50, p 69; Talbot

Plate I   c. Breamore (Hants)

d. Headbourne Worthy (Hants)

b. Marton (Lincs)

therefore support on stylistic and iconographical grounds for a late-tenth-or, perhaps, early-eleventh-century date for this sculpture as there is for Romsey and Breamore.[54]

Diocese of Dorchester-on-Thames

The other area particularly associated with Æthelwold is the East Midlands, where he revived monasteries at Peterborough, Ely, and Thorney.[55] Before the Viking invasions of the ninth century, there had been two dioceses in this area, Leicester and Lindsey: these seem to have been almost completely destroyed, with the Leicester bishopric moving its seat south to Dorchester-on-Thames where it remained after the reconquest even though it then incorporated Lindsey as well. There is a reference to a sculptured crucifix at Peterborough which is particularly interesting in the light of the remains from the Winchester area, and the site's connection with Æthelwold. The monastery there was plundered in 1070 by a Danish army led by Swein, and the Peterborough chronicle records that the raiders went into the church and:

> clumben upp to þe halge rode, namen þa þe kynehelm of ure Drih't'nes heafod eall of smeate gold, namen þa þet fotspure þe wæs undernæðen his fote, *þet* wæs eall of read golde.[56]

This rood was obviously high up, and apparently in deep relief if not in the round: presumably also it was made of something intrinsically valueless, like wood or stone, or it too would have been taken and not just its accoutrements. The story suggests an appropriate setting for a sculpture like Romsey II. The range of sculptures from the whole diocese, however, reflects its politically mixed fortunes. It may be interesting, for example, that the sculptures associated with the robed type omitted from the present paper are all from this area.

One sculpture from Northamptonshire looks earlier than the tenth century. This is the cross-shaft from Nassington (plate IIa). This has one figure-panelled face, on which parts of two panels survive, with the Crucifixion at the bottom. The moulding of the lower edge is missing, but unless the cross was set on a tall shaft as on Romsey I and Alnmouth, the scene could be substantially complete. The figure of Christ (type 1) has been deliberately defaced. Above the cross-arms the sun and moon are relief carvings enclosed within a slightly dished circle. That on the right may only have been a

---

Rice, *English Art 871-1100*, pl 53b.
[54] There has not been any very detailed study of this sculpture. Most commentators have been agreed on its 'Winchester' connections, for example, Quirk, 'Winchester New Minster and its Tenth Century Tower', 29 and Kendrick, *Late Saxon and Viking Art*, pp 46-7. Talbot Rice, *English Art 871-1100*, pp 99-100, seems to have seen it as more sharply differentiated from Breamore, because of its more static qualities, but some of the difference is probably due to the lack of surviving detail. The deep relief was apparently once evident in one of Christ's hands, found in the cavity at his head, but this was already missing by 1951: Green and Green, *Saxon Architecture and Sculpture in Hampshire*, pp 36-7.
[55] See Introduction, p 3.
[56] *The Peterborough Chronicle 1070-1154*, ed. C. Clark (Oxford, 1970, 2nd edn), s.a. 1070, p 2. '(The raiders) climbed up to the Holy Rood, then took the crown from Our Lord's head, all of pure gold, then took the footrest which was underneath his feet, which was all of red gold.'

frontal face; that on the left includes some other feature which impinges on the framing disc. It is not clear which is which. Below each arm is a frontal half figure: on Christ's right the spear-bearer holds up his spear in his right hand; on his left his companion is presumably the sponge- or cup-bearer.[57]

The other faces of the cross show, on the opposite broad face, three complete registers of an interlace pattern formed into a ring knot, incorporating a loose ring in the lowest register. The side to the right has a pattern of elaborate twists, not the simple figure of eight typical of much Midland work in the late pre-Conquest period; and that to the left has a continuous vine scroll with berry bunches and stem bindings. The layout and composition are reminiscent of early Northumbrian work, from sites such as Hexham, and also Mercian work of c.800, in that it has one figure-carved face and the other sides covered with continuous patterns, but the developed form of the interlace compares with work assigned to the late ninth century in Northumbria, from Hexham-derived centres such as Norham.[58]

The evidence from the Crucifixion scene itself includes the form of the cross which is found in association with the Crucifixion throughout the area, and so appears to be a regional motif. It is not a period fashion, although Anglo-Saxon ivory Crucifixions with this motif, among others, have usually been dated to the late tenth/ early eleventh century.[59] The sun and moon, especially if they were personified, derive from the expanded Carolingian image of the first half of the ninth century. The static frontal figures on either side are perhaps more unusual in Carolingian art, but not unknown.[60] As with Northumbrian Crucifixion scenes, however, these frontal half figures may have been an adaptation, a local solution to the problem of fitting the scene into a panel necessarily narrow in relation to its height. The mid to late ninth century is indicated for the production of this cross, which seems to show that pre-Viking traditions were still strong in the immediate aftermath of the Viking invasions.

Some of the surviving sculptures from the reform period or later are somewhat disappointing after this. There is a fragment from Marton (Lincs) which may be a panel without a border (plate IIb).[61] The cross is the same type with a sunken outline, and quarters the panel. Christ (type 2) sags to his right, but his legs are straight and his feet are side by side on a sloping *suppedaneum*. In the absence of subsidiary and indeed stylistic detail it is

---

[57] In Taylor and Taylor, *Anglo-Saxon Architecture*, p 455, these figures are described as too worn for identification, but they seem to me quite clear and to form a rather fine composition suited to the form of the cross-shaft. The most detailed previous discussion of this cross-shaft is in its first publication, J. R. Allen, 'Early Christian Sculpture in Northamptonshire', *Associated Architectural Societies Reports and Papers* 19 (1887-8), 398-423.

[58] See Hexham II, Cramp, *Corpus*, I, pl 173; and the Bakewell and Bradbourne crosses: Routh, 'A Corpus of the pre-Conquest Stones in Derbyshire', pls II, VIII, and IXa. The ring knot had appeared on late ninth-century work at Norham (Northumberland), and in a related cross at Kirk of Morham in a Pictish area much influenced by Northumbria. See G. Adcock, *A Study of the Types of Interlace on Northumbrian Sculpture* (unpubl. M.Phil., Durham, 1974), p 196 and pl 73; Cramp, *Corpus*, I, pl 205.

[59] Beckwith, *English Ivories*, pls 70 and 73.

[60] For example on a ninth-/ tenth-century ivory box in Brunswick; and see also an ivory panel c.900 in Cividale: Goldschmidt, *Elfenbeinskulpturen*, pls XLIV, no. 966 and LXXVIII, no. 166.

[61] First published in Taylor and Taylor, *Anglo-Saxon Architecture*, p 414; *ibid.*, 'Architectural Sculpture', 13.

d. Harmston (Lincs)

Plate II   c. Great Glen (Leics)

Plate III   a. Langford I (Oxon)

difficult to date this little slab more precisely than tenth to twelfth century – but it could be tenth century. The little crucifix from Ropsley (Lincs) has the same cross type, but is both worn and lacking in detail.[62] It is dated only by its architectural context. Another defaced fragment from Great Glen (Leics) may also be an unframed panel (plate IIc).[63] The cross here is a plain Latin cross which can be seen most clearly beneath Christ's arms where its outline is deeply grooved. Christ (type 2) appears to be turned slightly to the right, with his head also possibly turned to the right. As with Marton, the un-crossed feet suggest a pre-thirteenth century date, and there are none of the features of the developed Romanesque style of the twelfth century, but there is no really positive evidence of date. The slab above the tower arch at Barton-on-Humber adds nothing to our knowledge of the iconography of the Crucifixion in the late pre-Conquest period, though the style in which the head appears sunken into the background is very different from that associated with the reform period. It is a reminder, however, of the architectural uses of the unframed panel or slab.

It is almost a relief to turn to the more complete depiction on a cross shaft at Harmston (Lincs) which is almost certainly eleventh century, perhaps post-Conquest, even though it has some archaic features. The Crucifixion is set on one broad face and near the top of the shaft which could, however, be incomplete at both the top and bottom (plate IId).[64] Both broad faces are decorated with twist patterns in two vertical rows. The sides are ornamented with zigzag, and the angles of the shaft have a heavy cable moulding, that on the right of the Crucifixion having been cut away. The Crucifixion is inserted rather than panelled into the twist pattern which breaks off without terminating the design above and below. The upper spandrels of the cross are filled with narrower versions of the same pattern. Christ (type 1) is on a cross with very slightly expanded arms. There is a figure beneath each arm of the cross. These are presumably John and Mary, but it is difficult to distinguish them. The zigzag and the twists suggest that this is very late, and it in any case represents a native, regional taste which has again nothing to do with Winchester art. The Crucifixion, however, does show the effect of the southern type in its choice of John and Mary and in the inclusion of the *Manus Dei*: this, more than anything, indicates how much is lost that would have made the surviving remains intelligible.

At Langford (Oxon), however, there are two remarkable sculptures of the Crucifixion. One of these is the robed figure omitted from the present discussion; the other is that over the south door of the thirteenth-century south porch (plate IIIa). In this position Christ appears with distorted and downward curving arms and upraised hands, with Mary turning away from him on his left, and John turning away from him on his right. Most commentators have pointed out that Christ's arms and these figures have been transposed, which implies a reconstruction after a removal, as at Breamore.[65]

[62] *Ibid.*, 'Architectural Sculpture', 51.
[63] Found by Professor R. J. Cramp. Unpublished.
[64] D. S. Davies and A. W. Clapham, 'Pre-Conquest Carved Stones in Lincolnshire', *Arch. Journ.* 83 (1926), 1-20, esp. 13-14; Taylor and Taylor, *Anglo-Saxon Architecture*, pp 285-6.
[65] S. Casson, 'Late Anglo-Saxon Sculpture', *American Magazine of Art* 28 (1935), 330, seems to have accepted the arm position which he compares to Stepney, and also seems to have

If the arms and figures are restored to their original positions it is immediately clear that the group could not have been confined to such a restricted space: the slabs with the arms would have had to be higher, and the accompanying figures need not have been close under the arms. The need for realignment may also explain the current problem with the arms at Breamore: at Langford, the incorrect reconstruction has clearly been forced to fit the available space.

The cross has stepped terminals, with a roll moulding below the step on the upper arm, and the step on the lower arm forming the *suppedaneum*. Christ (type 3) is clearly meant to be hanging from his nailed hands, but there is no attempt at realistic portrayal of the strain on the arms and body which would result. The stone is worn, but the fine carving of the folds and pleats and the jagged undercut edge of the dress is quite clear. Mary, on his right, is a dignified and undramatic figure. She is frontal, with her nimbed head turned to the cross and her shoulders therefore partly turned. Her head tilts only slightly, which is consistent with the suggestion that she originally stood farther away. John, too, is a frontal figure, wearing a cloak of rather severe outline, slightly lifted by his right arm which rests on his breast. He holds a book beneath his left arm.

This sculpture is very important, both for our understanding of the development, in the art of late Anglo-Saxon England, of the iconography in which Christ sags in death on the cross, and also because it shows a relationship between Ottonian and Winchester art. In particular, the figure of Christ is a close parallel to that of the crucified Christ on the back of the gold altar cross of Lothar in the Palace Treasury at Aachen, except for the nimbus behind the head of the Langford figure.[66] The drooping head, straining arms, the body straight and almost frontal above the waist, with pectoral muscles and rib cage clearly marked, combined with the heavy sagging of the lower body and legs are very close. But the Lothar cross is also a type of altar-crucifix which must have helped to inspire the typical late Winchester-school cross at Stepney and in the miniature in the New Minster *Liber Vitae*.[67] The front face of the Lothar cross consists of a jewelled Latin cross with mouldings and stepped terminals. This cross is said to date from 980-9. In England, an interesting parallel is provided by the Crucifixion in the late-tenth-century Arenberg Gospels, which also has a cross with stepped terminals and a figure of Christ sagging almost as much.[68] There are similarities also in the treatment of Mary and John: Mary lifts the edge of a fluttering overdress with one hand, and John holds a book, and gestures

---

believed the Crucifixion was carved out of a single block. Kendrick, *Late Saxon and Viking Art*, p 47; Talbot Rice, *English Art 871-1100*, pp 98-9; Taylor and Taylor, *Anglo-Saxon Architecture*, p 372; and *ibid.*, 'Architectural Sculpture', 13, all accept that the sculpture has been wrongly assembled in its present position. Dating has varied, with Kendrick placing it in the twelfth century, and the Taylors (following Talbot Rice) in the period 1020-50.

[66] P. Lasko, *Ars Sacra 800-1200* (Harmondsworth, 1972), fig. 3, p 100.

[67] Lasko, *Ars Sacra*, pl 95, and also pp 99-104 and pls 93-4 for a discussion of the patronage of Mathilde, Abbess of Essen, granddaughter of Otto the Great, in connection with the Lothar cross and other crucifixes of the same form and style; for the *Liber Vitae*, London, British Library MS Stowe 944: see *Golden Age*, no. 62, p 78 and pl 62.

[68] See n 51, above.

Plate III b. Stepney (London)

Plate IV   a. Bradford-on-Avon (Wilts)

b. Bradford-on-Avon (Wilts)

with one hand held close to his face. This manuscript is believed to have a Canterbury provenance, but it and the sculpture belong remarkably together. However, the static, but also calm figures on the Langford slab are rather unlike any of the English miniatures, and the parallel folds are also different from anything found in painting in this period. Even the draperies of the Stepney Crucifixion slab appear to flutter more, but that sculpture also suggests that much three-dimensional work has been lost, in metal and wood as well as in stone.[69]

Wells

West of Winchester there are only traces of Crucifixion sculpture. At Muchelney (Som) there is a *suppedaneum* from a large rood, represented as a steeply sloping ledge outlined by a single roll moulding (plate IVd).[70] All that survives of Christ is his feet, carved in relief but with a flattened instep and long, almost finger-like toes, reminiscent of the treatment of Romsey II. There may have been a monastery here from a very early period, and Muchelney was certainly a reformed Benedictine monastery, within the sphere of influence of Glastonbury.[71]

Sherborne

At Winterbourne Steepleton, Dorset, there is a carving of an angel which indicates a large scale monumental sculpture, but it was probably not a Crucifixion (plate IVc).[72] The angel is carved on a single slab, and has a robe which wraps around his half-turned body, leaving one end flying free above, and upward-kicking legs. The one surviving wing sprouts from behind the nimbed head and flies parallel to the body. His head turns to look back at his feet. His body appears to be in a reclining posture, but this may be misleading, and partly the result of the damaged arms. He has a long, three-quarter view face with strongly marked features, possibly a moustache, and a tonsure conveyed by three curls, almost like a twisted fillet, around the crown of his head. Flying angels facing outwards are certainly found in Winchester art, for example in the New Minster Charter where they support a mandorla with Christ in Majesty, and the Benedictional of St Æthelwold in the Baptism miniature.[73] These are not particularly close in style, however, and neither are the backward-turned angels supporting a mandorla with a depiction of the Trinity which are found in a sketch, possibly an insertion of the mid eleventh century, in the Harley Psalter, which was made in Canterbury

---

[69] See below, p 181.
[70] Taylor and Taylor, *Anglo-Saxon Architecture*, p 452; *ibid*. 'Architectural Sculpture', 9.
[71] Knowles and Hadcock, *Mediaeval Religious Houses*, p 478. Foundations of a pre-Conquest church have been found within the chancel of a largely fifteenth-century abbey, and other fragments of pre-Conquest sculpture are displayed in the museum: Taylor and Taylor, *Anglo-Saxon Architecture*, pp 451-3 and fig. 216.
[72] This piece has often been mentioned together with the Bradford-on-Avon angels, as if they are linked in date if not in style, but see Kendrick, *Late Saxon and Viking Art*, p 43, where he notes Norman influence in style.
[73] Temple, *Anglo-Saxon Manuscripts*, pls 84 and 85.

between c.1010 and 1030.[74] Somewhat closer to the sculpture are the long-faced angels on either side of a Crucifixion scene on a boxwood box for which a West Midlands origin has been proposed.[75] These are only slightly more stylised, with a much flatter hair style. They are also clearly attending at the Crucifixion, and even the position of the wings is different. On the opposite side of the lid of the same box there are angels supporting a mandorla with Christ in Majesty: these are still not a perfect comparison, for the free-flying fold of the dress is lacking, and the focus of attention is again not in doubt. The closest comparison in style, in fact, is with an angel in the bottom right hand corner of a miniature in a troper which has been linked with this box, and which has been associated with Canterbury, but also with Hereford.[76] The long faces, the hair, the heavily emphasised upper lip are all found here, while the angel in the manuscript looks as if it has been adapted rather unsuccessfully from a horizontally flying figure: the stylistic connection seems unusually marked, not only with the troper but with the Hereford Gospels.[77] Both manuscripts are of the mid eleventh century, and the sculpture, like them, provides important evidence for the evolution of the Romanesque style in England. It almost certainly, however, provides no evidence for the iconography of the Crucifixion, and the scene of which it did form a part can only be guessed at.

Diocese of Ramsbury

Fragments of only one monumental composition have survived from this diocese, at Bradford-on-Avon (Wilts).[78] The recent history of this church and its rediscovery in the nineteenth century are well known, but the date of the remaining fabric has been much contested.[79] The original foundation could be as early as 705, but in 1001 the monastery was granted to the nuns of Shaftesbury by King Ethelred to provide a refuge for themselves and for the relics of Edward the Martyr. Dating of the sculptures has been related to the history of the fabric, and they have sometimes been placed in the tenth century or even earlier.

Each angel is carved on a single block of stone, shaped to accommodate the composition (plate IVa and b). Feet and wings extend beyond the

---

[74] London, British Library MS Harley 603, fol. 1: Temple, *Anglo-Saxon Manuscripts*, pl 210. These angels are also awkward adaptations of flying figures. The two above appear to be reclining, those below look upside down.
[75] *Golden Age*, no. 129, pp 125-6. The box is in the Cleveland Museum of Art, Cleveland, Ohio.
[76] London, British Library Cotton MS Caligula A. XIV, fol. 22.
[77] Cambridge, Pembroke College, MS 302: *Golden Age*, nos. 70, 71, p 86, and pl XXI.
[78] These angels have been discussed many times: G. B. Brown, *Anglo-Saxon Architecture. The Arts in Early England* II (2nd edn, London, 1925), pp 304-5; A. W. Clapham, *English Romanesque Architecture: I Before the Conquest* (Oxford, 1930), p 139; Kendrick, *Anglo-Saxon Art to A.D. 900*, p 220; *ibid.*, *Late Saxon and Viking Art*, pp 42 and 139; Talbot Rice, *English Art 871-1100*, p 93; M. Rickert, *Painting in Britain. The Middle Ages* (Melbourne, London and Baltimore, 1954), n 31, p 54; Quirk, 'Winchester New Minster and its Tenth-Century Tower', 30; Taylor and Taylor, 'Architectural Sculpture', 29-30; G. Zarnecki, '1066 and Architectural Sculpture', *Proceedings of the British Academy* 52 (1966), 89-90; Cramp, 'Anglo-Saxon Sculpture of the Reform Period', *Tenth-Century Studies*, p 196.
[79] Compare Taylor and Taylor, *Anglo-Saxon Architecture*, pp 86-9 with E. Fernie, *The Architecture of the Anglo-Saxons* (London, 1983), pp 145-50.

Plate IV   c. Winterbourne Steepleton (Dorset)

d. Muchelney (Som)

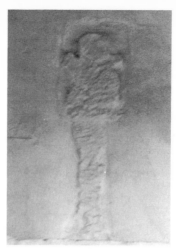

Plate V   a. Bibury (Gloucs)

b. Daglingworth I (Gloucs)

confines of the slab, however. As positioned now they fly towards some central feature, of which no fragment survives. The angels are identical in iconography, but not quite in execution: that on the left has more delicately carved drapery, and his left wing bends and folds so that it presents both an inner and an outer surface. The more ridge-like feathers on the same wing of the right-hand angel follow the shape of the wing more rigidly. Both have outstretched, veiled arms, long robes with a wide waistband and a loose fold at the back, and hair tied back with a double fillet. Their wings seem to frame their heads and arms. They have been compared to angels on a small ivory plaque from Winchester.[80] Half-figures of winged angels flying towards the Crucifixion appear on several English ivories, at least once with veiled hands.[81] Much more significant, however, are the almost full-length figures, very close in detail, depicted in the Crucifixion miniature in the Sherborne Pontifical, of the end of the tenth century. In this manuscript the angels also have fillets binding their hair.[82] In style and iconography these angels support a date in the early eleventh century for the building of which they formed a part.

Diocese of Worcester

There are the remains of several sculptures of the Crucifixion in this diocese. One of these, at Bitton (Gloucs) is a robed figure of Christ and so outside the scope of the present study. A fragment at Bibury (Gloucs) seems to be a fragment of a large composition as at Breamore or Headbourne Worthy, and it is indisputably *in situ* above the chancel arch. It is therefore disappointing that only a single figure survives in outline, to the left of centre (plate Va).[83] The outline of the head is clear, as is the width of the shoulders which are portrayed frontally. The unusual width suggests arms clasped close to the body, and a projection over the right shoulder suggests a hand raised to the face. The lower part of the body tapers sharply towards the feet, and also bends towards the centre at about knee level. Assuming that these manifestations are not the misleading result of damage, the posture described is perfectly consistent with one often ascribed to Mary at the cross, but in a particularly exaggerated form like that of Mary in the Ramsey Psalter. This manuscript was probably made in Winchester, either for use in Ramsey Abbey, or perhaps for Oswald, bishop of Worcester, the founder of Ramsey.[84]

At Wormington (Gloucs) there is a sculpture, from a site close to Winchcombe Abbey, on quite a different scale, which in spite of its near completeness has received comparatively little attention (plate Vc).[85] Here Christ is shown on the cross with only the slightest suggestion of sagging (type 2). The cross has expanded arms, and a sloping *suppedaneum*. The

[80] Beckwith, *English Ivories*, pl 39.

[81] Ibid., pls 38 and 69.

[82] See n 39, above.

[83] C. E. Keyser, 'A Visit to the Churches of Barnsley, Bibury ...', *Transactions of the Bristol and Gloucestershire Archaeological Society* 41 (1918-19), 171-204; Taylor and Taylor, *Anglo-Saxon Architecture*, p 65; *ibid.*, 'Architectural Sculpture', 8-9.

[84] See n 49, above.

[85] The only full discussion of this cross is H. M. Taylor, 'Iconography of the Wormington Crucifixion', *Antiquity* 39 (1965), 55-6, in which it is said to have a Lamb's head.

rounded head of a large nail is visible beside the ankle of Christ's left foot. His head, with its cruciferous nimbus, is inclined to his right and bowed down on his shoulder to his breast. His hair hangs down behind his head and tapers off along his left shoulder and he has a forked beard which is in the wrong position for a head tilted on its side, for it is hanging down instead of following the inclination of the head to the right. The error seems one of adaptation similar to that already noted for an eleventh-century troper in connection with the Winterbourne Steepleton angel.[86] Christ's right arm is slightly flexed, the left arm stretched tautly out, consistent with the extreme sagging of the head, but there is not the sagging at the hips which would justify this indication: like the beard, this suggests inept adaptation. His hands are missing, so the panel has either been cut down or formed part of a larger composition extending over several panels or building blocks. Christ wears a loincloth folded over at the waist, with one end of the garment tucked under the fold to appear again above. Deeply incised lines and rigidly stepped edges indicate stiff formal folds. The garment is drawn up at the centre.

Above Christ's head the *Manus Dei* appears out of a sleeve. It is held palm outwards with the little finger and third finger curled into the palm, a gesture of Benediction. Both the gesture in which the hand is held palm open, sometimes holding a wreath or crown of victory, and the pointing hand back-turned, seem more common in art outside England.[87] The Blessing gesture is a feature of the late pre-Conquest iconography of the Crucifixion, however, and can be found, for example, on a late tenth-/ early-eleventh-century ivory with stylistic links with Romsey I,[88] and in a miniature in a collection of prayers and church offices made for Ælfwine, abbot of the New Minster, Winchester, c.1023-35.[89] This miniature also shows Christ with his bearded head resting on his right shoulder. Christ's type 2 posture is also characteristic of the late pre-Conquest Crucifixion miniature: in, for example, the Ramsey Psalter, where Christ also has a forked beard, and the slight tense curve of the body here could have been copied by a less competent artist as an upright figure.[90] The same combination of characteristics appears in an ivory crucifix so like the Ramsey miniature in style that the two have been commonly linked.[91] The treatment of the loincloth in the ivory compares closely with the Wormington slab. This contrasts with the treatment of the same iconography in the Arenberg Gospels which is more exaggerated, and with that in the Sherborne Pontifical which is more stylised.[92] Another interesting comparison is with an unfinished drawing of the crucified Christ on a text page of a manuscript with associations with the scriptorium of Winchcombe Abbey (Gloucs) which has been dated to between 1030 and 1050.[93] The drawing has a similar, but less exaggerated, head position, with

[86] See above, p 175, and also n 85 above.
[87] Schiller, *Iconography of Christian Art*, II, pls 354, 365, 377, 379, 380, and 395.
[88] Beckwith, *English Ivories*, pl 72; and see above, p 167.
[89] London, British Library MS Cotton Titus D XXVII, fol. 65v: Temple, *Anglo-Saxon Manuscripts*, pp 94-5 and pl 246.
[90] See n 49 above.
[91] *Golden Age*, no. 118, pp 117-18 and pl XXVI.
[92] See nn 51 and 39 above.
[93] The Winchcombe Psalter, Cambridge University Library, MS Ff. 1. 23: Temple, *Anglo-*

Plate V   c. Wormington (Gloucs)

Plate V   d. Newent (Gloucs)

long hair straggling on the shoulders, and a looped and knotted loincloth. Winchcombe Abbey was a daughter house of Ramsey, so this parallel is particularly interesting, as well as providing some supporting evidence for a date for the sculpture in the first half or even, more specifically, the second quarter of the eleventh century.

There are two more Crucifixion panels from Gloucestershire, both at Daglingworth, where two other panels probably part of the same series, also survive.[94] Daglingworth I is an unframed slab, quartered by a cross with splayed arms and a *suppedaneum* (plate Vb). Christ (type 1) has been described as wearing a long, girdled tunic, but in fact this is a misunderstanding of the stylised physical details: it is collar bones, not a collar, which are represented.[95] He wears a loincloth which droops at the back, and down-pointing V-shapes indicate folds on either side of a central tie. On the other hand, both the spear-bearer on his right and the sponge-bearer on his left wear tunics with V-shaped openings at the neck and with parallel or zigzag lines indicating folds in the skirt. Daglingworth II is carved on a different stone and is more weathered, but the cross and the figure of Christ are almost identical in detail, only slightly stiffer. There are no accompanying figures.

The iconography of these panels affords no clue to their date: in this respect they can be paralleled from the ninth to the twelfth century. The style, however, particularly in the stylisation of hair and beard and other details, and in the figures with their heavy, rounded shoulders, is not easy to parallel in pre-Conquest art, but seems to fit more comfortably in the fully developed Romanesque sculpture of the late eleventh and twelfth centuries. A wood relief-crucifix in Naples of c.1100 has such a heavy-shouldered figure of Christ, and a similarly stylised loincloth with its girdle tied in an interlace knot like the robe of the seated figure of Christ at Daglingworth,[96] and an ivory crucifix from Spain (Leon) of the late eleventh century has a beard with spiralling curls and hair falling over his shoulders in long, thin locks.[97] The technique of cutting back from the surface has been seen as a pre-Conquest technique, and while this is true it is not confined to this period. There thus seems no reason for seeing the Daglingworth sculptures as earlier than the late eleventh century. In this case the appearance of the spear- and sponge-bearers also looks like a break with the Winchester tradition, for although these figures continued in popularity in the north, and appeared on some small ivory carvings of uncertain provenance, there is little trace of them in manuscripts from southern England in the late pre-Conquest period, and in the sculptures discussed here, the only example is on the ninth-century cross-shaft from Nassington, which also has links with the pre-Viking north.[98]

Saxon Manuscripts, pp 97-8. The Crucifixion drawing is in a copy of Bede's *Historia Ecclesiastica* (Cambridge, Corpus Christi College, MS 41, p 484): *ibid.*, pp 98-9 and pl 255.

[94] The fullest discussions of this piece are Kendrick, *Late Saxon and Viking Art* pp 50-1; A. W. Clapham, 'Some Disputed Examples of pre-Norman Sculpture', *Antiquity* 25 (1951), 94-5; Taylor and Taylor, *Anglo-Saxon Architecture*, pp 188-9; *ibid.*, 'Architectural Sculpture', 15-16.

[95] For comparison, Kendrick, *Late Saxon and Viking Art*, pp 50-1, refers to the depiction of the navel on a 'fully draped Christ' as a mistake by the sculptor.

[96] Schiller, *Iconography of Christian Art*, II, pl 498.

[97] G. Zarnecki, *Romanesque Art* (London, 1971), pl 155.

[98] There seems to be only one example in manuscript painting, in London, British Library

Diocese of Hereford

Only one sculpture with the Crucifixion has survived from this diocese, and that is the small and essentially private monument from Newent (Gloucs). This is quite crudely carved, but it also has the most elaborate iconography of any pre-Conquest depiction of the theme in any medium (plate Vd).[99] On the face opposite the Crucifixion, a large figure in priestly garments and with a cross on his breast holds a crozier in his right hand and in his left a staff cross with a ring head. He tramples a human figure beneath his feet. Above, on his left, another figure veils his face, while below two smaller figures fall head first. On the right below is a figure holding up a large sword, and above are two figures possibly ascending. Finally, in the top right corner is a figure disposed horizontally. This scene almost certainly represents Christ and the Harrowing of Hell.[100] The narrow edges have the names of all four evangelists: in this position it would seem that they stand as witnesses to both the Crucifixion and the Harrowing of Hell.

The Crucifixion scene is almost quartered by the cross with its splayed arms edged by a fine roll moulding, and a *suppedaneum*. Christ (type 1) dwarfs the rest of the scene. In the upper arm of the cross are two raised circles, and the same motif is repeated in the shaft below: they are therefore difficult to identify with the sun and moon, and perhaps they represent jewels. Above the rings in the upper arm are two affronted birds, perhaps the souls of the faithful departed,[101] with the *Manus Dei* between them descending palm outwards from the upper arm of the cross. In the side-arms figures fly above and below each of Christ's arms. The two on the left are certainly winged. The two below the arms carry an object, on the left a rod with a three-pronged end, on the right a circle. These must be attendant angels with instruments of the Passion (here the crown of thorns and the scourge), as on the Rothbury cross head.[102] In the shaft of the cross are two sorrowing figures in the attitudes associated with John and Mary.

In the top-left spandrel of the cross, in the outer corner, is an unidentifiable fragment of carving. Below it a winged angel flies towards Christ's head, its hands clasped in worship. The opposite side is very crowded, apparently containing a Nativity scene. In the top right-hand corner a tiny frontal figure, with its hands clasped before it, stands by a plant form. Possibly this is to be seen in association with the entombed figure in the bottom left spandrel, as a reference to Adam and the Fall. On either side of the shaft is a tall mourning

---

MS Cotton, Tiberius C. VI, f 13. This manuscript is ascribed to Winchester, c.1050, on palaeographical and stylistic grounds, but it has other features, including its prefatory cycle of sixteen full-page drawings of the lives of David and Christ, which suggest new sources of influence, not a harking back to an earlier native tradition. The cross of rough-hewn wood has other manuscript parallels, but none in pre-Conquest sculpture. See Temple, *Anglo-Saxon Manuscripts*, pp 115-17 and pl 311.

[99] G. Zarnecki, 'The Newent Funerary Tablet', *Transactions of the Bristol and Gloucestershire Archaeological Society* 72 (1953), 49-55.

[100] Schiller, *Iconography of Christian Art*, I, pl 156; *ibid.*, II, pl 379.

[101] *Ibid.*, II, pl 1. This would be very rare, however. The only other possibility seems to be a duplication of the dove symbolising the Holy Spirit, comparable with the duplication of the paired figures on either side of the cross.

[102] Coatsworth, *Iconography of the Crucifixion*, pp 200-7; Cramp, *Corpus*, 217-21 and pl 211.

figure. Possibly these also represent Mary and John, using a slightly different formula, but it is also possible that one or other of these pairs represents donor figures.[103]

The association of the Fall with the Crucifixion, though a commonplace of theology from very early times, seems to have found expression in art in the tenth century, and it was also a feature of late Old English homiletic literature.[104] This seems to support the late-tenth-/ early-eleventh-century date suggested on epigraphic grounds,[105] but for all its ambitious programme, the real crudity of the piece and its idiosyncratic nature leave surprisingly little evidence of its date.

Diocese of Canterbury

There are no surviving sculptures of the Crucifixion from the diocese of Canterbury, but I have commented on the evidence from a sixteenth-century description of a cross from Reculver in Kent.[106]

Diocese of London

A very interesting rectangular panel has survived from Stepney (plate IIIb).[107] This has a border of crude palmettes each enclosed by a border moulding above and below and a raised semi-circle on either side. Between each palmette is a narrow raised oval, becoming a tear shape at each corner. Within is a Latin cross with elaborately stepped terminals, each with an outer squared moulding and three inner roll mouldings. Christ (type 3) is one of the most competent depictions of the human figure among surviving Crucifixion scenes, comparable with Langford I, and Romsey II. He wears a loincloth folded over at the waist to a V-shaped fold at the front, and moulded closely over the legs beneath. It is knee-length but droops at Christ's back, and so is placed correctly on the left for the viewer. Above his head, the sun and moon are depicted as flat discs in relief against which are relieved weeping figures with bowed heads and veiled hands. The figures face the cross and are not differentiated in any way. Mary stands on Christ's right, and it is she, not John, who holds a book.

The layout of this panel suggests an enlarged version of an ivory relief panel of the Crucifixion, but the border with its partly enclosed leaf forms

---

[103] Donor figures/worshippers had appeared in connection with the Crucifixion, though rarely, since the ninth century: Schiller, *Iconography of Christian Art*, II, pl 354. See also Cnut and Ælfgifu presenting a cross to the New Minster, Winchester, in the New Minster *Liber Vitae*: *Golden Age*, pl 62, and the Crucifixion miniature in the Gospel Book of Judith of Flanders, of the second quarter of the eleventh century, New York, Pierpont Morgan Library, MS 709, fol. 1v: Temple, *Anglo-Saxon Manuscripts*, pl 289.

[104] See below, p 187. For scenes depicting the connection see Schiller, *Iconography of Christian Art*, II, pls 381, 387.

[105] E. Okasha, *Hand-List of Anglo-Saxon Non-Runic Inscriptions* (Cambridge, 1971), pp 102-3.

[106] See above, p 164.

[107] Ascribed to the late tenth/ early eleventh century by most commentators, although the fullest discussion (O. M. Dalton, 'A Relief Representing the Crucifixion in the Parish Church of St Dunstan's, Stepney', *Proceedings of the Society of Antiquaries of London* 22 (1908), 225-31) concluded that a pre-Conquest date, though possible, was difficult to prove.

compares quite closely with some tenth-/ eleventh-century ivories,[108] and also with some English manuscripts of the same period.[109] A pre-Conquest date is also suggested by the form of the cross, which compares very closely to the form of the cross given by Cnut and Ælfgifu to the New Minster, Winchester, as depicted in the *Liber Vitae*, and other crosses in late tenth- and eleventh-century manuscripts.[110] The heavily sagging figure of Christ is found in mid-eleventh-century manuscripts rather than earlier, notably in the Gospels of the Countess Judith, in which encircled personifications of the sun and moon also appear, and the unusual feature of Mary holding a book.[111] Personifications of the sun and moon without circles appear in several manuscripts, but the book appears only in manuscripts and other works of the eleventh century.[112] The accumulation of comparative detail suggests a pre-Conquest date for the sculpture, but the style is markedly different from that of the manuscripts: in particular the figures on the sculpture are more static and symmetrical. The panel seems to belong to the eleventh century rather than the tenth, and suggests the strength of the Winchester style at that period, but also an ability to develop or accommodate new motifs. The location of this sculpture, in the diocese of London and not far from Westminster, could be an indication of the new continental links of the time of Edward the Confessor.

The Crucifixion Sculptures in Context

One of the most interesting aspects of the Crucifixion in pre-Conquest sculpture is the distribution of some of its major features, especially over time. No doubt some of the blanks in the distribution map may be explained by the lack of locally available supplies of suitable stone, or by the accidents of survival and recovery:[113] nevertheless, it seems clear that there were great differences in the treatment of the theme of the Crucifixion, and in the conditions for its production in the medium of sculpture, between north and south, and between the periods before and after the Viking invasions (figs 1 and 2). All surviving sculptures with the Crucifixion which can be dated to the period before about the mid ninth century, for example, are from monastic sites in Northumbria and Mercia.[114] Only, one, from Hexham, is an

---

[108] Goldschmidt, *Elfenbeinskulpturen*, pls XXXVII, no. 88; and XXXVIII, no. 89.

[109] Borders in fragments of a gospel thought to have been written by the same scribe, Godeman, who wrote the Benedictional of St Æthelwold, show how this theme was carried out in manuscript painting: London, College of Arms, MS Arundel 22, fol. 84: *Golden Age*, no. 38, p 59 and pl VII.

[110] *Golden Age*, pl 62. See discussion of Langford, p 173 above; also the miniatures in the Arenberg Gospels and the Sherborne Pontifical, nn 39 and 51 above; also interesting is a post-Conquest miniature inserted in the mid-eleventh-century psalter, London British Library MS Arundel 60: Talbot Rice, *English Art 871-1100*, pl 79a.

[111] See n 103, above.

[112] BL Arundel 60 (see n 110 above), fol. 12v, contemporary with the manuscript: Temple, *Anglo-Saxon Manuscripts*, p 120, pl 312; see also the Crucifixion on the eleventh-century bronze doors at Hildesheim: Thoby, *Le Crucifix*, pl XXXIV.

[113] See E. M. Jope, 'The Saxon Building Stone Industry in Southern and Midland England', *Medieval Archaeology* 8 (1964), 91-118, esp. fig. 25. Rediscovery has often depended on the activities and interest of Victorian restorers, and, more recently, on archaeologists.

[114] See fig. 5.1 in R. J. Cramp, 'Monastic Sites', *The Archaeology of Anglo-Saxon England*,

architectural sculpture. In the later period, the greater proportion of survivals is from the north, and all these are on free-standing monuments: most are associated with churches or churchyards, but not with monastic sites. All the architectural sculptures from this late period have survived south of a line drawn between the Severn and the Humber, and the few examples in this area on free-standing monuments all come from the East Midlands. The distribution of iconographical features seems equally marked. In an analysis based on the typology of Christ, for example, the rare variations from the completely upright and frontal figure are all found south of the same line from Severn to Humber, with the exception of the remarkable crucifixion on the Ruthwell cross.[115] The distribution of the accompanying figures John and Mary, as opposed to spear-bearer and sponge-bearer, follows almost exactly the same pattern, with the one exception in the south at Nassington on a cross which in other respects also follows a traditional Northumbrian or Mercian pattern;[116] while the main exception in the north, two cross heads from Durham, also show new influences in the period immediately preceding the Norman Conquest.[117] It seems reasonable to infer that there was a different development south of the Humber after the Viking invasions which was in some way dependent on the area in which Wessex was politically dominant by the early tenth century, and/or on the revival of Benedictine monasticism throughout the same area through the influence of St Æthelwold and others. In neither case would influence from the earlier centres of Northumbria and Mercia seem to be an important factor. It is all the more important to extract the maximum information from the material remains themselves, since there are no direct documentary links between the extant sculptures and the social and intellectual *milieu* in which they were made. There are rare and frequently late references to actual sculptures with slight references to individual details and position,[118] but the very developed forms of iconography of the pre-Conquest Crucifixion attested in manuscripts as well as ivories and sculptures could scarcely have been deduced from these references or from the use of the theme in pre-Conquest literature, even though the Crucifixion as a theme is an important element in what survives of that.

The links between theological and literary narratives and concepts, and visual images (which can also be either narrative or symbolic) are complex. It is clear, for example, that the appearance of a theme in literary and visual media is not necessarily simultaneous: it is less clear whether influence between these different modes was always in one direction – from the verbal to the visual or *vice versa*. There are numerous examples of symbolic

---

ed. D. M. Wilson (London, 1976), pp 201-52.

[115] Coatsworth, *Iconography of the Crucifixion*, I, 188-96.

[116] See above, p 171.

[117] E. Coatsworth, 'The Four Crossheads from the Chapter House, Durham', *Anglo-Saxon and Viking Age Sculpture*, pp 85-92.

[118] For example, the reference to a crucifix in the refectory of Glastonbury which shook, causing Christ's diadem to fall between King Edgar and St Dunstan: William of Malmesbury, 'De Antiquitate Glastoniensis' in *Historiae Britannicae, Saxonicae, Anglo-Danicae*, ed. T. Gale, Scriptores XV, II (Oxford, 1691), p 304. It is tempting to see this as confirmation of the use of the diadem on the pre-Conquest crucifix, but the story is late, and related to a whole series of miracle stories connecting Dunstan with a speaking crucifix retailed by William of Malmesbury, Eadmer, and Osbern: see *Memorials*, pp 113, 211-12, and 308.

interpretations of the Crucifixion which had a wide circulation in theological literature for several centuries before appearing, sometimes only briefly, in the visual arts. The personifications of Ecclesia and Synagogue from the expanded Crucifixion image of Carolingian schools of the ninth century are a case in point.[119] The Carolingian image was also enriched by the beginnings of a dramatic emphasis on the sufferings of Christ. From this period onwards He appears in the vast majority of surviving examples, stripped to a loincloth, and in a few cases, but also increasingly, with a drooping head. This formed a notable break with the preceding practice, for from the sixth century Christ on the cross had commonly appeared as a robed, priestly figure.[120] The mid ninth century is also important, however, for commentary on the Crucifixion which broke with earlier traditions. Candidus, a monk from Fulda, emphasised that it was through Christ's death that he fulfilled the will of the Father: this was a shift in emphasis away from the theme of Christ's victory over death. Candidus specifically commented that the inclination of Christ's head signified his meek acceptance of his Father's will. Amalarius of Metz, and Paschasius Radbertus, from the monastery at Corbie, both expressed the view that the body of Christ which was born, suffered, and died on the cross, was the same as that offered daily in the mass. These views were opposed by Florus, a deacon of Lyons, and Ratramnus, also from Corbie. These discussions were probably important for the development of the iconography of the Crucifixion.[121] This controversy on the nature of the eucharist, though not yet fully developed, aroused some interest, and rumbled on until it became really divisive, and had to be settled for a time at least, at the Fourth Lateran Council in 1215. Its ninth-century beginnings have, however, been seen as having some influence on several fields, including Anglo-Saxon poetry, homiletic literature, and the liturgy, as well as on the visual arts.[122] It is by no means clear what the chronological relationship between the appearances of these new themes in the various fields, literary and visual, would have been, though it may be surmised that ideas were current before they were taken up by artists working in an ecclesiastical *milieu*. Clemoes, in his study of Cynewulf's image of the Ascension, concluded that it had been 'moulded by liturgical worship as well as by the visual arts'[123] but perhaps one might also expect, in a *milieu* in which ecclesiastical organisations were major producers as well as patrons of the arts and literature, that visual images might also have been moulded

---

[119] S. Ferber, 'Crucifixion Iconography in a Group of Carolingian Ivory Plaques', *Art Bulletin* 48 (1966), 323-34.

[120] K. Wessel, 'Die Entstehung des Crucifixus', *Byzantinische Zeitschrift* 53 (1960), 95-111; E. Coatsworth, 'The Decoration of the Durham Gospels', *The Durham Gospels*, ed. C. D. Verey, T. J. Brown, and E. Coatsworth, Early English Manuscripts in Facsimile 20 (1980), pp 53-63, esp. pp 58-62.

[121] As suggested by R. Haussherr, *Der Tote Christus am Kreuz. Zur Ikonographie der Gerokreuzes* (unpubl. diss., Bonn, 1963), pp 181-4.

[122] T. Klauser, trans. J. Halliburton, *A Short History of the Western Liturgy* (London, 1969), pp 46-7; M. McC. Gatch, *Preaching and Theology in Anglo-Saxon England* (Toronto and Buffalo, 1977), pp 64-5; R. E. Boenig, '*Andreas*, The Eucharist and Vercelli', *Journal of English and Germanic Philology* 79 (1980), 313-31.

[123] P. Clemoes, 'Cynewulf's Image of the Ascension', *England Before the Conquest*, ed. P. Clemoes and K. Hughes (Cambridge, 1971), pp 293-304, esp. p 302.

in response to liturgical and exegetical considerations, and perhaps even to personal and devotional ones as well.[124]

Can any of these ideas be traced in the literature of the reform period as clearly as the iconography of the Carolingian Crucifixion, and its Ottonian developments can be traced in late Anglo-Saxon art? The *Dream of the Rood* and its links with early art have often been discussed.[125] But the poem was written in the form in which we know it in southern England in the late tenth century. Christ's sufferings are emphasised: the piercing with the nails and shedding of blood from the side are both mentioned, though transferred to the cross. On the other hand, Christ hastens fearlessly to be raised on the cross, strips himself, and mounts the cross *modig on manigra gesyhðe*. The fragment of the poem on the Ruthwell Cross refers to the same moment, which suggests it belongs to an earlier, Northumbrian version of the poem.[126] Apart from any possible influence from the traditions of secular heroic poetry, the image of Christ willingly ascending the cross no doubt reflects the image of *Christus Victor* authoritative in literature and art at least until the beginning of the ninth century.[127] Christ stripped to a loincloth, however, does not occur in the visual tradition of seventh- and eighth-century Northumbria.[128] Both the Crucifixion on the Ruthwell cross and on the Rothbury cross-head, seem to represent a new influence in Anglian art of the late pre-Viking period, and in both there are clear traces of influence from the new Carolingian image of the ninth century.[129] It is perhaps this which is also reflected in the poem. The tenth-century version of the poem should therefore be seen in its contemporary as well as its archaic context: the deep personal apprehension of the suffering and death of Christ felt both by the cross and the dreamer may owe something to the emotional and pietistic approach originating on the continent in the ninth century, but transmitted to southern England in the tenth century through new and more direct contacts with continental centres as a result of the monastic reforms.[130] The emphasis on penance and judgment, and the dramatic use of the cross as a substitute for Christ are strongly linked with other poetry of the late ninth and tenth centuries, and with the development of the *Improperia* of the Good Friday *Adoratio Crucis* between the ninth and eleventh centuries.[131]

The poem *Christ III* has two lengthy references to the Crucifixion, both emphasising the theme of Judgment, but differing in detail. The first, in lines 1081-1198, reveals Christ and the cross as they will appear on Judgment

---

[124] Compare the 'one off' qualities of the Newent slab, above, p 180.

[125] B. Raw, 'The Dream of the Rood, and its Connections with Early Christian Art', *Medium Ævum* 39 (1970), 239-56.

[126] M. J. Swanton, ed., *The Dream of the Rood* (Manchester, 1970), pp 1-2.

[127] Haussherr, *Der Tote Christus am Kreuz*, pp 181-2, for the strength of this tradition. See also p 180 for a quotation from Ambrose (d.397), who refers to Christ ascending the cross as the conquering hero ascends the car.

[128] Coatsworth, 'The Decoration of the Durham Gospels'; and *ibid.*, 'Two Examples of the Crucifixion at Hexham', *Saint Wilfrid at Hexham*, pp 180-4.

[129] Coatsworth, *Iconography of the Crucifixion*, pp 188-96, 200-7; Cramp, *Corpus*, pp 217-21.

[130] F. A. Rella, 'Continental Manuscripts Acquired for English Centres in the Tenth and Eleventh Centuries: a Preliminary Checklist', *Anglia* 98 (1980), 107-16.

[131] C. L. Chase, '"Christ III", "The Dream of the Rood", and Early English Passion Piety', *Viator* 11 (1980), 11-33.

Day. Part of the narrative of the Passion and Crucifixion is recounted to emphasise the sufferings caused to Christ by men: the piercing of the hands and feet and of the side; the spitting, mocking and scourging; and the giving of the crown of thorns (which all precede the Crucifixion). The writer then contrasts the grief of dumb creation at the event with the sinfulness of men: the sun and moon are darkened, the temple veil is rent; the earth trembles, but also gives up its dead; and Hell and all creation know their lord, as those who pierced him will know on the last day. Even the sea and the trees acknowledge the lord. Later in the poem (lines 1428-58), Christ himself describes his passion: the mocking, scourging, and spitting; the crown of thorns; the giving of the bitter drink; the hanging on the high cross; the piercing of the side. The expanded Carolingian image of the ninth century might be said to give visual expression to these themes, with its personifications of sun and moon, Oceanus and Terra, but it also included many more elements: attendant angels, Ecclesia and Synagogue, Mary and John.[132] Some of the major elements picked out in the poem appear grouped in pre-Conquest sculptures of the Crucifixion: sun and moon; spear-bearer and sponge-bearer, but in the north (on crosses dating from c.800 and later) rather than in the south. A different reduced image with angels or sun and moon, Mary and John, appeared most often in the south.[133] It has been suggested that the poem *Andreas*, which incorporates some of the same details as the poem *Christ*, was influenced by the eucharistic controversy between Radbertus and Ratramnus and their followers.[134]

A devotional work once in the possession of Nunnaminster (Winchester) reinforces the suggestion that there was a developing tradition of personal devotion around the theme of the Crucifixion.[135] It includes a group of prayers on Christ's Passion, each of which concentrates on a different detail or aspect: the mocking; scourging and spitting; the crown of thorns; the mocking again; the stripping; Christ's neck, bowed in meek acceptance; Christ's arms and hands; the gift of the Holy Spirit; the Passion; the darkness; the vinegar and gall; the giving up of the spirit; Christ's eyes; his ears; his nostrils; and his wounded side. These prayers have been seen in an earlier, eastern tradition of prayer before a crucifix,[136] but the whole tenor of the prayers would be at home in a *milieu* influenced by the eucharistic theories of the ninth century.

The Anglo-Saxon homilies contain references to the Crucifixion, especially those of Ælfric, but none of the homilists attempts a dramatic word picture of the event: the sources are clearly other literary texts. As Ælfric was a pupil of Æthelwold, however, his views have particular interest. In his Sermon on the Passion, he refers to the cross on which Christ, fastened with

---

[132] Ferber, 'Crucifixion Iconography in a Group of Carolingian Ivory Plaques', 323-34; see A.S. Cook, *The Christ of Cynewulf* (repr. Connecticut, 1964), pp 195-6, for the suggestion that the poem, like the iconography, was influenced by exegesis, particularly that of St Gregory.
[133] See above, p 183.
[134] Boenig, '*Andreas*, the Eucharist, and Vercelli', pp 313-31.
[135] *An Ancient Manuscript of Nunnaminster, Winchester*, ed. W. de Gray Birch, Hampshire Record Society V (London, 1889), pp 67-78.
[136] H. Mayr Harting, *The Coming of Christianity to Anglo-Saxon England* (London, 1972), pp 187-9.

four nails, stretches to north, south, east, and west, and so hanging, redeems every region of the world.[137] The image is a striking one and the concept may in some way have been influential in the development of the iconography of the Crucifixion in the pre-Conquest period as a whole, where the cross was usually a dominant motif stretching the full height and width of the available space; but Ælfric himself is merely giving conventional instruction.[138] There are other conventional references, such as to the wound in the right side.[139] Ælfric too, however, seems to have been aware of the eucharistic theories of the ninth century. In the Sermon on the Passion already mentioned he adapts Ratramnus' treatise on the symbolic nature of Christ's presence in the mass, but a story taken from Radbertus' opposing work is also included.[140] It would seem that both views were in circulation and found interesting, but that the appeal to authority which both ninth-century writers expressed struck a stronger chord than the fact that they were actually in disagreement.

Ælfric also linked references to the bondage of Adam and Eve with the idea of the descent into hell as the starting point of salvation: this was a very influential idea, and one closely connected with the significance of the death of Christ.[141] This idea is also found in one of the Blickling Homilies, in which Christ's death and descent into hell introduce the figure of the Virgin, through whom the lamentations of Eve are brought to an end.[142] Possibly a renewed emphasis on the importance of the Virgin may explain the replacement of the spear- and sponge-bearers by St John and the Virgin in the iconography of the Crucifixion in the south of England in the late pre-Conquest period.

All writing is a product of its time, and the same is true of the work of artists and sculptors, but the links between the two forms of expression remain largely obscure for this period. Nevertheless there seems enough to suggest that there was a renewed emphasis on the theme of the Crucifixion in southern England commencing in the tenth century, shown both by new and impressive forms of monument and by several important changes in accompanying figures and motifs which differ from everything we know about the iconography of the Anglo-Saxon Crucifixion in the early period. A factor here may have been the decline of the old monastic order generally, leading to the need for reform, as well as the destruction brought about by the Viking invasions. In the north, indeed, the Viking invasions may have helped to preserve and fossilise old monuments and old monumental forms, which even enjoyed a revival there in the tenth and eleventh centuries. In the south, however, strong links in style and iconography in several instances

---

[137] *The Homilies of the Anglo-Saxon Church*, II, ed. B. Thorpe (London, 1844-6), pp 254-6.
[138] There are very similar passages in Bede: J. P. Migne, *Patrologia Cursus Completus. Series Latina* (Paris, 1844-64), 92, col. 913; and (possibly) Alcuin: *ibid.*, 101, col. 1208; cf. St Augustine on St John's Gospel, *Corpus Christianorum Series Latina* 36 (Turnholti and Brepols, 1953), p 657.
[139] *The Homilies of Ælfric. A Supplementary Collection*, ed. J. C. Pope, EETS 259, I (London, 1967), pp 468-9 (*De Sancte Trinitatis*).
[140] Gatch, *Preaching and Theology in Anglo-Saxon England*, pp 64-5.
[141] *Ibid.*, p 68.
[142] *The Blickling Homilies of the Tenth Century*, ed. R. Morris, EETS os 73 (London, 1880), pp 6-7.

with the work of the new monastic scriptoria suggest that these changes had their roots in the wider changes brought about by the monastic reform movement. This may be inferred particularly from those surviving from the diocese of Winchester, including the two from Romsey Abbey with its associations with Æthelwold and the royal family, and it is fortunate that such a large group has survived from this area. There also seem to be signs of a linked but distinct tradition related to Ramsey Abbey associated with the less well-known reformer, St Oswald. The spread of the surviving sculptures from the late tenth into the mid eleventh century shows that the situation was not static, a once and for all adoption of new models, but that the new artistic tradition was strong enough to go on developing and that artists were receptive to new ideas and new models throughout the period. However, the links with continental court art in both the tenth and eleventh centuries suggests that royal interest and patronage was also an important factor in the circulation of models. This perception is needed to balance the apparent links with monastic centres of the reform period in some areas. Given the fragmentary nature of the remains and the many blanks in the record, and the absence of any surviving large scale examples in wood or metal, it is not possible to present a more complete picture for the Crucifixion at this period.[143]

Pre-Conquest Sculptures with the Crucifixion from Southern England and the East Midlands: a Handlist

Sculptures lacking the central feature of Christ on the cross are marked*; those in which the iconography relates to the robed Christ are marked+. For typology of Christ, see n 29 above. For cross typology, see *Corpus*, fig. 2.

1.   BARTON-ON-HUMBER, Lincolnshire*   St Peter
Monument type: A slab or panel, without frame or edge mouldings.
Location: *In situ* above the hood mould of the eastern arch of the tower, on the west face.
Measurements: Height: c. 68.6cm; Width: 45.7cm.
Details: An upright, frontal head, possibly of Christ, type 1, is all that survives.

2.   BIBURY, Gloucestershire* (Plate Va)   St Mary
Monument type: An incomplete monumental rood.
Location: *In situ* above the chancel arch, on the west face.
Measurements: Too high to measure, but comparable to Breamore.
Details: Only one figure survives, to left of centre, cut back to the surface and showing only in outline: it appears to be Mary attendant at the Crucifixion.

---

[143] I would like to thank Professor Rosemary Cramp for reading a draft of this paper and making many helpful suggestions, and Mrs Y. Beadnell, Chief Technician of the Department of Archaeology, Durham, for redrawing figs. 1 and 2.

3. BITTON, Gloucestershire⁺   St Mary
Monument type: Three fragments of a monumental rood.
Location: A. Foot of a cross with Christ's feet and snake below: *in situ* on the west
face of the east wall of the nave, above the chancel arch, set immediately above a
square-sectioned string course and centred immediately below the gable. B. A head
of Christ, now in a room in the first floor of the tower, but found in 1850 blocking a
squint between the chancel and a destroyed north porticus. C. One arm of Christ on
the cross, now at the west end of the north aisle, but found with B.
Measurements: A. Too high to measure. B. Height: 25.4cm; Width: 29.2cm; Depth
(on right): 16.5cm; (on left): 31.8cm. C. Height: 38cm; Width: 87.6cm; Depth:
12.5cm; Depth of relief: 10cm.
Details: The fragments, in good condition, show a cross with mouldings and a
stepped termination (C), and a *suppedaneum* (A). Christ's head is bowed to his right
(B); and he wears a sleeved robe (C).

4. BRADFORD ON AVON, Wiltshire* (plate IVa and b)   St Laurence
Monument type: Two figures from a monumental sculpture, probably a rood.
Location: Built into the wall above the west face of the chancel arch. Found in this
wall in 1856-7, but later removed and replaced.
Measurements: A (left): Height: c.61cm; Width: 106.8cm. B (right): Height: c.53.4cm;
Width: 111.8cm.
Details: Two angels flying towards a central element, probably Christ on the cross.

5. BREAMORE, Hampshire (plate Ic)   St Mary
Monument type: A monumental rood carved on eight separate slabs, almost complete
but dressed back to the wall and so surviving mainly in outline.
Location: Built in the south face over the south door, inside the porch, where it was
reassembled apparently in the fifteenth century. Original position not known.
Measurements: Height (max.): 210cm; Width of cross at base: 48cm.
John: Height: c.158cm; Width at base: c.47.5cm. Mary: Height: c.163.5cm; Width
at base: c.47cm.
Details: Cross (type A1) with square-cut edge mouldings and square panels cut into
the ends of the side arms; sun and moon in these panels; *Manus Dei* above Christ's
head; Christ (type 3); Mary on his right; John on his left.

6. CONISHOLME, Lincolnshire⁺   St Peter
Monument type: An incomplete cross-head.
Location: On a window sill in the chancel. Found in 1925 in the churchyard, when
the ground shrank following a dry summer.
Measurements. Height: 49.5cm; Width: 25.4cm. Height of Christ figure: 29.8cm.
Details: Incomplete and partly defaced cross-head, used as a crucifix. Cross
(type B11); Christ (type 1) naked or defaced. Motif of two linked ovals above
Christ's head; one boss and trace of another or ?twist motif on Christ's left; two
bosses on his right.

7. GREAT GLEN, Leicestershire (plate IIc)   St Cuthbert
Monument type: Panel without a border or edge moulding: or, less likely, a fragment
of a cross shaft.
Location: Built into the east wall of the north aisle: no record of its discovery.
Measurements: Height: 50.8cm; Width: 34.4cm.
Details: Very worn and damaged. Cross (type A1); Christ (Type 2).

8. HARMSTON, Lincolnshire (plate IId)   All Saints
Location: Now set into a modern base at the west end of the nave of All Saints'
Church, Harmston. Found built into a wall at the Old Manor House.
Measurements: (Of shaft): Height: 104.2cm; Width: 29.9 > 24.2cm. (Of Crucifixion
scene): Height: 29.5cm; Width: 24.2cm.
Details: A Crucifixion scene set possibly near the top of a cross-shaft. It is set within
the edge mouldings of the shaft, but there are no upper or lower borders and the
surrounding twist decoration fills the upper spandrels of the cross. The scene is
complete and relatively unworn, but crudely carved. Cross (type A1 or B6) set on a
base; *Manus Dei* above Christ's head; Christ (type 1); figure beneath each cross arm,
distinguished in dress but individually unidentifiable: probably John and Mary.

9. HEADBOURNE WORTHY, Hampshire (plate Id)   St Swithun
Monument type: A monumental rood.
Location: Apparently *in situ* in the west face of the west wall above a door, and
inside a later porch.
Measurements: (Christ): Height: c.253cm; Width (across arms): c.134cm. (Cross-
shaft): Width: 54cm; (John): Height: c.78cm; Width (at feet): 20cm; (across ledge
below feet): 37cm. (Mary): Height: c.88cm; Width (at feet): 32cm; (across ledge
below feet): 40cm.
Details: Carved on at least five slabs. The outlines of the figures are clear, but the
whole has been cut back to the surface of the wall and Christ's head is severely
damaged. Cross with shaft narrowing from top to bottom and arms slightly raised
from the horizontal (Between type A1 and B6); *Manus Dei*; Christ (type 2); John on
Christ's left; Mary on his right.

10. LANGFORD I, Oxfordshire (plate IIIa)   St Matthew
Monument type: A monumental rood.
Location: Built into the late medieval south porch, above the south door, outside.
Evidence from incorrect assembly suggests that this was not its original or intended
position.
Measurements: (Of cross): Height: 156.5cm; Width: 114.5cm. (Of subsidiary
figures): c.84cm.
Details: Carved on five separate slabs and apparently designed for the subsidiary
figures to stand further out and not directly under the cross-arms. Wrongly assembled, with Christ's arms upside down, Mary and John on wrong sides, facing
away: otherwise in good condition. Cross (type A1) with stepped terminations
preceded by mouldings; Christ (type 3); Mary (should be on Christ's right); John
(should be on Christ's left).

11. LANGFORD II, Oxfordshire[+]   St Matthew
Monument type: A monumental rood.
Location: Built into the east wall of the late medieval south porch, outside.
Measurements: Height: 187cm; Width: (across arms of cross): c.231cm; (across
Christ's arms): 176cm.
Details: Incomplete but in good condition. Cross (type A1) with triangular mouldings
on side arms. Christ (type 1).

12. MARTON, Lincolnshire (plate IIb)   St Margaret
Monument type: A panel without border or edge mouldings.
Location: Now built into the north wall of the chancel, at the east end above the

altar. Found hidden by the organ and moved in 1907 to its present position.
Measurements: Height: 35cm; Width: 23.5cm.
Details: Complete but very worn or defaced. Cross (type B6); Christ (type 2).

13. MUCHELNEY, Somerset (plate IVd)   Dedication unknown
Monument type: A monumental rood.
Location: Now in the Abbey Museum. No record of discovery but the foundations
of a small pre-Conquest church have been found within the Norman chancel of the
largely fifteenth-century abbey; and there are other pre-Conquest fragments in the
Museum.
Measurements: Height: 34cm; Width 21 > 19cm; Depth: 18.5cm at bottom of sloping
ledge.
Details: A small fragment of a large monument, in good condition. The foot of a
cross (probably type A1); feet of Christ; sloping, ledge-like *suppedaneum*.

14. NASSINGTON, Northamptonshire (plate IIa)   St Mary
Monument type: An incomplete cross-shaft.
Location: Now in the north-west corner of the nave. Found built into the west wall
of the tower.
Measurements: Height: 84.5cm; Width: 42 > 36.8cm.
Details: Set in a panel low on one broad face of a cross-shaft. Possibly incomplete
and quite worn. Cross (type B6); sun and moon above cross-arms, probably personified as encircled faced or busts, but now individually indistinguishable; Christ
(type 1); spear-bearer on Christ's left; sponge- or cup-bearer on his right.

15. NEWENT, Gloucestershire (plate Vd)   St Mary
Monument type: Small square grave-marker.
Location: Now in a glass show case at the west end of the nave. Found in 1912 with
bones in excavation for a new vestry, to the north of the church.
Measurements: Height: 20.3cm; Width: 16.5cm.
Details: Worn and damaged in places but complete and generally in good condition.
Cross (type B6); *Manus Dei*; Christ (type 1); two pairs of mourning or worshipping
figures (one probably representing John and Mary: Mary figure on Christ's right);
birds; four circles; ?Adam in Eden and Adam entombed; angels and figures with
symbols of the Passion; ?Nativity scene.

16. RECULVER, Kent   Dedication unknown
Monument type: A round-shafted cross and head.
Location: Fragments possibly of this cross now in Canterbury Cathedral do not
include any elements identifiable with the Crucifixion. Early references suggest it
stood between nave and chancel, and a description of the Crucifixion by Leland has
survived (see p 164 above).
Measurements: Unknown.
Details: The Crucifixion scene seems to have been set at the top of the cross-shaft,
immediately below the head. Cross (type unknown); Christ (type unknown), but
fastened with four nails.

17. ROMSEY I, Hampshire (plate Ia)   St Mary and St Elflæda
Monument type: A panel with edge mouldings.
Location: Now set up as a reredos over the altar in St Anne's chapel at the east end
of the south aisle. Found by the Rev. E. Berthon (vicar 1860-92) in the walling of

St Mary's chapel, in the ambulatory, face inwards. Said to have occupied a position over the altar in the south choir aisle in 1742.

Measurements: Height: 66cm; Width: c.40cm.

Details: Complete and in good condition. Cross (type A3); Christ (type 1); John on Christ's left; Mary on his right; sponge-bearer on his left; spear-bearer on his right; Half figure of angel above each cross arm; plant ornament.

18.   ROMSEY II, Hampshire (plate Ib)   St Mary and St Elflæda
Monument type: A monumental rood.

Location: Built into the exterior of the twelfth-century west wall of the south transept, just outside the abbess's doorway.

Measurements: Height (overall): 202cm; (of figure): 162cm; Width (max.): 183cm.

Details: Worn and damaged in places, but generally in good condition. Complete figure of Christ on the cross, but uncertain whether composition complete. Cross (type A1); *Manus Dei*; Christ (type 1).

19.   ROPSLEY, Lincolnshire   St Peter
Monument type: Carved on a building stone, without frame or edge moulding.

Location: *In situ* in the north-west quoin of the nave, outside.

Measurements: Height: 28cm; Width: c.21.5cm.

Details: Complete, but crude and very weathered. Cross (type B6); Christ (type 1).

20.   STEPNEY, London (plate IIIb)   St Dunstan
Monument type: A panel with a decorative border.

Location: Now built into the east wall of the chancel, below the window. Formerly over the south door.

Measurements: Height: 98.5cm; Width: 68cm.

Details: Complete and in good condition. Cross (type A1) with mouldings and stepped terminations; sun and moon personified as undifferentiated, veiled, weeping faces, encircled; Christ (type 3); Mary on Christ's right; John on his left; plant decoration in border.

21.   WALKERN, Hertfordshire⁺   St Mary
Monument type: A monumental rood.

Location: *In situ* over former exterior doorway in the south face of the south arcade wall, near its western end.

Measurements: Height: c.155cm.

Details: ?Cross (type A1); *Manus Dei*; Christ (type 1).

22.   WINTERBOURNE STEEPLETON, Dorset* (plate IVc)   St Michael and All Angels
Monument type: A monumental sculpture, probably *not* a rood.

Location: Built into the south wall, outside. There is a tradition that it was originally set over or near the west door.

Measurements: Height: 39cm; Width: 64cm.

Details: One slab of an originally larger composition, some damage but in good condition. Angel.

23.   WORMINGTON, Gloucestershire (plate Vc)   Dedication unknown
Monument type: A panel without a frame.

Location: Now above the altar at the east end of the south aisle of St Catherine's church, but found below ground in the garden of Wormington House.

Measurements: Height: 85.5cm; Width: 46cm.

Details: Christ's hands are missing, therefore either the panel has been cut down; or, possibly, it formed part of a larger composition on more than one building stone. Worn in places. Cross (type B6); *Manus Dei*; Christ (type 1).

Sculptures incorrectly published as pre-Conquest Crucifixions

1. BARKING, Essex   St Margaret
Crucifixion sculpture which can be dated to the thirteenth century on stylistic grounds.

2. BROCKWORTH, Gloucestershire   St George
Thirteenth-century gable cross.

3. DAGLINGWORTH I, Gloucestershire (plate Vb)   Holy Rood

4. DAGLINGWORTH II, Gloucestershire   Holy Rood
Two panels, closely related in iconography and style, and very conservative in iconography, but on stylistic grounds more likely to be late eleventh/ twelfth century than earlier. (See p 179).

5. LANGTON BY SPILSBY, Lincolnshire
A thirteenth-century or later gable cross.

6. LUSBY, Lincolnshire   St Peter
A stone carved with a cross in relief, and decorated with incised circles. Set above the keystone of the blocked south door, outside.

7. NEW ALRESFORD, Hampshire   St John the Baptist
Post-Conquest, probably thirteenth century, based on the cutting of the cross and the possibility that Christ's feet are crossed.

INDEX OF MANUSCRIPTS

GENERAL INDEX